What experts say about

The questions in Practice Tests For The Digital SAT are very close to the actual test.

– Vaibhav Sharma SAT Math Coach

I would recommend high school and public libraries to consider purchasing this book for their patrons.

– Kelley Wilson, School Library Media Specialist, Brandywine High School

Because of the breadth, depth, and organization, I would recommend this book to students and teachers.

– Motz Maria, Purchasing Dept School Board Sarasota County

This page is intentionally left blank

VIBRANT
PUBLISHERS

PRACTICE TESTS FOR THE
Digital SAT®

2024 | SECOND EDITION

5 full-length tests

Questions framed **adhering**
to the **Digital SAT guidelines**

In-depth information
about the Digital SAT

Practice Tests For The Digital SAT
SECOND EDITION

Paperback ISBN 10 : 1-63651-187-2
Paperback ISBN 13 : 978-1-63651-187-0

Library of Congress Control Number: 2022951781

This publication is designed to provide accurate and authoritative information in regard to the subject matter covered. The author has made every effort in the preparation of this book to ensure the accuracy of the information. However, information in this book is sold without warranty either expressed or implied. The Author or the Publisher will not be liable for any damages caused or alleged to be caused either directly or indirectly by this book.

Vibrant Publishers books are available at special quantity discount for sales promotions, or for use in corporate training programs. For more information please write to **bulkorders@vibrantpublishers.com**

Please email feedback/corrections (technical, grammatical or spelling) to **spellerrors@vibrantpublishers.com**

To access the complete catalogue of Vibrant Publishers, visit **www.vibrantpublishers.com**

SAT˚ is a trademark registered by the College Board, which is not affiliated with, and does not endorse, this product.

Table of Contents

Dear Student,

Thank you for purchasing **Practice Tests for the Digital SAT®**. We are committed to publishing books that are content–rich, concise and approachable enabling more students to read and make the fullest use of them. We hope this book provides the most enriching learning experience as you prepare for your **SAT** exam. Should you have any questions or suggestions, feel free to email us at **reachus@vibrantpublishers.com**. Thanks again for your purchase. Good luck for your Digital SAT!

– Vibrant Publishers Team

ACT/SAT
Books in Test Prep Series

Math Practice Tests for the ACT ISBN: 978-1-63651-211-2	**Winning Strategies For ACT Essay Writing: With 15 Sample Prompts** ISBN: 978-1-63651-212-9
Digital SAT Math Practice Questions ISBN: 978-1-63651-189-4	**Digital SAT Reading and Writing Practice Questions** ISBN: 978-1-63651-188-7

For the most updated list of books visit

www.vibrantpublishers.com

This page is intentionally left blank

How To Get The Most Out Of This Book

Having no realistic practice to successfully take the Digital SAT test can make it look daunting. However, this book is specifically designed to give you a thorough practice of the new SAT. By attempting the practice tests in this book, you will become confident to face the real test.

The second edition of *Practice Tests For The Digital SAT* is improved and tailored according to your test prep needs. The questions in this edition are created after extensive research to give you a realistic practice of the skills tested on the Digital SAT.

This book includes *5 full-length Digital SAT tests* with a total of 490 practice questions for your continuous practice. The practice tests in this book follow the modular format for the Reading and Writing and Math sections. Each question has the most appropriate answer explanation and distractor explanations. The clear and elaborate explanations will aid you in understanding the reasoning behind each correct (or incorrect) answer and train your mind to logically answer the questions.

First, read the **About The Digital SAT** chapter in order to fully understand how the test is planned and administered before diving into the tests. As the College Board transitions from administering paper-and-pencil SAT tests to Digital tests, you need to be aware of all the appropriate information that can increase your chance of passing the test with a high score.

After reading through the information, consider taking one of the complete practice tests first. In the first test, give yourself as much time as you need rather than trying to finish within the allotted SAT time limit. However, write down how long each section and module takes to solve, so you can determine how to budget your time. Then, compare your answers with the correct answers given in the "Answer Key" section of each test. Understand what went wrong by referring to the detailed solutions given in the "Answer & Explanations" section. Look over the categories of questions that you have difficulty with or made errors on. This will help you identify your strengths and weaknesses and the areas you need to focus on.

You can get ample practice of Reading and Writing questions from *Digital SAT Reading and Writing Practice Questions* and Math questions from *Digital SAT Math Practice Questions.*

After completing your practice, try another complete practice test. This time, have your timer at hand and take breaks only at the intervals given in the real test. This more realistic testing experience will also show you how well you can concentrate for extended periods. After you complete the second practice test, check your answers and compare them with the answers given in the "Answer Key" section after each test and look for patterns in the questions you made errors on. Are they the same style as before, or do you have different weaknesses? Try reviewing these weaknesses before taking the next complete practice test.

Create a study schedule and stick with it. Attempt to take a practice test every week for 6 weeks. Use our *Mock Tests* for additional practice. This will help you get well-versed with the format of the SAT and also increase your confidence.

Continue alternating review of specific question types with complete practice tests throughout your preparation period. Do not worry if you miss a day on your study plan; just revise your schedule as needed so you can complete every practice test in this book. When the day arrives for your actual SAT, you will be comfortable with the new pattern of the test and ready to solve any style of question that might be on it, whether it is related to language or mathematics. You can be confident of getting your best possible score!

More so, practicing test questions and reviewing their corresponding answers will expose you to the format and structure of the real Digital SAT. Use this guide as a companion in understanding every aspect of the Digital SAT.

Good luck with your SAT journey!

Chapter 1

About the Digital SAT®

Introduction

Now that you have made the important decision to head to college/university, there is one last thing you need to do to achieve your goal — take the SAT. Most universities or colleges, including Ivy League schools, expect you to have a good SAT score to secure admission in any course of your choice.

But, there is a major change in how students will give the SAT. The College Board has decided to transition the famous pencil-and-paper test into a fully digital one. The College Board's decision to go digital is based on giving a fair testing experience to students. The digital test will be easier to take, easier to administer, will be more secure, and more relevant.

For giving the new test, you need to be aware of the format of the test, the time that will be given to you to answer each question, the possible complexity of the questions, and the scoring method employed to assess your performance in the test. In this chapter, you will discover important information including the SAT policy of inclusive accessibility, the newly introduced Multistage Adaptive Testing feature, the modular format of the test, and much more.

The College Board has also streamlined the method of delivery of the Digital SAT. With the latest test delivery platform for the digital SAT Suite assessments, students can have access to all their tests and their content, as well as enjoy the chance of practicing with the full-length, adaptive practice tests offered for free on the platform. More so, every question on the Digital SAT Suite is in a discrete (standalone) format. This indicates that test takers can answer each question independently. They don't necessarily need to refer to a common stimulus such as an extended passage.

If you are attempting the SAT for the first time, it could be scary not knowing exactly what to expect in the test. This is why this book is specifically designed to expose you to everything you need to know about successfully taking the Digital SAT Suite test.

Customized Test Delivery Platform

The College Board has set up a customized test delivery platform for the Digital SAT Suite assessments. This platform called Bluebook is designed according to the principles of UDA (Universal Design for Assessment) and the main goal of it is to make the testing experience accessible to a maximum number of students. The most useful features of this platform are that: (i) all test takers can have complete access to the tests and their content; (ii) students will be able to take full-length, adaptive practice tests for free on the platform so that they can assess their knowledge levels or have an understanding of similar test materials before attempting the real tests.

Multistage Adaptive Testing

The College Board is changing from a linear testing mode, which has been the primary mode of SAT administration to an adaptive mode.

The main difference between the linear and adaptive testing modes is that for the linear testing mode, students are given a test form that contains some questions that have already been set before the test day and do not change during testing, irrespective of the student's performance.

On the other hand, the adaptive testing model makes it possible for the test delivery platform to adjust the questions' difficulty level based on the performance of the individual test takers. Therefore, each student will be given test questions that match their level of understanding.

This adaptive test mode is known as **Multistage Adaptive Testing (MST).** The MST is administered in two stages, and each stage comprises a module or set of questions. The first module consists of test questions with different ranges of difficulty levels (easy, medium, and hard). The performance of the test takers in the first module is appropriately assessed, and the results are used to determine the level of difficulty of questions to be administered to them in the second module.

The set of an administered first-stage module and its second-stage module are referred to as a **panel**.

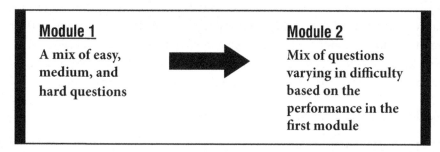

Module 1	Module 2
A mix of easy, medium, and hard questions	Mix of questions varying in difficulty based on the performance in the first module

Embedded Pretesting

The Digital SAT also includes embedded pretesting in its design. What this means is that a small number of pretest (unscored) questions are incorporated among the operational (scored) questions. Even though they are not administered for a score, you may not be able to distinguish these pretest questions from the operational questions on which your scores are based. It is advisable that you pay maximum attention and effort to these questions, which can be used in estimating your understanding levels to the difficulty of the questions. The number of pretest questions is few so you will not be asked to focus mainly on questions that won't be used to estimate your final SAT score. It is important to note that answers to pretest questions won't contribute to your final score. The pretest questions are mainly used to gather your performance information so that it can be utilized later to assess if these questions are appropriate for operational use later.

Discrete Questions

One interesting aspect of the Digital SAT is that all their questions are in discreet format; that is they are standalone. You can answer each question on its own, which doesn't necessarily require any reference to a common stimulus such as an extended passage. This is one of the striking differences between the paper-and-pencil SAT and the Digital SAT in the sense that the former uses both discrete and question sets. In practice, the question sets expect you to reference a common stimulus.

Scoring

Students will obtain a section score based on their final performance in the Reading and Writing and Math section. For the SAT, students can get a score between 400-1600. Hence, for each of the tests of the Digital SAT, there will be 3 scores reported: (1) A Reading and Writing section score; (2) A Math section score; (3) A total score, which is the sum of the two section scores. It is important to note that the scales for these scores have the same ranges as for the paper-based SAT. This indicates that the Digital SAT total score is on the familiar 400–1600 scale.

Reading and Writing	Math	Total Score
Between 200-800	Between 200-800	Between 400-1600

Overall Test Specifications

The Digital SAT is made up of two sections: A Reading and Writing (RW) section and a Math section. In the linear model, the test had separate sections for Reading and Writing. However, in the Digital SAT, both the Reading and Writing tests are combined in one section. The questions in these two sections concentrate primarily on the skills and knowledge that students need to use in college and/or for getting ready for their careers. The main parts of the digital SAT tests are similar to those of the paper-and-pencil SAT test assessments. More so, all the testing programs within the digital SAT Suite, whether it is the SAT, PSAT 10, PSAT 8/9, or PSAT/NMSQT have similar designs. Although, these tests allow for differences in test takers' ages and levels of understanding.

Digital SAT Suite: Overall Test Specifications

Characteristic	Reading and Writing section	Math section
Administration	Two-stage adaptive design; this section contains two separately timed modules	Two-stage adaptive design; this section contains two separately timed modules
Number of questions	54 questions; 25 questions in each module with 2 pretest ques	44 questions; 20 questions in each module with 2 pretest ques
Time	64 minutes	70 minutes
Time per question	1.19 minutes	1.59 minutes
Time per module	32 minutes	35 minutes
Content domains	Information and Ideas, Craft and Structure, Expression of Ideas, Standard English Conventions	Algebra, Advanced Math, Problem-Solving and Data Analysis, Geometry and Trigonometry

Test Length

There are a total of 54 questions for the Reading and Writing section. These 54 questions are divided into two equal-length modules; that is, one for each of the section's two stages. Out of the 27 questions for each module, 25 questions are operational—which means that test takers' performance on them is used to calculate their section score, and 2 questions are pretests.

For the Math section, the first module has 20 operational questions and 2 pretest questions. Then the second module consists of 20 operational questions and 2 pretest questions. In total, the Math section will comprise 44 questions.

Time Per Module

You will have 32 minutes to complete each module of the Reading and Writing section and 35 minutes to complete each module of the Math section. Once the time for the first module has expired, you will be automatically advanced to the second module. The second module may contain questions that are of higher or lower difficulty, depending on your performance in the first module. You will not have the opportunity to return to the first-module questions.

Total Time Allotted

You will have 64 minutes to complete the Reading and Writing section and 70 minutes to complete the Math section.

Average Time Per Question

You will, on average, have 1.19 minutes to answer each Reading and Writing question and 1.59 minutes to answer each Math question.

Question Format(s) used

The Reading and Writing section mostly utilizes four-option multiple-choice questions, and each question has a single best answer (which is referred to as the keyed response or key). Roughly 75 percent of questions in the Math section also adopt the same four-option multiple-choice format, while the remaining part of the test utilizes the student-produced response (SPR) format. This means that students will be required to answer the latter type of questions by giving their own responses and putting their responses in the field next to the question. These questions measure your ability to be able to solve math problems by yourself. It is possible for the SPR questions to have more than one correct response; however, you are required to provide only one answer.

Text Complexity

It is assumed that the complexity test takers can read is directly related to how ready they are for college and their careers. Therefore, the idea of text complexity is strictly considered when designing and developing the Digital SAT questions. The texts in the Reading and Writing section are given three complexity bands (grades 6–8, grades 9–11, and grades 12–14).

Texts for grades 12-14 have the highest complexity, followed by the texts for grades 9-11, while grades 6-8 have texts with the lowest complexity. While it is possible to use the same texts for grades 12-14 and grades 9-11, those difficult texts cannot be used for grades 6-8 because they don't appropriately assess the literacy knowledge and skills of students in eighth and ninth grades.

On the other hand, text complexity is not an issue in the Math section, because it is not formally measured. It is estimated that about 70 percent of Math questions don't necessarily have a context. You are only required to use the information/data provided to solve some questions that may be related to science, social studies, history, etc.

What is Changing

The College Board continues to maintain fairness and high quality in its administration of SAT Suite, and some aspects of its operations are changing. These changes include:

- Transitioning to digital testing by 2023 or 2024 latest. Once the transition is completed, students can no longer take the paper-and-pencil SAT tests.

- The digital SAT Suite tests are particularly shorter than their paper-and-pencil predecessors—it can be taken in 2 hours 14 minutes instead of 3 hours.

- You now have more time on their hands to answer each question.

- It is now possible for you to receive scores in days instead of weeks, faster than the predecessor paper-and-pencil SAT.

- The SAT Suite now connects students to opportunities based on their scores. They can be connected to information and resources concerning local 2-year colleges, career options, and workforce training programs.

- States, schools, and districts will be given more flexibility concerning when they could give the SAT Suite tests.

- The digital SAT will now have a single Reading and Writing section instead of separate Reading and Writing and Language sections. More importantly, the Reading and Writing section's passages are significantly shorter and more diverse.

- A single (discrete) question is associated with each passage (or passage pair) instead of having several questions associated with a small number of longer passages, as it is for the paper-and-pencil SAT Suite tests.

- You can now use calculators throughout the Math section.

What is Staying the Same

Despite the above-mentioned changes, some aspects of the SAT Suite tests are remaining the same, such as:

- The Digital SAT will still measure skills and knowledge that you are learning in school that can be used in college and/or your future career.

- The test will be scored on the same scales as the paper-and-pencil test.

- The test will be administered in schools and test centers with a proctor.

- You will still be connected to scholarships and the College Board National Recognition Programs.

- Support will be given to all students who need accommodations and/or support to access the tests and their content.

- The Reading/Writing passages will cover a wide range of academic disciplines and text complexities.

- The test will still have both multiple-choice and student-produced response question formats.

More Questions Answered about the Digital SAT

1. **When will I be able to register for the digital SAT tests?**

   The first digital SAT administrations at international test centers will start in the fall 2023.

2. **How will students take the digital SAT?**

   You can give the SAT on a laptop or tablet using a custom-built digital exam application called Bluebook that can be downloaded in advance of the test day.

3. **How will the Digital SAT be more secure?**

   At this moment, if one test form is compromised, it can mean that the scores for all the students in that group or at the same test centers will be canceled. However, going digital will make it possible to give every student a unique test form so that it won't be technically possible to share answers.

4. **How will the College Board address test day issues and technical support challenges?**

   The College Board has dedicated customer service resources ready to troubleshoot issues on test day for students and test centers. There is a technology coordinator for each test center to provide additional support and technical help when needed.

5. **What kinds of tools will be available for students taking the digital SAT?**

You can use the following tools while using the software:

- Flag questions to come back to them later

- A countdown clock to know when you are running out of time. You can decide to show or hide it at the top of the testing screen

- A built-in graphing calculator that you can use on the entire math section (or you can bring your own calculators)

- A reference sheet of basic math formulas

The Reading and Writing Section at a Glance

The table below summarizes the specifications of the types of questions and their distribution in the Reading and Writing section.

Content Domain	Skill/Knowledge	Question distribution
Information and Ideas	<ul><li>Central Ideas and Details</li><li>Command of Evidence (Textual and Quantitative)</li><li>Inferences</li></ul>	12-14 questions (26%)
Craft and Structure	<ul><li>Words in Context</li><li>Text Structure and Purpose</li><li>Cross-Text Connections</li></ul>	13-15 questions (28%)
Expression of Ideas	<ul><li>Rhetorical Synthesis</li><li>Transitions</li></ul>	8-12 questions (20%)
Standard English Conventions	<ul><li>Boundaries</li><li>Form, Structure, and Sense</li></ul>	11-15 questions (26%)

1. The term *"Anthropocene"* introduced by Dutch scientist, Paul Crutzen, in the mid-1970s, is often used in the context of pollution caused by human activity since the commencement of the Agricultural Revolution. Various start dates for the Anthropocene have been offered by scientists, ranging from the beginning of the first Agricultural Revolution, also known as the *Neolithic Revolution*, to as recently as the 1960s. However, the _____ has not been completed, and hence a formal, conclusive date remains to be finalized.

Which choice completes the text with the most logical and precise word or phrase?

A) ratification

B) investigation

C) legality

D) approval

Key: A

Level: Hard | **Domain:** CRAFT AND STRUCTURE

Skill/Knowledge: Words in Context

Key Explanation: Choice A is the correct option because "ratification" refers to the action of signing or giving formal consent to something, making it officially valid. This word is best suited to the context because the second sentence of the passage talks about how many scientists have offered dates, but a conclusive date has yet to be finalized. The keywords to focus on are "formal, conclusive date" which points to which option (A) might be most suitable in this context.

Distractor Explanations: Choice B is incorrect because there is no evidence provided that an investigation may have been initiated into the subject. Similarly, **Choice C** is incorrect because there is no mention of a legal aspect or the need for legal compliance in determining the start date of the Anthropocene. The sentence focuses on the completion of a process, rather than its legality. **Choice D** is incorrect because while "approval" is similar to "ratification," it doesn't capture the complete meaning in this context. The passage suggests that a formal, conclusive date remains to be finalized, indicating the need for a higher level of approval beyond a simple decision or agreement. "Ratification" better conveys the idea of a formal and authoritative confirmation or approval by relevant parties.

2. A recent study by a team of Yale scientists led by Dr. Laura Ingram investigated the impact of exercise on cognitive function in older adults. They postulated that regular physical activity would enhance cognitive abilities and memory. Participants aged 60 and above were divided into two groups: an exercise group and a control group. Over six months, the exercise group engaged in moderate-intensity aerobic exercises thrice weekly, while the control group maintained a sedentary lifestyle. Cognitive assessments were conducted at the study's beginning and end to measure memory, attention, and executive functions.

Which finding from the study, if true, would most directly support Dr. Ingram and her team's hypothesis?

A) The exercise group showed significant improvements in memory and attention compared to the control group, the latter demonstrating some cognitive enhancement.

B) Both the exercise and control groups displayed similar cognitive performance at the end of the study.

C) Older adults who did not participate in the exercise program experienced a decline in cognitive function.

D) The exercise group reported increased motivation and enjoyment in their daily activities, but cognitive improvements were inconclusive.

Key: C

Level: Medium | **Domain:** INFORMATION AND IDEAS

Skill/Knowledge: Command of Evidence (Textual)

Key Explanation: Choice C is the correct answer because if this finding were true, it would support the hypothesis that regular physical activity improves cognitive abilities in older adults. It suggests that exercise has a protective effect on cognitive function and highlights the specific benefits of engaging in regular physical activity.

Distractor Explanations: Choice A is incorrect because it does not directly support the hypothesis that regular physical activity improves cognitive abilities in older adults, as it suggests that both the exercise group and the control group demonstrated enhancements , albeit one more than the other. **Choice B** is incorrect because it implies that there was no significant difference in cognitive performance between the exercise group and the control group. If this finding were true, it would not support the hypothesis that regular physical activity improves cognitive abilities in older adults, as it indicates that exercise did not have a direct impact on cognitive functioning. **Choice D** is incorrect because it does not directly support the hypothesis that regular physical activity improves cognitive abilities in older adults. The mention of inconclusive cognitive improvements further weakens the connection between exercise and cognitive function.

The Math Section at a Glance

The table below summarizes the specifications of the types of questions and their distribution in the Math section.

Content Domain	Skill/Knowledge	Question Distribution
Algebra	• Linear equations in one variable • Linear equations in two variables • Linear functions • Systems of two linear equations in two variables • Linear inequalities in one or two variables	13-15 questions (35%)
Advanced Math	• Equivalent expressions • Nonlinear equations in one variable and systems of equations in two variables • Nonlinear functions	13-15 questions (35%)
Problem-Solving and Data Analysis	• Ratios, rates, proportional relationships, and units • Percentages • One-variable data: distributions and measures of center and spread • Two-variable data: models and scatterplots • Probability and conditional probability • Inference from sample statistics and margin of error • Evaluating statistical claims: observational studies and experiments	5-7 questions (15%)
Geometry and Trigonometry	• Area and volume • Lines, angles, and triangles • Right triangles and trigonometry • Circles	5-7 questions (15%)

1. Which expression is equivalent to $2x^2 + 3x + 1$?

   A) $(2x + 1)(2x + 1)$

   B) $(x + 2)(x + 1)$

   C) $(x - 2)(x - 1)$

   D) $(2x + 1)(x + 1)$

   Key: D

   Level: Easy | **Domain:** ADVANCED MATH

   Skill/Knowledge: Equivalent Expressions | **Testing Point:** Factoring a quadratic equation

   Key Explanation: Choice D is correct.
   To find the equivalent expression, factor the given quadratic equation by splitting the middle term.
   In $2x^2 + 3x + 1$, $a = 2$, $b = 3$ and $c = 1$ using the format $ax^2 + bx + c$.
   Getting the product of a and c yields $ac = (2)(1) = 2$
   The factors of 2 whose sum is the value of b (where $b = 3$) is 2 and 1.
   Hence, the equation can be written as $2x^2 + 2x + x + 1$.
   Grouping the binomials in the equation yields $(2x^2 + 2x) + (x + 1)$.
   Factoring $2x$ from the first group yields $2x(x + 1) + (x + 1)$.
   Factoring $x + 1$ from the two groups yields $(2x + 1)(x + 1)$.
   Therefore, Choice D is the correct answer.

   Distractor Explanation: Choices A, B, and C are incorrect and may result from a conceptual or calculation error.

2. The dog park charges $10 for a membership and $3 per hour for the dog to run around in their park. Mindy brings her dog to the park and spends less than $40. Which of the following inequalities represents Mindy's situation, where h is the number of hours at the park and C is the total amount Mindy paid?

   A) $3h + 10 < 40$

   B) $3C - 10 < 40$

   C) $3h + 10 = 40$

   D) $3h + 10 > 40$

   Key: A

   Level: Easy | **Domain:** ALGEBRA

   Skill/Knowledge: Linear inequalities in one or two variables | **Testing Point:** Create a linear inequality

   Key Explanation: Choice A is correct. To determine the inequality that represents the situation, first create the expression that is equal to the total amount that Mindy paid (C).

The total amount C is the sum of the membership fee ($10) and the fee for having the dog in the park in h hours. This yields $C = 10 + 3h$ or $C = 3h + 10$.

Since Mindy spent less than $40 in the dog park, then $C < 40$. Substituting the value of C in terms of h in the inequality yields $3h + 10 < 40$.

Therefore, the inequality $3h + 10 < 40$ is the correct answer.

Distractor Explanation: Choice B is incorrect. This option is wrong because C is the total amount paid by Mindy and not the rate per hour for the dog to run around the park. **Choices C** and **D** are incorrect. Mindy spent less than $40. Hence, the correct symbol to use is < not > or =.

Chapter 2

....

Practice Test 1

You are about to begin a full-length Practice Test. The test has four modules. The time allotted for each module is marked at the beginning of the module. Work on one module at a time. Use a timer to keep track of the time limits for every module.

Try to take the Practice Test under real test conditions. Find a quiet place to work, and set aside enough time to complete the test without being disturbed. At the end of the test, check your answers by referring to the Answer Key and fill in your raw score in the scorecard below. Also, note down the time taken by you for completing each module.

Pay particular attention to the questions that were answered incorrectly. Read the answer explanations and understand how to solve them.

....

My Score Card (Raw Score)

	Reading and Writing		Math	
	Module 1	Module 2	Module 1	Module 2
Out of	27	27	22	22
My Score	_____	_____	_____	_____
Time Taken	_____	_____	_____	_____

TEST BEGINS ON THE NEXT PAGE

Reading and Writing Test
27 QUESTIONS | 32 MINUTES

DIRECTIONS

The questions in this section address a number of important reading and writing skills. Each question includes one or more passages, which may include a table or graph. Read each passage and question carefully, and then choose the best answer to the question based on the passage(s). All questions in this section are multiple–choice with four answer choices. Each question has a single best answer.

1

Allowing goats to graze an area is one potential solution for removing unwanted weeds in terrain that is too rocky and remote to allow for cutting or herbicide spraying. Goats significantly reduce the incidence of the unwanted plants, but they must be quickly removed to prevent them from eating everything else as well; goats lack _____.

Which choice completes the text with the most logical and precise word or phrase?

A) bias

B) prejudice

C) discrimination

D) bigotry

2

Anyone interested in a career in business needs superior communication skills. Not only are they essential to convey ideas to colleagues and explain plans clearly to ensure that work is completed effectively in a timely manner, but also they are needed to make proposals _____ to clients and potential investors.

Which choice completes the text with the most logical and precise word or phrase?

A) charismatic

B) irresistible

C) attractive

D) fascinating

CONTINUE ➡

3

Explaining the coexistence of various plant and butterfly species is _____ to truly understand the region's biodiversity and the forces that sustain or reduce it. Such an understanding will help ecologists devise an appropriate plan that maximizes the limited funding available for conservation and that still allows for future development of the area.

Which choice completes the text with the most logical and precise word or phrase?

A) critical

B) perilous

C) condemning

D) analytical

4

The Hagia Sophia, built between 532 and 537 in Istanbul under the orders of the Roman Emperor Justinian I, has been alternately used for different religious purposes since that time. The cultural and historical value of the building and its contents are _____, as a wealth of splendid and unique details have been added over the centuries since its construction.

Which choice completes the text with the most logical and precise word or phrase?

A) congenial

B) incalculable

C) cumbersome

D) voluminous

5

The London and Northwestern Railway War Memorial is a First World War memorial outside Euston Station in London, England. The memorial was designed by Reginald Wynn Owen and _____ employees of the London and Northwestern Railway (LNWR) who were killed in the First World War.

Which word most logically completes the text?

A) commemorates

B) idolizes

C) celebrates

D) overlooks

6

By analyzing more than one million surface ocean observations from the Drake Passage, the researchers detected subtle differences between the CO_2 trends in the surface ocean and the atmosphere that suggest a strengthening of the carbon sink that is most pronounced during winter. Although the researchers aren't sure of the exact mechanism driving these changes, it's likely related to winter mixing with deep waters that have not had contact with the atmosphere for several hundred years. These results contrast with previous findings that showed that the Southern Ocean's CO_2 sink had been stagnant or weakening from the early 1990s to the early 2000s. "Given the importance of the Southern Ocean to the global oceans' role in absorbing atmospheric CO_2, these studies suggest that we must continue to expand our measurements in this part of the world despite the challenging environment," says Colm Sweeney, lead investigator on the Drake Passage study.

Which choice best states the main purpose of the text?

A) To emphasize the difficulty of collecting accurate data from the Southern Ocean

B) To illustrate the problems with amassing an adequate database on the Southern Ocean

C) To place the results of the Drake Passage study in the wider context of other studies

D) To highlight the need to correct the problem of CO_2 absorption before it is too late

7

The following text is from Oscar Wilde's 1888 short story "The Selfish Giant."

Every afternoon, as they were coming from school, the children used to go and play in the Giant's garden. It was a large lovely garden, with soft green grass. Here and there over the grass stood beautiful flowers like stars, and there were twelve peach–trees that in the spring–time broke out into delicate blossoms of pink and pearl, and in the autumn bore rich fruit. The birds sat on the trees and sang so sweetly that the children used to stop their games in order to listen to them.

Which choice best states the function of the underlined sentence in the text as a whole?

A) It sets up the description of location presented in the sentences that follow.

B) It establishes a sense of contrast with the description in the previous sentence.

C) It elaborates on the previous sentence's description of the characters.

D) It introduces an ominous undercurrent to the sentences that follow.

8

An antibody–based drug is one candidate for a more effective, longer lasting overdose treatment. To explore this possibility, a team at Scripps Research Institute led by Kim D. Janda first treated mice with a vaccine that stimulated the animals to produce a slew of different antibodies against fentanyl, some of which helped protect the mice from overdoses. In the new work, the team recovered antibodies from the mice, purified them, and screened them for their ability to bind fentanyl. The team evaluated six of these antibodies against nine fentanyl analogs commonly confiscated by law enforcement. One antibody, 6A4, demonstrated the best fentanyl– binding affinity and had a six–day half–life in mice.

Which choice best explains why the author most likely included the information that the drugs were "commonly confiscated by law enforcement"?

A) To explain how the researchers obtained drugs for experimentation

B) To indicate that the research would apply to overdoses in authentic cases

C) To eliminate the argument that the trials were improperly conducted

D) To establish why special permits were needed to experiment with the drugs

9

Text 1

Van Gogh's *Starry Night* depicts a night sky filled with swirling clouds, shimmering stars, and a radiant moon, captivating one's gaze using dynamic lines and spacing. While other Impressionists were moving away from such silhouettes, Van Gogh maintained the importance of fluidity in his compositions. His forms convey emotion, the dimness of the night sky almost reflecting his turbulent quest to overcome his illness.

Text 2

Art provides a glimpse into the artist's inner world, enabling a deeper understanding of diverse perspectives and serving as a powerful communication tool to evoke emotions and stimulate thought. However, the commercialization of art has raised concerns about its essence and transformative power. Artists like Warhol challenged capitalism, but their posthumous commodification ironically undermines their intentions.

Based on the texts, how would the author of Text 2 likely view the significance of "Starry Night" as described in Text 1?

A) By recognizing "Starry Night" as a valuable artwork that has successfully transcended the limitations of commercialization.

B) By considering "Starry Night" as a prime example of art's transformative power, offering a glimpse into the artist's emotions.

C) By criticizing "Starry Night" for not challenging capitalism, unlike Warhol.

D) By agreeing that it is captivating in its fluidity but not transformative like other Impressionists.

CONTINUE

The following text is adapted from Herman Melville's 1851 novel, *Moby Dick; or The Whale.*

Call me Ishmael. Some years ago—never mind how long precisely—having little or no money in my purse, and nothing particular to interest me on shore, I thought I would sail about a little and see the watery part of the world. It is a way I have of driving off the spleen and regulating the circulation. Whenever I find myself growing grim about the mouth; whenever it is a damp, drizzly November in my soul; whenever I find myself involuntarily bringing up the rear of every funeral I meet—then, I account it high time to get to sea as soon as I can. If they but knew it, almost all men in their degree, some time or other, cherish very nearly the same feelings towards the ocean with me.

What is the main idea of the text?

A) A ship captain describes the reasons for embarking on his career.

B) A sailor reminisces about the impetus for setting out on a voyage.

C) A merchant sailor develops an argument about his poor salary.

D) An impoverished man explains how he degenerated to his current condition.

The common solution of building more roads may not have the desired effect of reducing rush-hour traffic. For example, the Katy Freeway project in Houston cost millions of dollars and the upshot was that congestion got worse, with travel times increased by 55% during the evening rush hour and by a third in the mornings. The reason for that is something called "induced demand," a term introduced in the 1960s by economists. It relates to the phenomenon that if more of a good is produced, more is consumed. In the same way, if more roads are provided, more people are encouraged to drive.

According to the text, what is induced demand?

A) An idea that contradicts a widespread belief that congestion is the result of road building.

B) A phenomenon that is rarely taken into account when road systems are being planned.

C) A theory that is understood by city planners and has affected their traditional solutions to traffic congestion.

D) A concept that can be mitigated by educating consumers about the potential effects.

12

Published in 1794 by William Blake, "The Tyger" is a classic poem from a larger collection titled Songs of Experience. The poem uses the imagery of fire to delve into the question of who might have created such a dangerous creature: _____

Which quotation from "The Tyger" most effectively illustrates the claim?

A) "In what distant deeps or skies, / Burnt the fire of thine eyes?"

B) "In what furnace was thy brain? /What the anvil? what dread grasp / Dare its deadly terrors clasp?"

C) "When the stars threw down their spears, / And water'd heaven with their tears, / Did he smile his work to see?"

D) "Did he who made the Lamb make thee?"

13

Every year, Earth follows a slightly elliptical path around the sun, resulting in two significant points in its orbit. One day, known as perihelion, marks the closest proximity between Earth and the sun, while another day, called aphelion, represents the farthest distance between them. While perihelion and aphelion vary by millions of miles, their influence on Earth's temperatures is minimal. Scientists have determined that the primary factor responsible for the changing seasons is actually the 23.5-degree tilt of Earth's axis.

Which finding, if true, would most directly support the scientists' finding?

A) During perihelion, the continent on Earth that is directly facing the sun typically experiences temperatures that are 1.5°C higher than normal.

B) In July, the Southern hemisphere is tilted away from the sun and experiences shorter and colder days.

C) During aphelion, the continent on Earth that is facing away from the sun typically experiences temperatures that are 1.5°C lower than normal.

D) For each hemisphere, summer always occurs during perihelion and winter always occurs during aphelion.

CONTINUE

Chili Peppers Exposed to Salt Stress

NaCl concen-tration (mM)	Average days to first flower	Average days to first fruit	Average number of fruits
0	23.66	48	6
30	23.66	52	3
60	31.66	66	2
90	39.66	0	0
120	40.33	0	0

This study about salt in the soil of growing chili plants indicated that increasing NaCl concentrations significantly delayed flowering and fruit ripening and significantly reduced the fruits' number, size, fresh mass and vitamins B6, B12 and C concentrations, but increased capsaicinoid concentration and consequently the fruit's tangy flavor. For example, plants _____.

Which choice most effectively uses data from the table to complete the example?

A) subjected to high NaCl concentrations were highest in capsaicinoid.

B) subjected to high NaCl concentrations had lower nutritional value.

C) with a NaCl concentration of 90 mM took 16 extra days to flower beyond ones with no salt.

D) with a NaCl concentration of 30 mM averaged 52 chili fruits on the plant.

A new deep-sea mapping model used over 700,000 images from every angle to create a full-sized 3D reconstruction of the Titanic, the major shipwreck caused by an iceberg that was discovered in 1985. The scan shows the bow, the stern, the boat deck, and even intricate details from the personal possessions of the ship's passengers to the serial number on one of the propellers. In order to create such a comprehensive view, the deep-sea mapping team had to map every square centimeter of the shipwreck, even uninteresting parts like _____

Which choice most logically completes the text?

A) the type of fuel used decades ago by the Titanic.

B) the mud in between the debris of the shipwreck.

C) the cracks on the side of the ship caused by the impact from the iceberg.

D) the scale of the 40,000 ton ship.

MSCHF, a company based in New York, has created a minuscule replica of one of Louis Vuitton's luxury purses; the tiny bag, sized 657 by 222 by 700 micrometers, can balance on top of a fingertip. MSCHF's replica is predicted to command at least $15,000 at an auction. MSCHF's artists believe that some luxury bags that are in fashion are so small that they no longer serve the purpose of a bag: to be able to hold a range of items. This tiny purse is only one of a multitude of hyperbolic products created to

_____

Which choice most logically completes the text?

A) pay homage to the heritage of designer brands.

B) replicate the items used in daily life in forms of artistic expression.

C) satirize the absurdity of consumerism in fashion.

D) criticize the inflation of everyday products.

When Charles Darwin first encountered the Galapagos finches during his expedition in 1835, he was amazed by their remarkable diversity and unique adaptations. Each finch species had a distinct beak shape and size that was well-suited to its specific feeding habits. For example, some had long, slender beaks for probing flowers, while others had powerful beaks for cracking nuts. The Galapagos finches, which lay eggs but also raise _____ offspring with care, have since become a classic example of evolution through natural selection.

Which choice completes the text so that it conforms to the conventions of Standard English?

A) it's

B) their

C) they're

D) its

18

Yuval Noah Harari is an Israeli historian who regularly discussed global issues with world leaders. Considered one of the foremost thinkers of his time, his current interest is delving into difficult questions combining biology and history, such as asking whether people _____ happier since the Stone Age to the present.

Which choice completes the text so that it conforms to the conventions of Standard English?

A) become

B) are becoming

C) have become

D) will have become

19

Energy access and gender are deeply entwined components of the global development agenda. The transformative effect on women of access to affordable, reliable, and sustainable modern energy _____ well established by countless research studies.

Which choice completes the text so that it conforms to the conventions of Standard English?

A) are

B) were

C) has been

D) have been

20

In Shakespeare's timeless tragedy, Macbeth is driven to madness and despair after he encounters three witches who prophesy that he will become King of Scotland. Tempted by ambition and spurred on by Gruochj, _____ killed the current king and seized the throne.

Which choice completes the text so that it conforms to the conventions of Standard English?

A) she

B) they

C) it

D) he

21

Attending the cinema allows for the exercise of personal preferences and the human need for distinction. In a nutshell, cinema attendance can be a personally expressive experience, good _____ therapeutic at the same time.

Which choice completes the text so that it conforms to the conventions of Standard English?

A) fun, and,

B) fun, and

C) fun; and

D) fun—and

CONTINUE

22

In a 2022 paper written by Kyle Rupp and _____ the researchers explore the complex mechanisms behind the automatic ability that most people have to recognize features of the human voice, even to the point of distinguishing subtleties of emotion and intention.

Which choice completes the text so that it conforms to the conventions of Standard English?

A) associates

B) associates,

C) associates—

D) associates:

23

Even within a single musical tradition, there may be fine distinctions based on the character and color of the voice. _____ a lyric soprano has a light, refined tone and a dramatic soprano has a powerful, emotional tone.

Which choice completes the text so that it conforms to the conventions of Standard English?

A) For example among operatic voices

B) For example, among operatic voices:

C) For example: among operatic voices,

D) For example, among operatic voices,

24

The energy industry has long met demand by varying the rate at which it produces fuel. Controlling the output of an oil–fired power plant is much like changing the speed of a car—press the accelerator and more gas flows to the engine. _____ the wind cannot be turned up or down. Smart software is one solution to make wind farms more efficient and responsive.

Which choice completes the text with the most logical transition?

A) Nevertheless,

B) Despite this,

C) Furthermore,

D) However,

25

Social work can take a toll, but it is deeply rewarding when you can see a positive change in someone else's life. There are many different career paths in social work. _____ there are some administrative roles, most social workers deal directly with clients. So regardless of the field you choose, you are most likely to interact with people on a regular basis.

Which choice completes the text with the most logical transition?

A) However,

B) While

C) Nevertheless

D) Therefore,

26

The Paleo diet includes meat, fruit, and vegetables in an attempt to recreate the eating patterns of prehistoric hunter–gatherers. Although it is a popular way to lose weight in the short term, there is no long–term credible research confirming its efficacy. _____ many scientists point out that the diet is misguided because wild grains were consumed well before the advent of farming.

Which choice completes the text with the most logical transition?

A) Subsequently,

B) Nevertheless,

C) Moreover,

D) Therefore,

While researching a topic, a student has taken the following notes:

- Shakespeare's play, Macbeth, explores the themes of ambition, guilt, and the perils of unchecked power.

- Shakespeare explores themes of revenge, uncertainty, and madness in "Hamlet".

- Macbeth begins as an unwavering subject of King Duncan but eventually succumbs to ambition and power-hunger, becoming his master's worst nightmare.

- Hamlet, on the other hand, is paralyzed by indecision and consumed by his desire for revenge.

- Both plays provide examples of Shakespeare's expert use of soliloquies to explore characters' internal thoughts and struggles.

The student wants to emphasize the differences in the main themes explored in the plays "Macbeth" and "Hamlet". Which choice most effectively uses relevant information from the notes to accomplish this goal?

A) Both "Macbeth" and "Hamlet" showcase Shakespeare;s talent in employing soliloquies to illuminate their protagonists' inner turmoils.'

B) "Macbeth" explores themes of unbridled power and ambition leading to disaster, while "Hamlet" predominantly deals with revenge and indecision.

C) Macbeth undergoes a transformation driven by ambition and the pursuit of power, unlike Hamlet who is motivated by revenge and uncertainty.

D) While "Macbeth" delves into the themes of ambition, guilt, and unchecked power, "Hamlet" investigates the motifs of revenge, uncertainty, and madness.

Reading Test

27 QUESTIONS | 32 MINUTES

DIRECTIONS

The questions in this section address a number of important reading and writing skills. Each question includes one or more passages, which may include a table or graph. Read each passage and question carefully, and then choose the best answer to the question based on the passage(s). All questions in this section are multiple-choice with four answer choices. Each question has a single best answer.

1

Any country, city, or rural village could be, in fact, its own unique tourism magnet. The tourism business, though, is <u>broader</u> than just the destination. Considerations need to be made for transportation, hotels and guest accommodations, and services that link the various components of a trip, such as guide services in national parks or city bus tours.

As used in the text, what does the word "broader" most nearly mean?

A) More pronounced

B) More general

C) More spacious

D) More extensive

2

The following text is from Jane Austen's 1811 novel, "Sense and Sensibility."

Many were the tears shed by them in their last adieus to a place so much beloved. "And you, ye well-known trees," said Marianne, "but you will continue the same, unconscious of the pleasure or the regret you occasion, and <u>insensible</u> of any change in those who walk under your shade! But who will remain to enjoy you?"

As used in the text, what does the word "insensible" most nearly mean?

A) Comatose

B) Negligible

C) Unaware

D) Insentient

3

The following text is adapted from F. Scott Fitzgerald's 1922 novel, *The Beautiful and the Damned.*

Now Adam J. Patch left his father's farm in Tarrytown early in sixty–one to join a New York cavalry regiment. He came home from the war a major, charged into Wall Street, and amid much fuss, <u>fume</u>, applause, and ill will he gathered to himself some seventy–five million dollars.

As used in the text, what does the word "fume" most nearly mean?

A) Exhaust

B) Stench

C) Pollution

D) Ire

4

Sometimes, behaviors have underlying reasons that are not initially apparent, as shown through a classic experiment by Walter Mischel. During the 1960s, Mischel placed a marshmallow piece in front of 600 children aged 4–6. About a third were willing to wait 15 minutes to get a whole marshmallow, and those children got higher SAT scores years later. However, Mischel's theory that willpower contributed to future success was somewhat arbitrary. A later experiment conducted by Tyler Watts and associates included a broader analysis of ethnicity and social status and determined that economic background most closely predicted the demonstrated behavior.

Which choice best states the main purpose of the text?

A) It presents the study by Tyler Watts to show that most behavioral psychology experiments are flawed.

B) It argues that experiments regarding behavior should be performed multiple times in order to determine true correlations.

C) It explains a significant problem in the current understanding of willpower in young children.

D) It discusses the study by Walter Mischel to show that there may be alternate explanations in an apparently obvious situation.

5

The median annual wage for urban and regional planners was $73,050 in May 2018. <u>The median wage is the wage at which half the workers in an occupation earned more than that amount and half earned less.</u> The lowest 10 percent earned less than $45,180, and the highest 10 percent earned more than $114,170. Employment of urban and regional planners is projected to grow 11 percent from 2018 to 2028, much faster than the average for all occupations. Demographic, transportation, and environmental changes will drive employment growth for planners. Within cities, urban planners will be needed to develop revitalization projects and address issues associated with population growth, environmental degradation, the movement of people and goods, and resource scarcity.

Which choice best states the function of the underlined sentence in the text as whole?

A) To define a term provided in the passage

B) To point out that the median wage is an insufficient measurement

C) To suggest a possible reason for the wide range in salaries

D) To provide support for the claim that employment is predicted to grow

6

Text 1

Depression is an illness of brain circuitry and chemistry that causes and is caused by changes in mood, thinking, and behavior. Behavioral activation is a type of talk therapy that helps patients free themselves from negative mood spirals by identifying a connection between actions and emotions, and gradually add small and enjoyable actions back into their lives. The process decreases avoidance, bolsters peer connection, and improves engagement in activities. This non–intrusive solution takes time, but is much healthier than covering the problem with medications.

Text 2

Studies have shown that a single ketamine infusion can often rapidly relieve depressive symptoms within hours in people who have not responded to conventional antidepressants, which typically take weeks or months to work. However, widespread use of ketamine for treatment–resistant depression has raised concerns about side effects, including feelings of floating, queasiness, visual distortions, and numbness. These conditions occurred in at least half of the participants of one study, but none persisted for more than four hours. To overcome these problems, ongoing research is necessary to develop a more practical rapid–acting antidepressant that works in the brain similarly to ketamine.

Based on the texts, how would the author of Text 1 most likely view the conclusion drawn by the author in the final sentence of Text 2?

A) With agreement, because she knows most depression treatments are insufficient

B) With reservation, because she promotes less invasive ways to address depression

C) With confusion, because she feels that the drug does not need any modification

D) With disapproval, because she contends that drug therapies are unacceptable

7

The following text is adapted from Abraham Lincoln's last public address, given April 11, 1865.

Some twelve thousand voters in the heretofore slave-state of Louisiana have sworn allegiance to the Union, assumed to be the rightful political power of the State, held elections, organized a State government, adopted a free-state constitution, and empowered the Legislature to confer the elective franchise upon the colored man. Now, if we reject, and spurn them, we do our utmost to disorganize and disperse them. We in effect say to the white men, "You are worthless, or worse--we will neither help you, nor be helped by you." To the blacks we say, "This cup of liberty which these, your old masters, hold to your lips, we will dash from you, and leave you to the chances of gathering the spilled and scattered contents in some vague and undefined when, where, and how."

According to the text, what does the imagery of a cup of liberty mainly serve to emphasize?

A) The generosity of the Union in giving freed slaves certain benefits

B) The advances made by the Union in protecting the rights of former slaves

C) The unconscious way in which many people accept their freedoms

D) The precarious nature of the freedoms granted to former slaves in Louisiana

8

The following text is adapted from Jefferson Keel's 2011 statement, "The Indian Reorganization Act—75 Years Later."

Our predecessors had a shared vision. Indian reservations should be places where the old ways are maintained, our languages are spoken, and our children learn our traditions and pass them on. They are places where there are fish in the stream and game in the field, and food grows wild; places where our people can live and be Indian. At the same time, this vision includes modern life, economic development to sustain our people; safety and respectful relationships with our neighbors; and the blessings of education, health care and modern technology. This vision was shared by the U.S. Congress in 1934 when it passed the Indian Reorganization Act. With the IRA, Congress renewed its trust responsibility to protect and restore our tribal homelands and the Indian way of life.

What is the main idea of the text?

A) The Indian Reorganization Act is a policy in keeping with the view of the earlier Indian people themselves.

B) The Indian Reorganization Act was written by Indian predecessors in order to preserve traditional culture.

C) The Indian Reorganization Act was created in the effort to deny Native Americans the basic rights they wished for.

D) The Indian Reorganization Act has been successful in helping Native American cultures to thrive since it was enacted.

CONTINUE ➡

9

The following text is adapted from Fyodor Dostoevsky's 1848 short story collection, "White Nights and Other Stories."

I came back to the town very late, and it had struck ten as I was going towards my lodgings. My way lay along the canal embankment, where at that hour you never meet a soul. It is true that I live in a very remote part of the town. I walked along singing, for when I am happy I am always humming to myself like every happy man who has no friend or acquaintance with whom to share his joy. Suddenly I had a most unexpected adventure.

According to the text, what is the reason the narrator is walking along the embankment late at night?

A) He wanted to avoid meeting other people.

B) He was escaping the pressures of the city.

C) He was returning to his quarters.

D) He sought more excitement in his life.

10

The Red Planet, Mars, has long fascinated scientists and astronomers alike. With its distinct reddish hue and proximity to Earth, Mars has been the subject of numerous space missions and scientific investigations. Researchers have focused their attention on Mars' potential for harboring life and its geological features. The exploration of Mars involves the study of its atmosphere, surface, and subsurface, as well as the search for evidence of water. Recent missions, such as the Mars Rover expeditions, have provided valuable data about the planet's geology and the possibility of ancient microbial life. By understanding Mars, scientists gain insights into the conditions that could support life beyond our own planet.

What is the main idea of the text?

A) Mars has been the subject of scientific investigations and missions due to its potential for harboring life and its geological features.

B) Mars' reddish hue and proximity to Earth have fascinated scientists and astronomers for a long time.

C) Recent missions, like the Mars Rover expeditions, have provided valuable data about Mars' geology and the possibility of ancient microbial life.

D) By understanding Mars, scientists gain insights into the conditions that could support life beyond our own planet.

11

Over the past 30 years, scientists have discovered many dinosaurs from the group known as Carcharodontosauridae, but a lack of complete fossils led to many assumptions about their structure and movement. However, a recent find in Argentina of a species named *Meraxes gigas* gives new insights. Standing 11 meters (36 feet) and weighing 4 tons, the carnivore probably appeared very much like the unrelated *Tyrannosaurus rex*. This conclusion is partly based on the discovery of an almost intact arm bone that is extremely short like those of *T. rex*.

Which finding, if true, would most strongly support the scientists' conclusion?

A) *M. gigas* and *T. rex* were discovered to have lived in time periods separated by about 20 million years.

B) The skull bones from the *M. gigas* fossil are oversized in proportion to the body, as are those of *T. rex* fossils.

C) The average size of an adult *T. rex* varied greatly, between 5 tons and almost 7 tons.

D) Remains from both *T. rex* and M. gigas show that they both were carnivores which preyed on mostly herbivorous dinosaurs.

12

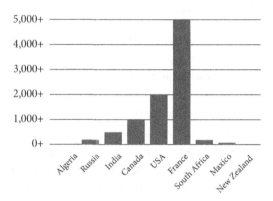

Daily new confirmed COVID-19 cases per million people, January 28, 2022

Effectively managing infectious diseases demands a comprehensive grasp of the factors that contribute to their transmission. While controlling highly infectious diseases such as the COVID-19 virus can depend on a variety of conditions and multiple sociodemographic, epidemiological, and geographic factors, a recent study has attempted to shed light on whether a country with a high number of COVID-19 cases can impact infection rates in a neighboring country. A prime example of the scope of this study can be observed in the case of _____

Which choice most effectively completes the text using information from the graph?

A) Canada, which had a lower number of daily new confirmed cases as compared to neighboring USA which was recording between 1000 to 2000 new cases daily.

B) Argentina, with more than 5000 daily new cases as compared to the rest of South America.

C) Russia, which had significantly higher case numbers than the 500 plus cases being reported daily in India.

D) India, which shares significant trade routes with Australia where daily case numbers exceeded 5000.

CONTINUE

13

The Smithsonian's National Museum of American History has curated an extensive photo exhibition of Disney's theme parks. Curator Bethanee Bemis believed that Disney World and Disneyland played significant roles in the national history of America, both reflecting American values and adapting based on its American visitors. For instance, a photo of a Japanese American family visiting the theme park in 1955 reflects the changes in attitudes towards Japanese immigrants after the end of Japanese internment camps in the US. Other historians would agree with Bemis' conclusion, _____

Which choice most logically completes the text?

A) referring to Disney theme parks as reflections of American culture and history.

B) stating that the majority of the parks' visitors are domestic American tourists.

C) comparing the varying impacts of Disneyland and Disneyworld on American culture.

D) also using photographs as the most accurate medium to capture Disney's influence.

14

The main and only method today for sterilizing female cats is an invasive surgical operation wherein the cat's reproductive organs are removed. Post-surgical complications can include infection, hemorrhaging, extreme stress, and other issues. Further, the amount of time and resources required to neuter stray cats can be challenging since the cats must be found, trapped, relocated, sterilized, monitored and then released. Finally, since the operation can only be done by medical experts, _____

Which choice most logically completes the text?

A) the locations and health conditions of stray cats may be difficult to identify and understand

B) all veterinary hospitals are authorized to perform sterilization surgeries.

C) the availability of suitable veterinarians is another limiting factor and downside of surgical sterilization.

D) more junior veterinarians should be trained to carry out sterilizations of stray female cats.

15

A recent study by the University of California has found that when a particular scent blew through the bedrooms of senior citizens every night for two hours over the course of six months, memories _____, with cognitive capacity in participants increasing by 226%. This revolutionizes our understanding of the connection between smell and memory, offering a potential non-intrusive method to mitigate the onset of dementia.

Which choice completes the text so that it conforms to the conventions of Standard English?

A) skyrocket

B) will skyrocket

C) skyrocketed

D) are skyrocketing

16

Scientists have discovered that Heliconius butterflies _____ the location of consistent pollen sources and create long-term traplines. Traplines are learned foraging paths, which involve revisiting the same food sources consistently over successive days. This effective foraging tactic mirrors the behavior observed in certain orchid bees and bumblebees.

Which choice completes the text so that it conforms to the conventions of Standard English?

A) can remember

B) will remember

C) have remembered

D) are remembering

17

Known best for his famous *Lord of the Rings* trilogy, author J.R.R. Tolkien also completed a translation of the epic poem "Beowulf" in 1926. His son found the manuscript and had it published in 2014, 40 years after _____ death.

Which choice completes the text so that it conforms to the conventions of Standard English?

A) Tolkein

B) Tolkiens

C) Tolkiens'

D) Tolkien's

18

Recently, astronomers discovered two new rocky planets approximately the size of Earth. Smaller than our Sun, _____ making the two planets orbiting it potentially close enough to study their atmospheres in detail. Since the cooler of the two is estimated to be 543 degrees Fahrenheit (284 degrees Celsius), there is little chance of life as we know it, though.

Which choice completes the text so that it conforms to the conventions of Standard English?

A) there are only 33 light years between the red dwarf star HD260655 and our Solar System,

B) only 33 light years separate the red dwarf star HD260655 from our Solar System,

C) our Solar System is only 33 light years away from the red dwarf star HD260655,

D) the red dwarf star HD260655 is only 33 light years away from our solar system,

19

In 1967, Kenyan writer Ngugi wa Thiong'o worked as a lecturer in the department of English at the University of _____ "A Grain of Wheat in July" in the same year. He became instrumental in a movement that advanced African literature.

Which choice completes the text so that it conforms to the conventions of Standard English?

A) Nairobi and published

B) Nairobi, and published

C) Nairobi and published,

D) Nairobi, and published,

20

People often join martial arts such as karate, judo, and taekwondo in order to increase their amount of weekly exercise in an interesting way. Those who participate for extended periods, though, typically cite the development of personal qualities—particularly _____ the reason they continue.

Which choice completes the text so that it conforms to the conventions of Standard English?

A) self-control—

B) self-control—as

C) self-control—which is

D) self-control— they say is

21

Rainwater harvesting is the collection of run–off from a structure or other impervious surface in order to store it for later use. Rainwater collection systems can be as simple _____ rain in a rain barrel or as elaborate as harvesting rainwater into large cisterns to supply your entire household demand.

Which choice completes the text so that it conforms to the conventions of Standard English?

A) as: collecting

B) as, collecting

C) as—collecting

D) as collecting

22

The delicate art of Kamāl ud–Dīn Behzād, who was born circa 1455, is often considered the apogee of Islamic miniature paintings. Director of a workshop in the Herat Academy, Behzād had great influence, and his work was copied extensively both _____ his lifetime.

Which choice completes the text so that it conforms to the conventions of Standard English?

A) during, and after

B) during and after,

C) during—and after

D) during and after

23

Most people have heard of search and rescue dogs, which assist the police and other responders in finding victims of crimes or natural disasters. There are two work methods that the dogs follow.. Trailing dogs follow the specific scent of one person along the path that the person took. _____ air–scent dogs sniff the general vicinity until they find any individual in the search region.

Which choice completes the text with the most logical transition?

A) Because of this,

B) By contrast,

C) Therefore,

D) Moreover,

24

It may seem that all mosquitoes hate the human race, but in reality, only the females require blood to obtain a specific protein needed to produce eggs. Males do not drink blood. _____ even if they wanted to, they do not have the mouthparts to pierce skin. It turns out that mosquitoes get most of their energy from plant nectar and fruit.

Which choice completes the text with the most logical transition?

A) Therefore,

B) Finally,

C) In fact,

D) Namely,

While researching a topic, a student has taken the following notes:

- James Joyce was an Irish writer famous for writing novels such as Ulysses which featured stream-of-consciousness narrative techniques.

- American author William Faulkner used similar methods in "The Sound and the Fury".

- Joyce's "Ulysses" centers around one day in Dublin and features multiple characters' inner thoughts.

- By contrast, Faulkner's "The Sound and the Fury" chronicles the decline of one family over three decades in America's South.

- As with his other works, Joyce experimented with form and language in Ulysses, which is best known for its humor, clever wordplay, dense prose, allusive references, and dense plot lines.

- Faulkner is known for his intricate narrative structures as well as for exploring Southern identity issues through moral issues in his stories.

The student wants to emphasize the differences between James Joyce's "Ulysses" and William Faulkner's "The Sound and the Fury". Which choice most effectively uses relevant information from the notes to accomplish this goal?

A) James Joyce's "Ulysses" takes place over one day in Dublin and features humor and wordplay; in contrast, William Faulkner's "The Sound and the Fury" spans over thirty years to explore Southern identity and morality.

B) Both "Ulysses" by Joyce and Faulkner's "The Sound and the Fury" employ a stream-of-consciousness narrative style, representing their literary connection.

C) James Joyce's "Ulysses" and William Faulkner's "The Sound and the Fury" both focus on multiple characters' internal thought processes, showing their depth.

D) Ulysses by Joyce and Faulkner's The Sound and the Fury are celebrated for their intricate narrative structures, signaling their prominence within literary works.

26

While researching a topic, a student has taken the following notes:

- The Greek tragedy "Oedipus Rex" is widely recognized for its sublime dramatic irony; audiences become aware of Oedipus' fate long before he does.

- "To Kill a Mockingbird" by Harper Lee utilizes dramatic irony through Boo Radley, initially seen as an intimidating figure but who later becomes an emblem of kindness and safety.

- "Pride and Prejudice" by Jane Austen makes effective use of dramatic irony; readers witness Darcy's increasing feelings for Elizabeth before even she realizes them.

- Shakespeare employs dramatic irony in "Macbeth" to draw his audience into his story, with everyone, including Macbeth, aware of Macbeth becoming King while Duncan, Banquo, and other characters are unaware.

The student wants to provide an explanation and example of dramatic irony in literature. Which choice most effectively uses relevant information from the notes to accomplish this goal?

A) Dramatic irony in literature allows audiences to gain more information than its characters, such as in "Oedipus Rex," where audiences know of Oedipus' fate while Oedipus remains unaware until its conclusion.

B) Boo Radley serves as an emblematic representative of dramatic irony in Harper Lee's "To Kill a Mockingbird". Initially seen as frightening and hostile, Boo eventually transforms into an unsuspected protector.

C) Jane Austen's classic novel "Pride and Prejudice" employs dramatic irony expertly; readers recognize Darcy's growing feelings for Elizabeth Bennet long before Elizabeth herself does.

D) Shakespeare's "Macbeth" employs dramatic irony by informing Macbeth himself about the prophecy predicting that he will become king, leaving Duncan and Banquo unaware.

27

While researching a topic, a student has taken the following notes:

- Cher is a famous musician and performer born in 1946.

- She was known for regularly changing her appearance and musical styles.

- In the 1970s, she starred in a TV series that ran for 3 years.

- She collaborated with her husband on her first pop/rock hit, "I Got You Babe" (1965).

- Her 1979 disco dance song "Take Me Home" brought her fame after a hiatus.

The student wants to emphasize a point using the two songs. Which choice most effectively uses relevant information from the notes to accomplish this goal?

A) "I Got You Babe" was performed in 1965 and "Take Me Home" was performed in 1979.

B) Cher changed styles regularly, using pop/rock for "I Got You Babe" and disco for "Take Me Home."

C) In the 1970s, Cher performed in a television series as well as sang "Take Me Home."

D) Cher both collaborated with her husband and performed a disco dance song.

STOP

No Test Material On This Page

No Test Material On This Page

Math

22 QUESTIONS | 35 MINUTES

DIRECTIONS

The questions in this section address a number of important math skills. Use of a calculator is permitted for all questions.

NOTES

Unless otherwise indicated: • All variables and expressions represent real numbers. • Figures provided are drawn to scale. • All figures lie in a plane. • The domain of a given function is the set of all real numbers x for which $f(x)$ is a real number.

REFERENCE

$A = \pi r^2$ $A = \ell w$ $A = \frac{1}{2}bh$ $c^2 = a^2 + b^2$ Special Right Triangles

$C = 2\pi r$

$V = \ell w h$ $V = \pi r^2 h$ $V = \frac{4}{3}\pi r^3$ $V = \frac{1}{3}\pi r^2 h$ $V = \frac{1}{3}\ell w h$

The number of degrees of arc in a circle is 360.

The number of radians of arc in a circle is 2π.

The sum of the measures in degrees of the angles of a triangle is 180.

For **multiple–choice questions,** solve each problem, choose the correct answer from the choices provided, and then circle your answer in this book. Circle only one answer for each question. If you change your mind, completely erase the circle. You will not get credit for questions with more than one answer circled, or for questions with no answers circled.

For **student–produced response questions,** solve each problem and write your answer next to or under the question in the test book as described below.

- Once you've written your answer, circle it clearly. You will not receive credit for anything written outside the circle, or for any questions with more than one circled answer.

- If you find more than one correct answer, write and circle only one answer.

- Your answer can be up to 5 characters for a positive answer and up to 6 characters (including the negative sign) for a negative answer, but no more.

- If your answer is a fraction that is too long (over 5 characters for positive, 6 characters for negative), write the decimal equivalent.

- If your answer is a decimal that is too long (over 5 characters for positive, 6 characters for negative), truncate it or round at the fourth digit.

- If your answer is a mixed number (such as 3.!. 2), write it as an improper fraction (7/2) or its decimal equivalent (3.5).

- Don't include symbols such as a percent sign, comma, or dollar sign in your circled answer.

CONTINUE ▶

1

If $4x + 16 = 24$, what is the value of $x + 4$?

A) 2

B) 4

C) 6

D) 8

2

Cocopine high school conducts annual surveys at its school to find out the number of teachers and students by gender. The results of the survey showed that there were 35 teachers and 245 students in the school.

	Students	Teacher
Male	131	
Female		16

Using the table above, if a person is chosen at random, what is the probability that the person is a male teacher?

A) $\dfrac{19}{280}$

B) $\dfrac{19}{150}$

C) $\dfrac{19}{131}$

D) $\dfrac{19}{35}$

3

$$|2x - 3| = 11$$

If a is a solution to this equation above and $a > 0$, what is the value of a?

4

Line k is a line perpendicular to line m. Given that the equation for line m is $5y = 4x + 15$, which of the following could be the equation for line k?

A) $y = \dfrac{4}{5}x - 12$

B) $y = \dfrac{5}{4}x + 6$

C) $y = -\dfrac{5}{4}x - 2$

D) $y = \dfrac{5}{4}x + 10$

5

What is the center of the circle, given that its equation is $x^2 + y^2 - 6x + 4y = 36$?

A) $(-3, 2)$

B) $(2, -3)$

C) $(3, -2)$

D) $(-2, 3)$

6

If $(8^x)^x \times 4^{2x}$ is equivalent to $\left(\dfrac{2^{ax}}{2^{-b}}\right)^x$, what is the value of a?

7

$$-6x + 3 < y$$
$$y < x + 6$$

If (x, y) is a solution to the above system of inequalities, which of the following could be (x, y)?

A) $(-2, -4)$

B) $(4, 7)$

C) $(-2, 1)$

D) $(-2, -4)$

8

If $f(x) = 2(x-3)^2 + 8$ is transformed to $g(x) = 2(x-5)^2 + 5$, which of the following describes the transformation?

A) The x coordinate moves to the right 2 units and the y coordinate moves 3 units down.

B) The x coordinate moves to the left 2 units and the y coordinate moves 3 units down.

C) The x coordinate moves to the right 2 units and the y coordinate moves 3 units up.

D) The x coordinate moves to the left 2 units and the y coordinate moves 3 units up.

9

Which of the following equation best represents the graph below?

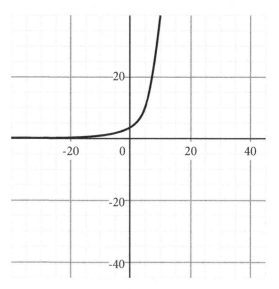

A) $y = 5(0.7)^x$

B) $y = 5(1.3)^x$

C) $y = 3(0.7)^x$

D) $y = 3(1.3)^x$

10

If triangle PQR (not shown) is similar to triangle DEF shown below and DE = 2PQ, what is the value of sin R?

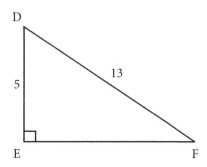

11

The average SAT score of 7 students in a class is 1,320. If a student with an SAT score of 1,460 joins the class, what will be the new average SAT score (rounded off to the nearest 10)?

A) 1,300

B) 1,340

C) 1,390

D) 1,460

12

A researcher studies bacteria in a pond and models a function that shows how the bacteria populate in the pond. Let t be the number of days since the bacteria began to populate the pond. Which of the following is the best interpretation of $(3)^{\frac{t}{14}}$ in the equation: $p(t) = 2,034(3)^{\frac{t}{14}}$?

A) The number of bacteria at the beginning of the study

B) The number of bacteria triples every two weeks

C) The number of bacteria increases by 3 every two weeks

D) The number of bacteria in the pond after two weeks

13

$$5(x+3) - 3(2-x) = px + 7$$

What is the value of p, if the equation above has no solutions?

14

$$3x - 4y = 16$$

$$-6x = -8y + 32$$

How many solutions does the above system of equations have?

A) One solution

B) Two solutions

C) Infinitely many solutions

D) No solution

15

What is the length of the minor arc AB, given that the diameter of the circle is 12 cm and the measure of the angle of sector AOB is 72°?

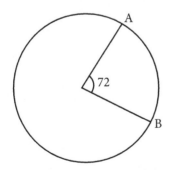

A) 2.4π

B) 28.8π

C) 12π

D) $\dfrac{\pi}{6}$

16

The expression $y = -2(x+3)^2 + 6$ is equivalent to $ax^2 + bx + c$, where $a < 0$ and $b < 0$. What is the value of c?

17

If the coordinates of the midpoint of line segment AB are (8, 10) and the coordinates of point A are (6, 11), which of the following would represent the coordinates of point B?

A) (7, 10.5)

B) (2, 0.5)

C) (10, 9)

D) (7, 11)

18

How many solutions does the equation $|x+3| = 0$ have?

A) None

B) One

C) Two

D) There is not enough information to answer the question.

19

What is the value of $|f(2)|$ where
$f(x) = x^2 - 20x + 9$?

A) -27

B) 27

C) 35

D) 53

20

The price of oil increased by 20% at the beginning of May. Some policies were then put in place which reduced the price of oil by 14% two weeks after the initial increase. What is the overall percentage increase or decrease in the oil?

21

A circle is inscribed in a square. If the length of one side of the square is $4\sqrt{2}$ and the area of the circle is $p\pi$, what is the value of p?

A) 8

B) 16

C) 32

D) 64

22

$-3x + 6 \leq 2 - x$

Which of the following is not a solution to the inequality above ?

A) 0

B) 2

C) 3

D) 4

No Test Material On This Page

Math

22 QUESTIONS | 35 MINUTES

DIRECTIONS

The questions in this section address a number of important math skills. Use of a calculator is permitted for all questions.

NOTES

Unless otherwise indicated: • All variables and expressions represent real numbers. • Figures provided are drawn to scale. • All figures lie in a plane. • The domain of a given function is the set of all real numbers x for which $f(x)$ is a real number.

REFERENCE

$A = \pi r^2$
$C = 2\pi r$

$A = \ell w$

$A = \dfrac{1}{2} bh$

$c^2 = a^2 + b^2$

Special Right Triangles

$V = \ell w h$

$V = \pi r^2 h$

$V = \dfrac{4}{3}\pi r^3$

$V = \dfrac{1}{3}\pi r^2 h$

$V = \dfrac{1}{3}\ell w h$

The number of degrees of arc in a circle is 360.

The number of radians of arc in a circle is 2π.

The sum of the measures in degrees of the angles of a triangle is 180.

For **multiple-choice questions,** solve each problem, choose the correct answer from the choices provided, and then circle your answer in this book. Circle only one answer for each question. If you change your mind, completely erase the circle. You will not get credit for questions with more than one answer circled, or for questions with no answers circled.

For **student-produced response questions,** solve each problem and write your answer next to or under the question in the test book as described below.

- Once you've written your answer, circle it clearly. You will not receive credit for anything written outside the circle, or for any questions with more than one circled answer.

- If you find more than one correct answer, write and circle only one answer.

- Your answer can be up to 5 characters for a positive answer and up to 6 characters (including the negative sign) for a negative answer, but no more.

- If your answer is a fraction that is too long (over 5 characters for positive, 6 characters for negative), write the decimal equivalent.

- If your answer is a decimal that is too long (over 5 characters for positive, 6 characters for negative), truncate it or round at the fourth digit.

- If your answer is a mixed number (such as 3.!. 2), write it as an improper fraction (7/2) or its decimal equivalent (3.5).

- Don't include symbols such as a percent sign, comma, or dollar sign in your circled answer.

1

If m and n are solutions to the equation $f(x) = 3x^2 + 9x - 27,$ what is the value of $m + n$?

A) -9

B) -3

C) 3

D) 9

2

Which of the following is equivalent to $3x^2 y + 5x - (3x^2 y^2 - 2x^2 y)$?

A) $6x^2 y - 3x^2 y^2 + 5x$

B) $x^2 y - 3x^2 y^2 + 5x$

C) $6x^2 y - 2x^2 y^2 + 5x$

D) $-3x^2 y^2 + 5x^2 y + 5x$

3

$$-2y + 2 < 6$$

What is the least integer value of y that satisfies the inequality above?

4

$$y = 2x - 5$$

$$y = 2x^2 - 18x + 45$$

How many solutions does the above system of equations have?

A) None

B) One

C) Two

D) Infinite

5

If $3x - y = 11$ and $2x - 2y = 2$, what is the value of $x + y$?

A) 3

B) 5

C) 9

D) 13

6

If $sin\ 32° = 0.551$, what is the value of $cos\ 58°$?

7

If 1 *foot* = 12 *inches*, what is the area of the triangle (not drawn to scale) below in ft^2?

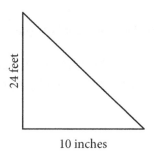

24 feet

10 inches

A) 10

B) 20

C) 120

D) 1440

8

For all values of $x > 0$, which of the following is equivalent to the following equation $\dfrac{-5}{x} - \dfrac{x}{x-4}$?

A) -6

B) $\dfrac{x^2 + -20}{4}$

C) $\dfrac{-x^2 - 5x + 20}{x^2 - 4x}$

D) $\dfrac{-9 - x}{x - 4}$

9

Which of the following equations best represents the equation of the following graph?

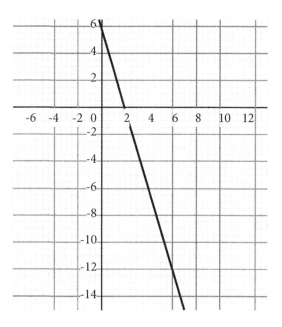

A) $3y - 9x = 18$

B) $3y + 9x = 18$

C) $6y - 12x = 36$

D) $5y + 20x = 30$

10

$$y - 7 = 3^x - 5$$

What is the *y*–intercept for the equation above?

11

For what value of x does the function

$h(x) = \dfrac{3x-5}{x^2 - 2x - 15}$ become undefined if $x < 0$?

A) −5

B) −4

C) −3

D) 5

12

If $f(3) = -1$ and $f(4) = -3$, what is the $x-$
intercept for the line represented by the function
$f(x)$?

A) −2

B) $\dfrac{2}{5}$

C) 2

D) 2.5

13

If $(x + 3) = 5x - 17$, what is the value of $f(2)$?

14

Amber travels from her home to the mall in

$1\dfrac{1}{2}$ *hours*. She completes her errands in one hour

and she then travels back home in $2\dfrac{1}{2}$ *hours*.

If the distance from the mall to her home is x
miles, find the average speed of her trip in terms
of x.

A) $\dfrac{x}{4}$

B) $\dfrac{x}{2}$

C) $\dfrac{2x}{5}$

D) $2x$

15

Given that the length of a rectangle is 3 *meters*
more than its width, what is the perimeter of the
rectangle given that the area is 28 *square meters*?

A) 11

B) 14

C) 22

D) 32

16

A study conducted by a school's medical board found that 23 out of the 48 students surveyed practice sanitary routines such as washing their hands before meals. If there are 2,280 students in the school, approximately how many students in the school do not practice sanitary routines (rounded up to the nearest whole number)?

17

Which of the following is the equation of $g(x) = 2x$ when it's moved 1 unit to the left and 1 unit up?

A) $y = 2x - 1$

B) $y = 2x + 1$

C) $y = 2x + 5$

D) $y = 2x + 3$

18

What is the *x coordinate* of the vertex for the parabola represented by the equation $y = 2x^2 + 8x + 12$?

A) -4

B) -2

C) 2

D) 6

19

If $\dfrac{x^2 - 6x + 10}{x + 2} = A + \dfrac{B}{x + 2}$, what is the value of B?

20

If triangle ABC is a right triangle and B is 90° and the longest side of the triangle is 61 and the shortest side is 11, what is the length of the third side of the triangle?

A) 40

B) 59

C) 60

D) 62

21

The psychology department of a school conducted a study on 20 random students in a third grade class of 58 students. 20 of the students were then offered a supplement. The study found that 15 of these students did better in their end–term exams compared to those who did not take the supplements. Which of the following statements can best be concluded from the above study?

A) Students who take supplements do better on exams.

B) Students who do not take supplements do not do well on their exams.

C) Supplements improve students' performance in their exams.

D) No conclusion can be drawn about the cause–and–effect relationship between test taking and supplement taking.

22

If $x + 3y = 9$ and $2x + 2y = 14$, what is the value of $y - x$?

A) -5

B) 1

C) 5

D) 6

STOP

No Test Material On This Page

Answer Key

Reading and Writing

Module 1

Questions	Correct	Mark your correct answers
1.	C	
2.	C	
3.	A	
4.	B	
5.	A	
6.	C	
7.	A	
8.	B	
9.	B	
10.	B	
11.	B	
12.	B	
13.	B	
14.	C	
15.	B	
16.	C	
17.	B	
18.	C	
19.	C	
20.	D	
21.	B	
22.	B	
23.	D	
24.	D	
25.	B	
26.	C	
27.	B	

Module 2

Questions	Correct	Mark your correct answers
1.	D	
2.	C	
3.	D	
4.	D	
5.	A	
6.	B	
7.	D	
8.	A	
9.	C	
10.	A	
11.	B	
12.	A	
13.	A	
14.	C	
15.	C	
16.	A	
17.	D	
18.	D	
19.	A	
20.	B	
21.	D	
22.	D	
23.	B	
24.	C	
25.	A	
26.	A	
27.	B	

Math

Module 1

Questions	Correct	Mark your correct answers
1.	C	
2.	A	
3.	7	
4.	C	
5.	C	
6.	3	
7.	B	
8.	A	
9.	D	
10.	$\frac{5}{13}$ or 0.384 or 0.385	
11.	B	
12.	B	
13.	8	
14.	D	
15.	A	
16.	−12	
17.	C	
18.	B	
19.	B	
20.	3.2	
21.	A	
22.	A	

Module 2

Questions	Correct	Mark your correct answers
1.	B	
2.	D	
3.	−1	
4.	B	
5.	C	
6.	0.551	
7.	A	
8.	C	
9.	B	
10.	3	
11.	C	
12.	D	
13.	−22	
14.	B	
15.	C	
16.	1,188	
17.	D	
18.	B	
19.	26	
20.	C	
21.	D	
22.	A	

1. **Level:** Easy | **Domain:** CRAFT AND STRUCTURE
   Skill/Knowledge: Words in Context

   Key Explanation: Choice C is the best answer because the underlined word is what goats "lack" or "do not have." The first half of the sentence indicates that the goats will eat "everything else" as well as "unwanted weeds." In other words, the goat does not care what it eats. **Choice C** refers to "judgment," or "refinement" about what it chooses, so fits the context of eating anything.

   Distractor Explanations: Choice A is incorrect because it refers to unfairness or partiality towards one thing. However, the goats are not deliberately trying to treat one plant poorly; they eat all without preferences. **Choice B** is incorrect because it refers to unfairness or partiality towards one thing. However, the goats are not deliberately trying to treat one plant poorly; they eat all without preferences. **Choice D** is incorrect because it refers to an obstinate and unchanging belief about the superiority of one's group over others, but the goats do not feel they are superior to others.

2. **Level:** Easy | **Domain:** CRAFT AND STRUCTURE
   Skill/Knowledge: Words in Context

   Key Explanation: Choice C is the best answer because the underlined word describes how clients and investors view the proposal that the person with a career in business makes. **Choice C** refers to something that is desirable. The resulting sentence, therefore, indicates that the businessperson helps make the plan desirable to others.

   Distractor Explanations: None of the other

choices adequately shows how the clients and investors need to view the proposals. **Choice A** refers to a personal quality that inspires others. It does not refer to something inanimate like a proposal. **Choice B** refers to something that is impossible to avoid the effect of. The clients and investors, though, are not forced to accept the proposal. **Choice D** refers to something that is extremely interesting so that it is impossible to stop paying attention to it. Although a proposal might be fascinating, the key is to make it desirable enough that others buy into it.

3. **Level:** Hard | **Domain:** CRAFT AND STRUCTURE
   Skill/Knowledge: Words in Context

   Key Explanation: Choice A is the best answer because "critical" is the author's view of what "explaining such coexistence" is. The sentence continues to say that the explanation is needed to "truly understand the region's biodiversity." **Choice A** refers to something absolutely necessary, so fits the context in saying that explaining coexistence is necessary to understand biodiversity and therefore developing an appropriate plan for managing the area.

   Distractor Explanations: None of the other choices accurately describes how essential "explaining such coexistence" really is. **Choice B** means "dangerous." **Choice C** refers to expressing criticism and disapproval. **Choice D** refers to using logic and reasoning.

4. **Level:** Medium | **Domain:** CRAFT AND STRUCTURE
   Skill/Knowledge: Words in Context

   Key Explanation: Choice B is the best answer because the blank portion needs to be a word that describes the "cultural and historical value of the building and its contents," which are described as being full of "splendid and unique details" from over the past 1,500 years. **Choice C** refers to something that is too great to mathematically determine or count. It fits the context that the building's value is so great it cannot be replaced by any money.

Distractor Explanations: None of the other choices adequately describe the precious nature of the "value of the building and its contents." **Choice A** refers to a place or thing that is pleasant and agreeable, not an intangible thing such as "value." **Choice C** refers to something that is physically large or bulky, not something intangible. **Choice D** also refers to something that is physically large or bulky, not something intangible.

5. **Level:** Medium | **Domain:** INFORMATION AND IDEAS
    Skill/Knowledge: Words in Context

    Key Explanation: Choice A is correct because to commemorate something means to remember the event and by doing so, to honor it. Here, the memorial commemorates the employees of LMWR killed in the First World War.

    Distractor Explanations: Choice B is incorrect because to idolize is to respect or admire someone extensively. Here, the memorial has been built to remember martyrs and not only to show respect. **Choice C** is incorrect because "celebrate" is not a word used to describe the purpose of a memorial. **Choice D** is incorrect because the memorial has been built for the fallen LNWR employees and hence, cannot overlook or ignore them.

6. **Level:** Hard | **Domain:** CRAFT AND STRUCTURE
    Skill/Knowledge: Text Structure and Purpose

    Key Explanation: Choice C is the best answer because the main point of the paragraph is that "these results contrast with previous findings" and emphasize that more studies are needed, indicating that the Drake Passage study did not provide all the answers. Therefore, the paragraph shows how the results of the Drake Passage study fits into "the wider context" or "bigger picture" of other studies.

    Distractor Explanations: Choice A is incorrect because the paragraph does not suggest that any of the data gathered so far is "inaccurate" or "not correct." Therefore, the paragraph is not being used to show how difficult it is to get correct data. **Choice B** is incorrect because the paragraph does not "illustrate" or "explain" why it is hard to "amass" or "gather" enough data. The paragraph mentions that the conditions are "challenging," but does not give any detail about why. **Choice D** is incorrect because, though the paragraph says that CO_2 absorption is important, it does not talk about "correcting" or "fixing" the problem. It only says that there needs to be more research done to understand the process better.

7. **Level:** Easy | **Domain:** CRAFT AND STRUCTURE
    Skill/Knowledge: Text Structure and Purpose

    Key Explanation: Choice A is the best answer. The underlined sentence shows that the garden was large and "lovely" or "appealing," and the following sentence gives various reasons that the garden was appealing to all the senses.

    Distractor Explanations: Choice B is incorrect because there is no contrast with the previous sentence; the garden was lovely, so that provides a reason for the children to want to play there. **Choice C** is incorrect because the underlined sentence does not refer to "characters" or "people," only to place. **Choice D** is incorrect because there is no "ominous undercurrent" or "scary implication" in the description of the garden. It could be that the giant is very nice and there is no problem with the children playing there.

8. **Level:** Easy | **Domain:** CRAFT AND STRUCTURE
   Skill/Knowledge: Text Structure and Purpose

   Key Explanation: Choice B is the best answer because the phrase is used to describe the "fentanyl analogs" or "drugs comparable to fentanyl." The fact that they were "commonly confiscated" or "often seized" by law enforcement shows that the drugs are ones in common use, and therefore are likely to be illegal drugs that overdose patients had access to and used. If this is true, the research on the drugs is likely to "apply" or "be relevant" to "authentic cases" or "real situations" in which a patient overdoses on an illegal drug.

   Distractor Explanations: Choice A is incorrect because the method of "obtaining" or "getting" the drugs is not mentioned. The researchers could have gotten the drugs from a variety of sources. **Choice C** is incorrect because the fact that the drugs were the kind seized by officers does not show that the trials were "improperly" or "incorrectly" done. **Choice D** is incorrect because there is no indication that the research required special permits to use the drugs. Therefore, the quote is not included to "establish" or "provide a reason" for a point that is not even mentioned.

9. **Level:** Medium | **Domain:** CRAFT AND STRUCTURE
   Skill/Knowledge: Cross–Text Connections

   Key Explanation: Choice B is the correct answer because it accurately draws upon the information provided in both texts. "Starry Night" is described in Text 1 as a painting that conveys the artist's emotions and reflects his turbulent quest to overcome illness. The author of Text 2 would likely view it as a significant example of art's transformative power.

   Distractor Explanations: Choice A is incorrect because it suggests that the author of Text 2 would acknowledge the value of "Starry Night" and its ability to go beyond the constraints of commercialization. However, there is no explicit mention in the texts about transcending the limits of commercialization. **Choice C** is incorrect because it does not rely on the information provided in the texts. There is no mention of comparing "Starry Night" to Warhol in terms of their challenges to capitalism. **Choice D** is incorrect because there is no mention of "Starry Night" being compared to other Impressionists in terms of its transformative nature.

10. **Level:** Medium | **Domain:** INFORMATION AND IDEAS
    Skill/Knowledge: Central Ideas and Details

    Key Explanation: Choice B is the best answer because "impetus" refers to a reason or motivation. The passage begins by explaining that the narrator will "take to the ship" whenever he is feeling morbid and needs a change.

    Distractor Explanations: Choice A is incorrect because there is no indication that the narrator is a captain. He also does not appear to be a sailor as a steady career, but instead when he feels tired of being on land. **Choice C** is incorrect because the narrator says he had no money, and therefore felt like going sailing; there is no discussion of a sailor's salary. He could have had a large salary aboard ship but spent it all. **Choice D** is incorrect because, while the narrator indicates that he was "impoverished" with "little or no money in my purse," he does not say how he got to that condition

11. **Level:** Medium | **Domain:** INFORMATION AND IDEAS
    Skill/Knowledge: Central Ideas and Details

    Key Explanation: Choice B is the best answer because the passage says that "induced demand" is a phenomenon in which making more of a product will lead to more people wanting it; in this case, "if more roads are provided, more people are encouraged to drive." However, the passage says that the "common solution" is to build more roads, showing that in the average or common case of wanting to reduce traffic jams, the effect is not considered. If it were "taken into consideration" or "thought about," then planners would probably use a different solution than just building roads.

    Distractor Explanations: Choice A is incorrect because, although the passage indicates that congestion continues as more roads are built, it does not say that induced demand "contradicts" or "goes against" that concept. There is also no hint that there is a "widespread belief" or "lots of people thinking" that building roads causes congestion; if so, the common solution would not be to build more. **Choice C** is incorrect because there is no hint that city planners are now incorporating the idea into their plans; if so, then there would not be situations like the example from Houston. **Choice D** is incorrect because

there is no discussion in the passage about how to "mitigate" or "reduce" the effect. The effect is just defined.

12. **Level:** Medium | **Domain:** INFORMATION AND IDEAS
    Skill/Knowledge: Command of Evidence (Textual)

    Key Explanation: Choice B is the best answer. The claim is that "the poem uses the imagery of fire to delve into the question of who might have created such a dangerous creature." In choice B, the words "furnace" and "anvil" are "imagery" or "symbols" that evoke heat and fire; they are tools used to heat metal to the melting point and form it into a shape. **Choice B** refers to "delving" or "asking" the question of who might have created the "dangerous creature," which causes "deadly terrors: what furnace, anvil, and grasp could create a tiger? These questions are asking who would dare to forge and hold the tiger.

    Distractor Explanations: Choice A is incorrect because it touches on the fire imagery in the "fire of thine eyes," but it does not refer to the question of who created such a creature. **Choice C** is incorrect because it only refers to the creator and the danger or fear caused by a tiger: tigers are scary enough that stars "throw down their spears" or "give up" and "water heaven with their tears" or "cry." **Choice C** does not use any fire imagery. **Choice D** also does not give any support to the claim that the poem uses fire imagery; it only wonders if someone who created a lamb could also create a tiger.

13. **Level:** Hard | **Domain:** INFORMATION AND IDEAS
    Skill/Knowledge: Command of Evidence (Textual)

Key Explanation: Choice B is correct. Scientists found that the seasons on Earth are caused by the Earth's tilt rather than the proximity to the sun. Therefore, the finding that the Southern hemisphere experiences their "winter" with colder and shorter days when it is tilted away from the sun directly supports the conclusion of the study.

Distractor Explanations: Choice A is incorrect because this choice describes how temperature changes are influenced by perihelion, which is refuted in the study. **Choice C is** incorrect because this choice describes how temperature changes are influenced by aphelion, which is refuted in the study. **Choice D** is incorrect because this choice describes how the seasons are influenced by perihelion and aphelion, which are refuted in the study.

14. **Level:** Easy | **Domain:** INFORMATION AND IDEAS

    Skill/Knowledge: Command of Evidence (Quantitative)

    Key Explanation: Choice C is the best answer because the figure lists "39.66" in the column of "average days to first flower" for 90nM of NaCl, and 23.66 days for 0 NaCl. Therefore, the difference is 16 days, which supports the claim that "increasing NaCl concentrations delayed significantly flowering" times.

    Distractor Explanations: Choice A is incorrect because only the passage refers to capsaicinoids; the table does not. **Choice B** is incorrect because only the passage refers to vitamins and minerals. Nutritional value is impossible to determine from the table. **Choice D** is incorrect because for the "NaCl concentration of 30 mM" line, the table says 54 days until the first fruit appeared; that is not the total number of fruits.

15. **Level:** Medium | **Domain:** INFORMATION AND IDEAS

    Skill/Knowledge: Inferences

    Key Explanation: Choice B is correct. The study states that all the parts of the shipwreck had to be mapped, even the seemingly mundane parts, to create a full view. This choice of mud in the debris is a seemingly uninteresting one, but it is a physical detail that is helpful in capturing the entire Titanic shipwreck.

    Distractor Explanations: Choice A is incorrect because the fuel used by the ship is not a physical detail that can be mapped as part of the deep-sea mapping of the shipwreck. **Choice C** is incorrect because the cracks caused by the iceberg which sunk the ship should be one of the most interesting parts since it led to this shipwreck. Therefore, it is not suitable to use this as an example of an "uninteresting part" of the shipwreck. **Choice D** is incorrect because the entire scale of the ship is not a small physical detail comprising a few square centimeters to be mapped.

16. **Level:** Medium | **Domain:** INFORMATION AND IDEAS

    Skill/Knowledge: Inferences

    Key Explanation: Choice C is correct. The text states that an absurdly small replica of a luxury purse was created by MSCHF, a company that has commented on the way popular luxury items can be so exaggerated that they lose their actual purpose. Therefore, these replicas and products are meant to make fun of or critique how consumers pay so much money to designer brands despite the products' lack of function.

Distractor Explanations: Choice A is incorrect because the text suggests that MSCHF is making fun of the products from luxury brands. Therefore, paying homage is not suitable here because it is typically a sign of admiration and respect. **Choice B** is incorrect because the text suggests that MSCHF has created a tiny replica of the bag not because it is an item used in daily life, but because the bag is an example of an expensive fashion product that is actually non-functional. **Choice D** is incorrect because the text suggests that MSCHF is focusing on the absurd price of luxury items rather than everyday products.

17. **Level:** Hard | **Domain:** STANDARD ENGLISH CONVENTIONS
    Skill/Knowledge: Form, Structure, and Sense

    Key Explanation: Choice B is the best answer. The possessive pronoun "their" is used to show ownership by multiple individuals. In the sentence, it refers to the Galapagos finches and indicates that they raise their offspring with care. Since the context mentions "Galapagos finches" (plural), using the plural possessive pronoun "their" is appropriate and grammatically correct.

    Distractor Explanations: Choice A is incorrect because "it's" is a contraction of "it is" or "it has," which is not suitable for indicating possession. In this sentence, we need a possessive pronoun, not a contraction. **Choice C** is incorrect because "they're" is a contraction of "they are," and it is not used to indicate possession. It would be grammatically incorrect to use "they're" in this context. **Choice D** is incorrect because "its" is a singular possessive pronoun used for one thing. In the sentence, we are referring to the offspring of multiple Galapagos finches, so using the singular form "its" is not appropriate.

18. **Level:** Medium | **Domain:** STANDARD ENGLISH CONVENTIONS
    Skill/Knowledge: Form, Structure, and Sense

    Key Explanation: Choice C is the best answer. The present perfect verb form using "has/have" is used to show that something started in the past and continues now. It fits the time context of the question that Harari poses, "from the stone age to the present."

    Distractor Explanations: Choice A incorrect because the verb is in simple present tense, and is without an auxiliary verb, rendering it grammatically wrong. **Choice B** is incorrect because even though it has an auxiliary verb, it doesn't include the idea of change from the distant past. **Choice D** is incorrect because it refers to something which has not yet occurred in the future, so does not describe "from the stone age to the present."

19. **Level:** Easy | **Domain:** STANDARD ENGLISH CONVENTIONS
    Skill/Knowledge: Form, Structure, and Sense

    Key Explanation: Choice C is the best answer. The subject of the sentence is long, "the transformative effect on women of access to affordable, reliable, and sustainable modern energy." However, it can be reduced to the singular "the effect." **Choice C** is a singular verb that shows that the studies were done in the past and still continue today.

    Distractor Explanations: All of the other choices can be eliminated because they are plural verbs, so cannot be used with the singular subject "the effect." **Choice A** is incorrect because it is a plural verb, and doesn't follow the rules of subject-verb agreement. **Choice B** is incorrect because it is also a plural verb. **Choice D** is also incorrect because it is a plural verb as well.

20. **Level:** Easy | **Domain:** STANDARD ENGLISH CONVENTIONS
Skill/Knowledge: Form, Structure, and Sense

Key Explanation: Choice D, is the best answer. In the passage, the subject is Macbeth, a male character, so the appropriate pronoun to use in this context is "he". The sentence is referring to Macbeth as the one who killed the curent king and seized the throne, so the pronoun "he" accurately completes the text.

Distractor Explanations: Choice A is incorrect because it would not conform to the conventions of Standard English in this context. The passage clearly states that the subject is Macbeth, a male character, so using the pronoun "she" would be grammatically incorrect and change the meaning of the sentence. **Choice B** is incorrect because it is a plural pronoun and would not agree with the singular subject "Macbeth." The sentence is describing actions performed by a single individual (Macbeth), so using the plural pronoun "they" would be grammatically incorrect. **Choice C** is incorrect because "it" is a singular pronoun typically used for inanimate objects or animals, not people. Referring to Macbeth as "it" would be grammatically incorrect and dehumanizing, as he is a character with emotions and agency in the story.

21. **Level:** Medium | **Domain:** STANDARD ENGLISH CONVENTIONS
Skill/Knowledge: Boundaries

Key Explanation: Choice B is the best answer. When three or more items are included in a list joined by "and," the items are followed by commas, but the "and" is not.

Distractor Explanations: Choice A is incorrect because there should be no comma after "and." **Choice C** is incorrect because a semi-colon is used to join two independent clauses, and using it here would be gramatically wrong. **Choice D** is incorrect because a single dash should be preceded by a complete idea, but the two items before the punctuation would need to be joined by "and" for the idea to be complete.

22. **Level:** Easy | **Domain:** STANDARD ENGLISH CONVENTIONS
Skill/Knowledge: Boundaries

Key Explanation: Choice B is the best answer. "In a 2022 paper written by Kyle Rupp and associates" modifies the main clause, "the researchers explore…" by giving the context of when and where the sentence occurs. Such a modifier at the start of the sentence should be divided from the main clause with a comma.

Distractor Explanations: Choice A is incorrect because with no punctuation, the reader does not know where the main clause begins. **Choice C** is incorrect because a single dash is used for emphasis, so it doesn't fit the context. **Choice D** are incorrect because a single dash or a colon should follow an independent clause, but the first person has no active verb ("written" modifies the noun "paper.")

23. **Level:** Easy | **Domain:** STANDARD ENGLISH CONVENTIONS
Skill/Knowledge: Boundaries

Key Explanation: Choice D is the best answer. The main clause starts, "a lyric soprano has…." The other words at the start of the sentence modify the main clause, so need to be divided with commas. "For example" is one separate idea that qualifies that the sentence is an illustration of the previous claim. "Among operatic voices" restricts the discussion to voices that are used in the opera.

Distractor Explanations: Choice A is incorrect because it has no punctuation separating the different elements of the sentence from each other, so it is hard for the reader to determine how the ideas relate to each other. **Choice B** is incorrect because a colon should follow a complete clause, but the preceding portion has no verb. **Choice C** is also incorrect because here too, the colon is not used correctly as it has no verb in the preceding portion.

24. **Level:** Medium | **Domain:** EXPRESSION OF IDEAS
    Skill/Knowledge: Transitions

    Key Explanation: Choice D is the best answer. "The wind cannot be turned up or down" is a contrast with the previous discussion, which explains that oil–powered plants can control output like adjusting the flow of gas to a car. **Choice D** is used to indicate that the following information is different from what has preceded, so it effectively warns the reader of the contrast to come.

    Distractor Explanations: Choice A is incorrect because "nevertheless" would establish a cause-and-effect relationship between power generated by oil-fired power plants and wind farms. **Choice B** is incorrect because it shows that even though one thing happens, another also

happens. It doesn't establish that the discussion is highlighting a difference between two things that might happen even if the other did not. **Choice C** is incorrect because it is used to add more information along the same idea to the preceding argument, not change to a contrasting thought.

25. **Level:** Easy **Domain:** EXPRESSION OF IDEAS
    Skill/Knowledge: Transitions

    Key Explanation: Choice B is the best answer. There is a contrast in the sentence between "some administrative roles" and the rest of people who do social work. **Choice B** is used at the start of a dependent clause to show a contrast between the clause it introduces and the main clause of the sentence.

    Distractor Explanations: Choice A can be discarded because "however" introduces a contradiction to previous statements. The sentence in question is building on the previous statements, rather than contradicting it. **Choice C** is incorrect because like "however", "nevertheless" also marks a variance between prior statements and the following one. **Choice D** can be eliminated because "therefore" is used to show that the next statement is a consequence of the former one(s).

26. **Level:** Easy | **Domain:** EXPRESSION OF IDEAS
    Skill/Knowledge: Transitions

    Key Explanation: Choice C is the best answer. The passage is structured with the first sentence defining the diet and the second sentence giving a reason to doubt that it is effective, a reason not to follow it. The final sentence gives another reason to question whether the diet should be used. **Choice C** is used to introduce an additional argument for the same topic, so fits the context well.

Distractor Explanations: The other choices can be eliminated because they are not used to add more detail on the same topic. **Choice A** is used for a time series, but there is no indication that the lack of research was followed in time by scientists being concerned. **Choice B** is used to stress that the previous point may be true, but that the following, opposing argument is more reasonable. Therefore, it does not fit the context of two concordant ideas. **Choice D** is used to introduce a logical conclusion based on what information is already given, not to bring up new ideas.

27. **Level:** Hard | **Domain:** EXPRESSION OF IDEAS
Skill/Knowledge: Rhetorical Synthesis

Key Explanation: Choice B is the correct choice because it effectively contrasts the themes from both plays. It demonstrates how "Macbeth" centers around unchecked power and ambition leading to ruin, while "Hamlet" focuses more on revenge and uncertainty.

Distractor Explanations: Choice A is incorrect and a good distractor because though it may be true that both plays highlight Shakespeare's use of soliloquies, this does not highlight and particular themes from either play that the student wants to emphasize. **Choice C** is incorrect as it focuses on character transformations rather than emphasizing differences in themes between both plays. As such, this choice does not adequately portray its objective of emphasizing these themes. **Choice D** is also incorrect because although it identifies the distinct themes in each play, it fails to delve deeper into the implications

of these themes, making it less effective than Choice B. While it states the unique themes of each play, it does not effectively contrast them, or describe the effects these themes have on the story or characters, which is a key factor in understanding their differences.

1. **Level:** Medium | **Domain:** CRAFT AND STRUCTURE
   Skill/Knowledge: Words in Context

   Key Explanation: Choice D is the best answer because "broader" is a comparative adjective that shows the difference between the tourism business and the destination. The paragraph shows that the tourism business contains many different aspects than just the sites: it also includes "transportation, hotels and guest accommodations, and services that link the various components of a trip." Choice D refers to something that covers a wide range of topics or deals with many elements of something, so accurately shows that tourism deals with many more elements than just the destination.

   Distractor Explanations: None of the other choices effectively establishes the relationship between the tourism business and the destination. **Choice A** refers to something that is more noticeable or clear. **Choice B** refers to something that is not detailed or only covers the main points. **Choice C** refers to something that is wide in physical space.

2. **Level:** Medium | **Domain:** CRAFT AND STRUCTURE
   Skill/Knowledge: Words in Context

   Key Explanation: Choice C is the best answer because "insensible" is a verb that shows what the trees do to the "any change in those who walk" under them. **Choice C** means "not notice," so it correctly shows that the trees do not notice that different people are present.

   Distractor Explanations: Choice A refers to an unconscious state, especially when someone is sick or injured. Therefore, it does not apply to trees that do not notice anything. **Choice B** means "trivial" or "unimportant," so does not describe

what the trees do to a change in the people under them. **Choice D** is incorrect because it refers to a lack of thinking or perception of the environment around something. Although trees do not think, Marianne is talking to them as if they were animate creatures that might perceive things if they wanted to.

3. **Level:** Hard | **Domain:** CRAFT AND STRUCTURE
   Skill/Knowledge: Words in Context

   Key Explanation: Choice D is the best answer because "fume" refers to one of the things relating to the way that Adam amassed millions of dollars in Wall Street. The other things are "fuss" or "commotion," "applause" or "praise," and "ill will" or "hard feelings." **Choice D** refers to anger that is often related to a conflict, so aptly shows that he was very aggressive or hurt others as he "charged in" and made money.

   Distractor Explanations: None of the other choices fits the list of emotional qualities reflecting what happened to Adam on Wall Street. **Choice A** refers to waste gasses, **Choice B** to an unpleasant smell, and **Choice C** to waste products.

4. **Level:** Medium | **Domain:** CRAFT AND STRUCTURE
   Skill/Knowledge: Text Structure and Purpose

   Key Explanation: Choice D is the best answer. The topic sentence points out that "sometimes behaviors have underlying reasons that are not initially apparent," and then gives Mischel's experiment as an example. The differing results of Watt's experiment show that a fuller analysis might reveal previously unconsidered explanations for a behavior such as deciding to wait to eat a marshmallow.

Distractor Explanations: Choice A is incorrect because, while Watt's experiment revealed a flaw in Mischel's experiment, there is no indication that "most" experiments are flawed. **Choice B** is incorrect because the passage does not say that all experiments should be performed more than once; it only gives an example of a situation where a second experiment revealed more information about a topic. **Choice C** is incorrect because the passage does not say there is a "significant problem" in the way we understand willpower now; the passage points out that a previous problem in understanding was rectified.

5. **Level:** Easy | **Domain:** CRAFT AND STRUCTURE
   Skill/Knowledge: Text Structure and Purpose

   Key Explanation: Choice A is the best answer because the definition explains what a median wage is. This definition clarifies that not all planners earned the median figure of $73,050. It also explains why a total of 20% of the planners earned less than $45,180 or more than $114,170. If the reader did not know the definition of median wage, then the reason for the wide range in salaries might not make much sense.

   Distractor Explanations: Choice B is incorrect because the author does not imply that the median wage is "insufficient" or "not good enough." The median wage does not give all the necessary details to know the range of salaries, but offers a valid middle point to use as a point of reference. The definition shows how the data can be used to better understand the salary that could be earned as a planner. **Choice C** is incorrect because there is no "reason" or "cause" given to explain why planners earn different amounts of money. **Choice D** is incorrect because there is no link between salary earned and number of jobs. Therefore, a

definition of how the salary in the passage was calculated does not support or prove that there will be more jobs in the future.

6. **Level:** Medium | **Domain:** CRAFT AND STRUCTURE
   Skill/Knowledge: Cross–Text Connections

   Key Explanation: Choice B is the best answer because the conclusion of Text 2 is that researchers need to develop a new drug to treat depression. The author of Text 1 would probably respond with "reservation" or "some doubt" because she promotes behavioral activation, a non–invasive method that does not use any medications at all, to retrain the brain into positive patterns. She probably would encourage avoiding invasive methods like introducing drugs into the body if possible.

   Distractor Explanations: Choice A is incorrect because the author of Text 1 indicates that behavioral activation is successful. She does not discuss any other method of treatment, so it is impossible to tell if she would say that "most" treatments do not work. **Choice C** is incorrect because the author of Text 1 does not refer to drug performance at all. **Choice D** is incorrect because there is not enough information to tell whether the author of Text 1 "contends" or "argues" that drugs are "unacceptable" or "not allowable." She may agree that drug therapies should be attempted when other methods fail.

7. **Level:** Medium | **Domain:** CRAFT AND STRUCTURE
   Skill/Knowledge: Central Ideas and Details

   Key Explanation: Choice D is the best answer because the cup of liberty is something that "your old masters" hold for the slaves. The imagery shows that the cup can be "dash[ed] from you" so that it is unclear when the "scattered contents" or "freedoms" will be given back. In other words, the imagery emphasizes the "precarious" or "unstable" nature of the freedoms. It is very easy to throw aside or break the gains that have been made.

Distractor Explanations: Choice A is incorrect because Lincoln is not saying that the Union is "generous" or "willing to give a lot." He is saying that a poor decision will remove everything that has been given so far. **Choice B** is incorrect because the cup of liberty is what "your old masters," who are slave-owners in Louisiana, hold for slaves. The cup of liberty is not the advances of the Union, only of Louisiana. **Choice C** is incorrect because the imagery does not include the reaction of people accepting the cup; it says the cup is easy to break.

8. **Level:** Medium | **Domain:** INFORMATION AND IDEAS
   Skill/Knowledge: Central Ideas and Details

   Key Explanation: Choice A is the best answer because Keel describes the "vision" or "dream" of the Indian's "predecessors" or "earlier people," then states that "This vision was shared by the U.S. Congress in 1934 when it passed…the Indian Reorganization Act." In other words, Keel feels that the vision was "shared" or "in keeping"—both mean "the same"—with each other.

   Distractor Explanations: Choice B is incorrect because Keel indicates that the IRA was written by the government, not by the predecessors, even though the goals were the same. **Choice C** is incorrect because the policy matched the desires of the Indians to "protect and restore our tribal homelands and the Indian way of life." The

policy did not "deny" or "remove" rights from the Indians. **Choice D** is incorrect because there is no indication of how well the policy has upheld its goals.

9. **Level:** Easy | **Domain:** INFORMATION AND IDEAS
   Skill/Knowledge: Central Ideas and Details

   Key Explanation: Choice C is the best answer because the passage says that the narrator's "way lay along the canal embankment," which shows that he was on the embankment because it was the "route" or "way" he needed to go. The first line says the reason he was taking that route was, "I was going towards my lodgings." "Quarters" and "lodgings" both refer to the place where one lives, so he was headed towards his quarters.

   Distractor Explanations: None of the other choices are supported by evidence from the passage. **Choice A** is incorrect because, although the embankment was usually deserted, "at that hour you never meet a soul," there is no proof that he was trying to avoid other people. **Choice B** is incorrect because he went on his walk to escape the pressures of the city, but the embankment was on his return trip as he was going home to his lodgings. **Choice D** is incorrect because the embankment was usually deserted, so that is not a place that he would have looked for excitement or adventure.

10. **Level:** Hard | **Domain:** INFORMATION AND IDEAS
    Skill/Knowledge: Central Ideas and Details

    Key Explanation: Choice A is the best answer because it summarizes the main idea of the text. The passage mentions that Mars has fascinated scientists and astronomers, and researchers have focused on its potential for life and geological features. It also discusses recent missions like the Mars Rover expeditions that have provided valuable data about Mars' geology and the possibility of ancient microbial life. All of these points contribute to the central idea that Mars has been a subject of scientific investigations and missions due to its potential for harboring life and its geological features.

Distractor Explanations: Choice B is incorrect because although the passage mentions Mars' distinct reddish hue and proximity to Earth as factors that have fascinated scientists and astronomers, these aspects alone do not encompass the main idea of the text, which focuses on scientific investigations and missions related to Mars' potential for life and its geological features. **Choice C** is incorrect because it narrows down the main idea to recent missions like the Mars Rover expeditions providing valuable data about Mars' geology and the possibility of ancient microbial life. While this information is mentioned in the passage, it does not encompass the broader scope of the main idea, which includes Mars' potential for life and the overall fascination and scientific attention it has garnered. **Choice D** is incorrect because although it mentions the importance of understanding Mars for gaining insights into conditions that could support life beyond our own planet, it does not encompass the full range of topics covered in the passage, such as Mars' potential for harboring life, its geological features, and recent missions providing valuable data.

11. **Level:** Hard | **Domain:** INFORMATION AND IDEAS
    Skill/Knowledge: Command of Evidence (Textual)

    Key Explanation: Choice B is the best answer. The scientists' conclusion is that "the carnivore

probably appeared very much like the unrelated *Tyrannosaurus rex*." **Choice B** gives a detail about the "appearance" or "how it looks" that show that there is a similarity: both species had a head that was "oversized" or "very large" when compared to the rest of the body. Therefore, they both looked like they had big heads.

Distractor Explanations: Choice A is incorrect because a long separation of time could mean that the dinosaurs had evolved in different ways and looked very different. **Choice C** is incorrect because it shows a way that the dinosaurs looked different rather than a way that they are similar. Both dinosaurs were large, but *T. rex* would have, in general, been much larger. **Choice D** is incorrect because it only shows a similarity in diet. It is possible that two carnivores have very different physical characteristics or appearances while still eating the same food.

12. **Level:** Hard | **Domain:** INFORMATION AND IDEAS
    Skill/Knowledge: Command of Evidence (Quantitative)

    Key Explanation: Choice A is the correct option as it effectively uses information provided in the map to explain the scope of the study mentioned in the text. Canada and USA are neighboring countries, but Canada's daily cases are between 500-1000 as opposed to USA's cases, which are almost double, at 1000-2000 cases daily. **Choice A** demonstrates the impact of high cases in one country on a neighboring country, similar to what the study is trying to understand..

Distractor Explanations: Choice B is incorrect because while it mentions Argentina's high daily new cases, it doesn't directly address the impact on a neighboring country. It focuses on South America as a whole rather than a specific neighboring country. **Choice C is** incorrect because it provides a comparison between Russia and India's case numbers but doesn't necessarily address the impact on a neighboring country. It focuses on two specific countries rather than the relationship between neighboring countries. **Choice D** is incorrect because it talks about trade routes between India and Australia, but it doesn't directly discuss the impact on a neighboring country due to high COVID-19 cases. It introduces a different factor (trade routes) rather than focusing on the relationship between neighboring countries.

13. **Level:** Medium | **Domain:** INFORMATION AND IDEAS
    Skill/Knowledge: Inferences

    Key Explanation: Choice A is correct. The text states Bemis believed that the Disney theme parks "played significant roles in the national history of America" and "reflect[ed] American values." This choice is synonymous with Bemis' belief.

    Distractor Explanations: Choice B is incorrect because the text does not suggest that Bemis drew a conclusion about the breakdown of where the parks' visitors were from. **Choice C** is incorrect because the text does not suggest that Bemis drew a conclusion about the difference between Disneyland and Disney World. **Choice D** is incorrect because the text does not suggest that Bemis drew a conclusion about the most accurate medium, or method, to portray Disney's influence on America.

14. **Level:** Medium | **Domain:** INFORMATION AND IDEAS
    Skill/Knowledge: Inferences

Key Explanation: Choice C is correct. The text is about the limitations and downsides of sterilization surgery for female cats. The last sentence states that the surgery can only be performed by experts, so this choice should state another limitation based on this reason. Therefore, the availability of such experts is another limitation since sterilizations are dependent on these experts.

Distractor Explanations: Choice A is incorrect because the locations and health conditions of cats do not relate to the fact that the operation can only be performed by experts. **Choice B** is incorrect because this choice states a positive aspect rather than a limiting factor. **Choice D** is incorrect because the text does not suggest that solutions should be identified. The text is focusing on listing out the various limitations of surgical operations, so it is not logical to propose a solution to train more veterinarians.

15. **Level:** Medium | **Domain:** STANDARD ENGLISH CONVENTIONS
    Skill/Knowledge: Form, Structure, and Sense

    Key Explanation: Choice C is the correct answer. The convention being tested is verb forms. Option C is correct because "skyrocketed" is in the past tense and correctly matches the timeline established by the earlier part of the sentence ("when a particular scent blew".") Since the sentence is discussing the outcome of the study as something that has already occurred, the past tense "skyrocketed" is the appropriate choice.

    Distractor Explanations: Choice A is incorrect because it doesn't match the tense of the sentence. The sentence has already established a past context (" when a particular scent blew... of six months,") Therefore, the verb should also be in the past tense to maintain consistency. **Choice B** is incorrect because it uses the future tense which doesn't fit with the past context of the sentence. The study's findings have already been presented as a past event, so using the future tense here would be grammatically incorrect. **Choice D** is incorrect because it uses the present continuous tense which doesn't match the past timeline of the sentence. The sentence is describing the results of a completed study, so the present continuous tense is not suitable here.

16. **Level:** Medium | **Domain:** STANDARD ENGLISH CONVENTIONS
    Skill/Knowledge: Form, Structure, and Sense

    Key Explanation: Choice A is the correct answer. The convention being tested is verb forms. Choice A is correct because "can remember" indicates the ability of Heliconius butterflies to retain a memory of the location of consistent pollen sources. It fits well with the context and the sentence's structure, as it describes a general ability.

    Distractor Explanations: Choice B is incorrect because "will remember" implies a future action. However, the context of the sentence is discussing a general discovery or observation about the behavior of Heliconius butterflies. Therefore, the future tense is not appropriate here. **Choice C** is incorrect because while "have remembered" (present perfect tense) is grammatically correct, it is not the best choice in this context. The sentence is not focusing on an action that started in the past and continues to the present. Instead, it is describing the general behavior of the Heliconius butterflies. **Choice D** is incorrect because "are remembering," which is in the present continuous tense, is not the best option to describe a general trait of Heliconius butterflies. Also, we see that the latter half of the sentence ("and create long-term

traplines") does not use the continuous tense, further making choice D an incorrect option.

17. **Level:** Medium | **Domain:** STANDARD ENGLISH CONVENTIONS
    Skill/Knowledge: Form, Structure, and Sense

    Key Explanation: Choice D is the best answer. An apostrophe and s are used to show possession for one person; in this case, the death of J.R.R. Tolkien.

    Distractor Explanations: Choice A is incorrect because the missing word should be a possessive noun. **Choice B** is incorrect because an s forms a plural noun, but does not indicate possession. **Choice C** is used to show the possession of more than one person, but the context implies that Tolkien died and his son was still alive to publish the manuscript.

18. **Level:** Medium | **Domain:** STANDARD ENGLISH CONVENTIONS
    Skill/Knowledge: Form, Structure, and Sense

    Key Explanation: Choice D is the best answer. "Smaller than our sun" is a modifier that should be followed by the noun it refers to, in this case, "the red dwarf star HD260655."

    Distractor Explanations: All of the other choices are incorrect because the modifier at the start of the sentence illogically describes the incorrect noun. In **Choice A**, "smaller than our Sun" refers to the generic "there." In **Choice B**, it refers to "only 33 light years," and in **Choice C** it refers to "our solar system."

19. **Level:** Easy | **Domain:** STANDARD ENGLISH CONVENTIONS
Skill/Knowledge: Boundaries

Key Explanation: Choice A is the best answer. In this text, "and" joins two verb phrases, "worked…" and "published…." Two verbs should not be divided by commas if they share the same subject; in this case, "Kenyan writer Ngugi wa Thiong'o" does both actions. There should also not be a comma between the verb "published" and its object, "A Grain of Wheat in July."

Distractor Explanations: Choice B is incorrect because there should be no comma after "Nairobi" because the "and" joins two verbs with the same subject. **Choice C** is incorrect because there should be no comma after "published." Similarly, **Choice D** is incorrect because there should be no comma after "Nairobi" and "published." A comma is needed between a verb and a quote only when the quoted information is a complete sentence, not when the marks are indicating the title of a book.

20. **Level:** Easy | **Domain:** STANDARD ENGLISH CONVENTIONS
Skill/Knowledge: Boundaries

Key Explanation: Choice B is the best answer. When additional information is included in a sentence using two dashes, then the main part of the sentence should remain grammatically correct. By removing the aside, it is easier to determine that the proper sentence structure uses the idiom "cite XX as YY." **Choice B** completes this structure.

Distractor Explanations: All of the other choices are incorrect because they create a grammatically incorrect main clause. **Choice A** places two nouns in a row without any particle or preposition showing how they relate to each other. **Choice**

C adds an additional subject (which) and verb. Similarly, **Choice D** adds an additional subject (they) and verb.

21. **Level:** Easy | **Domain:** STANDARD ENGLISH CONVENTIONS
Skill/Knowledge: Boundaries

Key Explanation: Choice D is the best answer. The idiom "as XX as YY" should have no punctuation dividing the elements from each other; they are part of the same idea.

Distractor Explanations: All of the other choices can be eliminated because they divide the standard idiom "as XX as YY" with punctuation. **Choice A** is incorrect because a colon in a sentence should follow a complete clause, but the idea in front of the punctuation is incomplete. **Choice B** is incorrect because commas are used to divide separate ideas from the main clause. **Choice C** is incorrect because a single dash in a sentence should follow a complete clause, but the idea in front of the punctuation is incomplete.

22. **Level:** Easy | **Domain:** STANDARD ENGLISH CONVENTIONS
Skill/Knowledge: Boundaries

Key Explanation: Choice D is the best answer. "Both" refers to the two ideas "during his lifetime" and "after his lifetime." No punctuation should separate the parts of an idea joined by "both," especially as the shared idea of "lifetime" is included at the end.

Distractor Explanations: All of the other choices include unnecessary punctuation. **Choice A** makes the preposition "during" stand on its own without a noun to clarify it; there needs to be something specifying "during what." **Choice B** divides "his lifetime" from the two prepositions that refer to it. **Choice C** is incorrect because a single dash should follow a complete sentence, but "during" is dangling.

23. **Level:** Easy| **Domain:** EXPRESSION OF IDEAS
    Skill/Knowledge: Transitions

    Key Explanation: Choice B is the best answer because the passage is discussing two kinds of dogs that track people in different ways. **Choice B** sets up the idea that the following information is going to be very different from what precedes, so it effectively shows that the two dogs work under two methods that are distinct.

    Distractor Explanations: Choice A is incorrect because it reflects that the previous statement(s) have helped reach the following statement, which isn't the case. **Choice C** is incorrect because "therefore" is used to show the result of an argument. However, the fact that air–scent dogs sniff an area is not the result of the discussion that trailing dogs follow a specific scent. **Choice D** is used to introduce more information on the same topic, so erroneously makes the reader think the discussion will continue with more details about trailing dogs.

24. **Level:** Easy | **Domain:** EXPRESSION OF IDEAS
    Skill/Knowledge: Transitions

    Key Explanation: Choice C is the best answer. **Choice C** is used to provide emphasis for a preceding claim by adding details that support that claim. **Choice C** therefore fits the context of adding the detail that males are physically not capable of drinking blood to the more general preceding claim that they do not drink blood.

    Distractor Explanations: Choice A is used to show a logical conclusion of an argument that

is being developed, but the fact that males do not have a special mouth is not necessarily the logical result of not drinking blood; it is more of a cause. It is possible for the males to have the special mouth but not use it. **Choice B** is used to summarize items in a list or conclude a section in a passage, but in this case, there is an additional idea which follows: mosquitos get energy from plants. **Choice D** is incorrect because it is used to add the specific example that illustrates a claim. However, the passage implies that there are more reasons for not drinking blood than the mouth shape. Rather, the reason is that they don't need the protein.

25. **Level:** Medium | **Domain:** EXPRESSION OF IDEAS
    Skill/Knowledge: Rhetorical Synthesis

    Key Explanation: Choice A is the optimal answer as it succinctly summarizes the differences between Joyce's "Ulysses" and Faulkner's "The Sound and the Fury". It emphasizes their distinct time frames, settings, and themes to meet the student's goal of emphasizing these distinctions.

    Distractor Explanations: Choice B is incorrect and acts as a distractor because it emphasizes similarities rather than differences between works by using the stream-of-consciousness technique to focus on similarities rather than emphasizing any particular aspects of them. While providing accurate information, this does not meet student goals of emphasizing differences. **Choice C** is incorrect because it draws attention to another similarity between the works: their focus on multiple characters' inner thoughts. Although accurate, this approach does not highlight their distinctions as desired by the student. **Choice D** is incorrect and acts as a distractor because while it accurately highlights both works' complex narrative structures, it only serves to draw attention to their similarity instead of emphasizing any differences. Thus it fails to meet its objective of emphasizing differences.

26. **Level:** Hard | **Domain:** EXPRESSION OF IDEAS
    Skill/Knowledge: Rhetorical Synthesis

    Key Explanation: Choice A is correct because it clearly and succinctly explains what dramatic irony is before providing a specific example from Oedipus Rex of its use in that story. This answer best fulfills the student's aim of providing both an explanation and an example of dramatic irony in literature.

    Distractor Explanations: While **Choice B** acknowledges dramatic irony within "To Kill a Mockingbird", it fails to define exactly what dramatic irony means and thus fulfills only part of its student objective. **Choice C** provides an example from "Pride and Prejudice", but doesn't elaborate on dramatic irony - making it less effective than Choice A. While **Choice D** does provide an example of dramatic irony from "Macbeth", it fails to offer a comprehensive and effective definition, making it less effective at helping students meet their goal of understanding dramatic irony.

27. **Level:** Hard | **Domain:** EXPRESSION OF IDEAS
    Skill/Knowledge: Rhetorical Synthesis

    Key Explanation: Choice B is the best answer. The student emphasizes the second bullet that Cher explored different styles by highlighting the point that the two songs are of different styles.

    Distractor Explanations: None of the other choices highlights a common feature. **Choice**

A only says that the songs were performed at different times. **Choice C** refers to a song and a television series, but there is no unifying theme about why those are notable. **Choice D** also refers to two unrelated facts: the reader does not know how or why they are significant.

1. **Level:** Easy | **Domain:** ALGEBRA
Skill/Knowledge: Linear equations in one variable
Testing point: Solving equations with one variable

Key Explanation: Choice C is correct. This question can be solved in two ways. The most efficient way to solve the equation is to factor out the 4 from the left side of the equation yielding $4(x+4)=24$. Dividing both sides of the equation by 4 yields $(x+4)=\dfrac{24}{4}$, which equates to $(x+4)=6$, which is **Choice C.**

The second way to solve this equation is to subtract 16 from both sides of the equation. The result is $4x+16-16=24-16$ which in turn translates to $4x=8$. Dividing both sides of the equation by 4 gets $x=2$. However, the question asks for the value of $x+4$, and not x, which will then be 2 + 4, or 6.

Distractor Explanations: Choice A is incorrect as this is the value of x. **Choice B** is incorrect as this is the value of $4x$ when 2 is subtracted from both sides of the equation. **Choice D** is incorrect as this answer may be the result of a conceptual error or miscalculation

2. **Level:** Medium | **Domain:** PROBLEM−SOLVING AND DATA ANALYSIS
Skill/Knowledge: Probability and conditional probability | **Testing point:** Conditional probability

Key Explanation: Choice A is correct. Given that there are 35 teachers in the school, according to the table, there are 16 female teachers. Thus, the number of male teachers in the school is 35 – 16 = 19. The number of people in the school is found by adding the number of teachers to the number of students as follows: 245 + 35 = 280. Therefore,

of the 280 people in the school, 19 are male teachers and the probability of selecting a male teacher is $\dfrac{19}{280}$.

Distractor Explanations: Choice B is incorrect since it is the probability of choosing a teacher given that he is already male. **Choice C** is incorrect as it is conceptually incorrect because it mixes students and teachers. **Choice D** is incorrect, since it's the probability of choosing a male given that he is already a teacher.

3. **Level:** Easy | **Domain:** ADVANCED MATH
Skill/Knowledge: Nonlinear equations in one variable and systems of equations in two variables
Testing point: Solving absolute value equations

Key Explanation: Absolute value equations usually have two solutions. The first step would be to remove the parentheses and set up two linear equations as follows:

$2x - 3 = 11$ and $2x - 3 = -11$

To solve for x in the first equation, add 3 to both sides of the equation as follows:

$2x - 3 + 3 = 11 + 3$

$2x = 14$

$x = 7$

To find the second solution solve for x in the second equation by adding 3 to both sides of the equation as follows:

$2x - 3 + 3 = -11 + 3$

$2x = -8$

$x = -4$

Thus, the positive solution for x is 7.

4. **Level:** Easy | **Domain:** ALGEBRA
Skill/Knowledge: Linear functions | **Testing point:** Perpendicular lines

Key Explanation: Choice C is correct.
Perpendicular lines meet at 90–degree angles and have opposite sign reciprocal slopes. Putting the given equation into slope–intercept form $y = mx + b$ by dividing all terms by 5, yields $y = \dfrac{4}{5} y + 3$. The m in the slope–intercept form of the equation represents the slope of the line. Therefore, the slope of the line is $\dfrac{4}{5}$ and the opposite reciprocal slope is $\dfrac{-5}{4}$, which is the slope of the perpendicular line. This makes **Choice C** the only correct answer.

Distractor Explanations: Choice A is incorrect as the line would be parallel to m rather than perpendicular as the lines have the same slope. **Choice B** is incorrect as it is the negative of the perpendicular slope. **Choice D** is incorrect as it is the negative of the perpendicular slope.

5. **Level:** Medium | **Domain:** GEOMETRY AND TRIGONOMETRY
    Skill/Knowledge: Circles | **Testing point:** Standard form of the equation of a circle and completing the square

    Key Explanation: Choice C is correct. To find the center of the circle, first transform the equation to its standard form $(x - h)^2 + (y - k)^2 = r^2$, where (h, k) is the center of the circle and r is its radius. To get the equation in standard form, complete the square. To do this, first, rearrange the terms in the equation to have all the x's and y's near each other as follows: $x^2 - 6x + y^2 + 4y = 36$. The standard form of a quadratic equation is $ax^2 + bx + c$ Next, working with just $x^2 - 6x$, with $a = 1$ and $b = -6$, add $\left(\dfrac{b}{2}\right)^2$ or $\left(\dfrac{-6}{2}\right)^2$ to both sides of the equation

to get $x^2 - 6x + 9 + y^2 + 4y = 36 + 9$. Next, working with just $y^2 + 4y$, with $a = 1$ and $b = 4$, add $\left(\dfrac{b}{2}\right)^2$ or $\left(\dfrac{4}{2}\right)^2$ to both sides of the equation to get $x^2 - 6x + 9 + y^2 + 4y + 4 = 36 + 9 + 4$ or 49. Next, factoring $x^2 - 6x + 9$ yields $(x - 3)^2$, and factoring $y^2 + 4y + 4$ yields $(y + 2)^2$, to get $(x - 3)^2 + (y + 2)^2 = 49$

Therefore, the center of the circle will be (3, –2).

Distractor Explanations: Choice A is incorrect because if the standard form of a circle equation is read incorrectly then $(-h, -k)$ would be incorrectly determined to be the center of the circle. **Choice D** is incorrect as the x and y coordinates have been reversed. **Choice B** is incorrect as this is the negative of incorrect **Choice D**.

6. **Level:** Hard | **Domain:** ADVANCED MATH
    Skill/Knowledge: Equivalent expressions | **Testing point:** Exponents and matching coefficients

    Key Explanation:
    $(8^x)^x \times 4^{2x} = ((2^3)^x)^x \times (2^2)^{2x} = 2^{3x^2} \times 2^{4x}$
    This yields $2^{3x^2 + 4x}$ using exponent rules.
    $\dfrac{2^{ax^2}}{2^{-bx}} = 2^{ax^2 + bx}$ using exponent rules.
    Therefore,
    $3x^2 + 4x = ax^2 + bx$
    $a = 3$

7. **Level:** Medium | **Domain:** ALGEBRA
    Skill/Knowledge: Linear inequalities in one or two variables | **Testing point:** Solving systems of linear inequalities

Key Explanation: Choice B is correct. The most efficient way to solve the problem is to substitute the given answer choices into the system of inequalities and see which answer makes both inequalities valid. Plugging in **Choice A** into the first inequality yields

$-6(-2) + 3 < -4$

$12 + 3 < -4$

$15 < -4$, which is false. Plugging in **Choice B** into the first inequality yields $-6(4) + 3 < 7$

$-24 + 3 < 7$

$-21 < 7$, which is true. Next, plug **Choice B** into the second inequality which yields

$7 < 4 + 6$

$7 < 10$. This is true, making **Choice B** the correct option.

Distractor Explanations: Choice A does not work as shown above. Plugging **Choice C** into the first inequality yields

$-6(-2) + 3 < 1$

$12 + 3 < 1$

$15 < 1$, which is not true. Plugging **Choice D** into the first inequality yields

$-6(-2) + 3 < -4$

$12 + 3 < -4$

$15 < -4$, which is not true.

8. **Level:** Hard | **Domain:** ADVANCED MATH
    Skill/Knowledge: Nonlinear functions | **Testing point:** Transformations of quadratic equations

    Key Explanation: Choice A is correct. The vertex form of the equation of a parabola is $y = (x − h)^2 + k$, where (h, k) is the vertex of the parabola. Thus, the vertex of the $f(x)$ equation is $(3, 8)$ and the vertex of the $g(x)$ equation is $(5, 5)$. Therefore, the x coordinate moves to the right 2 units from $f(x)$ to $g(x)$, and the y coordinate moves down 3 units.

Distractor Explanations: Choice B is incorrect as the x coordinate is moving to the right, not the left. A student may pick this option if he or she assumes that since h has reduced by 2 units it is moving to the left. **Choice C** is incorrect because the y coordinate is moving down not up. **Choice D** is incorrect. This incorrect answer may be selected if the student transformed $g(x)$ onto $f(x)$ instead of the other way around.

9. **Level:** Easy | **Domain:** ADVANCED MATH
    Skill/Knowledge: Nonlinear functions | **Testing point:** Identifying the equation of an exponential function from a graph

    Key Explanation: Choice D is correct. The graph depicts an exponential growth equation, which has its standard equation $y = ab^x$, where if in an exponential equation $b > 1$, then the equation represents exponential growth. The value of a in the equation represents the initial value of the equation when $x = 0$. Using the process of elimination, choices A and C can be ruled out as their b values are less than 1 and thus represent exponential decay, not growth. **Choice A** can also be ruled out as it gives an initial value of 5 whereas the graph shows a smaller initial value. **Choice D** is correct as it is the only equation that shows that the graph is increasing exponentially and has a y–intercept of less than 5.

    Distractor Explanations: See the process of elimination answer explanations above.

10. **Level:** Medium | **Domain:** GEOMETRY AND TRIGONOMETRY
    Skill/Knowledge: Right triangles and trigonometry | **Testing point:** Similar triangles and use of SOHCAHTOA

Key Explanation: Since triangle *DEF* and triangle *PQR* are similar, angles *F* and *R* are congruent. Therefore, *sin R = sin F*. Therefore using *SOHCAHTOA* the *sin* of an angle is equal to the length of the opposite side to the angle divided by the length of the hypotenuse of the triangle. Thus, the *Sin* of *F* is $\frac{5}{13}$.

11. **Level:** Easy | **Domain:** PROBLEM-SOLVING AND DATA ANALYSIS
    Skill/Knowledge: One-variable data: distributions and measures of center and spread | **Testing point:** Finding the mean

    Key Explanation: Choice B is correct. To find the average of a set of data, divide the total sum of the values of the data by the number of items. The average of the SAT scores of the 7 students is 1,320. Therefore, the sum of their scores would be 1,320 × 7 = 9,240. Adding in the SAT score of the 8th student, the new sum of the SAT scores will be 9,240 + 1,460 = 10,700. The new average SAT score will be $\frac{10,700}{8} = 1,337.5$, which is 1,340 rounded to the nearest tens place.

    Distractor Explanations: Choice A is incorrect as this is the mean score if the new higher score is subtracted from the sum of the current sum of scores and divided by 6. **Choice C** is incorrect as this is the average of the average SAT scores of the 7 students and the score of the new student $\frac{(1,320+1,460)}{2}$. **Choice D** is incorrect as this answer incorrectly assumes that the new score will be the new average SAT score.

12. **Level:** Easy | **Domain:** PROBLEM-SOLVING AND DATA ANALYSIS
    Skill/Knowledge: Two-variable data: models and scatterplots | **Testing point:** Exponential function interpretation

    Key Explanation: Choice B is correct. The 3 in the exponential equation above represents the growth factor. It indicates a tripling of the bacteria. When $t = 14$ the growth factor in the equation becomes $3^{\frac{14}{14}}$, which is 3, and therefore at $t = 14$ days the amount of bacteria triples. There are 14 days in two weeks which makes **Choice B** the correct answer.

    Distractor Explanations: The equation for an exponential model is $y = ab^x$, where a represents the initial amount of the data. **Choice A** is incorrect because $a = 2,034$ would represent the amount of bacteria at the beginning of the study and not the given term. **Choice C** is incorrect because it assumes that the model is linear, however, the model is exponential. **Choice D** is incorrect as this answer gives $rp(t)$ and not the given term in the equation.

13. **Level:** Easy | **Domain:** ALGEBRA
    Skill/Knowledge: Linear equations in one variable
    Testing point: Linear equation with no solutions

    Key Explanation: The first step is to use the distributive property to expand out the terms on the left side of the equation as follows:

    $5(x+3) - 3(2-x)$

    $5x + 15 - 6 + 3x$

    Combining like terms on the left side of the equation yields $8x + 9$

    Therefore, for the equation below to have no solutions, the lines represented by both sides of the equation need to be parallel, and thus have the same slope and different *y-intercepts*. Since the equations are in slope–intercept form $y = mx + b$, with different *y-intercepts*, the slope of the line represented by $8x + 9$ is 8 and thus $p = 8$.

14. **Level:** Hard | **Domain:** ALGEBRA

    Skill/Knowledge: Systems of two linear equations in two variables | **Testing point:** Finding the number of solutions in a system of equations

    Key Explanation: Choice D is correct. To compare the equations, do math operations to get the equations in the slope–intercept form $y = mx + b$, where m is the slope of the line and b is the *y-intercept*. First, simplify the second equation by dividing out a 2 from all terms to get: $-3x = -4y + 16$. Adding $4y$ to both sides of the equation and adding $3x$ to both sides of the equation yields $4y = 3x + 16$. Dividing all terms in the equation by 4 to get it into slope–intercept form yields $y = \dfrac{3}{4}x + 4$. Adding $-3x$ to both sides of the first equation yields $-4y = -3x + 16$. Dividing all terms in the equation by -4 yields $y = \dfrac{3}{4}x - 4$. Looking at the revised equations the lines have the same slope but different *y-intercepts*, making the lines parallel. Parallel lines do not intersect, and therefore there is no solution to the system of equations.

    Distractor Explanations: Choice A is incorrect because to have one solution, the slopes of both equations should not be equal, and they are. **Choice B** is incorrect because linear systems cannot have 2 solutions. **Choice C** is incorrect because to have infinitely many solutions the equations would need to represent the same line and thus be the same (the slopes and *y-intercepts* of the two lines would be the same); they are not.

15. **Level:** Medium | **Domain:** GEOMETRY AND TRIGONOMETRY

    Skill/Knowledge: Circles | **Testing point:** Finding the length of a minor arc

    Key Explanation: Choice A is correct. The length of the minor arc is found by using the formula $\dfrac{\theta}{360}\pi d$, where theta is the measure of the central angle and d is the diameter of the circle. Therefore, the length of minor arc AB is $\dfrac{72}{360}\pi(12) = 2.4\pi$, which is **Choice A.**

    Distractor Explanations: Choice B is incorrect as it gives the area of the minor sector AOB. **Choice C** is incorrect as it is the circumference of the whole circle. **Choice D** is incorrect as it is $\dfrac{12\pi}{72} = \dfrac{\pi}{6}$ and may be due to a calculation error.

16. **Level:** Medium | **Domain:** ADVANCED MATH

    Skill/Knowledge: Equivalent expressions | **Testing point:** Matching coefficients

    Key Explanation: $(x + 3)^2$ is equal to $(x+3)\times(x+3)$. Using the foiling method to multiply out the terms, yields $x^2 + 3x + 3x + 9$, or $x^2 + 6x + 9$. Using the distributive property, $-2(x^2 + 6x + 9) + 6 = -2x^2 - 12x - 18 + 6$, which is equivalent to $-2x^2 - 12x - 12 = ax^2 + bx + c$. Therefore, $c = -12$.

17. **Level:** Easy | **Domain:** GEOMETRY AND TRIGONOMETRY

    Skill/Knowledge: Lines, angles, and triangles | **Testing point:** Midpoint between two points on a line

    Key Explanation: Choice C is correct. To find the midpoint between two points on a line (x_1, y_1)

and (x_2, y_2), use the midpoint coordinates formula

$$\left(\frac{x_1 + x_2}{2}, \frac{y_1 + y_2}{2}\right)$$

Therefore the coordinates of the midpoint of line segment AB can be found from the following

equations: $\frac{6 + x_2}{2} = 8$ and $\frac{11 + y_2}{2} = 10$. Using

cross products, solve $x_2 + 6 = 16$, or $x_2 = 10$, and y_2 + 11 = 20, or $y_2 = 9$. Therefore, the coordinates of point B are (10, 9).

Distractor Explanations: Choice A is incorrect and is found when the midpoint formula is used incorrectly with (8, 10) and (6, 11) as the points. **Choice B** is incorrect and is found by subtracting in the midpoint formula instead of adding. **Choice D** is incorrect and may be arrived at through a conceptual error.

18. **Level:** Easy | **Domain:** ADVANCED MATH
Skill/Knowledge: Nonlinear functions | **Testing point:** Finding the number of solutions to an absolute value equation

Key Explanation: Choice B is correct. Since the absolute value is equal to zero, the only value that makes the absolute value equation equal to zero is $x = -3$. Thus, there is only one solution.

Distractor Explanations: Choice A is incorrect because for an absolute value to have 0 solutions, it must be equal to a negative number and zero is not a negative number **Choice C** is incorrect as to have two solutions the absolute value must be equal to a positive number. Zero is not a positive number. **Choice D** is incorrect as there is enough information to answer the question.

19. **Level:** Easy | **Domain:** ADVANCED MATH
Skill/Knowledge: Nonlinear functions | **Testing point:** Absolute value and value of a function

Key Explanation: Choice B is correct. To find $f(2)$, substitute 2 for all values of x in the equation as follows:

$(2)^2 - 20(2) + 9 = -27$.

To find $|f(2)|$ take the absolute value of -27 which is 27, or **Choice B**.

Distractor Explanations: Choice A is incorrect as the question requires the absolute value of the function value and not the function value itself. **Choices C** is incorrect and can be arrived at through miscalculations. **Choice D** is incorrect and can be arrived at through miscalculations

20. **Level:** Easy | **Domain:** PROBLEM–SOLVING AND DATA ANALYSIS
Skill/Knowledge: Percentages | **Testing point:** Percentage increase and decrease

Key Explanation: Assume that the initial price of the oil was x. The price of oil after the 20% increase would be $1.2x$. This price is then decreased by 14%. Thus, 86% of the oil price remains and thus $0.86 \times 1.2x = 1.032x$. This shows that after the two changes, the price of oil has increased overall by 3.2%.

21. **Level:** Easy | **Domain:** GEOMETRY AND TRIGONOMETRY
Skill/Knowledge: Circles | **Testing point:** Area of a circle inscribed in a square

Key Explanation: Choice A is correct. The length of a side of the square is equal to the diameter of the circle. The area of a circle can be found using the formula πr^2, where r is the radius of the circle.

The radius of a circle is half of its diameter, so the radius of the circle is $\frac{4\sqrt{2}}{2}$ or $2\sqrt{2}$. Therefore, the area of the circle is $\left(2\sqrt{2}\right)^2 \times \pi$ or 8π.

Therefore, $p = 8$.

Distractor Explanations: Choice B is incorrect. This is the value of two times the diameter of the circle. **Choice C** is incorrect. This is the value of the area of the square and not the circle. **Choice D** is incorrect. This is the value of the area of the circle if the radius is equal to 8.

22. **Level:** Medium | **Domain:** ALGEBRA
Skill/Knowledge: Linear inequalities in one or two variables | **Testing point:** Solving a linear inequality

Key Explanation: Choice A is correct. To solve, first add x to both sides of the equation to get: $-2x + 6 \leq 2$. Next, subtract 6 from both sides of the equation to get: $-2x \leq -4$ Finally, divide both sides by -2 which flips the inequality sign yielding $x \geq 2$. Only **Choice A** is not in the domain of the equation.

Distractor Explanations: Choice B is incorrect. This answer choice is solution to the inequality and answer the opposite of what the question is asking. **Choice C** is incorrect. This answer choice is solution to the inequality and answer the opposite of what the question is asking. **Choice D** is incorrect. This answer choice is solution to the inequality and answers the opposite of what the question is asking.

1. **Level:** Easy | **Domain:** ADVANCED MATH
    Skill/Knowledge: Nonlinear functions | **Testing point:** Sum of the solutions

    Key Explanation: Choice B is correct. The equation represents a quadratic in the form $ax^2 + bx + c$, where $a=3$, $b=9$, and $c=-27$. The sum of the solutions to a quadratic equation is given by the formula $\left(\dfrac{-b}{a}\right)$, Therefore, the sum of the solutions of the quadratic equation would be $\left(\dfrac{-9}{3}\right)$, or -3.

    Distractor Explanations: Choice A is incorrect because it is the product of the solutions to the quadratic equation and not the sum of them. The product of the solutions of a quadratic equation is given by the formula $\left(\dfrac{c}{a}\right)$, which is $\left(\dfrac{-27}{3}\right)$ or -9. **Choice C** is incorrect as it is $\left(\dfrac{b}{a}\right)$, not $-\left(\dfrac{b}{a}\right)$. **Choice D** is incorrect as it is the negative of the product of the solutions.

2. **Level:** Easy | **Domain:** ADVANCED MATH
    Skill/Knowledge: Equivalent expressions | **Testing point:** Combining like terms

    Key Explanation: Choice D is correct. First, distribute the negative to the terms in the parentheses as follows: $3x^2y + 5x - 3x^2y^2 + 2x^2y$. Combining like terms yields $5x^2y + 5x - 3x^2y^2$ which is **Choice D** when the terms are arranged in standard form.

    Distractor Explanations: Choice A is incorrect due to miscalculation or lack of concept knowledge. **Choice B** is incorrect. The sign changes of the terms in the parentheses when the negative sign is distributed to these terms and the parenthesis is removed. **Choice C** is incorrect due to miscalculation or lack of concept knowledge

3. **Level:** Medium | **Domain:** ALGEBRA
    Skill/Knowledge: Linear inequalities in one or two variables | **Testing point:** Solving for a linear inequality

    Key Explanation: To solve the inequality, first subtract 2 from both sides to get: $-2y + 2 - 2 < 6 -2$. Next, divide both sides by -2 to get: $y > -2$ Note that multiplying or dividing by a negative number in an inequality flips the inequality sign. -1 is the least possible integer value of y which satisfies the inequality $y > -2$.

4. **Level:** Easy | **Domain:** ADVANCED MATH
    Skill/Knowledge: Nonlinear equations in one variable and systems of equations in two variables **Testing point:** Discriminant and solving for linear and quadratic equations

    Key Explanation: Choice B is correct. Using the substitution method, substitute the first equation for y in the second equation yielding $2x - 5 = 2x^2 - 18x + 45$. Next, subtract the $2x$ from both sides to get $-5 = 2x^2 - 20x + 45$. Add 5 to both sides of the equation to get $0 = 2x^2 - 18x + 50$. The discriminant of a quadratic equation is $b^2 - 4ac$, when the quadratic equation is in the form $ax^2 + bx + c$. In the quadratic equation $a = 2$, $b = -20$, and $c = 50$. The value of the discriminant determines the number of solutions for a quadratic equation. Therefore, plugging in the values of a, b, and c into the discriminant, yields $(-20)^2 - 4(2)(50)$ which yields $400 - 400 = 0$ Therefore, the system will have one solution as the discriminant $= 0$.

    Distractor Explanations: Choice A is incorrect, most likely due to a miscalculation. **Choice C** is incorrect due to miscalculations. **Choice D** is incorrect. Quadratic equations can't have an infinite number of solutions.

5. **Level:** Easy | **Domain:** ALGEBRA
Skill/Knowledge: Systems of two linear equations in two variables | **Testing point:** Solving linear systems using elimination or substitution

Key Explanation: Choice C is correct. The most efficient way to solve the system of equations is to subtract the two equations resulting in $x + y = 9$.

The system of equations can also be solved using the elimination or substitution methods to find x and y individually and then adding the values of x and y to find the answer.

Distractor Explanations: Choice A is incorrect as it is due to a miscalculation or a conceptual error. **Choice B** is incorrect as it is the value of x only and not $x + y$. **Choice D** is incorrect as it is found by the sum of the two equations which instead yields $5x - 3y = 13$, which does not give the value of $x + y$.

6. **Level:** Easy | **Domain:** GEOMETRY AND TRIGONOMETRY
Skill/Knowledge: Right triangles and trigonometry | **Testing point:** Trigonometric identities

Key Explanation: There is a trigonometric identity which states that $sin\ x = cos\ (90° - x)$

Therefore, $sin\ 32° = cos\ 58°$ and thus $cos\ 58° = 0.551$.

7. **Level:** Hard | **Domain:** GEOMETRY AND TRIGONOMETRY
Skill/Knowledge: Lines, angles, and triangles | **Testing point:** Conversion of measurements and area of triangles

Key Explanation: Choice A is correct. The area of a triangle is found by the formula $A = \frac{1}{2} \times$ base $\times$ height. Since the answer is required in *ft squared*, we will need to convert any lengths of the sides of the triangle that are in *inches* to *feet*.

Therefore, 10 *inches* can be converted to *feet* by multiplying it by $\frac{1}{12}$, which gives $\frac{10}{12}$ feet. This reduces to $\frac{5}{6}$ *ft*.

Using the area of a triangle formula, the area is $\frac{1}{2} \times \frac{5}{6} \times 24 = 10\ ft$.

Distractor Explanations: Choice B is incorrect as this is the area of the triangle without having converted any of the side *lengths* to *feet*. **Choice C** is incorrect as this is the area if all the side lengths were in inches instead of *feet*. **Choice D** is incorrect as even though the measurements have been converted to feet, the formula for the area used was *base* × *height* which is not the correct formula.

8. **Level:** Hard | **Domain:** ADVANCED MATH
Skill/Knowledge: Equivalent expressions | **Testing point:** Subtracting fractions with variable denominators

Key Explanation: Choice C is correct. All the given answer choices have one term, and not two like the original expression. Thus, the two fractional expressions need to be combined into one fraction by getting them both over the least common denominator. The least common denominator of the two terms is $x\ (x - 4)$. To get both terms over the least common denominator the first term needs to be multiplied by $\frac{(x-4)}{(x-4)}$ and the second term needs to be multiplied by $\frac{x}{x}$, yielding

$$\frac{-5(x-4)}{x(x-4)} = \frac{x(x)}{x(x-4)}$$

Since the denominators of the fractions are equal, the numerators can be combined over a single fraction as follows:

$$\frac{-5(x-4)-x(x)}{x(x-4)} = \frac{-5x+20-x^2}{x^2-4x},$$

which is **Choice C.**

Distractor Explanations: Choice A is incorrect as the question asked to simplify the terms and not solve for anything. **Choice B** is incorrect and may be due to a conceptual error or miscalculation. **Choice D** is incorrect and may be due to a conceptual error or miscalculation

9. **Level:** Easy | **Domain:** ALGEBRA
    Skill/Knowledge: Linear equations in two variables | **Testing point:** Identifying linear equations from graphs

    Key Explanation: Choice B is correct. The slope–intercept equation of a line is $y = mx + b$, where m is the slope and b is the y–intercept of the equation. The slope m of a line can be found using the equation $m = \frac{(y_2 - y_1)}{(x_2 - x_1)}$, where (x_1, y_1) and (x_2, y_2) represent any two points on the line Pick two points on the line that are easy to find on the graph. The x and y intercepts of the line are two good points to use. Using points (2, 0) and (0, 6), the slope of the line can be found by plugging these points into the slope formula, yielding $\frac{(6-0)}{(0-2)}$, or $\frac{6}{-2} = -3$. The y–intercept of the line is 6. Therefore $y = -3x + 6$. All of the answer choices are written in an offset of the standard equation of a line $ax + by = c$. Adding $3x$ to both sides of the slope–intercept form of the equation gives the standard equation of the line as $3x + y$

= 6. Multiplying all terms of the equation by 3 to better match the form of the answer choices yields $9x + 3y = 18$, which matches **Choice B**.

Distractor Explanations: Choice A is incorrect as this equation represents a line with a positive slope. From the graph the slope of the line is negative. **Choice C** is incorrect because the slope of the line is –3 and not 2. **Choice D** is incorrect because the slope of the line is –3 and not –4 .

10. **Level:** Easy | **Domain:** ADVANCED MATH
    Skill/Knowledge: Nonlinear functions | **Testing point:** Finding y–intercept

    Key Explanation: The y–intercept occurs where $x = 0$, $y - 7 = 3^0 - 5$. Anything to the power of zero = 1, so $y - 7 = 1 - 5$. Adding 7 to both sides of the equation to solve for y yields $y - 7 + 7 = 1 - 5 + 7$, $y = 3$.

11. **Level:** Medium | **Domain:** ADVANCED MATH
    Skill/Knowledge: Nonlinear functions | **Testing point:** Finding the value that makes a function undefined

    Key Explanation: Choice C is correct. A function is undefined when the denominator is equal to 0. To find what values of x make this occur, solve the equation $x^2 - 2x - 15 = 0$ for x. Use the grouping method of factoring to determine what two numbers multiply to –15 but add up to –2. The two numbers would be –5 and 3. Thus, the middle term of the quadratic equation can be written as $-5x + 3x$, instead of $-2x$ as follows: $2 - 5x + 3x - 15 = 0$. Grouping the terms and factoring out the greatest common factor of each group, yields $x(x - 5) + 3(x - 5) = 0$. $(x+3)(x-5) = 0$, $x = -3$, and $x = 5$. Only the solution to the quadratic equation $x = -3$ meets the question condition that x be less than zero. Thus, C is the correct answer.

Distractor Explanations: Choice A is incorrect as it gives the negative value 5, which could be the result of factoring incorrectly. **Choice B** is incorrect. It may be due to a miscalculation. **Choice D** is incorrect since this is the positive x value of the solution and the value needs to be less than zero.

12. **Level:** Medium | **Domain:** ALGEBRA
Skill/Knowledge: Linear functions | **Testing point:** Finding the x–intercept given two points

Key Explanation: Choice D is correct. $f(3) = -1$ and $f(4) = -3$ represent the x and y values of two points on a line. The points are $(3, -1)$ and $(4, -3)$. To find the x–intercept of the line represented, the equation of the line first needs to be determined. The slope–intercept form of the equation of the line, $y = mx + b$ is easiest to use. In this equation, m represents the slope of the line and b its y–intercept. The slope of a line can be found using the slope formula $m = \dfrac{(y_2 - y_1)}{(x_2 - x_1)}$. Plugging in the two points into the slope formula yields $m = \dfrac{-3 - (-1)}{4 - 3} = -2$.

Therefore the equation of the line is $y = -2x + b$.

To find b, plug either point into the equation and solve for b. Using the point $(3, -1)$ yields $-1 = -2(3) + b$, $-1 = -6 + b$, $b = 5$. Therefore the equation of the line is $y = -2x + 5$. The x–intercept of a line occurs where $y = 0$. Plugging in zero for y into the equation and solving for x gives the following x–intercept:

$0 = -2x + 5$, $2x = 5$, $x = 2.5$ or $\dfrac{5}{2}$.

Distractor Explanations: Choice A is incorrect as this is the slope of the line. **Choice B** is incorrect as this is the y–intercept. **Choice C** is incorrect and

is the result of a miscalculation in solving for the x–intercept.

13. **Level:** Hard | **Domain:** ALGEBRA
Skill/Knowledge: Linear functions | **Testing point:** Transformations and Solving for function values

Key Explanation: The function $f(x + 3)$ is moved to the left by 3 units, therefore we should also move the x value in $f(x)$ to the left by 3 units to get $2 - 3$ or $f(-1)$

Therefore $f(-1)$ is found by substituting -1 into the equation for x as follows:
$5(-1) - 17 = -22$.

14. **Level:** Hard | **Domain:** PROBLEM–SOLVING AND DATA ANALYSIS
Skill/Knowledge: Ratios, rates, proportional relationships, and units | **Testing point:** Calculating average speed with unknown variable

Key Explanation: Choice B is correct. Average speed is calculated by taking the total distance traveled divided by the total time to travel that distance. The total distance traveled would be $x + x = 2x$. The total time taken would be 2.5 hrs + 1.5 hrs = 4 hrs

Therefore, the average. speed = $\dfrac{2x}{4} = \dfrac{x}{2}$

Distractor Explanations: Choice A is incorrect as it does not account for the fact that there is a return trip. **Choice C** is incorrect as it incorrectly accounts for the time it took Amber to do her errands. **Choice D** is incorrect as it may be due to a conceptual error or the student incorrectly found the total distance traveled.

15. **Level:** Easy | **Domain:** GEOMETRY AND TRIGONOMETRY

    Skill/Knowledge: Area and volume | **Testing point:** Perimeter of a rectangle

    Key Explanation: Choice C is correct. If the width of the rectangle is w, the length would be $w+3$. The area of a rectangle can be found by multiplying the width of the rectangle by its length.

    Therefore the area of the rectangle would be $w(w+3)=28$. Using the distributive property, the equation can be expanded out to:

    $$w^2+3w=28$$
    $$w^2+3w-28=0$$

    Factoring the equation yields $(w+7)(w-4)=0$ Setting both factors of the equation equal to 0 results in $w=-7$ and $w=4$. Since the width of a rectangle cannot be negative, -7 is not a valid width for the rectangle. Therefore the width of the rectangle would be 4 and the length would be $4+3$ or 7. The perimeter of a rectangle is found by the formula $P=2(l+w)$. Plugging in the determined values for w and l yields $2(7+4)=22$ or **Choice C**

    Distractor Explanations: Choice A is incorrect as this value is the sum of the length and the width and not two times the sum. **Choice B is incorrect** as this is half the area. **Choice D is incorrect** and may be due to conceptual error.

16. **Level:** Easy | **Domain:** PROBLEM–SOLVING AND DATA ANALYSIS

    Skill/Knowledge: Inference from sample statistics and margin of error | **Testing point:** Inference from sample statistics

    Key Explanation: The students surveyed who do not practice sanitary routines are $(48 - 23) = 25$.

    It can therefore be extrapolated that $\dfrac{25}{48}$ of all the

students in the school donot practice sanitary routines. Therefore $\left(\dfrac{25}{48}\right) \times 2,280$ or 1,187.5 students. This rounds up to 1,188 students.

17. **Level:** Medium | **Domain:** ALGEBRA

    Skill/Knowledge: Linear functions | **Testing point:** Linear transformations

    Key Explanation: Choice D is correct. To move one unit up, 1 is added to the equation. To move 1 unit to the left, 1 is added to the x term in the equation as follows

    $y = 2(x+1) + 1$

    $y = 2x + 2 + 1$

    $y = 2x + 3$

    Distractor Explanations: Choice A is incorrect as this is moving the line to the right 1 unit and up by 1 unit. **Choice B is incorrect** as this is moving the line only up by one unit and not moving it to the left. **Choice C is incorrect** as this answer may be due to a conceptual issue.

18. **Level:** Medium | **Domain:** ADVANCED MATH

    Skill/Knowledge: Nonlinear equation in one variable and systems of equations in two variables
    Testing point: Finding the vertex of a parabola

    Key Explanation: Choice B is correct. The standard form of a parabola is represented by the equation $y = ax^2 + bx + c$. In the equation given, $a = 2$, $b = 8$, and $c = 12$. The x coordinate of the vertex is found using the formula $\left(\dfrac{-b}{2a}\right)$. Thus, $\left(\dfrac{-8}{2(2)}\right) = -2$

    Distractor Explanations: Choice A is incorrect as this is the sum of the solutions to the quadratic equation. **Choice C is incorrect** and is found by incorrectly using $\left(\dfrac{b}{a}\right)$ **Choice D** is incorrect as this is the product of the solutions to the quadratic equation.

19. **Level:** Easy | **Domain:** ADVANCED MATH
Skill/Knowledge: Equivalent expressions | **Testing point:** Long division and remainder theorem

Key Explanation: B is the remainder when $x^2 - 6x + 10$ is divided by $x + 2$. When the divisor is equated to 0, we find $x = -2$, we can then find the remainder by substitute -2 in place of x $\left(-2^2 - 6(-2) + 10\right)$ which yields 26, this is the value of B.

20. **Level:** Easy | **Domain:** GEOMETRY AND TRIGONOMETRY
Skill/Knowledge: Lines, angles, and triangles | **Testing point:** The pythagorean theorem

Key Explanation: Choice C is correct. The Pythagorean theorem states that the sum of the squares of the lengths of the sides of a right triangle is equal to the square of the length of the hypotenuse of the triangle, or $a^2 + b^2 = c$. Plugging in 11 for a and 61 for c yields $11^2 + b^2 = 61^2$

$b^2 = 61^2 - 11^2$

$b^2 = 3{,}721 - 121$

$b^2 = 3{,}600$

Therefore, $b = 60$.

Distractor Explanations: Choice A is incorrect and may be due to conceptual or calculation errors.**Choice B** is incorrect and may be due to conceptual or calculation **Choice D** is incorrect and can be found by adding $61^2 + 11^2$ and finding the square root instead of subtracting the two numbers.

21. **Level:** Easy | **Domain:** PROBLEM-SOLVING AND DATA ANALYSIS
Skill/Knowledge: Evaluating statistical claims: observational studies, and experiments | **Testing point:** Observational experiments

Key Explanation: Choice D is correct. This statement is true because it is not certain that taking supplements would directly equate to an improvement in student performance. It is not known if all other variables were kept constant. Therefore, a direct cause-and-effect relationship cannot be determined. Also, the sample size is too small to generalize to a larger population.

Distractor Explanations: Choice A is incorrect. This statement is false and imply that there is a relationship between student performance and taking supplements. **Choice B** is incorrect. This statement is false and imply that there is a relationship between student performance and taking supplements. **Choice C** is incorrect. This statement is false and imply that there is a relationship between student performance and taking supplements.

22. **Level:** Easy | **Domain:** ALGEBRA
Skill/Knowledge: Systems of two linear equations in two variables | **Testing point:** Solving for system of linear equations

Key Explanation: Choice A is correct. The most efficient way to answer this question is to not solve the system of equations for x and y individually, but rather to subtract the second equation from the first, yielding $-x + y = -5$. Therefore $y - x = -5$.

Distractor Explanations: Choice B is incorrect. This is the value of y. **Choice C** is incorrect. This is the negative value of option A and is due to a calculation mistake. **Choice D** is incorrect. This is the value of x.

This page is intentionally left blank

Chapter 3

....

Practice Test 2

You are about to begin a full-length Practice Test. The test has four modules. The time allotted for each module is marked at the beginning of the module. Work on one module at a time. Use a timer to keep track of the time limits for every module.

Try to take the Practice Test under real test conditions. Find a quiet place to work, and set aside enough time to complete the test without being disturbed. At the end of the test, check your answers by referring to the Answer Key and fill in your raw score in the scorecard below. Also, note down the time taken by you for completing each module.

Pay particular attention to the questions that were answered incorrectly. Read the answer explanations and understand how to solve them.

....

My Score Card (Raw Score)

	Reading and Writing		Math	
	Module 1	Module 2	Module 1	Module 2
Out of	27	27	22	22
My Score	_____	_____	_____	_____
Time Taken	_____	_____	_____	_____

TEST BEGINS ON THE NEXT PAGE

Reading and Writing Test

27 QUESTIONS | 32 MINUTES

DIRECTIONS

The questions in this section address a number of important reading and writing skills. Each question includes one or more passages, which may include a table or graph. Read each passage and question carefully, and then choose the best answer to the question based on the passage(s). All questions in this section are multiple-choice with four answer choices. Each question has a single best answer.

1

Hyraxes are small, furry, herbivorous mammals with short tails that live primarily in Africa; one species is also found in the Middle East. These little animals spend time in trees or rocky outcrops. They _____ resemble guinea pigs, but in reality, are much more closely related to sea cows and elephants.

Which choice completes the text with the most logical and precise word or phrase?

A) logically

B) customarily

C) superficially

D) universally

2

The following text is adapted from a publication by Jefferson Keel's 2011 publication, "The Indian Reorganization Act—75 Years Later: Renewing our Commitment to Restore Tribal Homelands and Promote Self-determination."

Today, the Indian Reorganization Act (IRA) is as necessary as it was in 1934. The purposes of the IRA were frustrated first by World War II and then by the termination era. Work did not begin again until the 1970s with the self-determination policy, and since then, Indian tribes have been building economies from the ground up.

As used in the text, what does the word "frustrated" most nearly mean?

A) Annoyed

B) Unfulfilled

C) Dissatisfied

D) Thwarted

CONTINUE

3

The following text is adapted from Mother Jones's speech to coal miners in West Virginia in 1912

The guards of the mining companies beat, abuse, maim, and hold up citizens without process of law; deny freedom of speech, a provision guaranteed by the Constitution; deny the citizens the right to assemble in a peaceable manner for the purpose of discussing questions in which they are concerned.

As used in the text, what does the word "provision" most nearly mean?

A) Allocation

B) Arrangement

C) Contingency

D) Requirement

4

The following text is from Frances Hodgson Burnett's 1905 novel "A Little Princess."

If Sara had been older or less punctilious about being quite polite to people, she could have explained herself in a very few words. But, as it was, she felt a flush rising on her cheeks. Miss Minchin was a very severe and imposing person, and she seemed so absolutely sure that Sara knew nothing whatever of French, that she felt as if it would be almost rude to correct her. The truth was that Sara could not remember the time when she had not seemed to know French.

Which choice best states the function of the underlined sentence in the text as a whole?

A) It gives a description of the physical appearance of one of the characters.

B) It establishes why one of the characters was not comfortable in the situation.

C) It reinforces an emotional state alluded to in the previous sentence.

D) It introduces the interaction between two characters in the following sentences.

5

The following text is adapted from Charlotte Bronte's 1847 novel Jane Eyre. In the novel, Jane Eyre has come to live at Thornfield Hall to be the governess of a young girl named Adele.

I found my pupil sufficiently docile, though disinclined to apply: she had not been used to regular occupation of any kind. I felt it would be injudicious to confine her too much at first; so, when I had talked to her a great deal, and got her to learn a little, and when the morning had advanced to noon, I allowed her to return to her nurse. I then proposed to occupy myself till dinner-time in drawing some little sketches for her use.

Which choice best states the function of the underlined sentence in the text as a whole?

A) It shows that the speaker is anxious to spend some time drawing.

B) It establishes that the speaker is frustrated with her pupil's lack of focus.

C) It demonstrates how the speaker attempts to teach her pupil in a way that will work best for the pupil's ability.

D) It introduces how the speaker interacts with her student in a teaching style that is most comfortable for the speaker.

6

The following text is adapted from F. Scott Fitzgerald's 1922 novel, "The Beautiful and the Damned."

At fifty-seven years old Adam Patch determined, after a severe attack of sclerosis, to consecrate the remainder of his life to the moral regeneration of the world. He became a reformer among reformers. He levelled a varied assortment of uppercuts and body-blows at liquor, literature, vice, art, patent medicines, and Sunday theatres. From an armchair in the office of his Tarrytown estate he directed against the enormous hypothetical enemy, unrighteousness, a campaign which went on through fifteen years, during which he displayed himself a rabid monomaniac, an unqualified nuisance, and an intolerable bore. The year in which this story opens found him wearying; <u>1861 was creeping up slowly on 1895;</u> his thoughts ran a great deal on the Civil War, somewhat on his dead wife and son, almost infinitesimally on his grandson Anthony.

Which choice best states the function of the underlined portion in the text as a whole?

A) It indicates that Adam Patch was living in the past rather than the present.

B) It provides a reason Adam Patch did not reflect often on the deaths of his wife and son.

C) It offers the reason that Adam Patch dedicated most of his time to campaigning against vices.

D) It clarifies the previous claim that Adam Patch was an intolerable bore.

7

Why does the sky turn red at sunrise and sunset? <u>The reason is Rayleigh Scattering, which is actually the same effect that you see in a rainbow when light hits rain.</u> Light travels in waves, with red waves being the longest visible light and blue being the shortest. The shorter the wave, the easier it scatters into different directions. During the day, the Sun shines directly down on the atmosphere, so all wavelengths enter and the sky looks blue to a viewer. However, when the Sun gets lower on the horizon, the light is traveling through a much larger distance of the atmosphere to reach the same place on the Earth's surface. At that angle, many of the shorter blue waves get scattered into outer space, and only the longer, red waves, which travel in a straighter line before being scattered, reach the viewer.

Which choice best describes the function of the underlined sentence in the text as a whole?

A) It explains where waves of light originate.

B) It offers an example that the reader might recognize.

C) It presents an exception to a general rule.

D) It shows why blue waves scatter more easily than red waves.

8

The following text is adapted from Tien Nguyen's 2019 publication, "Antibodies Reverse Synthetic Opioid Overdoses in Mice."

Medical professionals have only one treatment option, a drug called naloxone, against acute opioid overdoses, which is a growing problem that in 2017 killed more than 47,000 people in the US. The fast–acting treatment, sold as Narcan, races towards the brain where it blocks opioid receptors, denying the drugs access to them. But naloxone breaks down after about an hour, which allows a relapse into overdose unless the drug is re–administered. Naloxone's short lifetime also makes it less effective against powerful synthetic opioids like fentanyl and carfentanil, which are 100– and 10,000–fold stronger than morphine, respectively.

Which choice best explains why naloxone is not completely desirable as a solution for patients who have overdosed on opiates?

A) Naloxone is only able to protect a patient for a limited period.

B) Naloxone is more expensive than other available treatment options.

C) Naloxone offers no results for overdoses of many opiate drugs.

D) Naloxone has harmful side effects which can injure the patient.

9

Nanoparticles (NPs) are small particles with sizes from 1 to 100 nanometers, possessing excellent catalytic and adsorptive properties. They fall under nanomaterials (NMs) and are categorized based on their properties, shapes, and sizes. NPs exhibit distinct chemical and physical properties due to their nanoscale size and large surface area. They find applications in various fields, including composite materials like nanocomposites (NCPs) and as building blocks for new dielectric and magnetic materials. NPs can self-assemble into unique structures, and their unique properties are being harnessed in areas such as medicine, agriculture, and energy. Plant-mediated biological approaches are used for eco-friendly NP synthesis.

What is the main idea of the text?

A) Nanoparticles (NPs) exhibit distinct chemical and physical properties due to their nanoscale size and large surface area, finding applications in various fields.

B) Nanoparticles (NPs) are small particles categorized under nanomaterials (NMs) based on their properties, shapes, and sizes, with applications in composite materials and as building blocks for new materials.

C) Nanoparticles (NPs) possess unique properties and find applications in medicine, agriculture, energy, and other fields, with eco-friendly synthesis methods.

D) Nanoparticles (NPs) self-assemble into unique structures, and their properties are being harnessed for various purposes.

10

A recent study led by geophysicists reveals that powerful supershear earthquakes, previously considered rare, are actually more prevalent than believed. By analyzing all strike-slip earthquakes worldwide with magnitudes of 6.7 or greater since 2000, the researchers identified 12 supershear events, accounting for approximately 14% of the total. Prior to this discovery, the expected percentage of supershear earthquakes was previously less than 6%. Strike-slip earthquakes occur when tectonic plates slide sideways against each other, and supershear quakes are a subset of these events, characterized by faster fault ruptures than the speed of shear waves. The energy buildup and release during supershear earthquakes can result in more intense shaking and potentially greater destruction compared to earthquakes of similar magnitudes.

Which finding, if true, would most directly undermine the geophysicists' finding?

A) Supershear quakes are also a subset of dip-slip earthquakes.

B) Supershear quakes only occur in earthquakes with a magnitude of at least 6.7.

C) Supershear quakes can be detected by examining the speed of fault ruptures.

D) Strike-slip quakes always have a magnitude of at least 6.7.

11

The US Cities with the Greatest Percentage of Residents who Commute by Bicycle

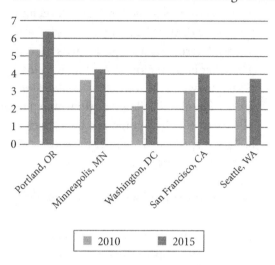

Based on data from the US Census Bureau

Why do people ride bicycles to work? Weather is not everything, as there is an annual average of 156 days of rain in the top commuting city, Portland, Oregon. Making cycling safer by adding protected bike lanes can increase ridership. Another option is making bikes more accessible, such as was done in the District of Columbia, which added 400 bike share depots since 2010. The success of such programs is evident: _____

Which choice most effectively uses data from the graph to complete the example?

A) Ridership in Washington, DC, increased from just over 2 percent in 2010 to 4 percent in 2015.

B) Washington, DC, used to have lower ridership than any other of the top five cities for bicycle commuters in 2010.

C) Portland, Oregon, now boasts over 6 percent of commuters who ride bikes and Washington, DC, has increased to 4 percent.

D) Washington, DC now has more bicycle commuters than San Francisco, California or Seattle, Washington.

12

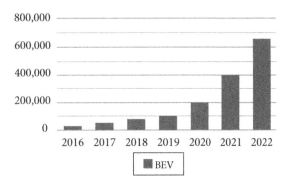

Cumulative number of battery-electric cars in
the UK (2016 to date)

Source: SMMT, December 2002

According to a study released by The Society of
Motor Manufacturers and Traders (SMMT), the
number of electric cars registered in the United
Kingdom has increased dramatically over the
years, showing increasing customer preference
for battery-electric cars over traditional cars.
However, this customer preference for battery-
electric cars has not increased uniformly over the
years. For instance, _____

Which choice most effectively uses data from the
graph to complete the text?

A) between 2016 to 2019, less than 200,000
battery-electric cars were registered in the UK

B) in 2020, less than 300,000 battery-electric cars
were registered in the UK

C) by 2022, almost 700,000 electric cars had been
registered

D) while the number of registered electric cars
rose by 200,00 between the years 2020 and
2021, there was a spike of almost 300,000
additional cars registered in 2022

13

A new species of salamander, *Tylototriton
phukhaensis,* was named in 2020. The defining
feature is a distinct head ridge, though it also
has head horns and a stripe down its back. A
molecular examination shows that it is closely
related to two of the four other *Tylototriton*
species found in Thailand. First identified from
a 20–year–old photograph in a travel magazine,
biologists speculated whether the species still
existed in the wild, but _____

Which choice most logically completes the text?

A) had to base their assessments on the
Tylototriton species that were more readily
available to them.

B) were able to locate living specimens that could
provide enough information for a positive
identification.

C) spent years vainly scouring the tropical
rainforests before determining that it was
probably indeed extinct.

D) finally concluded that the photograph might
have been inaccurate or was possibly even
created as a hoax.

14

Rhizobia are types of bacteria in the soil that live in the roots of plants. Rhizobia and plants are thought to have a mutualistic relationship where the bacteria produce and provide the nitrogen that plants require and the plants provide a habitat and carbon for a source of food. However, new research shows that some rhizobia do not produce much nitrogen and still benefit from the resources provided by the plants. As a result, plants that detect such rhizobia often adapt by becoming inhospitable environments. The only plants that may allow low-nitrogen producing rhizobia to continue to inhabit its roots are plants _____

Which choice most logically completes the text?

A) living in nutrient-low soil that desperately require nitrogen, however little.

B) that do not require any nitrogen at all.

C) that can produce its own nitrogen.

D) living in nutrient-rich soil that do not depend on rhizobia for nitrogen.

15

There's nothing like homemade red Thai chili paste to enliven a meal. Most cooks opt for store-bought substitutes, however, because traditionally it takes over 30 minutes of grinding ingredients such as chili pepper, lemongrass, cilantro, _____ in a mortar and pestle.

Which choice completes the text so that it conforms to the conventions of Standard English?

A) shallots and, lime

B) shallots, and lime

C) shallots, and lime,

D) shallots, and, lime

16

William Shakespeare is often misquoted, but at other times, phrases are used in a context very different from what they were intended to be. While "now is the winter of our _____ frequently used to mean a horrible time, it actually signals a time of change for the better in the drama "Richard III."

Which choice completes the text so that it conforms to the conventions of Standard English?

A) discontent." It is

B) discontent," is

C) discontent", is

D) discontent" is

17

Algeria marks its 53rd year of independence this _____ bitter struggle for freedom in the late 1950s and early 1960s became a central focus of the global movement against colonialism. It also influenced the evolving forms of oppression and resistance in apartheid South Africa.

Which choice completes the text so that it conforms to the conventions of Standard English?

A) month, the

B) month—the

C) month: the

D) month. The

18

In 2021, archaeologists unearthed remarkably preserved ice-age mammoths, including an infant and two young adults, on a privately owned piece of land in Cotswolds, Gloucestershire. Further mammoth discoveries_____, but access to the site was withdrawn by the owner, raising concerns about the preservation of these artifacts.

Which choice completes the text so that it conforms to the conventions of Standard English?

A) are anticipated

B) would be anticipated

C) were anticipated

D) was anticipated

19

The second smallest country by area in the world after Vatican City, Monaco is a mere 2.1 square kilometers. Most famous for the Monte Carlo Casino, _____. In fact, Monaco is a pioneer in marine conservation with one of the first protected marine areas in the world.

Which choice completes the text so that it conforms to the conventions of Standard English?

A) there is also an oceanographic museum in the country which is world–class.

B) the country also is home to a world–class oceanographic museum.

C) a world–class oceanographic museum is also in the country.

D) a museum of oceanography which is world–class is also in the country.

20

In what manner does the specificity of place influence art, enough to transform from background to foreground, shifting from a mere context to a significant character? This inquiry _____ at the heart of art historian Prudence Peiffer's groundbreaking survey, "The Slip: The New York City Street That Forever Altered American Art."

Which choice completes the text so that it conforms to the conventions of Standard English?

A) lie

B) lies

C) is lying

D) was lying

21

Formed in February 2019 and disbanded a mere ten months later, The Independent Group for Change, aka, Change UK, emerged as a centrist British political party with a pro-European Union stance. The party's primary objective was to champion a second referendum on European Union membership, advocating for continued EU affiliation. Its dissolution followed the loss of all _____ seats during the 2019 general election.

Which choice completes the text so that it conforms to the conventions of Standard English?

A) it's MPs'

B) its MP's

C) its MPs'

D) it's MPs

22

Those who paid attention to the music industry started to notice the decades–long trend of Billboard–topping tracks that directly incorporated inspiration from their predecessors in the form of sampling. _____ Drake sampled Ms. Lauryn Hill, who sampled Wu Tang Clan, who sampled Gladys Knight and the Pips.

Which choice completes the text with the most logical transition?

A) Ultimately,

B) In addition,

C) Furthermore,

D) For example,

23

Since it was completed in 1911, the Stoclet House in Belgium has been among the finest examples of the Vienna Secession of the Art Nouveau style. The integrity of the exterior architecture and garden remains almost untouched, and the interior has undergone few changes. Even much of the furniture is original. _____ the house fulfills the architectural criteria necessary for a UNESCO World Heritage site, which it became in 2009.

Which choice completes the text with the most logical transition?

A) Subsequently,

B) Otherwise,

C) Therefore,

D) However,

24

Messier 47 is a well–known star cluster that contains mostly massive, hot blue stars. It was first identified in 1654 by an Italian astronomer named Giovanni Hodierna. Charles Messier, without knowledge of Hodierna's discovery, independently cataloged the cluster about a hundred years later. _____ he wrote down erroneous coordinates, so the Messier 47 remained lost until its presence was confirmed by T.F. Morris in 1957.

Which choice completes the text with the most logical transition?

A) Finally,

B) Ironically,

C) Specifically,

D) Accordingly,

25

While researching a topic, a student has taken the following notes:

1. The African grey hornbill (Lophoceros nasutus) is a member of the Hornbill family of mainly tropical near-passerine birds found in the Old World.

2. It is a widespread and common resident breeder in much of sub-Saharan Africa and the southwest of the Arabian Peninsula.

3. The African grey hornbill has escaped or been deliberately released into Florida, USA, but there is no evidence that the population is breeding and may only persist due to continuing releases or escapes.

4. At 45–51 cm (18–20 in) in length, the African grey hornbill is a large bird, although it is one of the smaller hornbills.

5. The African grey hornbill is widespread over much of sub-Saharan Africa. It prefers open woodland and savannah.

The student wants to emphasize that it is unlikely that the African grey hornbill will rapidly multiply in Florida. Which choice most effectively uses relevant information from the notes to accomplish this goal?

A) The African grey hornbill is a smaller hornbill and is easier to hunt down

B) It seems likely that the presence of the African grey hornbill is due to a deliberate release or escape, with no proof of breeding

C) The African grey hornbill is only commonly found in sub-Saharan Africa where the climate is highly unlike Florida

D) It is a tropical bird that is only widespread in open woodland and savannah areas

26

While researching a topic, a student has taken the following notes:

- The United States operates under a federal system in which powers are divided between the national government and individual states.

- In contrast, China is a unitary state wherein its central government holds the majority of political power.

- Federal systems tend to grant more local autonomy, reflecting the distinctive needs of different regions within a country. Unitary systems tend to follow more uniform policies that reduce disparities but often neglect local needs.

- Critics contend that unitary systems may lead to an excess concentration of power while federal systems can create policy inconsistencies and inefficiencies.

The student wants to emphasize the contrasting principles of power distribution between federal and unitary systems. Which choice most effectively uses relevant information from the notes to accomplish this goal?

A) Federal systems like that found in the United States provide greater regional autonomy than unitary ones like China's, where policy uniformity could lead to potential neglect of local needs.

B) In contrast with China's unitary system that accumulates excessive power, the United States operates under a federal system, resulting in policy inconsistency and inefficiency.

C) Although both countries possess effective governance systems, their approaches to power distribution differ; with the United States emphasizing local autonomy while China favoring uniform policies.

D) While federal systems, such as the one in the United States, encourage regional autonomy that allows for addressing diverse local needs, China's unitary system centralizes political power, leading to uniform policies that might neglect these local specificities.

27

While researching a topic, a student has taken the following notes:

- In modern politics, populism refers to any political approach which attempts to appeal to ordinary citizens who feel their needs and concerns have been overlooked by established elite groups.

- Populism can be seen at both ends of the political spectrum: on one end are nationalistic right-wing movements that focus on anti-immigration sentiment while the other advocate for economic justice and workers' rights.

- Social media and the internet have played an enormous part in driving populism forward, providing direct channels of communication between political leaders and their constituents.

- Populism's critics warn it can lead to authoritarianism, as populist leaders exploit public discontent to consolidate power.

The student wants to emphasize the effects of populism in modern politics. Which choice most effectively uses relevant information from the notes to accomplish this goal?

A) Political populism has been amplified by social media and the internet, providing direct channels for political leaders to engage their constituents directly.

B) Populism, an appeal to ordinary people who feel left behind by elites, has experienced an explosion due to social media, which could potentially lead to authoritarianism if left unchecked.

C) Social media has acted as a catalyst in propelling populism, serving as a platform for ordinary citizens who feel their concerns have been ignored by elite establishments.

D) Critics warn of populism's rise as an appeal to ordinary people feeling neglected by elites; critics fear this trend can create a pathway toward authoritarianism.

Reading Test

27 QUESTIONS | 32 MINUTES

DIRECTIONS

The questions in this section address a number of important reading and writing skills. Each question includes one or more passages, which may include a table or graph. Read each passage and question carefully, and then choose the best answer to the question based on the passage(s). All questions in this section are multiple-choice with four answer choices. Each question has a single best answer.

1

Tourism is a growing sector of the global economy. Travel and tourism jobs are increasing worldwide, but Africa as a whole attracts less than 5 percent of total world tourists. However, Sub-Saharan Africa has a strong supply-side potential to attract tourists. Beach resorts alone create a large _____. The coastal waters of the Indian Ocean boast some of the finest beaches in the world, with plenty of opportunities for water sports.

Which choice completes the text with the most logical and precise word or phrase?

A) haul

B) persuasion

C) draw

D) connection

2

Noted for his contributions to understanding seventeenth-century art in the Netherlands, John Montias had a formal education in cultural economics. His studies of art auction sales from the period led to breakthroughs in the understanding of the _____ painter Johannes Vermeer.

Which choice completes the text with the most logical and precise word or phrase?

A) conspicuous

B) eminent

C) radiant

D) absolute

The following text is from The Best Plays of the Old Dramatists by Havelock Ellis.

"The earliest known edition of The Tragical History of Doctor Faustus is that of 1604; there is a second edition with date of 1609, agreeing in almost every particular with the first; a third edition with new scenes and many alterations, was published in 1616…

It is very doubtful if any of the additions to the edition of 1616 are by Marlowe; Mr. Bullen thinks that some of them are. They are often ingenious, and sometimes, they are improvements. They appear to be written by a clever and <u>facile</u> imitator of Marlowe's style."

As used in the text, what does the word "facile" most nearly mean?

A) Accomplished

B) Successful

C) Effortless

D) Superficial

The term "ghost kitchen" may make you think of a haunted house. In reality, it is just a physical space to prepare food that will be eaten elsewhere. The number of ghost kitchens is actually _____, since multiple brands or restaurants can share a low–rent space to make meals sold on delivery food apps.

Which choice completes the text with the most logical and precise word or phrase?

A) multiplying

B) inflating

C) skyrocketing

D) getting bigger

5

Horses have been demonstrated to possess complex thought processes that involve associations, memories, and recognition of emotions in other species. For example, in one experiment, horses were shown photographs of human faces that were angry or happy. <u>The people in the photographs were all strangers to the horses.</u> Several hours later, the actual person entered the field and stood near the horse with a neutral expression. In every case, the horses avoided approaching the people whose photographs had displayed anger.

What is the purpose of the underlined sentence in the overall structure of the text?

A) It explains how the subjects were selected for the experiment.

B) It points out that horses have a limited range of human contacts.

C) It highlights the importance of expression in communication.

D) It shows the researchers eliminated one possible weakness in the study.

6

The following text is from Gwendolyn Brooke's 1963 poem "We Real Cool." In this poem, the speaker is describing a group of teenagers who are spending time at a pool hall.

The Pool Players.
Seven at the Golden Shovel.
We real cool. We
Left school. We
Lurk late. We
Strike straight. We
Sing sin. We
Thin gin. We
Jazz June. We
Die soon.

Which choice best states the main purpose of the text?

A) To detail the carefree lifestyle of a group who will probably face consequences

B) To analyze how living a defiant lifestyle will certainly result in problems

C) To characterize a group of teenagers as being defiant and rebellious

D) To call attention to a group of teenagers enjoying themselves

Text 1

Chromosomes were unknown in 1834 when Gregor Mendel proposed his classic concept of heredity. In the late 1880s, scientists finally could stain cell structures with the clarity to see chromosomes. Walter Sutton and Theodor Boveri, in 1902 and 1903 respectively, independently published papers suggesting that genes were located in specific places on the chromosomes, which came in matched pairs except for the male Y chromosome.

Text 2

Thomas Hunt Morgan criticized the Sutton–Boveri chromosome theory of inheritance. However, he noticed some unusual trends while conducting experiments on fruit flies. A few males had white rather than red eyes, so he bred them and observed the results. He determined that white was a recessive mutation which did not appear in any first–generation females, though it might resurface in subsequent generations. After careful documentation, he published his conclusion that eye color genes were located on the X chromosome.

Based on the texts after his experiments, how would Thomas Hunt Morgan (Text 2) most likely describe the view Sutton and Boveri presented in Text 1?

A) It is largely correct, but it required some adjustment concerning minor details.

B) It is not compelling because he had definitive data contradicting the theory.

C) It may seem plausible, but it is not supported by scientific findings.

D) It probably holds true despite his initial skepticism of it.

Giant anteaters are neotropical mammals that, as their name suggests, consume ants, termites, and grubs, though they do occasionally eat fruit. Their habitat ranges from Central to South America in swamps, forests, and grasslands where their favored prey is common. The solitary foragers have specialized tongues so they can consume thousands of ants in a few minutes after breaking open a nest, and they quickly abandon the site when soldier ants emerge to protect the colony.

Which choice best states the main idea of the text?

A) Giant anteaters live alone in neotropical areas that have not been disturbed by humans.

B) There are fewer opportunities for giant anteaters to eat since soldier ants are more vigilant.

C) Giant anteaters have adapted so that they are able to gather sufficient food.

D) Despite the danger of soldier ants, giant anteaters prefer to eat ants over other food sources.

Scientist James Clark and graduate student Jason McLachlan of Duke University published findings from a study analyzing tree pollen extracted from ancient lake sediments in the journal Nature. According to Clark, the purpose of their study was to address a central scientific problem in explaining the diversity of tree species in a forest. "In the mathematical models ecologists use to describe how different species compete for resources such as light, moisture and nutrients, it can be difficult to get species to coexist," he said. "In models, slight advantages allow one species to 'out-compete' the other, leading to extinction, that is, loss of biodiversity. And so, ecologists have put a lot of effort into trying to understand the differences among species that would allow one species to coexist with another species."

According to the text, what is the primary purpose of analyzing tree pollen extracted from ancient lake sediments?

A) To explore the ramifications of a mathematical model

B) To isolate factors that allow a phenomenon to happen

C) To identify the causes of an unusual incident

D) To isolate the flaws in a common theory

Robert Henri (1865–1929) was an American painter and teacher who disliked the conservative restrictions placed on the highly-polished art by artists affiliated with the National Academy of Design. With several colleagues, he introduced a new style that depicted the seedy underside of urban life in a bold, realistic fashion. Critics dubbed the artists with the title of "Ashcan School" because they drew sketches in the streets of New York and depicted dirty snow, laundry hanging out to dry, and other scenes of everyday life.

Based on the text, what is most likely true about artists affiliated with the National Academy of Design?

A) They used a bold, realistic style for their paintings.

B) They did not live or work in New York City.

C) They avoided subjects that were undignified.

D) They preferred to draw scenes related to summertime.

11

Robin Williams (1951–2014) has often been considered one of the best American comedians of all time. Famous for creating engaging characters at the spur of the moment, Williams began his career as a stand–up comic and moved on to win many prestigious awards for his roles in motion pictures. Everyone who knew him described him as full of natural talent and energy: _____

Which quotation most effectively illustrates the claim?

A) "Williams helped us grow up." (Alyssa Rosenberg)

B) "He gave his…talent freely and generously to those who needed it most—from our troops stationed abroad to the marginalized on our own streets." (Barack Obama)

C) "The world is forever a little darker, less colorful and less full of laughter in his absence." (Zelda Williams)

D) "He came in like a hurricane…there goes my chance in show business." (David Letterman)

12

Deaths from Drug Overdoses in the United States by Year

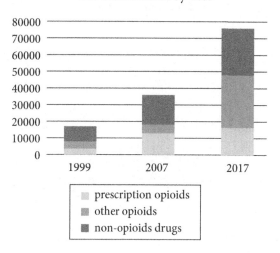

Data from National Institute on Drug Abuse, 2019.

In a potential advance in treating opioid overdose, researchers have developed long–lasting monoclonal antibodies that selectively bind potent synthetic opioids and reverse their effects in mice. The researchers propose that the antibodies could one day be administered as a stand–alone treatment or as part of a more effective combination treatment against opioid overdoses. This is extremely important, given that in 2017 alone, there were approximately _____

Which choice most effectively uses data from the graph to complete the example?

A) 18,000 deaths caused by any drug overdoses.

B) 38,000 deaths caused by any type of opiate drug overdose.

C) 48,000 deaths caused by drug overdoses on any opiate.

D) 75,000 deaths caused by prescription opiate drug overdoses.

CONTINUE

13

Population change in the EU Member States during 2019 *(per 1,000 residents)*

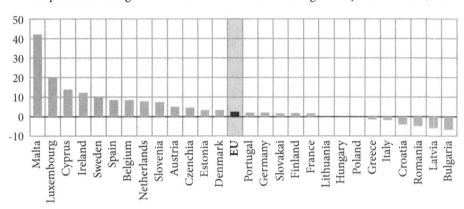

During 2019, there was an increase in population in eighteen EU member states. By far the highest population increase was recorded in Malta, followed by Luxembourg, Cyprus, Ireland, and Sweden. Conversely, _____

Which choice most effectively uses data from the graph to complete the text?

A) the largest population decreases were recorded in Bulgaria, Latvia, Romania, Croatia, and Italy.

B) Italy recorded a negative population growth.

C) only a few countries recorded an increase in population.

D) 4.7 million deaths were registered in the EU in 2019.

14

Animals that consume the flesh or nectar from fruits typically ingest small amounts of alcohol as well because the sugar from the fruit can turn into ethanol, a type of alcohol. Researchers studied hummingbirds to determine whether the level of alcohol will impact the birds' consumption behavior. The results showed that the hummingbirds began consuming less sugar water only when the alcohol volume reached 2% of total volume, with no difference in behavior observed for 1% of alcohol volume. Based on the findings, researchers speculate that _____

Which choice most logically completes the text?

A) naturally occurring levels of alcohol in the hummingbirds' typical diet likely do not exceed 2% in nature.

B) hummingbirds may be able to tolerate more than 2% if the taste of alcohol is masked.

C) naturally occurring levels of alcohol in the hummingbirds' typical diet likely do not exceed 1% in nature.

D) different types of food in the hummingbirds' diet will naturally have varying levels of alcohol volume.

15

Waterfalls come in many shapes. One classic form is the punchbowl, such as at Eagle Falls in Oregon. In such a _____ water flows down a narrow chute into a wide pool at the bottom. It is easy to swim in the tranquil waters at the base.

Which choice completes the text so that it conforms to the conventions of Standard English?

A) waterfall

B) waterfall,

C) waterfall:

D) waterfall;

16

Scott Evans is a golf ball diver. In other words, he dives into the water hazards placed on golf courses to collect and recycle the balls which accidentally landed there. His job may sound fun, but it is not _____ spends hours in murky water and can get trapped by unseen obstacles.

Which choice completes the text so that it conforms to the conventions of Standard English?

A) easy, he

B) easy; because he

C) easy. Since he

D) easy. He

17

Northern New Zealand is home to some of the oldest forests on Earth. Forests filled with kauri, the Maori name for the *Agathis australis* tree, _____ back to the Jurassic period over 135 million years ago.

Which choice completes the text so that it conforms to the conventions of Standard English?

A) date

B) dating

C) they date

D) those forests date

18

While training departments try to give us what we need to stay ahead in the competitive market, research _____ that they are also falling behind: employees rate their Learning & Development departments lower than almost any other product in the consumer landscape.

Which choice completes the text so that it conforms to the conventions of Standard English?

A) are showing

B) will show

C) showed

D) shows

19

Sceloporus malachiticus, commonly referred to as the emerald swift or green spiny lizard, belongs to the *Phrynosomatidae* family and hails from Central America. These lizards stand out with their vibrant green hue, with males often _____ more captivating features than females, such as vivid blue patches adorning both sides of their bellies.

Which choice completes the text so that it conforms to the conventions of Standard English?

A) exhibiting

B) are exhibiting

C) will exhibit

D) exhibit

20

The German pianist Clara Schumann (1819–1896) is considered one of the finest performers of the Romantic period. Her career spanned over sixty years, much of which was spent traveling around Europe. In addition to giving concert performances, _____ composed many works for the piano.

Which choice completes the text so that it conforms to the conventions of Standard English?

A) she

B) her

C) hers

D) she's

21

Many organizations are turning to a policy called "job sharing" in an effort to retain good employees. Dividing one full-time job between two employees _____ a company to recruit talented workers who do not have the time or inclination to work 40 hours every week.

Which choice completes the text so that it conforms to the conventions of Standard English?

A) allow

B) allows

C) allowing

D) to allow

22

The collection of rainwater is known by many names throughout the world. _____ from rainwater collection to rainwater harvesting to rainwater catchment. Rainwater harvesting is a viable technology in an urban setting, as all that is needed to take advantage of this resource is to capture the free water falling onto a roof and direct it to a storage tank.

Which choice completes the text so that it conforms to the conventions of Standard English?

A) They ranges

B) Their range

C) These range

D) The names ranges

23

Italian physicist Alessandro Volta, known for his pioneering work in electricity, made significant advancements in the field by inventing the first electric battery. His invention, the Voltaic Pile, produced a continuous flow of electricity. _____ Volta's groundbreaking discovery laid the foundation for the development of modern electrical systems.

Which choice completes the text with the most logical transition?

A) Hence,

B) Moreover,

C) Similarly,

D) Nonetheless,

24

Guernica, a painting in oil on canvas, is one of Pablo Picasso's masterpieces and arguably one of the most influential anti-war paintings of all time. Though Picasso typically painted in private, he allowed influential visitors into his studio to observe the progress in order to promote awareness of the Spanish Civil War. _____ the completed painting was exhibited around the world to raise funds for war relief efforts.

Which choice completes the text with the most logical transition?

A) In addition,

B) By contrast,

C) Consequently,

D) For instance,

25

Ethiopian Prime Minister Abiy Ahmed was awarded the 2019 Nobel Peace Prize for his efforts to end the ongoing stalemate between Ethiopia and Eritrea. At the beginning of his tenure, he was lauded for progressive decisions. _____ he was accused of restricting the freedom of the press and detaining innocent people who held opposing views.

Which choice completes the text with the most logical transition?

A) Additionally,

B) Accordingly,

C) Subsequently,

D) Consequently,

CONTINUE

26

While researching a topic, a student has taken the following notes:

- Cold War politics were marked by fierce rivalry between the United States and the Soviet Union.

- The United States was known to practice a capitalist economic system and foster democratic governance.

- The Soviet Union was an authoritarian communist state with a centrally planned economy.

- Throughout the Cold War, both superpowers engaged in political propaganda, espionage, and military confrontation known as "proxy wars".

- In 1991, the dissolution of the Soviet Union signaled an end to Cold War rivalries and heralded an era dominated by America alone.

The student wants to emphasize the fundamental ideological differences between the United States and the Soviet Union during the Cold War. Which choice most effectively uses relevant information from the notes to accomplish this goal?

A) Throughout the Cold War, both nations engaged in various military confrontations that highlighted their profound ideological differences.

B) During the Cold War, the United States upheld a capitalist and democratic ideology, engaging in military confrontations with the Soviet Union, which staunchly defended its communist and centrally-planned economic framework.

C) The Cold War was defined by the ideological clash between the capitalist United States and the communist Soviet Union, made evident through their practices of political propaganda and espionage.

D) The fall of the Soviet Union in 1991 marked the end of both the Cold War and the ideological contest between the United States and the Soviet Union.

27

While researching a topic, a student has taken the following notes:

1. Ludovico Maria Enrico Einaudi is an Italian pianist and composer who trained at the Conservatorio Verdi in Milan.

2. He has composed the scores for a number of films and television productions and has won several awards for his compositions.

3. Einaudi is most known for being the most-streamed classical artist of all time with his music reaching over 1 million streams daily, and 2 billion streams in total.

4. His latest album Seven Days Walking: Day One has become the fastest-streamed classical album of all time since its release on 15 March 2019. The project is a series of digital albums released monthly over seven consecutive months.

5. Day One interweaves piano and string and focuses on several main themes that will recur in different forms on subsequent albums.

The student wants to emphasize Einaudi's most well-known achievement. Which choice most effectively uses relevant information from the notes to accomplish this goal?

A) Among his many achievements, composer Ludovico Maria Enrico Einaudi trained at the Conservatorio Verdi in Milan and has won multiple awards.

B) He has composed for multiple films and television shows.

C) Einaudi is known as the most-streamed classical artist of all time, with 2 billion streams in total.

D) Einaudi has come up with highly innovative projects, including combining recurring notes of piano and string in different albums.

STOP

No Test Material On This Page

Math

22 QUESTIONS | 35 MINUTES

DIRECTIONS

The questions in this section address a number of important math skills. Use of a calculator is permitted for all questions.

NOTES

Unless otherwise indicated: • All variables and expressions represent real numbers. • Figures provided are drawn to scale. • All figures lie in a plane. • The domain of a given function is the set of all real numbers x for which $f(x)$ is a real number.

REFERENCE

$A = \pi r^2$
$C = 2\pi r$

$A = \ell w$

$A = \frac{1}{2} bh$

$c^2 = a^2 + b^2$

Special Right Triangles

$V = \ell w h$

$V = \pi r^2 h$

$V = \frac{4}{3} \pi r^3$

$V = \frac{1}{3} \pi r^2 h$

$V = \frac{1}{3} \ell w h$

The number of degrees of arc in a circle is 360.

The number of radians of arc in a circle is 2π.

The sum of the measures in degrees of the angles of a triangle is 180.

For **multiple–choice questions,** solve each problem, choose the correct answer from the choices provided, and then circle your answer in this book. Circle only one answer for each question. If you change your mind, completely erase the circle. You will not get credit for questions with more than one answer circled, or for questions with no answers circled.

For **student–produced response questions,** solve each problem and write your answer next to or under the question in the test book as described below.

- Once you've written your answer, circle it clearly. You will not receive credit for anything written outside the circle, or for any questions with more than one circled answer.

- If you find more than one correct answer, write and circle only one answer.

- Your answer can be up to 5 characters for a positive answer and up to 6 characters (including the negative sign) for a negative answer, but no more.

- If your answer is a fraction that is too long (over 5 characters for positive, 6 characters for negative), write the decimal equivalent.

- If your answer is a decimal that is too long (over 5 characters for positive, 6 characters for negative), truncate it or round at the fourth digit.

- If your answer is a mixed number (such as 3.!. 2), write it as an improper fraction (7/2) or its decimal equivalent (3.5).

- Don't include symbols such as a percent sign, comma, or dollar sign in your circled answer.

1

Ash has a walking and cycling routine. For every minute she walks, she burns 20 calories. And for every minute she cycles, she burns 35 calories. If she burns 340 calories on a particular day after walking for x minutes and cycling for y minutes, which of the following equations best represents her routine?

A) $340 - 20x = 35y$

B) $35y - 20x = 340$

C) $340 - 20y = 35x$

D) $35x - 20y = 340$

2

The graph below shows velocity (y–$axis$) plotted against time (x–$axis$). For how many data points is the actual value higher than the predicted values on the line of best fit?

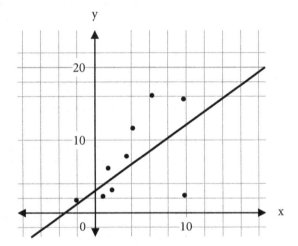

A) 2

B) 3

C) 6

D) 9

3

x	f(x)
−2	30
0	12
3	0
5	2

Which of the following is a factor of $f(x)$?

A) $(x+2)$

B) $(x-3)$

C) x

D) $(x-5)$

4

$$(t-5)+2(s-3)=8$$

$$2(t-5)-3(s-3)=-19$$

What is the value of s for the above system of equations?

5

$$3(x-2)-2(x-1)=-x+2(x+2)-8$$

How many solutions does the equation above have?

A) None

B) One

C) Two

D) Infinite

6

Which of the following is equivalent to $2g^{\frac{4}{5}}g^{\frac{2}{5}}$?

A) $\sqrt[5]{2g^6}$

B) $\sqrt[5]{32g^6}$

C) $2\sqrt[6]{g^5}$

D) $\sqrt[6]{2g^5}$

7

A researcher found the mean mass of all cheetahs in a park. He found that the mean mass of all cheetahs in the park is between 120 *lbs* and 182 *lbs*. What is the value of the margin of error for the mean mass of the cheetahs in the park?

8

What is the value of $f(6)$, if $f(2x) = 9x - 7$?

A) 11

B) 20

C) 47

D) 101

CONTINUE

9

A teacher takes note of the shoe sizes for 21 students in his class and creates the table below. Which of the following statements is true about the data below?

Shoe size	Frequency
1	3
2	4
3	4
4	7
5	2
6	1

A) The mean is greater than the median

B) The mean is the same as the median

C) The median is greater than the mean

D) There isn't enough information to answer the question.

10

$27^x \div 81^{-x} = 3^{ax}$?

What is the value of the above equation?

11.

If the value of the sum of interior angles of the hexagon is $b\pi$, what is the value of b?

A) 0.25

B) 1

C) 2

D) 4

12

What is the value when 80 is increased by 200%?

A) 160

B) 200

C) 240

D) 280

13

If $1 + \dfrac{a\sqrt{2}}{2}$ is a solution to the equation

$2x^2 - 4x - 7 = 0$, what is the possible value of a?

14

A real estate company kept a track of the number of houses it sold in October. Its team came up with the model $h(t) = 262 - 8t$, and t represents the number of days. Which of the following best represents 262?

A) The number of houses at the end of October

B) The number of houses at the beginning of October

C) The number of houses sold per day in October

D) The number of houses sold in the first 8 days of October.

15

ABC is a right–angled triangle, where B is 90° and angle C is 30°. If AC = 32, what is the area of triangle ABC.

A) $128\sqrt{3}$

B) $128\sqrt{2}$

C) $16\sqrt{3}$

D) $16\sqrt{2}$

16

If $(5xy + 3) - (6xy - 2xy^2 + 2) = axy^2 + bxy + c$, what is the value of $a + b$?

17

What is the product of the roots for the equation $3x^2 + 6x - 24 = 0$?

A) −8

B) −2

C) 2

D) 3

18

Which of the following best represents the equation of the graph below?

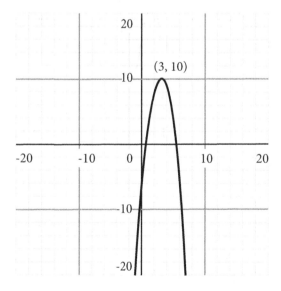

A) $y = 2(x + 3)^2 + 10$

B) $y = -2(x - 3)^2 + 10$

C) $y = 2(x - 3)^2 + 10$

D) $y = -2(x + 3)^2 + 10$

19

If $-3(-2 + 2x) = ax + b$, what is the value of ab?

20

Find the average rate of change when $x = 2$ and $x = 0$.

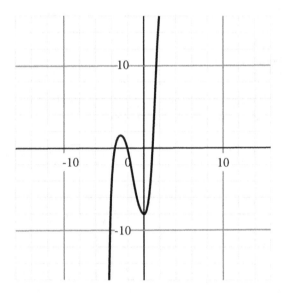

A) −8

B) −4

C) 4

D) 8

21

If $\frac{3}{4}(x - 5) = 27$, what is the value of $x - 5$?

A) $\frac{81}{4}$

B) 31

C) 36

D) 41

22

$$y > -2x - 1$$

$$3y < x + 9$$

Which of the following coordinates would be true for the above system of inequalities?

A) (−2, 1)

B) (4,1)

C) (3,1)

D) (−3, 3)

No Test Material On This Page

Math

22 QUESTIONS | 35 MINUTES

DIRECTIONS

The questions in this section address a number of important math skills. Use of a calculator is permitted for all questions.

NOTES

Unless otherwise indicated: • All variables and expressions represent real numbers. • Figures provided are drawn to scale. • All figures lie in a plane. • The domain of a given function is the set of all real numbers x for which $f(x)$ is a real number.

REFERENCE

$A = \pi r^2$
$C = 2\pi r$

$A = \ell w$

$A = \frac{1}{2} bh$

$c^2 = a^2 + b^2$

Special Right Triangles

$V = \ell w h$

$V = \pi r^2 h$

$V = \frac{4}{3} \pi r^3$

$V = \frac{1}{3} \pi r^2 h$

$V = \frac{1}{3} \ell w h$

The number of degrees of arc in a circle is 360.

The number of radians of arc in a circle is 2π.

The sum of the measures in degrees of the angles of a triangle is 180.

For **multiple–choice questions,** solve each problem, choose the correct answer from the choices provided, and then circle your answer in this book. Circle only one answer for each question. If you change your mind, completely erase the circle. You will not get credit for questions with more than one answer circled, or for questions with no answers circled.

For **student–produced response questions,** solve each problem and write your answer next to or under the question in the test book as described below.

- Once you've written your answer, circle it clearly. You will not receive credit for anything written outside the circle, or for any questions with more than one circled answer.

- If you find more than one correct answer, write and circle only one answer.

- Your answer can be up to 5 characters for a positive answer and up to 6 characters (including the negative sign) for a negative answer, but no more.

- If your answer is a fraction that is too long (over 5 characters for positive, 6 characters for negative), write the decimal equivalent.

- If your answer is a decimal that is too long (over 5 characters for positive, 6 characters for negative), truncate it or round at the fourth digit.

- If your answer is a mixed number (such as 3.!. 2), write it as an improper fraction (7/2) or its decimal equivalent (3.5).

- Don't include symbols such as a percent sign, comma, or dollar sign in your circled answer.

1

$$|3x - 1| = 2$$

If p and q are solutions to the equation above, which of the following best represents $p+q$?

A) $\dfrac{-1}{3}$

B) $\dfrac{1}{3}$

C) $\dfrac{2}{3}$

D) 1

2

Which of the following coordinates lie on the circle whose equation is $(x-3)^2 + y^2 + 8y = 84$?

A) $(1, 7)$

B) $(-2, 5)$

C) $(-3, 4)$

D) $(3, -6)$

3

If $sin\ C = 0.986$ and $cos\ 63 = 0.986$, what is the value of C?

4

If $\dfrac{2-2i}{3+4i}$ is equal to $a + bi$. What is the value of a?

A) $\dfrac{-2}{25}$

B) $\dfrac{-14}{25}$

C) $\dfrac{-1}{2}$

D) $\dfrac{2}{3}$

5

$$y = 2x^2 - 9x + 7$$

$$y = 2x - 2$$

Which of the following can be the value of x for the system of equations above

A) -1

B) $\dfrac{7}{2}$

C) $\dfrac{9}{2}$

D) $\dfrac{11}{2}$

6

$$3|3x - 2| - |6x - 4| = 7$$

What is the positive solution to the above equation?

7

Which of the following represents a *line l* (not shown) which is perpendicular to the *line m* (shown below)?

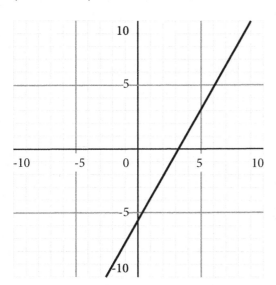

A) $3y = 5x - 15$

B) $5y = 3x + 15$

C) $5y = -3x + 15$

D) $3y = 5x + 10$

8

What is the circumference of the circle whose equation is $x^2 + 6x + y^2 - 4y = 51$

A) 8π

B) 14.28π

C) 16π

D) 64π

9

In the triangle ABC (not drawn to scale) shown below, $\angle ABC = 2x - 2$ and $\angle BAC = x + 3$. If $\angle ACD = 118°$, what is the value of x?

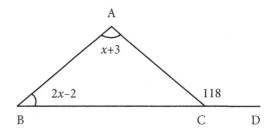

10

It takes 4 carpenters to build a bed in 3 days, how many carpenters will it take to build the bed in 2 days?

A) 6

B) 8

C) 12

D) 24

11

Which of the following is equivalent to $(5xy + 3x)(x - 2y)$?

A) $5x^2y - 6xy$

B) $5x^2y + 3x^2 + 10xy^2 - 6xy$

C) $5x^2y + 3x^2 - 10xy^2 - 6xy$

D) $-5x^2y^2 + 3x^2 - 6xy$

12

What is the value of y, if $7x - 4y = 1$ and $5x + 2y = 8$?

13

$$-2x \leq 8 - x$$

Which of the following is NOT a solution to the above equation?

A) -10

B) -8

C) -7

D) 2

14

If an unfair coin is tossed 20 times, and it lands on heads 14 times. What would be the probability of it landing on heads the 21st time?

A) 0.3

B) 0.5

C) 0.7

D) 0.20

15

What is the value of $x - y$ if $3y - 2x = 16$ and $5x + y = -6$?

A) -6

B) -2

C) 4

D) 6

16

A student conducted research on how many fish there are in a pond after m months and came up with the model, $f(x) = 1,200(1.03)^m$.

He wanted to have the time on the model in d days instead, as shown below

(assuming 1 month has 30 days)

$$f(x) = 1,200(1.03)^{ad}$$

What is the value of a?

CONTINUE

17

If the radius of a circular cylinder is 6, what is the volume of the cylinder if the height is twice its radius?

A) 108π

B) 216π

C) 432π

D) 864π

18

What is the value of the angle EOD, if the angle DRE is 35°?

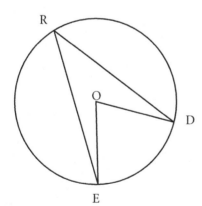

A) 35°

B) 55°

C) 60°

D) 70°

19

Which of the following is equivalent to

$$\frac{4x^2 - 3}{2x + \sqrt{3}}?$$

A) $2x - \sqrt{3}$

B) $2x + \sqrt{3}$

C) $2x - 3$

D) $2x + 3$

20

$$9x - 14y = -3$$

$$ax - by = 6$$

If the system of equations above has infinite solutions, what is the value of b?

21

If $3x + 5y = ax - 4x - by$, what is the value of a?

A) −5

B) 1

C) 3

D) 7

CONTINUE

22

$$3x + 2 < -5(x + 6)$$

Which of the following values is a solution to inequality?

A) −5

B) −4

C) 3

D) 4

STOP

No Test Material On This Page

Answer Key

Reading and Writing

	Module 1			Module 2	
Questions	**Correct**	**Mark your correct answers**	**Questions**	**Correct**	**Mark your correct answers**
1.	C		1.	C	
2.	D		2.	B	
3.	D		3.	D	
4.	C		4.	C	
5.	C		5.	D	
6.	A		6.	A	
7.	B		7.	D	
8.	A		8.	C	
9.	C		9.	B	
10.	A		10.	C	
11.	A		11.	D	
12.	D		12.	C	
13.	B		13.	A	
14.	A		14.	A	
15.	B		15.	B	
16.	D		16.	D	
17.	D		17.	A	
18.	C		18.	D	
19.	B		19.	A	
20.	B		20.	A	
21.	C		21.	B	
22.	D		22.	C	
23.	C		23.	A	
24.	B		24.	A	
25.	B		25.	C	
26.	A		26.	B	
27.	B		27.	C	

Math

	Module 1			Module 2	
Questions	**Correct**	**Mark your correct answers**	**Questions**	**Correct**	**Mark your correct answers**
1.	A		1.	C	
2.	C		2.	C	
3.	B		3.	27°	
4.	8		4.	A	
5.	D		5.	C	
6.	B		6.	3	
7.	31		7.	C	
8.	B		8.	C	
9.	A		9.	39	
10.	7		10.	A	
11.	D		11.	C	
12.	C		12.	$\frac{3}{2}$ or 1.5	
13.	3				
14.	B		13.	A	
15.	A		14.	C	
16.	1		15.	A	
17.	A		16.	$\frac{1}{30}$ or 0.0333	
18.	B				
19.	−36		17.	C	
20.	B		18.	D	
21.	C		19.	D	
22.	C		20.	−28	
			21.	D	
			22.	A	

1. **Level:** Medium | **Domain:** CRAFT AND STRUCTURE
   Skill/Knowledge: Words in Context

   Key Explanation: Choice C is the best answer because the blank portion shows how hyraxes resemble guinea pigs. **Choice C** refers to something that is only on the outside or surface, so fits the context of saying that the hyrax and guinea pig look similar, but they are not really related.

   Distractor Explanations: None of the other choices accurately explain how hyraxes resemble guinea pigs. **Choice A** refers to something that makes sense through reasoning, but one would reason that if the hyrax is related to an elephant, then it should look more like one. **Choice B** refers to something that happens by habit or tradition, but appearance is not based on habit. **Choice D** refers to something that happens in all cases or everywhere, so does not establish that some people see a general similarity.

2. **Level:** Medium | **Domain:** CRAFT AND STRUCTURE
   Skill/Knowledge: Words in Context

   Key Explanation: Choice D is the best answer because "frustrated" refers to what World War II and the termination era did to the purposes of the IRA. Choice D means "blocked" or "prevented," which fits the context of showing that events prevented the goals of the IRA from being completely fulfilled; that is why it is still needed today.

   Distractor Explanations: Choices A and C can be eliminated because they are emotional responses, but "the purposes of the IRA" are inanimate and cannot experience emotions. **Choice A** means "irritated" and **Choice D** means "not happy

with something." **Choice B** is incorrect because "fulfilling" refers to something doing the act of making another thing happen. However, it does not fit the context because World War II and the termination era were not things that could "fulfill" or make the IRA's goals happen. They were obstacles that stopped other things from fulfilling the purposes of the IRA.

3. **Level:** Hard | **Domain:** CRAFT AND STRUCTURE
   Skill/Knowledge: Words in Context

   Key Explanation: Choice D is the best answer because "provision" is something that is guaranteed by the Constitution, freedom of speech. **Choice D** refers to something that is necessary or must happen, so it fits the context of saying that freedom of speech is a right or need to be guaranteed by the highest law of the country.

   Distractor Explanations: None of the other choices adequately shows what is guaranteed by the Constitution. **Choice A** refers to the process of sharing something. **Choice B** refers to plans or preparations, but does not include the idea that they must occur. **Choice C** is a future event that might occur but cannot be accurately predicted.

4. **Level:** Medium | **Domain:** CRAFT AND STRUCTURE
   Skill/Knowledge: Text Structure and Purpose

   Key Explanation: Choice C is the best answer. The underlined sentence says that Sara flushed, which typically happens in anger or embarrassment. In this context, she appears embarrassed because she is not old or experienced enough—and was too "punctilious" or "careful"—to explain how she felt in a few words. The fact that she flushes highlights her sense of awkwardness and embarrassment.

Distractor Explanations: Choice A is incorrect because the sentence only says that Sara flushed. It does not explain what she looked like; she could be tall, short, dark–haired or blonde, dressed nicely, etc. **Choice B** is incorrect because the underlined sentence only establishes that Sara blushes. It does not give a reason why; the following sentences show she could speak French but was reluctant to tell Miss Minchin so. **Choice D** is incorrect because there is no interaction between characters in the following sentences. The underlined portion is expanded upon with a reason for blushing, not actions.

5. **Level:** Hard | **Domain:** CRAFT AND STRUCTURE
   Skill/Knowledge: Text Structure and Purpose

   Key Explanation: Choice C is the best answer since it bases the inference on the information found in the passage. The speaker shows patience with her student and does not overwhelm her with too much work at first since "it would be injudicious to confine her too much at first."

   Distractor Explanations: Choice A is incorrect because although she does draw after working with her student, there is no indication that she is impatient to work on this hobby. **Choice B** is wrong since it reflects an attitude opposite to the speaker's behavior. **Choice D** is incorrect since the passage clearly states that she conducts her lesson in a manner that would work well for her student, not for herself.

6. **Level:** Hard | **Domain:** CRAFT AND STRUCTURE
   Skill/Knowledge: Text Structure and Purpose

   Key Explanation: Choice A is the best answer because the phrase implies that Adam Patch still

felt he was living in 1861, whereas really years had passed the times were changing. The phrase gives a reason for him to "weary" and become tired… he had been so wrapped up in reforms, but his causes were not current or relevant any more. His thoughts were still focused on events such as the Civil War rather than on everyday life or his grandson.

Distractor Explanations: Choice B is incorrect because the passage implies that Adam focused on things that interested him. The fact that the wife and son died in the past is not the reason that he thinks about them infrequently; he doesn't really care about them as much as he does about things that happened earlier, like the Civil War. **Choice C** is incorrect because the fact that the times changed was the reason that his campaign against vices started to fade. The changing times is not why he started to fight against vice. **Choice D** is incorrect because someone can be interesting even if the times change. The reason that Adam was a bore was his actions during that time.

7. **Level:** Easy | **Domain:** INFORMATION AND IDEAS
   Skill/Knowledge: Text Structure and Purpose

   Key Explanation: Choice B is the best answer. The text is summarizing a potentially confusing effect that involves bending light waves. The reader has presumably seen a rainbow, however, so that image might help the reader visualize light bending when it hits the atmosphere as being similar to light bending when it hits rain.

   Distractor Explanations: Choice A is incorrect because "originate" means "begin," but light does not begin in a rainbow. **Choice C** is incorrect because the example of the rainbow shows the rule or effect of Rayleigh Scattering, it is not an "exception" or "not part of" the rule. **Choice D** is incorrect because the idea of a rainbow does not tell the reader "why" or "the reason" blue scatters more easily; a rainbow just offers an image which shows that colors separate in different ways when they hit something like rain or the atmosphere.

8. **Level:** Easy | **Domain:** INFORMATION AND IDEAS
   Skill/Knowledge: Central Ideas and Details

   Key Explanation: Choice A is the best answer because the text says that naloxone breaks down quickly, "after about an hour." This is "not completely desirable" or "unwanted" because it means that the drug needs to be carefully administered and the progress of the patient watched or the patient could "relapse" or "return to the original condition."

   Distractor Explanations: Choice B is incorrect because there is no discussion of price in the text. **Choice C** is incorrect because the passage does not say that naloxone has "no results" for some drugs. It only claims that it is less effective, meaning it has results that are not as strong, for "powerful synthetic opioids like fentanyl and carfentanil." **Choice D** is incorrect because there is no evidence of side effects related to naloxone. The only negative effect implied is that it needs to be readministered because it wears off quickly.

9. **Level:** Hard | **Domain:** INFORMATION AND IDEAS
   Skill/Knowledge: Central Ideas and Details

   Key Explanation: Choice C is the best answer because it accurately summarizes the main idea of the text. The passage discusses how nanoparticles (NPs) possess unique properties due to their nanoscale size and large surface area. It mentions their applications in medicine, agriculture, energy, and other fields. Additionally, it highlights the use of eco-friendly synthesis methods involving

plant-mediated biological approaches. All of these points contribute to the central idea that NPs possess unique properties and find applications in various fields, with an emphasis on eco-friendly synthesis methods.

Distractor Explanations: Choice A is incorrect because it focuses solely on the distinct chemical and physical properties of nanoparticles (NPs), without encompassing their categorization under nanomaterials, their applications in various fields, and the eco-friendly synthesis methods mentioned in the passage. **Choice B** is incorrect because although it mentions the categorization of nanoparticles (NPs) under nanomaterials (NMs) based on their properties, shapes, and sizes, it does not encompass the broader range of topics covered in the passage. The main idea extends beyond categorization to include the unique properties of NPs, their applications, and eco-friendly synthesis methods. **Choice D** is incorrect because it narrows down the main idea to the self-assembly of nanoparticles (NPs) into unique structures and the harnessing of their properties. While these aspects are mentioned in the passage, they do not fully capture the broader scope of the main idea, which includes the unique properties of NPs, their applications, and the emphasis on eco-friendly synthesis methods.

10. **Level:** Hard | **Domain:** INFORMATION AND IDEAS
    Skill/Knowledge: Command of Evidence (Textual)

    Key Explanation: Choice A is correct. The study states that scientists were shocked to discover that the proportion of supershear quakes was higher than expected at an estimated 14%. However, the study only examined strike-slip earthquakes. If supershear quakes are also a subset of dip-slip earthquakes, then there is a whole set of data that was not examined by the scientists and the proportion of supershear quakes could either be lower or higher than 14%.

Distractor Explanations: Choice B is incorrect because this choice still supports the conclusion of the study, since the scientists studied earthquakes with a magnitude of 6.7 or higher. **Choice C** is incorrect because this choice only describes a way to detect supershear quakes, but it does not undermine the finding of the study. **Choice D** is incorrect because this choice still supports the conclusion of the study, since the scientists studied strike-slip earthquakes with a magnitude of 6.7 or higher.

11. **Level:** Medium | **Domain:** INFORMATION AND IDEAS

    Skill/Knowledge: Command of Evidence (Quantitative)

    Key Explanation: Choice A is the best answer. The claim is that "such programs" are successful. There are two programs listed, making cycling safer and making bikes accessible. There are no specific examples of increasing safety, but the passage describes the details making bikes accessible by adding bike share depots in DC. **Choice A** shows that the program in DC, which started in 2010, probably has strong results, as ridership increased by over a percent in the five years after that policy was started.

    Distractor Explanations: Choice B is incorrect because it only says that DC had low ridership, but there is no indication of change. The reader does not know that the ridership increased after the program started. **Choice C** is incorrect because it focuses on Portland, but there is no indication that Portland did anything to make cycling safer or more accessible. **Choice C** also refers to DC, but the percentage of commuters is lower than that of Portland, so it could appear that the program was

not very successful. **Choice D** is incorrect because the reader does not know whether the program helped make the number of commuters in DC greater. It is possible that all along, there have been more commuters than the other cities. It is even possible that ridership in DC decreased after the program started.

12. **Level:** Medium | **Domain:** INFORMATION AND IDEAS

    Skill/Knowledge: Command of Evidence (Quantitative)

    Key Explanation: Choice D is correct because it shows an example of the inconsistent growth between the years 2020 to 2022. The previous sentence in the text talks about how the customer preference for electric cars has not increased uniformly. Choice D further illustrates this idea.

    Distractor Explanations: All the other choices are incorrect because the text must be completed with an example that illustrates the uneven rise in customer preference for battery-electric cars. **Choice A** is incorrect because it only states the number of electric cars registered between 2016-2019. **Choice B** is incorrect because it only states the number of electric cars registered between 2020. **Choice C** is incorrect because it does not offer a comparison that shows an uneven increase.

13. **Level:** Medium | **Domain:** INFORMATION AND IDEAS

    Skill/Knowledge: Inferences

    Key Explanation: Choice B is the best answer. The third sentence refers to "a molecular examination" which established genetic relationships with other species. Therefore, the biologists must have had molecules from actual salamanders to work with. In other words, they must have found at least one specimen in the wild to compare with the four Thai *Tylototriton* species.

Distractor Explanations: All of the other choices are incorrect because a molecular examination only of the species that were available, not using *T. phukhaensis*, would not be able to determine the molecular characteristics of *T. phukhaensis* well enough to know what species are related or not. The other choices all give scenarios in which the scientists did not find examples of the new species for comparison.

14. **Level:** Hard | **Domain:** INFORMATION AND IDEAS
    Skill/Knowledge: Inferences

Key Explanation: Choice A is correct. The text describes how plants only allow rhizobia to inhabit its roots because rhizobia provides nitrogen. When rhizobia is not providing sufficient nitrogen, plants will make it hard for rhizobia to live off of their roots. The remaining plants that may still allow such rhizobia to inhabit them must be plants that cannot get nitrogen from anywhere else and depend on the rhizobia from nitrogen, even if the amount is very low.

Distractor Explanations: Choice B is incorrect. Based on the text, if the plants do not require nitrogen at all, there is no purpose in allowing the rhizobia to inhabit their roots. **Choice C** is incorrect. Based on the text, if the plants can produce their own nitrogen, there is no purpose in allowing the rhizobia to inhabit their roots. **Choice D** is incorrect. Based on the text, if the plants can get nitrogen from other sources like the soil, there is no purpose in allowing the rhizobia to inhabit their roots.

15. **Level:** Medium | **Domain:** STANDARD ENGLISH CONVENTIONS
    Skill/Knowledge: Boundaries

Key Explanation: Choice B is the best answer. The proper structure for joining a list of over two nouns with "and" is to place a comma after each of the nouns that precedes "and." In this case, there should be a comma after "chili pepper," "lemongrass," "cilantro," and "shallots." No other punctuation is needed because "such as…lime" restricts the type of "ingredients" to specific ones that are ground together.

Distractor Explanations: Choices A and **D** are incorrect because there should be no comma after "and" in a list. The comma after "shallots" is sometimes omitted, but would only be acceptable if there were no other commas in the underlined portion. **Choice C** is incorrect because there should be no comma after "lime." The following portion is necessary to the understanding of the main sentence, so should not be separated with any punctuation.

16. **Level:** Medium | **Domain:** STANDARD ENGLISH CONVENTIONS
    Skill/Knowledge: Boundaries

Key Explanation: Choice D is the best answer. When a phrase is used as part of a sentence, the punctuation aside from the quotation marks should adhere to usual structures. In this case, the quotation is part of a clause subordinated by the conjunction "while." Replacing the quotation with XX, it is easier to see that the quote is the subject and "is used" is the verb, so no punctuation should divide the underlined portion: "While XX is frequently used…"

Distractor Explanations: Choice A is incorrect because the portion before the period is not a complete sentence because there is no active verb. **Choices B** and **D** are incorrect because no comma should divide the subject from the verb in a clause; the placement inside or outside the quote mark is irrelevant in this context.

17. **Level:** Easy | **Domain:** STANDARD ENGLISH CONVENTIONS
Skill/Knowledge: Boundaries

Key Explanation: Choice D is the best answer. There are two independent clauses that can stand on their own as sentences on either side of the underlined portion. Therefore, they should be divided into two separate sentences with a period.

Distractor Explanations: Choice A is incorrect because it is a comma splice between two independent clauses. **Choices B** and **C** can be eliminated because a single dash or colon can follow an independent clause, but the following portion needs to explain or add more detail to the previous sentence. In this case, the following portion changes to a different topic, from the 53rd year of independence to the struggle for freedom.

18. **Level:** Medium | **Domain:** STANDARD ENGLISH CONVENTIONS
Skill/Knowledge: Form, Structure, and Sense

Key Explanation: Choice C is the correct answer. The convention being tested is verb forms. This choice is correct because it uses the past tense "were anticipated," which aligns well with the overall context and tense usage of the text. It indicates that the anticipation of further mammoth discoveries existed in the past, parallel to the events mentioned earlier in the sentence.

Distractor Explanations: Choice A is incorrect because the sentence is primarily in the past tense, discussing events that occurred in 2021 and the subsequent withdrawal of access. Therefore, using the present tense does not provide the correct alignment of tenses. **Choice B** is incorrect because "would be anticipated" suggests a hypothetical scenario based on a condition. "Would be" is usually used in a sentence where an "if" situation exists. However, in this case, the sentence is

talking about a straightforward expectation based on the circumstances and not a hypothetical scenario. This makes choice B incorrect. **Choice D** is incorrect because it uses the singular form "was anticipated" which doesn't agree with the plural subject "Further mammoth discoveries." The subject "discoveries" is plural, and therefore, the correct verb form should be plural as well.

19. **Level:** Medium | **Domain:** STANDARD ENGLISH CONVENTIONS
Skill/Knowledge: Form, Structure, and Sense

Key Explanation: Choice B is the best answer. "Most famous for the Monte Carlo Casino" is a modifier which needs to refer to the following noun. In this case, the modifier describes "the country" and shows what the country is most famous for.

Distractor Explanations: All of the other choices can be eliminated because the modifier "Most famous for the Monte Carlo Casino" refers to something other than the country. In **Choice A**, the modifier is followed by the generic "there." In addition, "which is world–class" appears to refer to the preceding noun, "the country" rather than the "oceanographic museum." In **Choices C** and **D**, the modifier refers to the museum; the placement of "world–class" does not affect the answer choice.

20. **Level:** Medium | **Domain:** STANDARD ENGLISH CONVENTIONS
Skill/Knowledge: Form, Structure, and Sense

Key Explanation: Choice B is the correct answer. The convention being tested is subject-verb agreement. This choice is correct because it uses the correct singular form "lies," which matches the singular subject "this inquiry."

Distractor Explanations: Choice A is incorrect because it uses the plural form "lie," which is incorrect because the subject ("this inquiry") is singular. The verb should agree in number with the subject. **Choice C** is incorrect because the present continuous tense "is lying" cannot be suitably used here. This tense is used to describe ongoing actions, and it doesn't fit the context of a statement about a specific inquiry being at the heart of a survey. **Choice D** is incorrect because "was lying" is in the past continuous tense and is not suitable in the given sentence. This tense is used to describe ongoing actions in the past, and it doesn't fit the context of the text.

21. **Level:** Medium | **Domain:** STANDARD ENGLISH CONVENTIONS
    Skill/Knowledge: Form, Structure, and Sense

    Key Explanation: Choice C is the correct answer. The convention being tested is plurals and possessives. This choice is correct because it uses the plural possessive form "its MPs'" to indicate possession by multiple Members of Parliament. The placement of the apostrophe after "MPs" correctly shows that multiple MPs had lost their seats.

    Distractor Explanations: Choice A is incorrect due to the incorrect use of the contraction "it's," which means "it is" or "it has." **Choice B** is incorrect because it uses the singular possessive form "MP's," which indicates possession by a single MP. The sentence is referring to the seats of multiple Members of Parliament (MPs), so the plural form is required. **Choice D** is incorrect because it includes the incorrect use of the contraction "it's." Additionally, this choice lacks the apostrophe after "MPs" needed to indicate possession of seats by multiple Members of Parliament (MPs).

22. **Level:** Easy | **Domain:** EXPRESSION OF IDEAS
    Skill/Knowledge: Transitions

    Key Explanation: Choice D is the best answer because it is used to introduce an "example" or "illustration" that supports a claim. The part preceding the underline is a claim that people noticed that sampling occurred. The following portion is a specific illustration of that claim, a list of people who sampled each other's music.

    Distractor Explanations: None of the other choices adequately shows the relationship between the preceding and following sentences. **Choice A** refers to the final statement in a list or the result of an action. **Choices B** and **C** are used to provide different ideas that support the same claim rather than an example of the preceding claim.

23. **Level:** Easy | **Domain:** EXPRESSION OF IDEAS
    Skill/Knowledge: Transitions

    Key Explanation: Choice C is the best answer because it is used to introduce the conclusion of an argument. In this case, the text explains why the Stoclet House is important, and the conclusion is that the house qualifies to be a UNESCO World Heritage site.

    Distractor Explanations: Choice A is incorrect because it is used to introduce something that comes later in a series, but the qualification to be a World Heritage site does not come after the building is created as a classic in its style and in good condition, it is because the building is in good condition. **Choice B** is incorrect because it shows something that would happen in a different situation, but in this case, the qualification and the described situation both occurred. **Choice D** is used to show a contrast or change in ideas, not continue a logical train of thought.

24. **Level:** Medium | **Domain:** EXPRESSION OF IDEAS
Skill/Knowledge: Transitions

Key Explanation: Choice B is the best answer because it refers to something that is wryly humorous because it was in error or had something other than the intended result. **Choice B** fits the context of saying that Messier named the cluster but lost it due to writing "erroneous" or "wrong" information about it.

Distractor Explanations: Choice A is incorrect because it is used to introduce the last item in a list or discussion, but the text continues the story with what happens several hundred years later. **Choice C** is incorrect because it signifies that the following is an example or clarification of the previous claim, but making an error is not an example of cataloging stars. **Choice D** is used to show that the following is done in a way appropriate for the circumstances, so does not fit the context of making an error.

25. **Level:** Medium | **Domain:** EXPRESSION OF IDEAS
Skill/Knowledge: Rhetorical Synthesis

Key Explanation: Choice B is the best answer. The notes mention that "there is no evidence that the population is breeding" and that the small population of the African grey hornbill in Florida "may only persist due to continuing releases or escapes."

Distractor Explanations: Choice A is incorrect because it does not explain why the bird will not rapidly multiply in Florida. **Choice C** is incorrect because the notes offer no comparison between the climate in sub-Saharan Africa and Florida. **Choice D** is incorrect because the notes do not mention that the African grey hornbill is only

widespread in open woodland and savannah areas. Instead, it mentions that "it prefers open woodland and savannah."

26. **Level:** Hard | **Domain:** EXPRESSION OF IDEAS
Skill/Knowledge: Rhetorical Synthesis

Key Explanation: Choice A is correct because it best illustrates the diverging principles of power distribution between federal and unitary systems; federal systems provide "more regional autonomy", while unitary tend toward policy uniformity that may neglect local needs. This choice aligns perfectly with the student intent in emphasizing these differences between power distribution systems.

Distractor Explanations: Choice B is incorrect because it frames both systems largely negatively: federal systems as leading to "policy inconsistencies and inefficiencies", and unitary ones leading to excessive power concentration. Students' goal should not be criticizing rather than underscoring differences; hence this choice would not meet this aim. **Choice C** is incorrect and a good distractor because it explores various approaches to power distribution. Unfortunately, however, it fails the task due to not covering the potential consequences of these different forms of distribution of power - something the student wishes to emphasize. **Choice D** is also incorrect and a good distractor because though it provides accurate information about both federal and unitary systems, it falls short in directly contrasting the power distribution principles, emphasizing the outcomes more than the fundamental differences in the allocation of power. The student's aim to underscore contrasting principles isn't met in full here.

27. **Level:** Hard | **Domain:** EXPRESSION OF IDEAS
    Skill/Knowledge: Rhetorical Synthesis

    Key Explanation: Choice B is correct because it not only covers the effects of populism but also addresses potential dangers associated with unchecked populism outlined by student notes. Furthermore, this answer effectively synthesizes all major points presented.

    Distractor Explanations: Choice A is incorrect because it does not adequately explore the risks and consequences associated with populism, thus falling short of meeting its task requirements. **Choice C** is incorrect and a good distractor because while it successfully identifies the role social media plays in enhancing populism and emphasizes the populists' appeal to ordinary citizens, it fails to address the potential risks of unchecked populism, particularly its possible descent into authoritarianism, as highlighted in the student's notes. **Choice D** is incorrect as it only focuses on the widespread presence of populism across the political spectrum and its resonance with the ordinary citizen. It fails to address the significant role that social media and the internet have played in amplifying the reach of populist leaders and movements. Moreover, it does not mention the potential danger of populism leading to authoritarianism, thereby not fully capturing all effects of populism as highlighted in the notes.

1. **Level:** Medium | **Domain:** CRAFT AND STRUCTURE
    Skill/Knowledge: Words in Context

    Key Explanation: Choice C is the best answer because in the sentence, the underlined word is what beach resorts create. Choice C refers to the trait of being attractive and interesting enough to entice people to come. It fits the context of saying that even if there were no other tourist destinations, beach resorts are very attractive and interesting to tourists.

    Distractor Explanations: Choice A is incorrect because it refers to a large number of items collected by someone, but the beach resorts do not have a lot of things that they bought or amassed. **Choice B** refers to the act of convincing someone to do something. However, the beaches do not try to make people come; they are just interesting enough that people want to visit. **Choice D** relates to a link or attachment rather than something that pulls from afar

2. **Level:** Easy | **Domain:** CRAFT AND STRUCTURE
    Skill/Knowledge: Words in Context

    Key Explanation: Choice B is the best answer. The blank needs an adjective that describes the painter named Johannes Vermeer. "Eminent" refers to someone or something famous in a given field. In this context, it shows that the painter Johannes Vermeer is well–known in the field of art.

    Distractor Explanations: None of the other choices create a logical sentence. **Choice A** refers to something that is easy to see. Vermeer is from the seventeenth century, so although his art is famous, he is no longer visible. **Choice C** refers to something glowing or shining, which does not accurately describe a person. **Choice D** refers to

something complete or not modified, so it does not effectively describe a person.

3. **Level:** Hard | **Domain:** CRAFT AND STRUCTURE
    Skill/Knowledge: Words in Context

    Key Explanation: Choice D is the correct option. The author says that of the additions to the 1616 edition, many are clever but only sometimes they are improvements. Therefore, as used in the last sentence of the passage, "facile" refers to a superficial or shallow imitation of Marlowe's style of writing.

    Distractor Explanations: Choice A is incorrect because the sentence does not talk about the accomplishments of the imitator. In fact, the previous sentence points to how only some of the additions are improvements. **Choices B** is incorrect because there is no evidence to point out that all the additions to the 1616 edition are successful. **Choice C** is incorrect because because there is no evidence to point out that all the additions to the 1616 edition are effortless.

4. **Level:** Medium | **Domain:** CRAFT AND STRUCTURE
    Skill/Knowledge: Words in Context

    Key Explanation: Choice C is the best answer. It implies a very fast rate, so indicates that the number of ghost kitchens is increasing extremely fast.

    Distractor Explanations: Choices A and **D** are incorrect because they only indicate an increase; they do not include any hint that the rate is fast. **Choice B** is incorrect because it includes undertones of getting too big too fast, implying that the number may decrease soon, such as when the economy inflates and then collapses.

5. **Level:** Medium | **Domain:** CRAFT AND STRUCTURE
    Skill/Knowledge: Text Structure and Purpose

    Key Explanation: Choice D is the best answer because the underlined sentence explains that the photographs were of strangers. That detail can eliminate the weakness that the horses already knew the people and were reacting according to their experiences rather than that they were identifying an emotion from a picture of a face.

    Distractor Explanations: Choice A is incorrect because the sentence does not say how the "subjects" or "people in the experiment" were "selected" or "chosen." For example, they could have answered an advertisement or they could have been students in a class. **Choice B** is incorrect because the sentence does not say how many people the horses know; they could know many people. **Choice C** is incorrect because the entire text shows that expression is important for interspecies communication, but the underlined sentence does not stress that point

6. **Level:** Hard | **Domain:** CRAFT AND STRUCTURE
    Skill/Knowledge: Text Structure and Purpose

    Key Explanation: Choice A is the best answer as the poem is about a group, "we", that has left school, stays out late, drinks, and behaves in a generally carefree manner. It is clear that they will face consequences since the poem ends with the lines "We/Die soon"; the result of their reckless lifestyle.

    Distractor Explanations: Choice B is incorrect because it is not a question of if they will face problems, but when. The poem ends with the certainty that the group will die soon, not that they probably will. **Choice C** is wrong because it is too narrow. While it does detail the lifestyle of teens and arguably "characterizes" them, it ignores the larger issue of the theme which

should always be considered when determining an author's purpose. **Choice D** is wrong because it also ignores the bigger picture of the poem, which is serious. The last lines show that their fate will not be a positive one because of their lifestyle.

7. **Level:** Medium | **Domain:** CRAFT AND STRUCTURE
    Skill/Knowledge: Cross–Text Connections

    Key Explanation: Choice D is the best answer. The Sutton–Boveri theory is "that genes were located in specific places on the chromosomes." The passage says that Morgan "criticized the theory" at first or was "initially skeptical," but "after careful documentation," determined that certain genes are located on the X chromosome, showing that he had changed his mind and thought that there were indeed at least some genes in specific places on chromosomes.

    Distractor Explanations: Choice A is incorrect because there is no indication that details needed to be adjusted for the theory to be correct. **Choice B** is incorrect because Morgan found "definitive" or "convincing" data that supported, not "contradicted" or "went against" the theory. **Choice C** is incorrect because Morgan derived scientific findings that supported the theory, even though he originally thought it was not "plausible" or "realistic."

8. **Level:** Medium | **Domain:** INFORMATION AND IDEAS
    Skill/Knowledge: Central Ideas and Details

    Key Explanation: Choice C is the best answer. Giant anteaters have physically adapted by evolving "specialized tongues" that help them eat. They have also adapted behaviorally by living in an area where "their favored prey is common" and by learning to abandon the nest when soldier ants arrive.

Distractor Explanations: Choice A is incorrect because there is no indication that giant anteaters do not live in areas disturbed by humans; they could still live in swamps, forests, and grasslands around people. **Choice B** is incorrect because the passage does not say that ants are "more vigilant" or that there are "fewer opportunities." The passage only says that the ants are "vigilant" in protecting. **Choice D** is incorrect because the passage does not specify which food the anteaters prefer. It is possible that they might like grubs better, but they have fewer chances to eat them.

9. **Level:** Medium | **Domain:** INFORMATION AND IDEAS
   Skill/Knowledge: Central Ideas and Details

   Key Explanation: Choice B is the best answer because the text states that "the purpose of their study was to address a central scientific problem in explaining the diversity of tree species in a forest." In other words, the purpose was to "isolate factors" or "determine elements" that permit the "phenomenon" or "situation" of coexisting tree species to occur.

   Distractor Explanations: Choice A is incorrect because "ramifications" are "consequences." The study does not establish the consequences of the models; it is trying to explain why in reality there are coexisting species, whereas mathematical models have not solved that question. **Choice C** is incorrect because an "incident" refers to a specific event or occurrence, not an ongoing process. The researchers are trying to find a general explanation that holds valid for more than one specific event. **Choice D** is incorrect because the study does not point to "flaws" or "errors" in proposed theories. It is trying to find an answer to a question that was unexplainable at the time.

10. **Level:** Easy| **Domain:** INFORMATION AND IDEAS
    Skill/Knowledge: Central Ideas and Details

    Key Explanation: Choice C is the best answer because Henri produced work that was "a new style" than that of the National Academy of Design, which he "disliked." The passage says that his style had "depicted the seedy underside of urban life," meaning he painted things that were not considered fashionable or proper; they were "undignified" or "not majestic." Therefore, it is likely that the Academy artists "avoided" or "did not draw" such things.

    Distractor Explanations: Choice A is incorrect because the text says Henri used a "bold, realistic style" and that the Academy artists used a "highly–polished" style. Since Henri was trying to create a new way of painting, the two styles probably have little overlap. **Choice B** is incorrect because the text does not say that the artists were not in New York; it only implies that they did not draw sketches in the streets. **Choice D** is incorrect because "dirty snow" is only one example of Henri's art. It is possible that the artists drew winter scenes, but they avoided the dirt and squalor in their pictures.

11. **Level:** Hard | **Domain:** INFORMATION AND IDEAS
    Skill/Knowledge: Command of Evidence (Textual)

    Key Explanation: Choice D is the best answer. The claim is that Williams was "full of natural talent and energy." **Choice D** gives the idea of energy through a comparison with a hurricane, a powerful weather phenomenon. The fact that the speaker was worried about his own chances in show business alludes to the idea that Williams was so talented that no one else had a chance.

    Distractor Explanations: The other choices can be eliminated because they do not encompass both ideas of talent and energy. **Choice A** is incorrect because it only states that Williams was kind or helpful. **Choice B** shows that he was talented, but not that he was energetic. **Choice C** also implies that he was talented and less exciting when he was around, but does not convey the idea of energy.

12. **Level:** Easy | **Domain:** INFORMATION AND IDEAS

Skill/Knowledge: Command of Evidence (Quantitative)

Key Explanation: Choice C is the best answer because "any opiate" would include both users of prescription opiates and users of non–prescription opiates. In Figure 1, any opiate refers to the combination of the bottom and middle sections of the column. The right–hand column for 2017 has a combined amount of about 48,000 deaths, since the second section of the bar reaches to just under the 50,000 line.

Distractor Explanations: Choice A is incorrect because there were 18,000 deaths by "any" or "all combined" drug overdoses in 1999, not 2017. In 2017, there were 18,000 deaths caused by prescription opiates, the bottom section, but not all drugs combined; the latter is over 70,000. **Choice B** is incorrect because "any type of opiate" would refer to both prescription and non–prescription, the bottom two sections of the columns. However, none of the columns have those two sections total 38,000. **Choice D** is incorrect because 75,000 is the approximate total number of deaths in 2017, not the total for prescription opiates, which is just the bottom section of the column.

13. **Level:** Medium | **Domain:** INFORMATION AND IDEAS

Skill/Knowledge: Command of Evidence (Quantitative)

Key Explanation: Choice A is the best choice. The previous sentence in the text talks about the countries that recorded the highest growth in population. The sentence to be completed begins with "conversely". Thus, an opposite example must be provided which mentions the countries with a decrease in population.

Distractor Explanations: Choice B is incorrect because it only mentions one country. Since the previous sentence in the text mentions the top 5 countries that recorded a population increase, the ideal choice would be an example that mentions the top 5 countries with a population decrease. **Choice C** is incorrect because it does not provide an example that it is the opposite of the previous sentence. **Choice D** is incorrect because the text does not mention anything about the number of deaths registered.

14. **Level:** Medium | **Domain:** INFORMATION AND IDEAS

Skill/Knowledge: Inferences

Key Explanation: Choice A is correct. In a controlled environment, scientists found that hummingbirds change their behavior and consume less food when the alcohol volume reaches at least 2%. Therefore, it is likely that hummingbirds are able to eat a normal amount in nature because their typical diet in the real world does not contain more than 2% alcohol volume.

Distractor Explanations: Choice B is incorrect because the study does not suggest that hummingbirds are impacted specifically by the taste of alcohol. **Choice C** is incorrect because the study found that hummingbirds only change their behavior when the alcohol volume is 2%, not 1%. **Choice D** is incorrect because this choice is not relevant to the findings of the study.

15. **Level:** Easy | **Domain:** STANDARD ENGLISH CONVENTIONS
Skill/Knowledge: Boundaries

Key Explanation: Choice B is the best answer. "In such a waterfall" is a prepositional phrase that indicates a situation. Phrases should be divided from the main clause in a sentence by a comma.

Distractor Explanations: Choice A is incorrect because without any punctuation, it is unclear where the prepositional phrase ends and the main clause begins. **Choice C** is incorrect because colons should follow a complete independent clause, but the preceding portion cannot stand on its own as a sentence. **Choice D** is incorrect because semicolons should follow a complete independent clause, but the preceding portion cannot stand on its own as a sentence.

16. **Level:** Easy | **Domain:** STANDARD ENGLISH CONVENTIONS
Skill/Knowledge: Boundaries

Key Explanation: Choice D is the best answer. There are two ideas with subjects and verbs, so they can be divided into separate sentences.

Distractor Explanations: Choice A is incorrect because it is a comma splice between two independent clauses. **Choice B** is incorrect because "because" subordinates the following information. A semicolon should not be followed by a subordinate clause, only an independent clause. **Choice C** is incorrect because "since" creates a subordinate clause which cannot stand on its own as a sentence.

17. **Level:** Easy | **Domain:** STANDARD ENGLISH CONVENTIONS
Skill/Knowledge: Form, Structure, and Sense

Key Explanation: Choice A is the best answer. The portion between the italics, "the Maori… tree," modifies "kauri." To better see the structure of the main clause, remove the portion between the italics. It is then clear that the subject "Forests filled with kauri" needs to be followed by a verb, in this case, the phrasal verb "date back."

Distractor Explanations: Choice B is incorrect because it leaves the main clause without an active verb—"dating back…" is subordinated, but there is no complete clause before it. **Choice C** is incorrect because they include an extra noun. **Choice D** is incorrect because they include an extra noun. Two nouns should not be used in a row within a clause without subordinating one of them.

18. **Level:** Easy | **Domain:** STANDARD ENGLISH CONVENTIONS
Skill/Knowledge: Form, Structure, and Sense

Key Explanation: Choice D is the best answer. Research results are presented in the present tense as "universal truths."

Distractor Explanations: All of the other choices can be eliminated because they do not use the standard form for showing currently accepted research results. **Choice A** is a progressive tense, though "research" can be used in the plural. **Choice B** is a future tense. **Choice C** is the past tense, which is only acceptable if the results have subsequently been proven erroneous.

19. **Level:** Medium | **Domain:** STANDARD ENGLISH CONVENTIONS
Skill/Knowledge: Form, Structure, and Sense

Key Explanation: Choice A is the correct answer. The convention being tested is verb forms. This choice is correct because it uses the present participle "exhibiting," which is the correct form to complete the sentence. It maintains the parallel structure of the sentence and correctly indicates the ongoing behavior of the males exhibiting more captivating features

Distractor Explanations: Choice B is incorrect because it uses the present continuous tense "are exhibiting," which does not fit the context here. The present continuous tense is used for things that are occurring now, but which are temporary or may change. Therefore, because the male frogs display more captivating features than females (i.e., a permanent feature,) using present continuous tense in this context would be incorrect. **Choice C** is incorrect because the future tense "will exhibit," does not fit the context of the sentence. The sentence is describing a general behavior that males of the species typically have, rather than predicting a future action. **Choice D** is incorrect because the sentence is discussing a characteristic behavior of the male lizards that is ongoing or habitual. Using the simple present tense here doesn't convey the ongoing nature of the behavior.

20. **Level:** Easy | **Domain:** STANDARD ENGLISH CONVENTIONS
Skill/Knowledge: Form, Structure, and Sense

Key Explanation: Choice A is the best answer. The underlined portion needs to be a subject that is followed by the verb "composed."

Distractor Explanations: Choice B is incorrect because it indicates possession and needs to be followed by a noun. **Choice C** is incorrect because it is an object rather than a subject. **Choice D** is incorrect because it shows possession and needs to be followed by a noun. Alternatively, it could be a contraction for "she is," which does fit the past–tense context or the verb "composed."

21. **Level:** Easy | **Domain:** STANDARD ENGLISH CONVENTIONS
Skill/Knowledge: Form, Structure, and Sense

Key Explanation: Choice B is the best answer. The underlined portion is the main verb of the sentence. The entire preceding portion, "dividing one full–time job between two employees," is the subject. Though it may appear plural, the subject can be simplified to "dividing." When a verb ending in "–ing" is used as a subject, it is considered singular, and **Choice B** is a singular verb.

Distractor Explanations: Choice A is incorrect because it is plural, so does not agree with the singular "dividing." **Choice C** can be eliminated because it doesn't facilitate the formation of a complex sentence; the underlined portion should be an active verb form. Similarly, **Choice D** can be eliminated because it doesn't create a complete sentence.

22. **Level:** Medium | **Domain:** STANDARD ENGLISH CONVENTIONS
Skill/Knowledge: Form, Structure, and Sense

Key Explanation: Choice C is the best answer. "They" is plural, so correctly refers to the plural noun "many names" from the previous sentence. "Range" is plural, so it agrees with the plural noun.

Distractor Explanations: Choice A can be eliminated because "ranges" is used with a singular subject. Similarly, **Choice D** can be eliminated because "ranges" is singular, so does not agree with the plural noun. **Choice B** is incorrect because it is a noun rather than a noun and verb. As a result, the sentence is a fragment with no active verb.

23. **Level:** Hard | **Domain:** EXPRESSION OF IDEAS
    Skill/Knowledge: Transitions

    Key Explanation: Choice A, "Hence," is the best answer. "Hence" is used to indicate a logical conclusion or result based on the preceding information. In this case, it signifies that the following sentence is a direct outcome or consequence of Volta's invention. By using "hence," the sentence that follows logically connects to the previous information, suggesting that Volta's groundbreaking discovery directly led to the subsequent development of modern electrical systems.

    Distractor Explanations: Choice B, "Moreover," is incorrect because it suggests that the following sentence will provide additional supporting information. However, the sentence that follows does not offer additional supporting details. Instead, it presents a cause-and-effect relationship between Volta's invention and the development of modern electrical systems, which is better captured by the word "hence." **Choice C,** "Similarly," is incorrect because it implies that the following sentence will present information that is similar or comparable to the preceding information. However, the sentence that follows introduces a cause-and-effect relationship rather than presenting a similarity. The word "similarly" would be inappropriate in this context as it does not convey the intended cause-and-effect connection. **Choice D,** "Nonetheless," is incorrect because it indicates a contrasting idea or point. However, there is no logical contrast or contradiction between Volta's invention and the development of modern electrical systems. The word "nonetheless" would introduce an unnecessary contradiction or conflict in this context.

24. **Level:** Easy | **Domain:** EXPRESSION OF IDEAS
    Skill/Knowledge: Transitions

    Key Explanation: Choice A is the best answer because it is used to add another detail to develop a discussion. In this context, **Choice A** adds what happened to the finished painting after the discussion of what Picasso did while making the painting.

    Distractor Explanations: Choice B is incorrect because it is used to introduce an opposing or conflicting idea, but the final sentence continues the theme of the painting being influential for the cause against war. **Choice C** is incorrect because it shows the logical result of a series of actions. Though the final sentence expands on the idea of the anti–war protests, it is not necessarily given that after showing people the painting, Picasso would exhibit the painting to raise funds. **Choice D** is incorrect because it is used to add an example of a previous claim, but the following sentence discusses a time sequence rather than giving more detail about the visitors who entered his studio.

25. **Level:** Medium | **Domain:** EXPRESSION OF IDEAS
    Skill/Knowledge: Transitions

    Key Explanation: Choice C is the best answer. The passage is structured with the first two sentences explaining the good that Ahmed did. The portion following the underline has a different tone from receiving the Nobel Prize. **Choice C** is used to show something that happened at a later time, so fits the context of saying that first he was praised but later he was accused of certain problems.

    Distractor Explanations: Choice A is incorrect because it is used to add more information on the same topic, so it does not effectively show that the praise changed to concern over Ahmed's actions. **Choice B** is incorrect because it means that the following is fitting or appropriate given the preceding information, but in this case, being accused of bad things is not appropriate for a winner of a Nobel Prize. **Choice D** is incorrect because it is used to introduce the logical result of the preceding argument, but the following is not a logical result of winning a peace prize.

26. **Level:** Hard | **Domain:** EXPRESSION OF IDEAS
Skill/Knowledge: Rhetorical Synthesis

Key Explanation: Choice B provides a concise and comprehensive outline of the ideological disparities between the United States and the Soviet Union during the Cold War era. It emphasizes that the United States stood for capitalist economics and democratic governance, which were fundamentally contrasting to the communist and centrally-planned economy adhered to by the Soviet Union. This choice effectively highlights the key ideological differences that underpinned the Cold War dynamics, using the relevant information provided in the student's notes.

Distractor Explanations: Choice A is incorrect and a distractor because although it acknowledges the military confrontations of the Cold War, it does not directly connect these with ideological differences between the United States and the Soviet Union. **Choice C** is incorrect because, although it mentions the ideological differences and the tools (political propaganda and espionage) used during the Cold War, it inaccurately suggests that these tools were a direct manifestation of the ideological tension between the United States and the Soviet Union. While it is true that both nations employed these methods, the notes provided by the student do not specifically state that these practices were primarily driven by their

ideological clash. Therefore, this choice might potentially overstep the information given in the notes, implying a causative relationship that isn't explicitly stated. **Choice D** is incorrect and a distractor because although the dissolution of the Soviet Union marked an end to the Cold War, this statement doesn't completely capture its ideological dynamics; rather, its primary focus was more on the outcome of the conflict rather than the inherent differences between the two superpowers.

27. **Level:** Medium | **Domain:** EXPRESSION OF IDEAS
Skill/Knowledge: Rhetorical Synthesis

Key Explanation: Choice C is the best answer. The notes mention that is he most known for being the most-streamed classical artist of all time.

Distractor Explanations: Choice A is incorrect because this is not his most significant achievement. **Choice B** is also incorrect as the notes do not mention this as being his most significant achievement. **Choice D** is incorrect because the statement only describes his music projects and not a significant achievement.

No Test Material On This Page

1.   **Level:** Easy | **Domain:** ALGEBRA
Skill/Knowledge: Linear equations in two variables | **Testing point:** Converting English to Algebra to create a two variable equation

Key Explanation: Choice A is correct. She burns 20 calories when she walks every minute. Therefore, she burned $20x$ calories after x minutes. She also burns 35 calories every minute she cycles and therefore burns $35y$ calories after y minutes. The equation would therefore be $20x + 35y = 340$. Subtracting $20x$ from both sides of this equation yields $35y = 340 - 20x$.

Distractor Explanations: Choice B is incorrect because it states that the difference between the calories burned from cycling and burned from walking is equal to 340. **Choice C** is incorrect. The rate of 20 calories per minute can only be multiplied by x minutes of walking. And the rate of 35 calories per minute can only be multiplied by y minutes of cycling. **Choice D** is incorrect because The rate of 20 calories per minute can only be multiplied by x minutes of walking. And the rate of 35 calories per minute can only be multiplied by y minutes of cycling.

2.   **Level:** Easy | **Domain:** PROBLEM-SOLVING AND DATA ANALYSIS
Skill/Knowledge: Two-variable data: models and scatterplots | **Testing point:** Identifying points on a scatter plot

Key Explanation: Choice C is the correct answer because the number of dots that have a higher value than the line of best fit are the dots above the line i.e 6.

Distractor Explanations: Choice A is incorrect; it may be a conceptual error or lack of understanding of the question. **Choice B** is

incorrect as this is the number of dots below the line of best fit. **Choice D** is incorrect as this is the number of dots on the graph.

3.   **Level:** Easy | **Domain:** ADVANCED MATH
Skill/Knowledge: Nonlinear functions | **Testing point:** Using the remainder theorem

Key Explanation: Choice B is correct. The remainder theorem states that if $f(x)$ is divided by $x-a$, the remainder would be $f(a)$. Therefore when $f(a) = 0$, then $x-a$ is a factor of the function $f(x)$. In this case, $f(3)= 0$, therefore $x-3$ is a factor of the equation $f(x)$.

Distractor Explanations: Choice A is incorrect. Based on the table, dividing $(x+2)$, x, or $(x-5)$ from $f(x)$ will not yield a remainder of 0. **Choice C** is incorrect. Based on the table, dividing $(x+2)$, x, or $(x-5)$ from $f(x)$ will not yield a remainder of 0. **Choice D** is incorrect. Based on the table, dividing $(x+2)$, x, or $(x-5)$ from $f(x)$ will not yield a remainder of 0.

4.   **Level:** Easy | **Domain:** ALGEBRA
Skill/Knowledge: System of two linear equations in two variables. | **Testing point:** Solving for one variable in a system of linear equations

Key Explanation: Simplify the first equation by using the distributive property which yields $t - 5 + 2s - 6 = 8$. Adding 5 and 6 to both sides of the equation yields $t + 2s = 19$. Simplify the second equation by using the distributive property which yields $2t - 10 - 3s + 9 = -19$. Adding 10 and subtracting 9 from both sides of the equation yields $2t - 3s = -18$. To find the value of s, use the elimination method and multiply -2 by the first equation. This yields $-2t -4s = -38$. Then, add the two equations which yield $-7s = -56$. Dividing -7 from both sides of the equation yields $s = 8$.

5. **Level:** Easy | **Domain:** ALGEBRA
Skill/Knowledge: Linear equations in one variable
Testing point: Solving linear equations in one variable

Key Explanation: Choice D is correct. Simplify the equation by using distributive property, which yields $3x - 6 - 2x + 2 = -x + 2x + 4 - 8$. Combining like terms yields $x - 4 = x - 4$. This shows that the equation is the same on both sides. So, any value of x makes the equation true. Therefore, the equation has infinitely many solutions.

Distractor Explanations: Choice A is incorrect because to have no solutions, solving the equation will result in a false statement. **Choice B** is incorrect because to have one solution, solving the equation will yield x equal to a number. **Choice C** is incorrect because linear equations do not have 2 solutions.

6. **Level:** Hard | **Domain:** ADVANCED MATH
Skill/Knowledge: Equivalent expressions |
Testing point: Converting between exponents and radicals

Key Explanation: Choice B is correct. To simplify the variable with different exponents, add the exponents of $g^{\frac{4}{5}}$ and $g^{\frac{2}{5}}$ which yields $g^{\frac{6}{5}}$. Making 2 have the same exponent as g yields $32^{\frac{1}{5}} \cdot g^{\frac{6}{5}}$.

Putting them inside the radical sign yields $\sqrt[5]{32g^6}$

Distractor Explanations: Choice A is incorrect because the 2 did not have any exponent and thus should have been left outside the root or converted to the fifth. **Choice C** is incorrect and may result from interchanging the numerator and denominator of the exponent. **Choice D** is incorrect and may result from interchanging the numerator and denominator of the exponent.

7. **Level:** Medium | **Domain:** PROBLEM−SOLVING AND DATA ANALYSIS
Skill/Knowledge: Inference from sample statistics and margin of error | **Testing point:** Finding the margin of error.

Key Explanation: To find the margin of error, first find the midpoint of the sample mean mass.

This yields $\frac{120 + 182}{2} = 151$. The margin of error would be the difference between the midpoint and either of the sample mean masses. Subtracting 151 from 182 yields 31.

8. **Level:** Hard | **Domain:** ALGEBRA
Skill/Knowledge: Linear functions | **Testing point:** Solving a linear function

Key Explanation: Choice B is correct. To find $f(6)$, first find the value of x which will be plugged into the equation $f(2x)$. Equating $2x$ to 6 and solving for x yields $x = 3$. Plugging 3 to $9x-7$ yields 20. Therefore, $f(6) = 20$.

Distractor Explanations: Choice A is incorrect and may result from plugging 2 directly into the equation. **Choice C** is incorrect and may result from plugging 6 directly into the equation. **Choice D** is incorrect and may result from substituting x with $2x$ and plugging 6 into the equation.

9. **Level:** Medium | **Domain:** PROBLEM−SOLVING AND DATA ANALYSIS
Skill/Knowledge: One−variable data: distributions and measures of center and spread | **Testing point:** Finding the mean and median

Key Explanation: Choice A is correct because. The median of the above data set of 21 students will be the $\frac{21+1}{2}$, which is the 11th shoe size, which is then represented by 3. The mean shoe size can then be calculated by adding the products of the shoe size and their corresponding frequency and dividing the sum by the total number of students. This yields a sum of 67. Dividing the sum by 21 yields a mean of 3.19. Therefore, the mean will be larger than the median.

Distractor Explanations: Choice B is incorrect as it is a false statement. **Choice C** is incorrect as it is a false statement. **Choice D** is incorrect because there is sufficient information to answer the question.

10. **Level:** Medium | **Domain:** ADVANCED MATH
Skill/Knowledge: Equivalent expressions |
Testing point: Using exponent rules

Key Explanation: To solve for a, first make the bases equal. Converting 27^x to a base 3 yields 3^{3x}. Converting 81^{-x} to a base 3 yields $(3^4)^{-x}$ or 3^{-4x}. The equation will now become $3^{3x} \div 3^{-4x} = 3^{ax}$. On the right side of the equation, the bases are divided, which means that the exponents must be subtracted. Subtracting the exponents yields $3^{(3x - (-4x))} = 3^{ax}$ or simply $3^{7x} = 3^{ax}$. Equating the exponents yields $7x = ax$. Dividing both sides of the equation by x yields $7 = a$.

11. **Level:** Hard | **Domain:** GEOMETRY AND TRIGONOMETRY
Skill/Knowledge: Lines, angles, and triangles |
Testing point: Finding the sum of the Interior angles of a polygon

Key Explanation: Choice D is correct. The sum of interior angles in a polygon is represented by $180°(n-2)$. A hexagon has 6 sides and therefore the sum of interior angles in the hexagon will be

$180(6-2) = 720°$. 720 degrees in radian form will be $\frac{720}{180} = 4\pi$. Therefore $b = 4$.

Distractor Explanations: Choice A is incorrect and may result in calculating $\frac{180}{720}$. **Choice B** is incorrect and may result in calculating $\frac{720}{720}$. **Choice C** is incorrect and may result in calculating $\frac{720}{360}$.

12. **Level:** Easy | **Domain:** PROBLEM-SOLVING AND DATA ANALYSIS
Skill/Knowledge: Percentages | **Testing point:** Finding the percentage increase

Key Explanation: Choice C is correct. If 80 is increased by 200%, that means that the new value will be 300% of 80 which is 240. An alternative solution is to find 200% of 80 and add it to 80 which yields 240.

Distractor Explanations: Choice A is incorrect because it is the increase without adding the original. **Choice B** is incorrect because it is the percentage. **Choice D** is incorrect because it is the sum of 80 and 200.

13. **Level:** Easy | **Domain:** ADVANCED MATH
Skill/Knowledge: Nonlinear functions | **Testing point:** Using the quadratic formula

Key Explanation: To solve for the quadratic equation, use the quadratic formula $\frac{-b \pm \sqrt{b^2 - 4ac}}{2a}$, where $a = 2$, $b = -4$ and $c = -7$. Substituting the values to the formula yields

$\dfrac{-(-4)\pm\sqrt{(-4)^2-4(2)(-7)}}{2(2)}$. Simplifying this yields

$\dfrac{4\pm\sqrt{72}}{4}$ or $1\pm\dfrac{\sqrt{72}}{4}$. Simplifying $\sqrt{72}$ yields

$6\sqrt{2}$. Therefore, the expression becomes $1\pm\dfrac{6\sqrt{2}}{4}$

or $1\pm\dfrac{3\sqrt{2}}{2}$. Since the expression is now in the

same format as $1\pm\dfrac{a\sqrt{2}}{2}$, then $a = 3$.

14. **Level:** Easy | **Domain:** ALGEBRA
Skill/Knowledge: Linear functions | **Testing point:** Interpretation of terms in a linear function

Key Explanation: Choice B is correct. This is because 262 is the *y–intercept* of the model and represents the number of houses on day 0, which is the beginning of October.

Distractor Explanations: Choice A is incorrect because the number of houses at the end of October is represented by $h(x)$. **Choice C** is incorrect as the number of houses sold per day would be 8. **Choice D** is incorrect as the number of houses sold on the first day of October is represented when $x = 8$.

15. **Level:** Medium | **Domain:** GEOMETRY AND TRIGONOMETRY
Skill/Knowledge: Right triangles and trigonometry | **Testing point:** Working with special triangles

Key Explanation: Choice A is correct. A 90 – 60 – 30 triangle has a hypotenuse of 2x, a shorter leg of x, and a longer leg of $x\sqrt{3}$. The area of this triangle can then be found by the formula

$\dfrac{1}{2}\times base\times height$. Substituting the base and the

height yields $\dfrac{1}{2}\times x\times x\sqrt{3}$ or $\dfrac{x^2\sqrt{3}}{2}$. The given

side AC is the hypotenuse of the triangle. So, 32 = 2x which yields x = 16. Substituting 16 to the

formula yields $\dfrac{16^2\sqrt{3}}{2}$ or $128\sqrt{3}$.

Distractor Explanations: Choice B is incorrect and may result from using $\sqrt{2}$ instead of $\sqrt{3}$. **Choice C** is incorrect because this is one of the sides of the triangle. **Choice D** is incorrect and may result from using $\sqrt{2}$ instead of $\sqrt{3}$

16. **Level:** Easy | **Domain:** ADVANCED MATH
Skill/Knowledge: Equivalent expressions | **Testing point:** Matching coefficients

Key Explanation: Using distributive property on the left side of the equation yields
$5xy + 3 – 6xy + 2xy^2 – 2 = axy^2 + bxy + c$.
Combining like terms yields $2xy^2 – xy + 1 = axy^2 + bxy + c$. Comparing the coefficients on both sides of the equation, yields $a = 2$, $b = -1$, and $c = 1$ Therefore, $a + b = 1$.

17. **Level:** Easy | **Domain:** ADVANCED MATH
Skill/Knowledge: Nonlinear equations in one variable and systems of equations in two variables **Testing point:** Finding the product of the roots of a quadratic equation

Key Explanation: Choice A is correct. In a quadratic equation ($ax^2 + bx + c = 0$), the product

of the roots can be found by $\dfrac{c}{a}$, Using the given

equation, $c = -24$ and $a = 3$. Thus, the product of

the roots will be $\dfrac{-24}{3}$ or –8.

Distractor Explanations: Choice B is incorrect and may result from calculating the sum of the roots which is $\left(\dfrac{-b}{a}\right)$. **Choice C** is incorrect and may result from calculating $\dfrac{b}{a}$. **Choice D** is incorrect as this is the value of a.

18. **Level:** Medium | **Domain:** ADVANCED MATH
    Skill/Knowledge: Nonlinear functions | **Testing point:** Using the vertex form of a quadratics equation

    Key Explanation: Choice B is correct. The general equation of a parabola is given by $y = a(x - h)^2 + k$, where (h, k) denotes the coordinate of the vertex. In this case, $h = 3$ and $k = 10$. Thus, the equation becomes $y = a(x - 3)^2 + 10$. The sign of a denotes the orientation of the parabola. If a is positive, the parabola opens upward. If a is negative, the parabola opens downwards. In this case, the parabola opens downward so the value of a must be negative. Therefore, the equation of the parabola is $y = -2(x - 3)^2 + 10$.

    Distractor Explanations: Choice A is incorrect since their a is positive which would suggest that the graph opens upwards however the graph opens downward. **Choice C** is incorrect since their a is positive which would suggest that the graph opens upwards however the graph opens downwards. **Choice D** is incorrect and may result from using $(-3, 10)$ as the vertex instead of $(3, 10)$.

19. **Level:** Easy | **Domain:** ALGEBRA
    Skill/Knowledge: Linear equations in one variable
    Testing point: Matching coefficients

    Key Explanation: Using the distributive property, the equation becomes $6 - 6x = ax + b$ or $-6x + 6 = ax + b$. Comparing the coefficient and the constant

on both sides of the equation yields $a = -6$ and $b = 6$. Therefore, the product of a and b is -36.

20. **Level:** Easy | **Domain:** ADVANCED MATH
    Skill/Knowledge: Nonlinear functions | **Testing point:** Finding the average rate of change

    Key Explanation: Choice B is correct. To find the average rate of change between two points on a curve is the same as finding the gradient between the two points. In this case, the points are $(0, -8)$ and $(2, -16)$. $\dfrac{(-16)-(-8)}{0-2}$ which yields the slope as -4.

    Distractor Explanations: Choice A is incorrect as this is the negative value of option D. **Choice C** is incorrect as this is the negative value of option B. **Choice D** is incorrect. This is the value of the difference in the y *coordinates* between the two points.

21. **Level:** Medium | **Domain:** ALGEBRA
    Skill/Knowledge: Linear equations in one variable
    Testing point: Finding the value of x in a linear equation

    Key Explanation: Choice C is correct. To find the value of x, multiply both sides of the equation by $\dfrac{4}{3}$.
    This yields $(x - 5) = 27 \times \dfrac{4}{3}$ or simply $(x - 5) = 36$.

    Distractor Explanations: Choice A is incorrect and may result from multiplying $\dfrac{3}{4}$ to both sides of the equation instead of $\dfrac{4}{3}$. **Choice B** is incorrect and may result from conceptual or calculation errors. **Choice D** is incorrect and may result from calculating the value of x.

22. **Level:** Hard | **Domain:** ALGEBRA

Skill/Knowledge: Linear inequalities in one or two variables | **Testing point:** Finding solution to a system of linear inequalities

Key Explanation: Choice C is correct. To solve such questions, the best method would be to substitute the points to the inequalities and check if the statements are true or false.
Substituting $(3, 1)$ to the first inequality yields $1 > -2(3) -1$ or $1 > -7$, which is true.
Substituting $(3, 1)$ to the second inequality yields $3(1) < 3 + 9$ or $3 < 12$, which is also true. Therefore, the coordinate $(3, 1)$ lies inside the intersection of the two inequalities.

Distractor Explanations: Choice A is incorrect. Substituting $(-2, 1)$ to both inequalities will result in one false statement. **Choice B** is incorrect. Substituting $(1, 4)$ to both inequalities will result in one false statement. **Choice D** is incorrect. Substituting $(-3, 3)$ to both inequalities will result in false statements.

1. **Level:** Easy | **Domain:** ADVANCED MATH
   Skill/Knowledge: Nonlinear equations in one variable and system of equations in two variables | **Testing point:** Solving absolute value equations

   Key Explanation: Choice C is correct. To calculate the two solutions (p & q), equate the contents of the absolute value symbol to both the positive and negative values of the number on the other side of the equation. To obtain the first solution (p), solve for x in the equation $3x - 1 = 2$. Adding 1 to both sides of the equation yields $3x = 3$. Dividing 3 from both sides of the equation yields $x = 1$. Thus, $p = 1$. To obtain the second solution (q), solve for x in the equation $3x - 1 = -2$. Adding 1 to both sides of the equation yields $3x = -1$. Dividing 3 from both sides of the equation yields $x = -\dfrac{1}{3}$. Thus, $q = -\dfrac{1}{3}$. Adding 1 and $-\dfrac{1}{3}$ yields $\dfrac{2}{3}$. Therefore, $p + q = \dfrac{2}{3}$.

   Distractor Explanations: Choice A is incorrect as these are the two solutions to the equation. **Choice B** is incorrect and may result from multiplying the second solution (q) by –1. **Choice D** is incorrect as these are the two solutions to the equation.

2. **Level:** Medium | **Domain:** GEOMETRY AND TRIGONOMETRY
   Skill/Knowledge: Circles | **Testing point:** Using equation of a circle

   Key Explanation: Choice C is correct. To solve this question, plug each point into the equation of the circle. A coordinate that lies on the circle means that the equation will be equal on both ends. Plugging the point (–3, 4), the equation becomes $(-3 - 3)^2 + 4^2 + 8(4) = 84$. Simplifying the equation, this yields $84 = 84$.
   Therefore, point (–3, 4) lies on the circle.

   Distractor Explanations: Choice A is incorrect. Plugging the point (1, 7) into the equation yields $109 = 84$. Therefore, it lies outside the circle. **Choice B** is incorrect. Plugging the point (–2, 5) into the equation yields $90 = 84$. Therefore, it lies outside the circle. **Choice D** is incorrect. Plugging the point (3, –6) into the equation yields $-12 = 84$. Therefore, it does not lie on the circle.

3. **Level:** Easy | **Domain:** GEOMETRY AND TRIGONOMETRY
   Skill/Knowledge: Right triangles and trigonometry | **Testing point:** Using trigonometry identities

   Key Explanation: $Sin\ x = cos\ (90 - x)$. So, if $sin\ C$ and $cos\ 63$ are equal, then the angles would add up to 90°. Therefore, $63° + C = 90°$. Subtracting 63° from both sides of the equation yields $C = 27°$.

4. **Level:** Hard | **Domain:** ADVANCED MATH
   Skill/Knowledge: Equivalent expressions | **Testing point:** Working with complex numbers

   Key Explanation: Choice A is correct. Rationalize the denominator of $\dfrac{2 - 2i}{3 + 4i}$ by multiplying the fraction by the denominator's conjugate which is $\dfrac{3 - 4i}{3 - 4i}$. This yields $\dfrac{6 - 6i - 8i + 8i^2}{9 - 16i^2}$. Substituting –1 to i^2 yields $-\dfrac{2}{25} - \dfrac{14}{25}i$. Matching the coefficients yields $a = -\dfrac{2}{25}$ and $b = -\dfrac{14}{25}$.

   Distractor Explanations: Choice B is incorrect as this would be the value of b. **Choice C** is incorrect and may result from miscalculation or conceptual errors. **Choice D** is incorrect and may result from miscalculation or conceptual errors.

5. **Level:** Medium | **Domain:** ADVANCED MATH
Skill/Knowledge: Nonlinear equations in one variable and systems of equations in two variables
Testing point: Solving system of linear and quadratic equations

Key Explanation: Choice C is correct. To solve for x, we can equate the two equations.
This yields $2x - 2 = 2x^2 - 9x + 7$.
Subtracting $2x$ and adding 2 to both sides of the equation yields $2x^2 - 9x + 7 - 2x + 2 = 0$.
Combining like terms yields $2x^2 - 11x + 9 = 0$. To solve the quadratic equation use either the factor method or the quadratic formula. Using the factor method, get the two factors of $18x^2$ whose sum is $-11x$.
The two factors are $-2x$ and $-9x$ which makes the equation $2x^2 - 2x - 9x + 9 = 0$.
Grouping the first two terms together and the last two terms together yields $(2x^2 - 2x) - (9x - 9) = 0$
Factoring out the greatest common factor yields $2x(x - 1) - 9(x - 1) = 0$.
Factoring out the common binomial yields $(x - 1)(2x - 9) = 0$. Equating both factors to 0 yields the two solutions, which are $x = 1$ and $x = \dfrac{9}{2}$ or 4.5.

Distractor Explanations: Choice A is incorrect as it is the negative of one of the solutions. **Choice B** is incorrect and may result from getting the difference between the solutions. **Choice D** is incorrect and may result from adding the two solutions.

6. **Level:** Hard | **Domain:** ADVANCED MATH
Skill/Knowledge: Nonlinear equations in one variable and systems of equations in two variables
Testing point: Solving absolute equation

Key Explanation: To obtain the solutions, first simplify the equation by factorization. Factoring out 2 from $|6x - 4|$ yields $2|3x - 2|$. Factoring out $|3x - 2|$ from $3|3x - 2| - 2|3x - 2| = 7$ yields $(3 - 2)|3x - 2| = 7$ or $|3x - 2| = 7$. Then, equate the

contents of the absolute value symbol to both the positive and negative values of the number on the other side of the equation. To obtain the first solution, solve for x in the equation $3x - 2 = 7$. Adding 2 to both sides of the equation yields $3x = 9$. Dividing 3 from both sides of the equation yields $x = 3$. To obtain the second solution, solve for x in the equation $3x - 2 = -7$. Adding 2 to both sides of the equation yields $3x = -5$. Dividing 3 from both sides of the equation yields $x = \dfrac{-5}{3}$. Therefore, the positive solution to the equation is 3.

7. **Level:** Easy | **Domain:** ALGEBRA
Skill/Knowledge: Linear functions | **Testing point:** Creating equations from graphs

Key Explanation: Choice C is correct. Calculating the slope of the given line using the points $(-5, 0)$ and $(3, 0)$ yields $\dfrac{5}{3}$. A slope of a line perpendicular to this will be the negative reciprocal of the slope of the given line.
Therefore, a line perpendicular to this should have a slope of $\left(\dfrac{-3}{5}\right)$.
To get the slope of a line from the equation, convert the equation to slope–intercept form. Dividing both sides of the equation by 5, **Choice C** becomes $y = -\left(\dfrac{3}{5}\right)x + 3$.
Since the coefficient of x is $-\left(\dfrac{3}{5}\right)$, then this line is perpendicular to the given line.

Distractor Explanations: Choice A is incorrect as this is the equation of the line in the graph. **Choice B** is incorrect as this is the equation of a line that has a slope of $\dfrac{3}{5}$. **Choice D** is incorrect as this is the equation of a line that has a slope of $\dfrac{5}{3}$

making it parallel to the given line.

8. **Level:** Easy | **Domain:** GEOMETRY AND TRIGONOMETRY
Skill/Knowledge: Circles | **Testing point:** Finding the circumference of a circle given it's equation

Key Explanation: Choice C is correct. To find the circumference of a circle, first, find the radius of the circle or the diameter. Rewrite the given equation into the standard form for the equation of a circle, by completing the squares. This yields $x^2 + 6x + 9 + y^2 - 4y + 4 = 51 + 9 + 4$. Simplifying the equation yields $(x + 3)^2 + (y - 2)^2 = 64$. Since the equation is now in standard form, then $r^2 = 64$. Solving for r yields 8 as the radius. Using the formula of the circumference which is $2\pi r$ yields 16π.

Distractor Explanations: Choice A is incorrect and may result from using πr instead of $2\pi r$ to solve for the circumference. **Choice B** is incorrect and may result from using $\sqrt{51}$ as the radius of the circle. **Choice D** is incorrect and may result from solving for the area of the circle instead of the circumference.

9. **Level:** Medium | **Domain:** GEOMETRY AND TRIGONOMETRY
Skill/Knowledge: Lines, angles and triangles | **Testing point:** Using the exterior angle theorem

Key Explanation: According to the Exterior Angle Theorem, the exterior angle of a triangle is equal to the sum of the opposite and non-adjacent interior angles.

Therefore, $\angle ABC + \angle BAC = \angle ACD$.
The equation will now become $2x - 2 + x + 3 = 118$.

Combining like terms yields $3x + 1 = 118$.
Subtracting 1 from both sides of the equation yields $3x = 117$.
Dividing 3 from both sides of the equation yields $x = 39$.

10. **Level:** Easy | **Domain:** PROBLEM-SOLVING AND DATA ANALYSIS
Skill/Knowledge: Ratio, rates, proportional relationships, and units | **Testing point:** Creating and solving rate equation

Key Explanation: Choice A is correct. The question presents an inverse proportion problem where the number of carpenters (x) is inversely proportional to the number of days it requires to build a bed (y). Using the formula $xy = k$ and the given data $x = 4$ and $y = 3$ yields 12 as the value of k. Thus, the inverse proportion equation becomes $xy = 12$. To solve for the corresponding number of carpenters, substitute 2 with y which then yields $2x = 12$. Solving for x yields 6 as the number of carpenters needed to build the bed in 2 days.

Distractor Explanations: Choice B is incorrect as this is the product of four carpenters and 2 days. **Choice C** is incorrect as this represents the value of the constant k. **Choice D** is incorrect as this is a miscalculation or conceptual error.

11. **Level:** Easy | **Domain:** ADVANCED MATH
Skill/Knowledge: Equivalent expressions | **Testing point:** Using the FOILing method to multiply expressions

Key Explanation: Choice C is correct. Using distributive property yields, $5xy (x - 2y) + 3x (x - 2y)$. Simplifying the expression yields $5x^2y + 3x^2 - 10xy^2 - 6xy$.

Distractor Explanations: Choice A is incorrect and may result from applying the distributive property incorrectly. **Choice B** is incorrect and may result from a miscalculation error in multiplying $5xy$ and $-2y$. **Choice D** is incorrect and may result from applying the distributive property incorrectly.

12. **Level:** Medium | **Domain:** ALGEBRA
Skill/Knowledge: Systems of two linear equations in two variables | **Testing point:** Solving for a variable in a system of linear equations

Key Explanation: To solve for y, use the elimination method. Multiplying 2 to the second equation yields $10x + 4y = 16$. Adding the first and second equations yields $7x + 10x - 4y + 4y = 1 + 16$. Combining like terms yield $17x = 17$. Dividing 17 from both sides of the equation yields $x = 1$. Substituting the value of x to the first equation yields $7(1) - 4y = 1$ or $7 - 4y = 1$. Subtracting 7 from both sides of the equation yields $-4y = -6$. Dividing -4 from both sides of the equation yields $y = \dfrac{3}{2}$ or 1.5.

13. **Level:** Easy | **Domain:** ALGEBRA
Skill/Knowledge: Linear inequalities in one or two variables | **Testing point:** Solving for x in an inequality

Key Explanation: Choice A is correct. Adding x to both sides of the equation yields $-2x + x \le 8 - x +x$ or $-x \le 8$. Dividing both sides of the equation by -1 yields $x \ge -8$. Therefore, x is greater than or equal to -8. And -10 is the only option that is less than -8.

Distractor Explanations: Choice B is incorrect. This value will make the inequality true and be considered solution. **Choice C** is incorrect. This value will make the inequality true and be considered solution. **Choice D** is incorrect. This value will make inequality true and be considered solution.

14. **Level:** Easy | **Domain:** PROBLEM-SOLVING AND DATA ANALYSIS
Skill/Knowledge: Probability and conditional probability | **Testing point:** Finding the probability of an event

Key Explanation: Choice C is correct. The unfair coin is tossed 20 times and 14 of these land on heads making the probability of the unfair coin landing on heads $\dfrac{14}{20} = 0.7$. Therefore the probability of the coin landing on heads the 21st time will be 0.7.

Distractor Explanations: Choice A is incorrect as it gives the probability of the unfair coin landing on tails. **Choice B** is incorrect as this is the probability of landing on heads on a fair coin. **Choice D** is incorrect and may result from a miscalculation or conceptual error.

15. **Level:** Medium | **Domain:** ALGEBRA
Skill/Knowledge: Systems of two linear equations in two variables | **Testing point:** Solving for x and y in a system of linear equations

Key Explanation: Choice A is correct. Solve for x and y either by substitution or by elimination. Using the elimination method, multiply 3 by both sides of the second equation. This yields ($5x + y = -6$) 3 or $15x + 3y = -18$. Subtracting the second equation from the first equation yields $-17x = 34$. Dividing both sides of the equation by -17 yields $x = -2$. Substituting the value of x to the second equation yields $5(-2) + y = -6$. Simplifying the equation yields $y = 4$. Subtracting y from x yields $-2, -4$, or -6.

Distractor Explanations: Choice B is incorrect as it is the value of x. **Choice C** is incorrect because it is the value of y. **Choice D** is incorrect and may result from subtracting x from y.

16. **Level:** Easy | **Domain:** ADVANCED MATH
Skill/Knowledge: Nonlinear functions |
Testing point: Converting the unit on exponential functions

Key Explanation: Since the equations are still equal, then $1,200(1.03)^m = 1,200(1.03)^{ad}$. Dividing both sides of the equation by 1,200 yields $(1.03)^m = (1.03)^{ad}$. Since the bases are equal, equate the exponents which yield $m = ad$. Since 1 *month* = 30 *days*, then $1 = a(30)$. Dividing 30 from both sides of the equation yields $\frac{1}{30} = a$.

17. **Level:** Easy | **Domain:** GEOMETRY AND TRIGONOMETRY
Skill/Knowledge: Area and volume | **Testing point:** Finding the volume of a cylinder

Key Explanation: Choice C is correct. The volume of a cylinder is given by the formula $\pi r^2 h$. Using the given data, $h = 2r$. Therefore, $h = 2(6)$ = 12. Therefore, the volume will be $\pi(6)^2 (12) = 432\pi$.

Distractor Explanations: Choice A is incorrect and may result from conceptual or calculation errors. **Choice B** is incorrect and may result from calculating the surface area of the cylinder instead of volume. **Choice D** is incorrect and may result from interchanging the values of r and h.

18. **Level:** Easy | **Domain:** GEOMETRY AND TRIGONOMETRY

Skill/Knowledge: Circles | **Testing point: Using circle theorems**

Key Explanation: Choice D is correct. An angle subtended at any point of the circle is half the angle subtended at the center. This means that $\angle$ DOE = 2 $\angle$ DRE. Therefore, $\angle$ DOE = 2(35°) = 70°.

Distractor Explanations: Choice A is incorrect because it implies that the angles are equal. **Choice B** is incorrect and this maybe due to conceptual or calculation errors. **Choice C** is incorrect and this maybe due to conceptual or calculation errors.

19. **Level:** Easy | **Domain:** ADVANCED MATH
Skill/Knowledge: Equivalent expressions | **Testing point:** Factoring using the difference of two squares

Key Explanation: Choice D is correct. This question can be solved using factorization. Using the difference of squares, $x^2 - a^2$ becomes $(x + a) (x - a)$.
Transforming the numerator of $4x^2 - 3$ to the format $x^2 - a^2$ yields $(2x)^2 - \left(\sqrt{3}\right)^2$. Factoring the expression yields $(2x + \sqrt{3})(2x - \sqrt{3})$.
This would result to $\dfrac{\left(2x + \sqrt{3}\right)\left(2x - \sqrt{3}\right)}{\left(2x + \sqrt{3}\right)}$.
Canceling out the binomial $2x + \sqrt{3}$ from both numerator and denominator yields $2x - \sqrt{3}$.

Distractor Explanations: Choice A is incorrect and would result if the student mistook the denominator for a minus sign. **Choice B** is incorrect and may result from conceptual or calculation errors. **Choice C** is incorrect and may result from conceptual or calculation errors.

20. **Level:** Hard | **Domain:** ALGEBRA
Skill/Knowledge : Systems of two linear equations in two variables | **Testing point:** Working with systems of equations with Infinite solution

Key Explanation: Equations that have infinite solutions are equations that are the same line just written differently. They have the same slope and the same *y–intercept*.

In the above equation, neither are similar. To make them similar, multiply the top equation by -2 which yields $-18x + 28y = 6$.
Comparing the coefficients of the first and second equations yields $a = -18$ and $b = -28$.

21. **Level:** Easy | **Domain:** ALGEBRA
Skill/Knowledge: Linear equations in two variables | **Testing point:** Matching coefficients

Key Explanation: Choice D is correct. To find the value of a, we have to first group like terms together.
Adding $4x$ to both sides of the equation yields $3x + 5y + 4x = ax - 4x - by + 4x$
or simply $7x + 5y = ax - by$. This makes $a = 7$ and $b = -5$

Distractor Explanations: Choice A is incorrect because this would be the value of b instead. **Choice C** is incorrect because this would be the value of a if the $-4x$ had been ignored. **Choice B** is incorrect and may result from conceptual or calculation errors.

22. **Level:** Easy | **Domain:** ALGEBRA
Skill/Knowledge: Linear inequalities in one or two variables | **Testing point:** Solving for x in an inequality

Key Explanation: Choice A is correct. Using the distributive property yields $3x + 2 < -5x - 30$. Adding $5x$ and subtracting 2 from both sides of the equation yields $3x + 5x < -30 - 2$ or $8x < -32$. Dividing 8 from both sides of the equation yields $x < -4$. Since -5 is less than -4, then it is a solution to the inequality.

Distractor Explanations: Choice B is incorrect because the value of x must be less than and not equal to -4. **Choice C** is incorrect because it is greater than -4. **Choice D** is incorrect because it is greater than -4.

Chapter 4

....

Practice Test 3

You are about to begin a full-length Practice Test. The test has four modules. The time allotted for each module is marked at the beginning of the module. Work on one module at a time. Use a timer to keep track of the time limits for every module.

Try to take the Practice Test under real test conditions. Find a quiet place to work, and set aside enough time to complete the test without being disturbed. At the end of the test, check your answers by referring to the Answer Key and fill in your raw score in the scorecard below. Also, note down the time taken by you for completing each module.

Pay particular attention to the questions that were answered incorrectly. Read the answer explanations and understand how to solve them.

....

My Score Card (Raw Score)

	Reading and Writing		Math	
	Module 1	Module 2	Module 1	Module 2
Out of	27	27	22	22
My Score	_____	_____	_____	_____
Time Taken	_____	_____	_____	_____

TEST BEGINS ON THE NEXT PAGE

Reading and Writing Test

27 QUESTIONS | 32 MINUTES

DIRECTIONS

The questions in this section address a number of important reading and writing skills. Each question includes one or more passages, which may include a table or graph. Read each passage and question carefully, and then choose the best answer to the question based on the passage(s). All questions in this section are multiple–choice with four answer choices. Each question has a single best answer.

1

The researchers compiled data on side effects from 163 patients with major depressive disorder or bipolar disorder and 25 healthy <u>controls</u> who participated in one of five placebo–controlled clinical trials conducted at the NIH Clinical Center over 13 years. The study did not address the side effects associated with repeated infusions or long–term use.

As used in the text, what does the word "controls" most nearly mean?

A) Authorities

B) Restraints

C) Benchmarks

D) Commands

2

A large percentage of the organisms in the world are parasitic, meaning they derive nutrients from another species, but almost none of them are mammalian. One notable _____ is the vampire bat, which feeds on the blood of cows and other mammals.

Which choice completes the text with the most logical and precise word or phrase?

A) peculiarity

B) exception

C) distortion

D) idiosyncrasy

3

Salt stress, too much salt in the soil for plants to thrive, is one of the major environmental constraints limiting agricultural productivity and influencing the _____ of bioactive compounds of vegetables.

Which choice completes the text with the most logical and precise word or phrase?

A) attentiveness

B) dedication

C) concentration

D) centralization

4

Dogs have long been considered to be man's best friend. However, animal behaviorists have long wondered if dogs may end up taking on the personalities of their owners. Because dogs spend a considerable amount of time with humans, human personality could influence dog behavior. In 2012, dog behavior was reported by owners and friends to see if there was a similairity to their owner's personality.

Which choice best states the main purpose of the text?

A) To argue that dogs are man's best friend

B) To call attention to a connection between dogs and humans

C) To recall a memory of a dog and its owner

D) To explain a dog breed's behavior

5

In general, deep ocean habitats may be negatively affected by tidal current energy systems due to the change of water flows, materials on the ocean floor, and movement of sediment. Potential other effects include mortality of fish passing through turbines (blade–strike) and the collision risk of marine mammals with tidal stream farms. A study showed that change in sediment patterns will most likely follow the installation of tidal arrays, impacting the local underwater habitat, and in turn, animal and plant species. However, in their review, Frid et al. conclude that "there is little scientific literature to suggest that operation of underwater tidal energy devices will cause elevated levels of mortality to organisms such as fish and marine mammals." Also, Lewis et al. mention that, "while current technologies have moving parts that may harm marine life, there is no evidence to date of harm from tidal current devices to marine life."

What is the main function of the quotes from Frid et al. and Lewis et al. in the overall structure of the text?

A) They show reputable scientists that hold very different views from each other.

B) They provide authoritative viewpoints that oppose that of the author.

C) They undermine conclusions which emphasize safety of tidal energy systems.

D) They introduce expert opinions that reinforce the authors' primary claim.

6

Extraterrestrial life, that familiar science–fiction trope, that kitschy fantasy, that CGI nightmare, has become a matter of serious discussion, a "risk factor," a "scenario." How has ET gone from sci–fi fairytale to a serious scientific endeavor modeled by macroeconomists, funded by fiscal conservatives, and discussed by theologians? Because, following a string of remarkable discoveries over the past two decades, the idea of alien life is not as far–fetched as it used to seem. Discovery now seems inevitable and possibly imminent.

Which choice best states the function of the underlined sentence in the text as a whole?

A) To point out the ever–changing image of how extraterrestrial creatures appear

B) To encourage readers to imagine the possible variety of extraterrestrial life

C) To interject a lighthearted note into an otherwise serious passage

D) To emphasize that there is credibility in something that once was believed impossible

Text 1

A 1979 paper by father–and–son team Luis and William Alvarez identified their discovery of unusual quantities of a rare element called iridium in a layer of sediment about 65 million years ago. They contended that the iridium was indicative of a massive meteor impact that sent clouds of dust into the atmosphere, cooling the Earth enough to trigger the mass extinction of the dinosaurs at the end of the Cretaceous period.

Text 2

Though dramatic, the idea of a meteor strike wiping out the dinosaurs is far–fetched, say modern paleontologists. They agree a strike occurred but claim that there was actually no simultaneous or instantaneous event that could be classified as a mass extinction. Instead, species slowly died out over millions of years, with the last major representatives living to approximately the end of the Cretaceous period.

Based on the texts, which choice would the authors of the text most likely agree about?

A) A massive meteorite impact occurred, though it may not have caused a mass extinction.

B) Though the earth cooled due to a meteor impact, it was not enough to kill the dinosaurs.

C) There was actually no mass extinction of dinosaurs, though eventually they all died.

D) Most dinosaur species died prior to the period after the Cretaceous period.

The concept of sustainable agriculture has gained traction in recent years as the global population continues to rise. Sustainable farming practices aim to minimize the environmental impact of agriculture while ensuring long-term food security. This involves techniques such as organic farming, crop rotation, and precision agriculture. Organic farming eliminates the use of synthetic pesticides and fertilizers, promoting soil health and biodiversity. Crop rotation helps prevent soil erosion and nutrient depletion by alternating the cultivation of different crops. Precision agriculture employs technologies like GPS and remote sensing to optimize resource usage, reducing waste and increasing efficiency. Embracing sustainable agriculture is crucial for maintaining a healthy ecosystem and ensuring food availability for future generations.

What is the main idea of the text?

A) Sustainable agriculture has gained traction in recent years due to the rising global population.

B) Organic farming promotes soil health and biodiversity.

C) Sustainable agriculture practices aim to minimize environmental impact and ensure long-term food security.

D) Precision agriculture employs technologies to optimize resource usage.

The *GRL* paper focuses on one region of the Southern Ocean extending from the tip of South America to the tip of the Antarctic Peninsula. "The Drake Passage is the windiest, roughest part of the Southern Ocean," says Colm Sweeney, lead investigator on the Drake Passage study and co–author on the GRL paper, "The critical element to this study is that we were able to sustain measurements in this harsh environment as long as we have—both in the summer and the winter, in every year over the last 13 years. This data set of ocean carbon measurements is the densest ongoing time series in the Southern Ocean." The team was able to take these long–term measurements by piggybacking instruments on the Antarctic Research Supply Vessel *Laurence M. Gould,* which makes nearly 20 crossings of the Drake Passage each year, transporting people and supplies to and from Antarctic research stations.

According to the text, why are the results of the Drake Passage study unique?

A) They used more complete measurements than any other study of the region.

B) They were derived using equipment that had not previously been used.

C) They incorporated chemical measurements as well as other forms of data.

D) It was the first study to focus only on the Southern Ocean.

The following text is adapted from Jefferson Keel's 2011 statement, "The Indian Reorganization Act—75 Years Later: Renewing our Commitment to Restore Tribal Homelands and Promote Self–determination."

Two years ago, our shared vision and the Federal responsibility to Indian tribes were threatened by the Supreme Court's interpretation of the IRA in *Carcieri v. Salazar.* There are at least 14 pending cases where tribes and the Secretary of Interior are under challenge. There are many more tribes whose land–to–trust applications have simply been frozen while the Department of Interior works through painstaking legal and historical analysis. We are seeing harassment litigation against tribes who were on treaty reservations in 1934 with a BIA superintendent. Land acquisitions are delayed. Lending and credit are drying up. Jobs are lost or never created. We fear that this will continue to get worse until Congress acts. Even worse, this decision will create two classes of Indian tribes: those who will benefit from Federal trust responsibility and those who will not.

According to the text, why is the Carcieri decision especially problematic?

A) It did not adhere to the exact wording of the original 1934 legislation.

B) It asserted that the 1934 legislation only applies to specific Native Americans.

C) It created new methods by which the Native Americans could regain lands.

D) It set precedents that facilitated the establishment of tribal governments.

Emily Dickinson's poems were edited by her friends before publication to match the tastes of the times. Her personal style still shines through, as in the way she personifies books in her poem "In a Library": _____

Which quote from "In a Library" most effectively illustrates the claim?

A) "A precious, mouldering pleasure 't is / To meet an antique book, / In just the dress his century wore;"

B) "What interested scholars most, / What competitions ran / When Plato was a certainty."

C) "When Sappho was a living girl, / And Beatrice wore / The gown that Dante deified."

D) "Facts, centuries before, / He traverses familiar, / As one should come to town"

If we manage to separate out a clean signal from a planet outside our solar system and find some features in the light spectrum that might be indicative of life, we will need to work hard to think of any non–biological process that might account for them. "Life is the hypothesis of last resort," noted astronomer Carl Sagan. This requires some understanding of what processes might operate on worlds that we will know relatively little about; what we find on Earth can serve as a guide but also has potential to lead us astray.

Which finding, if true, would most directly undermine Carl Sagan's hypothesis?

A) A rover that was sent to Mars discovers a bacteria–like organism when it drills deep into the core of the planet.

B) An astronomer realizes that the atmosphere of a planet is too hot to sustain life even though it has oxygen.

C) A scientist finds a planet with a large amount of oxygen in its atmosphere so claims that the oxygen is produced by living creatures.

D) A new telescope finds a new planet orbiting a star that was previously believed to have no planets.

13

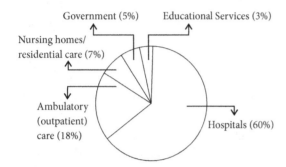

Percentage of Registered Nurses by Field

Data from US Bureau of Labor Statistics, June, 2021

Nursing is one of the fields in most demand, with an anticipated annual growth rate of 7 percent through 2029. Although some nurses work only in hospitals, there are actually many options, especially as the population ages and nurses are needed to tend to the daily needs of seniors. For example, _____

Which choice most effectively uses data from the graph to complete the example?

A) educational services employed about 3 percent of the registered nurses in 2021.

B) fewer registered nurses worked for the government than in ambulatory care.

C) the percentage of registered nurses working in nursing homes increased by 7 percent in 2021.

D) about 7 percent of registered nurses in 2021 worked in nursing or residential homes.

14

Engineering and Computer Science Stereotypes

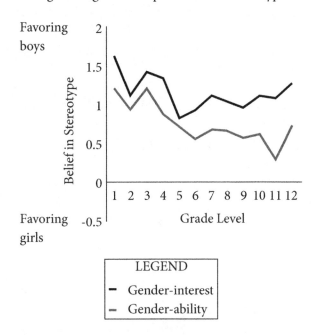

Scientists ran an experiment where they found that a diverse set of students believed gender-interest stereotypes favoring boys in computer science and engineering. Students developed these stereotypes at a very young age. They also found that: Gender-interest stereotypes were stronger than gender-ability stereotypes. Girls who believed the stereotypes were _____.

Which choice most effectively uses data from the graph to complete the text?

A) less skilled than interested in computer science and engineering.

B) equally skilled and interested in computer science and engineering.

C) less interested in participating in computer science and engineering.

D) more interested in participating in computer science and engineering.

15

Many proponents of using robots for space exploration believe robots can both accomplish better results and cost less than human explorers. Unmanned robots not only mitigate the typical safety hazards associated with space exploration, but also collect data with high accuracy and precision. Humans have various physical limitations, but robots may be able to collect thousands of samples on a daily basis and conduct highly technical analyses of the samples. However, data and understanding should not be misconstrued to be the same: _____

Which choice most logically completes the text?

A) having the context and foundations of scientific knowledge may be required to draw insightful conclusions from the collected data.

B) similarly, accuracy and precision are not the same.

C) robots have the capability to understand far-reaching implications, but humans may only be able to organize the data.

D) possessing enough data is required to draw accurate and relevant conclusions.

16

In the Solomon Islands, cowry shells were sewn into long pieces of cloth as a form of currency, and although _____ use has declined, they have not been completely replaced by modern coinage.

Which choice completes the text so that it conforms to the conventions of Standard English?

A) its

B) their

C) there

D) they're

17

Numerous theorists have offered minimum wage as a mechanism for leveling economic inequality by enabling lower-paid workers to earn more money. However, Professor David Neumark, in conjunction with Dr. William Wascher of the Federal Reserve Board, _____ with this view. The results of their literature survey covering over 100 papers revealed that only 10 percent reported positive results and over two-thirds documented increased disparity.

Which choice completes the text so that it conforms to the conventions of Standard English?

A) dissent

B) dissents

C) dissenting

D) have dissented

18

Volcanoes come in all sizes and shapes, but they all fall into three basic structural patterns known as cinder cone, _____ shield formations.

Which choice completes the text so that it conforms to the conventions of Standard English?

A) composite (or stratovolcano), and

B) composite, (or stratovolcano), and

C) composite (or stratovolcano) and,

D) composite, (or stratovolcano) and,

19

People in developed nations often take water for _____ over 2 billion people in the world do not have access to safe drinking water; 670 million people have no handwashing facilities at all.

Which choice completes the text so that it conforms to the conventions of Standard English?

A) granted but;

B) granted; but

C) granted, but

D) granted but

20

Wheat and rice are the most common cereal crops in the world and are consumed as the staple part of diets in many countries, but there are many other cereal _____ that can be eaten directly or fed to meat animals.

Which choice completes the text so that it conforms to the conventions of Standard English?

A) crops—such as rye and sorghum—

B) crops, such as rye, and sorghum,

C) crops—such as rye and sorghum,

D) crops, such as rye and sorghum—

21

Inuit is the common name for a group of indigenous people who live in the arctic and subarctic regions. The term was originally used by the Alaskan Inupiat people, so is not always used in self–reference by all the _____ Labrador, Quebec, Nunavut, and the Northwest Territories.

Which choice completes the text so that it conforms to the conventions of Standard English?

A) sub–groups in Greenland,

B) sub–groups in: Greenland,

C) sub–groups in: Greenland

D) sub–groups; in Greenland,

22

Creating a culture of support can have a significant impact on employee engagement and productivity. Research shows that _____ in their work tend to be more engaged and productive. This can lead to lower turnover rates, higher job satisfaction, and ultimately, better business outcomes.

Which choice completes the text so that it conforms to the conventions of Standard English?

A) employees who feel valued and supported

B) employees, who feel valued and supported,

C) employees - who feel valued and supported -

D) employees (who feel valued and supported)

23

There are so many sub–fields in science that sometimes the distinctions are hard to determine, and many overlap. _____ paleontology is the study of ancient life, including creatures ranging from as small as microbes to as large as dinosaurs, but paleoichthyology focuses exclusively on the study of prehistoric fish.

Which choice completes the text with the most logical transition?

A) Or else,

B) Even so,

C) For instance,

D) On the whole,

24

Echolocation is a form of sonar in which an animal emits a sound and, using the resulting echo, can locate and identify various objects. Echolocation is highly developed in only a few species, such as bats, whales and dolphins. _____ it is also present in a limited form among shrews and two species of cave–dwelling birds.

Which choice completes the text with the most logical transition?

A) However,

B) Consequently,

C) Accordingly,

D) Clearly,

25

It turns out that 21.6 percent of the population in the United States are bilingual and speak a language other than English in their homes. _____ that may seem like a large percentage, it is far lower than the worldwide average of 43 percent of the population speaking at least two languages.

Which choice completes the text with the most logical transition?

A) Although

B) Because

C) Despite

D) Since

26

While researching a topic, a student has taken the following notes:

- Maya Angelou was a famous civil rights activist, poet, and author, though she held many other roles throughout her life.

- *I Know Why the Caged Bird Sings* (1969) is one of her most acclaimed books; it publicly reveals details about her private life up to the age of 17.

- She was asked to read the poem "On the Pulse of Morning" at President Bill Clinton's inaugural ceremony in 1993.

- She directed her first movie, *Down the Delta,* in 1996, though she had previously participated in acting and production of other movies.

- Published in 2013 when she was 85 years old, *Mom & Me & Mom* recounts her complex relationship with her own mother.

- At her death in 2014, she was working on a new book about her experiences with different world leaders.

The student wants to emphasize an underlying theme in some of Maya Angelou's books. Which choice most effectively uses relevant information from the notes to accomplish this goal?

A) Maya Angelou wrote a wide variety of works in her later years, including *Down the Delta* and *Mom & Me & Mom*.

B) Many of Maya Angelou's works, such as *I Know Why the Caged Bird Sings* and *Mom & Me & Mom*, are autobiographical.

C) Maya Angelou had close contact with many world leaders, as shown by reading "On the Pulse of Morning" at President Bill Clinton's 1993 inaugural ceremony and writing a book on the subject prior to her death.

D) While some of her books received great critical acclaim, such as *I Know Why the Caged Bird Sings*, others were not popular, such as Mom & Me & Mom.

27

While researching a topic, a student has taken the following notes:

- Cryptocurrencies, like Bitcoin and Ethereum, have seen exponential market value gains in recent years.

- Bitcoin was introduced as open-source software in 2009 and is widely regarded as the first decentralized cryptocurrency.

- Ethereum stands apart from Bitcoin by including smart contracts - these allow for the programmatic execution of tasks when certain conditions are met.

- Due to Bitcoin's decentralized nature, transactions take longer and attract higher fees compared to centralized systems.

- Ethereum's blockchain enables more complex instructions, making it ideal for applications such as decentralized finance and non-fungible tokens.

A student wishes to emphasize the unique features of both Bitcoin and Ethereum. Which choice best uses relevant information from his notes to accomplish this objective?

A) Cryptocurrencies such as Bitcoin and Ethereum have experienced exponential market value gains.

B) Bitcoin, the pioneer of decentralized cryptocurrency, faces longer transaction times and higher fees due to its decentralized nature, contrasting Ethereum which includes programmable smart contracts making it ideal for complex applications like decentralized finance and non-fungible tokens.

C) Bitcoin is the first decentralized cryptocurrency, followed by other cryptocurrencies such as Ethereum, which distinguishes itself through the integration of smart contracts, allowing for more intricate operations like decentralized finance and non-fungible tokens

D) Given its decentralized system, Bitcoin transactions typically involve longer processing times and higher fees when compared with Ethereum.

No Test Material On This Page

Reading and Writing Test

27 QUESTIONS | 32 MINUTES

1

The cane toad (*Rhinella marina*) was _____ to South America but was transported to Australia in 1935 in an attempt to control the beetle infestations on sugarcane plantation.

Which choice completes the text with the most logical and precise word or phrase?

A) innate

B) congenital

C) pandemic

D) endemic

2

Guggenheim Fellowships are grants that have been awarded annually since 1925 (98 years ago) by the John Simon Guggenheim Memorial Foundation to those "who have _____ exceptional capacity for productive scholarship or exceptional creative ability in the arts."

Which choice completes the text with the most logical and precise word or phrase?

A) accomplished

B) demonstrated

C) renounced

D) relinquished

3

Harvard University is a private Ivy League research university in Cambridge, Massachusetts. Founded in 1636 as Harvard College and named for its first benefactor, the Puritan clergyman John Harvard, it is the oldest institution of higher learning in the United States and one of the most prestigious universities in the world.

As used in the text, what does the word "benefactor" most nearly mean?

A) Patron

B) Founder

C) Antagonist

D) Beneficiary

4

The following is from the "Gift of the Magi" by O. Henry written in 1906.

One dollar and eighty–seven cents. That was all. And sixty cents of it was in pennies. Pennies saved one and two at a time by bulldozing the grocer and the vegetable man and the butcher until one's cheeks burned with the silent imputation of parsimony that such close dealing implied. Three times Della counted it. One dollar and eighty–seven cents. And the next day would be Christmas. There was clearly nothing to do but flop down on the shabby little couch and howl. So Della did it. Which instigates the moral reflection that life is made up of sobs, sniffles, and smiles, with sniffles predominating.

Which choice best states the function of the underlined sentence in the text as a whole?

A) It establishes that Della is very frugal

B) It explains why Della is worried about money

C) It demonstrates that Della despises Christmas

D) It argues that Christmas is Della's favorite holiday

CONTINUE

5

In order to learn more about the properties of fire in space, scientists aboard the International Space Station have conducted many experiments. Their goal is to gain valuable insight into the mechanisms of fire that will ultimately help prevent fires on spacecraft or offer solutions to quickly extinguish such fires. Flames act very differently in an environment devoid of gravity than they do on Earth. For example, spheres of light form, and the flames can ignite at extremely low temperatures. <u>On Earth, a standard gas stove burns at about 3100 degrees Fahrenheit</u>, but a sustained flame can burn at 900 degrees in the International Space Station.

What is the main purpose of the underlined portion in the overall structure of the text?

A) It highlights the motivation for conducting the experiments.

B) It outlines the methodology the scientists are using to conduct the experiments.

C) It offers a point of comparison for the results of the experiments.

D) It presents an example of the phenomenon viewed in the experiments.

6

This passage is adapted from Emma Lazarus's poem *Spring Star*.

> Over the lamp–lit street,
>
> Trodden by hurrying feet,
>
> Where mostly pulse and beat
>
> Life's throbbing veins,
>
> See where the April star,
>
> Blue–bright as sapphires are,
>
> Hangs in deep heavens far,
>
> Waxes and wanes.

What is the main structure of the text?

A) It establishes a contrast between two images.

B) It shows the futileness of an action.

C) It offers a solution to a problem.

D) It elaborates on an extended metaphor.

7

The amygdala, a small almond-shaped structure located deep within the brain, plays a crucial role in processing emotions and emotional memories. It is an essential component of the limbic system, which regulates emotions, behavior, and motivation. The amygdala receives sensory information from the environment and triggers emotional responses, such as fear or pleasure. It is also involved in the formation and storage of emotional memories. Dysfunction of the amygdala can lead to mood disorders and impaired emotional processing. Studying the amygdala's function and connectivity with other brain regions provides valuable insights into the complex nature of human emotions and related psychological disorders.

What is the main idea of the text?

A) The amygdala regulates emotions, behavior, and motivation.

B) Dysfunction of the amygdala can lead to mood disorders and impaired emotional processing.

C) The amygdala is involved in the formation and storage of emotional memories.

D) The amygdala's function and connectivity provide insights into human emotions and psychological disorders.

8

A study led by Sarah Mann aimed to provide a fuller picture of the vegan diet in which no animal products are eaten, encompassing the health of the vegan diet as well as related ethical beliefs by studying scientific and popular literature in tandem. Furthermore, the study aimed to provide an insider's perspective of the vegan diet as a means of combating stereotypes and making the diet more relatable/understandable to those who are not vegan. The research was conducted in two parts – literature review and interview study. The interviews included questions targeting personal history, related health beliefs, factors influencing the decision to become vegan, and diet.

Based on the text, why did Mann include personal interviews in her study?

A) She assumed she would find a conflict between interviews and scientific studies.

B) She expected to resolve an outstanding debate about the health benefits of veganism.

C) She decided that most of the current literature was biased against the subject of veganism.

D) She hoped to better understand the viewpoint of people who opted to become vegan.

9

George Herman "Babe" Ruth, Jr. (1895–1948) played 22 seasons of Major League baseball. He started as a left–handed pitcher but made his fame as an outfielder and powerful batter, earning the title "Home Run King." Despite the decades that have passed since he stepped off the field, Babe Ruth is still a household name and considered one of the greatest American sports heroes. He was fortunate in that respect, as fans celebrated his triumphs against the background of news from World War I and the 1918 influenza pandemic.

Based on the text, what is one reason why Babe Ruth became so famous?

A) He was an excellent pitcher.

B) He showed people success during a grim time.

C) He fought in World War I.

D) He suffered from the 1918 influenza pandemic.

10

A study analyzed data from 641 brain-dead heart donors in Sweden. Among the donors, 24% showed signs of acute stress-induced cardiomyopathy, which impairs cardiac function in a specific part of the heart while the rest functions normally. This condition is caused by a surge in stress hormones during brain death. The transplantation center in the study did not experience issues with transplanting hearts affected by stress-induced cardiomyopathy, suggesting this impairment is only transient. The researchers observed that the cardiac function of these hearts quickly recovered, suggesting that the impairment is temporary and unrelated to underlying heart diseases like coronary artery disease.

Which finding, if true, would most directly undermine the study's finding?

A) Transplanted hearts that were affected by stress-induced cardiomyopathy go into heart failure approximately 21.2 years after the surgical transplant in 44% of cases.

B) Transplanted hearts that were affected by stress-induced cardiomyopathy take approximately 6 months to fully adapt and function normally in the recipients' bodies.

C) Transplanted hearts that were affected by stress-induced cardiomyopathy are sometimes rejected by the recipients' bodies in approximately 15% of cases.

D) Recipients must keep up a healthy and active lifestyle in order to avoid heart-related health issues.

11

Risk of different pathogen X outbreaks within the next 5 years
under current conditions or with always on vaccines available

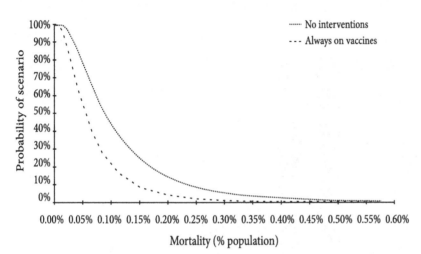

New global risk modeling has revealed a 27.5% probability of a pandemic as lethal as
COVID-19 occurring within the upcoming decade. The escalation of high-risk outbreak
occurrences can be attributed to various key factors, including climate change, the
expansion of international travel, a burgeoning global population, and the escalating
menace of zoonotic diseases. Additionally, research indicates that had the original
COVID-19 strain possessed the same transmissibility as the Omicron variant, the actual
death toll would have been nearly three times the actual toll. However, if effective vaccines
are administered within days of identifying a new pathogen, _____

Which choice most effectively completes the text using information from the graph?

A) the likelihood of encountering a pandemic with a comparable fatality rate to
COVID-19 does not change greatly.

B) the mortality rate may reduce marginally.

C) the likelihood of encountering a pandemic with a comparable fatality rate to
COVID-19 diminishes greatly.

D) the mortality rate will remain unchanged as pathogens rapidly transform themselves
to increase their transmissibility.

12

Global forest loss: deforestation vs forest degradation between 2001 and 2015

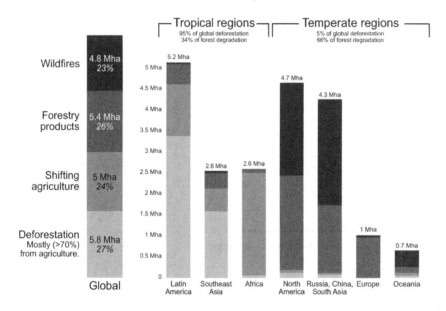

While examining global forest loss, Philip Curtis and team employed satellite imagery to determine that global deforestation accounts for a quarter of all forest loss. Nonetheless, a stark contrast emerges when evaluating tropical and temperate areas, revealing significant disparities in the prominence of each driver of forest loss on a global scale. Notably, a staggering 95% of deforestation incidents transpire within tropical regions, underscoring the preeminent role these regions play in this phenomenon. Within the tropics, clearing forests for purposes such as cultivating palm oil and soy crops, as well as establishing pastures for beef production, stands as the primary catalyst, accounting for almost two-thirds of the overall forest loss. In comparison, _____

Which choice most effectively completes the text using information from the graph?

A) Europe's tree loss is mainly due to logging to create forestry-based products, such as paper

B) Oceania also suffers from wildfires, but does not contribute much to forest loss due to its smaller geographical area

C) Most of Africa's forest loss comes from employing traditional shifting agriculture.

D) forest loss across temperate North America, Russia, China, and South Asia is the result of tree loss in wildfires.

CONTINUE

13

Dupuytren's disease, a medical disorder in which the patient's fingers become frozen in a bent position, is commonly found in Northern European countries and is likely genetic as it runs in families. It is commonly believed that the disease is caused by mutations of the EPDR1 protein. Swedish geneticist Dr. Hugo Zeberg speculated that the disease may be linked to Neaderthal DNA after observing that there are very few cases of Dupuytren's disease in Africa. This speculation is based on the established finding that _____

Which choice most logically completes the text?

A) Neanderthals lived in Northern Europe millenniums ago.

B) Africans have limited Neanderthal ancestry.

C) the ancestors of Neanderthals can be found in every continent on Earth.

D) Africans have high levels of Neanderthal ancestry.

14

The extreme temperatures on the planet Mercury make it unlikely that there is any life on the planet in a form we would recognize. Mercury is closest to the Sun, and therefore the daytime temperatures are extremely hot, up to 800 degrees Fahrenheit (430 degrees Celsius). Since there is only a residual atmosphere, nights are much colder. In fact, despite its proximity to the Sun, Mercury_____

Which choice most logically completes the text?

A) has an egg–shaped orbit which changes its distance from the Sun.

B) rotates around the Sun faster than any other planet, in only 88 days.

C) is approximately the same size as Earth's moon and covered with craters.

D) might even be cold enough to have permanent water ice near the poles.

CONTINUE ➡

15

The first seven months of 2023 have seen fires consume over 200,000 hectares across the European Union; fire season is far from over. Despite the _____ that are on permanent standby to combat wildfires, critics argue that the bloc has largely neglected preventive actions, such as actively managing forests.

Which choice completes the text so that it conforms to the conventions of Standard English?

A) European Unions firefighting airplanes'

B) European Union's firefighting airplane's

C) European Union's firefighting airplanes

D) European Unions firefighting airplane's

16

A classic image of colonial cooperation, _____. Martha kept detailed records of her experiences in the American frontier for over three decades.

Which choice completes the text so that it conforms to the conventions of Standard English?

A) the diary of an 18th–century midwife named Martha Ballard documents several quilting bees

B) an 18th–century midwife named Martha Ballard documented several quilting bees in her diary

C) Martha Ballard, an 18th–century midwife, documented several quilting bees in her diary

D) several quilting bees were documented in the diary of an 18th–century midwife named Martha Ballard

17

Most tourists organize their initial Italian trip around Rome, Florence, and Venice. While this trio provides an incredible array of experiences for travelers, Italy's treasures extend well beyond these cities. Most tourists never realize the allure of the countless other charming villages that grace the Italian countryside. In this nation, a lifetime of exploration ____ those who seek the less-trodden path.

Which choice completes the text so that it conforms to the conventions of Standard English?

A) await

B) has awaited

C) is awaiting

D) awaits

18

Volunteers of America is a non–profit organization which helps homeless, disabled, senior, and other underserved individuals regain a balanced life. Over the past 125 years, the _____ have helped an average of 1.5 million people annually.

Which choice completes the text so that it conforms to the conventions of Standard English?

A) volunteers efforts'

B) volunteer's efforts

C) volunteers' efforts

D) volunteers's efforts'

19

Henry Wadsworth Longfellow's detailed poems greatly influenced the perception of various historical events, such as Paul Revere's nighttime ride during the American Revolutionary war, even though he sometimes _____ to make the poems more engaging.

Which choice completes the text so that it conforms to the conventions of Standard English?

A) sacrificed accuracy for eloquence

B) sacrificed—accuracy for eloquence—

C) sacrificed: accuracy for eloquence

D) sacrificed (accuracy for eloquence)

20

Archaeologists determined that a pair of sandals made from sagebrush bark that were found in a cave in Oregon in 1939 are actually the oldest extant example of shoes in the _____ specimens have been dated to between 7,000 and 8,000 BCE.

Which choice completes the text so that it conforms to the conventions of Standard English?

A) world; and the

B) world. Because the

C) world, the

D) world. The

21

Inflation is when the prices of goods and services generally increase, resulting in a decrease in the purchasing power of money. Economists debate about the effects of low levels of _____ high levels of inflation are universally accepted as disruptive to an economy.

Which choice completes the text so that it conforms to the conventions of Standard English?

A) inflation,

B) inflation;

C) inflation:

D) inflation

22

Edward Tingatinga's professional art career only lasted four years. _____ he is considered one of the most influential modern African painters and was the founder of an art style now archetypal in Tanzania.

Which choice completes the text with the most logical transition?

A) Therefore,

B) Even so,

C) Specifically,

D) Moreover,

23

Dogs trained for search and rescue have the same goal of finding humans, but there are actually two main methods that the dogs use to reach this goal. One is called air scent, in which a dog sniffs its surroundings and makes a straight line for the target once the scent is detected. _____ a dog sniffs the ground and follows the specific route that the person took, even if the path is very convoluted. This method is called tracking.

Which choice completes the text with the most logical transition?

A) Furthermore,

B) Precisely,

C) However,

D) Alternatively,

24

Tropical saltwater fish are beautiful to watch, but they take a lot of time and special equipment to maintain properly. That equipment is not cheap, either. A standard tank with fish can easily cost around $2,000 to set up, and there are monthly expenses such as food, salt, and minerals, which can run over $35 a month for a 50–gallon tank. _____ the upkeep alone is equivalent to over two coffee lattes from a specialty store every week.

Which choice completes the text with the most logical transition?

A) On the other hand,

B) Even so,

C) In addition,

D) In other words,

25

While researching a topic, a student has taken the following notes:

- Company A is an innovative electronics producer with more than 100 years of history, regularly offering cutting-edge products.

- Company B, another top-tier electronics firm, was only established two decades ago but quickly rose to prominence due to its ground-breaking designs.

- Company A takes great pride in its comprehensive research and development program, which ensures the production of superior electronics products.

- Company B operates differently, taking an approach of rapid design and iteration that often yields multiple versions of a product within short intervals.

- Both companies enjoy strong consumer bases; with Company A drawing long-term customers to its fold while Company B targeting an older, tech-savvy demographic.

The student wants to emphasize the distinct operational strategies of Company A and Company B. Which choice most effectively uses relevant information from the notes to accomplish this goal?

A) Both Companies A and B enjoy strong customer bases; with Company A's clientele being comprised mainly of long-standing customers while Company B appeals more heavily to younger demographics.

B) Company A has achieved innovation through an exhaustive research and development program, while Company B relies on rapid design iteration to stay at the cutting edge.

C) Company B has risen to prominence in only two decades, an achievement credited to its rapid design and iteration model.

D) Despite Company A's long history in the electronics industry, Company B has managed to achieve prominence in a shorter period with its quick design and iteration approach.

26

While researching a topic, a student has taken the following notes:

- Digitalization has had an enormous impact on businesses, facilitating customer access and efficient functioning.

- Unfortunately, digitalization also exposes businesses to risks like cyberattacks, data breaches, and digital fraud.

- Traditional businesses operate within a specific region and cater to a select group of consumers.

- Traditional businesses benefit greatly from developing direct, personal relationships with their customers, which allows for immediate feedback and timely service delivery.

- Adopting digital tools typically involves significant financial investments in technology and training, creating an additional financial burden on businesses.

The student wants to emphasize the contrast between digital and traditional businesses. Which choice most effectively uses relevant information from the notes to accomplish this goal?

A) Digital businesses enjoy greater customer access and efficiency, but may be vulnerable to cyber attacks; traditional businesses tend to benefit more from personal interactions between customers, and have a select group of customers to deal with.

B) Adopting digital tools into a business requires significant investments; traditional businesses with a focus on direct interactions have few challenges in this regard.

C) While digital businesses provide convenient access and efficiency, they also face the unique threat of data breaches, and digital fraud compared to their counterparts in traditional businesses.

D) Traditional businesses tend to operate within a specific geographical region, while digital enterprises have global reach with cyber threats as a major concern.

27

While researching a topic, a student has taken the following notes:

- The Internet has transformed communication by making it faster and more globalized.

- Historically, telegram was an innovative breakthrough in long-distance communication when first created in the 19th century.

- The Pony Express was an iconic mail service of the American West during the mid-1800s that marked a breakthrough in long-distance communication.

- Johannes Gutenberg's invention of the printing press in 15th-century Europe revolutionized information dissemination.

The student wants to highlight the revolutionary nature of the Internet as a communication tool compared to historical methods. Which choice most effectively uses relevant information from the notes to accomplish this goal?

A) The Internet, in enabling instantaneous global communication, represents a leap from historical advances in long-distance communication methods such as the telegram or the Pony Express.

B) While printing presses, telegrams, and the Pony Express were once revolutionary advances, in terms of communication speed, they were not as fast as the Internet.

C) Much like Gutenberg's printing press, the Internet marked an important turning point in how humans communicate and access information.

D) Though groundbreaking in their time, Pony Express and Telegram lack the global reach and speed of the Internet in their communication capacity.

· ·

STOP

No Test Material On This Page

No Test Material On This Page

Math

22 QUESTIONS | 35 MINUTES

DIRECTIONS

The questions in this section address a number of important math skills. Use of a calculator is permitted for all questions.

NOTES

Unless otherwise indicated: • All variables and expressions represent real numbers. • Figures provided are drawn to scale. • All figures lie in a plane. • The domain of a given function is the set of all real numbers x for which $f(x)$ is a real number.

REFERENCE

$A = \pi r^2$
$C = 2\pi r$

$A = \ell w$

$A = \frac{1}{2} bh$

$c^2 = a^2 + b^2$

Special Right Triangles

$V = \ell w h$

$V = \pi r^2 h$

$V = \frac{4}{3} \pi r^3$

$V = \frac{1}{3} \pi r^2 h$

$V = \frac{1}{3} \ell w h$

The number of degrees of arc in a circle is 360.

The number of radians of arc in a circle is 2π.

The sum of the measures in degrees of the angles of a triangle is 180.

CONTINUE ➡

For **multiple–choice questions,** solve each problem, choose the correct answer from the choices provided, and then circle your answer in this book. Circle only one answer for each question. If you change your mind, completely erase the circle. You will not get credit for questions with more than one answer circled, or for questions with no answers circled.

For **student–produced response questions,** solve each problem and write your answer next to or under the question in the test book as described below.

- Once you've written your answer, circle it clearly. You will not receive credit for anything written outside the circle, or for any questions with more than one circled answer.

- If you find more than one correct answer, write and circle only one answer.

- Your answer can be up to 5 characters for a positive answer and up to 6 characters (including the negative sign) for a negative answer, but no more.

- If your answer is a fraction that is too long (over 5 characters for positive, 6 characters for negative), write the decimal equivalent.

- If your answer is a decimal that is too long (over 5 characters for positive, 6 characters for negative), truncate it or round at the fourth digit.

- If your answer is a mixed number (such as 3.!. 2), write it as an improper fraction (7/2) or its decimal equivalent (3.5).

- Don't include symbols such as a percent sign, comma, or dollar sign in your circled answer.

CONTINUE

1

Which of the following describes the transformation of a circle with the equation $(x - 3)^2 + (y + 6)^2 = 49$ to a circle with the equation $(x - 2)^2 + y^2 + 8y = 33$?

A) The circle moves 1 to the right and 2 up

B) The circle moves 1 to the right and 2 down

C) The circle moves 1 to the left and 2 up

D) The circle moves 1 to the left and 2 down

2

$$(x - 1)(x + 2) = x (x - 3)$$

How many solutions are there to the equation above?

A) None

B) One

C) Two

D) Four

3

$$3(x - 6) - 2 (x + 2) = px - 5x - 22$$

If the system above has an infinite number of solutions, what would be the value of p ?

4

If the number of weeds on a farm is represented by the function $f(x) = 1,300(1.995)^x$, where x is in weeks, which of the following statements is true about the model?

A) The number of weeds on the farm in the beginning was 1.995

B) The number of weeds on the farm increases by 1.995 every x weeks

C) The number of weeds on the farm increases by 99.5% every x weeks

D) The number of weeds on the farm increases by 1,300 every x weeks

5

$$(x - 2)^2 (x + 2)^2$$

Which of the following is equivalent to the above equation?

A) $x^4 - 8x^2 + 16$

B) $x^4 - 16$

C) $x^4 + 8x + 16$

D) $x^4 + 16$

6

A food scientist measures 27 different foods whose calorie content is shown below. What is the difference between the mean and the median of the calorie content of the 27 foods, rounded to the nearest tenth of a calorie?

Calorie content	Frequency
100	6
180	9
280	11
350	1

7

What is the x–intercept for the following equation

$x = 3^{y-1} + \dfrac{5}{3}$?

A) $\dfrac{1}{3}$

B) $\dfrac{5}{3}$

C) 2

D) 3

8

30 Grade 11 students in a summer math class were asked what is the hardest subject for them. 80% of the students said that Statistics was the hardest while the rest chose Physics as the hardest subject. Which of the following statements can best be concluded from this information?

A) 80% of the students in the summer math class think Statistics is the hardest subject.

B) 20% of the Grade 11 students think Statistics is the hardest subject.

C) 80% of the Grade 11 students in the math summer class think Physics is the hardest subject.

D) 20% of the grade 11 students in the math summer class think Physics is the hardest subject.

9

If $-3(x + 3)^2 + 9 + x = ax^2 + bx + c$, what is the value of $a + b + c$?

10

If the maximum point for a quadratic equation $f(x)$ is (3, 2), and it passes through the point (2, 0), which of the following is a solution for x to the quadratic equation?

A) −16

B) −2

C) 4

D) 12

11

What is the value of the slope of a line that passes through the origin and point (3, 5)?

A) $-\dfrac{3}{5}$

B) $-\dfrac{5}{3}$

C) $\dfrac{3}{5}$

D) $\dfrac{5}{3}$

12

$$y \geq 2\,(x-3)^2 + 5$$

$$y \leq x + 3$$

If (a, b) is a solution to the above system of inequalities, which of the following represents the minimum value of b?

A) −5

B) −3

C) 3

D) 5

13

What is the volume of a sphere with a radius of 3?

14

$$3x - 4y = 8$$

$$px + 8y + 6 = 0?$$

If the system of equations above has no solution, which of the following would be a possible value of p?

A) −6

B) −2

C) 2

D) 6

15

$$x^2 + 6x + y^2 - 6y = 63$$

What is the center for the equation of the circle given above?

A) $(3, -3)$

B) $(6, -6)$

C) $(-6, 6)$

D) $(-3, 3)$

16

$$3x^2 - 6x - 11$$

If one of the solutions for the quadratic equation above is $\dfrac{3 + \sqrt{g}}{3}$, what is the value of g?

17

$$-2x \geq -4 - x$$

Which of the following is NOT a solution to the above inequality?

A) 2

B) 3

C) 4

D) 5

18

$$\sqrt{2x + 5} = x - 5$$

What are the possible solutions to the equation above?

A) 2

B) 10

C) 2 and 10

D) −2 and −10

19

If $\dfrac{5}{x} = \dfrac{2}{y}$ and $\dfrac{4}{x} - \dfrac{2}{y} = -\dfrac{1}{5}$, what is the value of xy?

20

If $\dfrac{3x^2 + 7x + 9}{x - 2} = 3x + 13 + \dfrac{A}{x - 2}$. What is the value of A?

A) −23

B) 7

C) 19

D) 35

21

A zookeeper conducted a study on the mass of penguins in the zoo. He found that the mean mass of the penguins in the zoo is 67.9 *kgs*. He estimated that the margin of error for the mean mass is 4.5 *kgs*. Which of the following statements can best be concluded from the study he conducted?

A) The mass of the penguins in the zoo is between 72.4 *kgs* and 63.4 *kgs*.

B) The mass of all penguins is 67.9 *kgs*.

C) The median mass of penguins in the zoo lies between 72.4 *kgs* and 63.4 *kgs*.

D) The mean mass of the penguins in the zoo lies between 72.4 *kgs* and 63.4 *kgs*.

22

$$3(x - 3) + 2(x + y) = 5x + 2y - 9$$

How many solutions does the system above have ?

A) None

B) One

C) Two

D) infinite

No Test Material On This Page

Math

22 QUESTIONS | 35 MINUTES

DIRECTIONS

The questions in this section address a number of important math skills. Use of a calculator is permitted for all questions.

NOTES

Unless otherwise indicated: • All variables and expressions represent real numbers. • Figures provided are drawn to scale. • All figures lie in a plane. • The domain of a given function is the set of all real numbers x for which $f(x)$ is a real number.

REFERENCE

$A = \pi r^2$
$C = 2\pi r$

$A = \ell w$

$A = \frac{1}{2}bh$

$c^2 = a^2 + b^2$

Special Right Triangles

$V = \ell w h$

$V = \pi r^2 h$

$V = \frac{4}{3}\pi r^3$

$V = \frac{1}{3}\pi r^2 h$

$V = \frac{1}{3}\ell w h$

The number of degrees of arc in a circle is 360.

The number of radians of arc in a circle is 2π.

The sum of the measures in degrees of the angles of a triangle is 180.

For **multiple–choice questions,** solve each problem, choose the correct answer from the choices provided, and then circle your answer in this book. Circle only one answer for each question. If you change your mind, completely erase the circle. You will not get credit for questions with more than one answer circled, or for questions with no answers circled.

For **student–produced response questions,** solve each problem and write your answer next to or under the question in the test book as described below.

- Once you've written your answer, circle it clearly. You will not receive credit for anything written outside the circle, or for any questions with more than one circled answer.

- If you find more than one correct answer, write and circle only one answer.

- Your answer can be up to 5 characters for a positive answer and up to 6 characters (including the negative sign) for a negative answer, but no more.

- If your answer is a fraction that is too long (over 5 characters for positive, 6 characters for negative), write the decimal equivalent.

- If your answer is a decimal that is too long (over 5 characters for positive, 6 characters for negative), truncate it or round at the fourth digit.

- If your answer is a mixed number (such as 3.!. 2), write it as an improper fraction (7/2) or its decimal equivalent (3.5).

- Don't include symbols such as a percent sign, comma, or dollar sign in your circled answer.

1

$3(x + 5)^2 - 2(x - 5)^2 + 2x$

Which of the following equations is equal to?

A) $x^2 + x + 125$

B) $3x^2 + 52x + 25$

C) $x^2 - 2x - 25$

D) $x^2 + 52x + 25$

2

Which of the following is equivalent to

$\dfrac{1}{x-2} + \dfrac{2x}{5-x}$, for all values of x, where $x \neq 2$ and

$x \neq 5$?

A) $\dfrac{2x^2 - 5x + 5}{-x^2 + 7x - 10}$

B) $\dfrac{2x + 1}{-3}$

C) $\dfrac{2x + 1}{3}$

D) $\dfrac{2x + 1}{(5 - x)(x - 2)}$

3

$3(x - 2) + 5y = 2$

$y = -2(x - 5)$

What is the value of y for the system above ?

4

Which of the following best describes the line of best fit for the graph below?

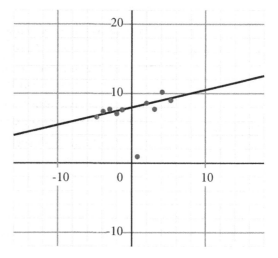

A) $y = \dfrac{1}{4}x + 8$

B) $y = 4x + 8$

C) $y = \dfrac{1}{4}x - 8$

D) $y = \dfrac{-1}{4}x + 8$

5

If angle AOB is $\dfrac{7}{12}\pi$, what is the value of the arc length AB, given that the radius of the circle is 6 cm?

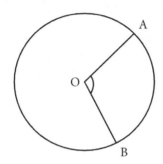

A) 12π cm

B) 36π cm

C) $\dfrac{7}{2}\pi$ cm

D) $\dfrac{21}{2}\pi$ cm

6

$$2x^2 + 6x + 4 = 0$$

What is the sum of the roots for the equation given above?

A) −3

B) −2

C) 2

D) 3

7

If the difference of the sum of the interior angles in a hexagon and that of a heptagon is $a\pi$, what is the value of a?

8

Given that $f(3) = 2$ and $f(6) = -3$, which of the following functions best describes $f(x)$?

A) $f(x) = -\dfrac{5}{3}x + 7$

B) $f(x) = \dfrac{2}{3}x - 6$

C) $f(x) = -\dfrac{3}{5}x$

D) $f(x) = \dfrac{3}{5}x + 2$

9

Given that $2(x + 4) = 18$, what is the value of $x + 6$?

A) −4

B) 5

C) 9

D) 11

10

An educational fair is attended by students and parents in a state. If 2,000 students attended the fair, and the ratio of students to parents in the fair is 5:3.5, how many people attended the fair?

11

Find the percent decrease from the actual value y for when $x = 4$ and the predicted value y for when $x = 4$.

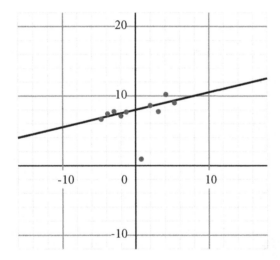

A) 18.18%

B) 22.22%

C) 33.33%

D) 50%

12

$$y > -3x + 5$$

$$y > 2x$$

Which of the following coordinates represent a solution to the above system of inequalities?

A) (2, 4)

B) (1, 4)

C) (4, 3)

D) (2, 1)

13

$$3\,|x - 4| = 6$$

What is one possible positive solution to the equation above?

14

If AB = DC and segment AD is parallel to segment BC, and AD = 12, DC = 10, and BC = 28, find the area of the figure ABCD below (not drawn to scale).

A) 48

B) 60

C) 96

D) 120

15

$$2\,|\,x+3\,|-3\,|\,x+3\,| = -2$$

How many solutions does the equation above have?

A) None

B) One

C) Two

D) There isn't sufficient information to answer the question.

16

What is the value of the slope of a line perpendicular to the line $5x - 6y + 30 = 0$

17

Which of the following is equivalent to $cos\,72°$?

A) $sin\,18°$

B) $cos\,18°$

C) $sin\,72°$

D) $tan\,18°$

18

The weather channel predicted that there will be a 0.26 chance that it will rain this week. What is the probability that it will not rain this week?

A) 0.26

B) 0.62

C) 0.74

D) 1

19

$$v(t) = -3t^2 + 9t + 12$$

What is the maximum value of t for the above equation $v(t)$?

20

If the semi–circle below has a radius of 7 and angle PQR = 60°, what is the length of side PR?

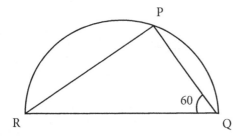

A) 7

B) $7\sqrt{2}$

C) $7\sqrt{3}$

D) 14

21

$$|x + 3| > 4$$

Which of the following is a solution to the inequality ?

A) −9

B) −7

C) −5

D) −2

22

If $3x + 4y = 31$ and $2x + 3y = 22$, what is the value of $x + y$?

A) 4

B) 5

C) 9

D) 11

STOP

No Test Material On This Page

Answer Key

Reading and Writing

Module 1

Questions	Correct	Mark your correct answers
1.	C	
2.	B	
3.	C	
4.	B	
5.	B	
6.	D	
7.	D	
8.	C	
9.	A	
10.	B	
11.	A	
12.	C	
13.	D	
14.	C	
15.	A	
16.	B	
17.	B	
18.	A	
19.	C	
20.	A	
21.	A	
22.	A	
23.	C	
24.	A	
25.	A	
26.	B	
27.	B	

Module 2

Questions	Correct	Mark your correct answers
1.	D	
2.	B	
3.	A	
4.	B	
5.	C	
6.	A	
7.	D	
8.	D	
9.	B	
10.	A	
11.	C	
12.	D	
13.	B	
14.	D	
15.	C	
16.	D	
17.	D	
18.	C	
19.	A	
20.	D	
21.	B	
22.	B	
23.	D	
24.	D	
25.	B	
26.	A	
27.	A	

Math

Module 1

Questions	Correct	Mark your correct answers
1.	C	
2.	B	
3.	6	
4.	C	
5.	A	
6.	29.3	
7.	C	
8.	D	
9.	−38	
10.	C	
11.	C	
12.	D	
13.	36π	
14.	A	
15.	D	
16.	42	
17.	D	
18.	B	
19.	10	
20.	D	
21.	D	
22.	D	

Module 2

Questions	Correct	Mark your correct answers
1.	D	
2.	A	
3.	−2	
4.	A	
5.	C	
6.	A	
7.	1	
8.	A	
9.	D	
10.	3,400	
11.	A	
12.	B	
13.	2 or 6	
14.	D	
15.	C	
16.	$\dfrac{-6}{5}$	
17.	A	
18.	C	
19.	$\dfrac{3}{2}$ or 1.5	
20.	C	
21.	A	
22.	C	

1. **Level:** Hard | **Domain:** CRAFT AND STRUCTURE
    Skill/Knowledge: Words in Context

    Key Explanation: Choice C is the best answer because it refers to something that is used as a standard of comparison. It fits the context of saying that 25 healthy people were used as comparisons for the 163 patients with major depressive disorder or bipolar disorder.

    Distractor Explanations: None of the other choices describe the 25 healthy patients. **Choice A** refers to "experts," but the experts on the subject were conducting the experiment, not taking placebos as part of the test. **Choice B** refers to limitations rather than comparisons. **Choice D** refers to orders.

2. **Level:** Easy | **Domain:** CRAFT AND STRUCTURE
    Skill/Knowledge: Words in Context

    Key Explanation: Choice B is the best answer because the text is describing a trend among parasites: almost none are mammals. The blank portion is a noun that describes the vampire bat, which is a parasitic mammal. **Choice B** refers to something that does not follow the general rule, so perfectly describes a parasite that does not fit the usual pattern.

    Distractor Explanations: Choice A is incorrect because it refers to a strange or unusual habit or characteristic that stands out, not to an object that does not fit a rule. **Choice C** is incorrect because it refers to something that is not the same shape or quality, such as sound or appearance. **Choice D** is incorrect because it refers to an individual preference that is unusual.

3. **Level:** Easy | **Domain:** CRAFT AND STRUCTURE
    Skill/Knowledge: Words in Context

    Key Explanation: Choice C is the best answer because C refers to the gradual amassing or acquisition of something. It fits the context of describing what aspect of bioactive compounds—in this case, nutrients—in vegetables is affected by salt stress. The sentence can be paraphrased by saying that salt changes the rate that bioactive compounds amass.

    Distractor Explanations: None of the other choices fits the context of describing what aspect of biological compounds is affected by salt. **Choice A** refers to how well one focuses one's thoughts, so it does not apply to inanimate things. **Choice B** also does not refer to inanimate things, as it describes the emotion of being committed to a purpose. **Choice D** is incorrect because it refers to bringing activities, not things, into one place under one form of control or leadership.

4. **Level:** Easy | **Domain:** CRAFT AND STRUCTURE
    Skill/Knowledge: Text Structure and Purpose

    Key Explanation: Choice B is the best answer because the passage explores that because of the time a dog and his owner spend together influences a dog's personality. Hence, the connection between the two has attention called to it by the author of the passage.

    Distractor Explanations: Choice A is incorrect as the passage is not trying to convince readers that dogs are man's best friends. One can certainly draw their own conclusion that dogs are a man's best friend from the information provided, but the author is not reaching this conclusion himself or herself. **Choice C** is wrong because the passage does not describe a particular instance of an owner and his experience with his dog. **Choice D** is wrong because the passage is not focusing on the behavior of one dog breed in particular, but all dogs in general.

5. **Level:** Medium | **Domain:** CRAFT AND STRUCTURE
    Skill/Knowledge: Text Structure and Purpose

    Key Explanation: Choice B is the best answer because the paragraph is outlining various potential problems to underwater habitats. The author indicates that there are many different potential problems, so "deep ocean habitats may be negatively affected." The quotations come after this discussion and are preceded with "however," which shows that they are a contradiction to the previous idea. Therefore, they are included to show the opposite side of the argument. They indicate that as yet, despite the author's concerns, there has been no "elevated levels of mortality" or "evidence…of harm."

    Distractor Explanations: Choice A is incorrect because the claims made in the quote support the same idea: very little damage occurs to ocean creatures. Therefore, the views are not different from each other. **Choice C** is incorrect because "undermine" refers to weakening an argument. However, the quotes strengthen rather than weaken the idea that systems are safe. **Choice D** is incorrect because the conclusions oppose rather than strengthen the paragraph's main claim that there are risks from tidal energy systems to aquatic habitats and creatures.

6. **Level:** Hard | **Domain:** CRAFT AND STRUCTURE
    Skill/Knowledge: Text Structure and Purpose

Key Explanation: Choice D is the best answer because the author follows the phrases about extraterrestrial life with a question that asks how such life has changed from "sci–fi fairytale to a serious scientific endeavor." The author is emphasizing the transition in how people perceive extraterrestrial life. In the past, it was viewed as something "impossible" or "not real," and the phrases highlight that image. The phrases provide a strong contrast to the "credible" or "believable" nature of extraterrestrial life today, which the author summarizes in the concept that the search for life is "modeled by macroeconomists, funded by fiscal conservatives, and discussed by theologians."

Distractor Explanations: Choice A is incorrect because the author never describes the appearance of extraterrestrial life. The phrases may evoke images, but they do not act as a contrast for the current beliefs about what life outside Earth might look like. **Choice B** is incorrect because the images evoked by the phrases are all theatrical forms of aliens. They do not necessarily reflect what scientists think actual extraterrestrial life might look like, and do not "encourage" or "suggest" that the reader think about anything other than the stereotypes. **Choice C** is incorrect because, while the phrases may be "lighthearted," the purpose is not to make the reader laugh. The purpose is to emphasize the important point that the new view of extraterrestrial life is very serious compared to views of such life in the past.

7. **Level:** Medium | **Domain:** CRAFT AND STRUCTURE
    Skill/Knowledge: Cross–Text Connections

    Key Explanation: Choice D is the best answer that both authors would agree upon. The author of Text 1 says that there was a mass extinction at the end of the Cretaceous period, indicating that most species did not survive past that time: they died before the next period. The author of Text 2 says that there was no mass extinction, but that the "last major representatives liv[ed] to approximately the end of the Cretaceous period." In other words, they died off slowly over time until the end of the period, and most did not live into the next period.

Distractor Explanations: Choice A is incorrect because the author of Text 1 says that a meteorite "triggered" or "caused" a mass extinction. **Choice B** is incorrect because the author of Text 2 does not say whether the Earth cooled or not; in addition, the author of Text 1 says that the change was enough to cause a mass extinction. **Choice C** is incorrect because Text 1 refers to a mass extinction.

8. **Level:** Hard | **Domain:** INFORMATION AND IDEAS
   Skill/Knowledge: Central Ideas and Details

Key Explanation: Choice C is the best answer because it accurately summarizes the main idea of the text. The passage discusses the concept of sustainable agriculture and its importance in minimizing environmental impact and ensuring long-term food security. The passage mentions techniques like organic farming, crop rotation, and precision agriculture, which are all part of sustainable agriculture practices. The main idea centers around the goal of sustainable agriculture, which is to reduce environmental impact while ensuring food security.

Distractor Explanations: Choice A is incorrect because it focuses only on the reason for the rise of sustainable agriculture (global population),

but it doesn't encompass the broader scope of the passage, which discusses the techniques and goals of sustainable agriculture. **Choice B** is incorrect because it only highlights one aspect of sustainable agriculture (organic farming) and does not cover the other techniques or the overarching goal of ensuring long-term food security. **Choice D** is incorrect because it only mentions precision agriculture, without including the other techniques or the broader objective of minimizing environmental impact and ensuring food security.

9. **Level:** Medium | **Domain:** INFORMATION AND IDEAS
   Skill/Knowledge: Central Ideas and Details

Key Explanation: Choice A is the best answer because, according to Sweeney, "The critical element" or "important point" of the study was that the researchers "were able to sustain measurements in this harsh environment as long as [they] have—both in the summer and the winter, in every year over the last 13 years." In other words, the results of the study were "unique" or "one of a kind" because they relied on "measurements" or "data" that did not lack large blocks of time. No previous study had such complete data to work with: the Drake Passage data "is the densest ongoing time series in the Southern Ocean."

Distractor Explanations: Choice B is incorrect because there is no discussion of what equipment or methods the scientists used to collect their data. They could have used very common tools. **Choice C** is incorrect because there is no evidence that previous studies did not "incorporate" or "use" chemical measurements. The only difference brought up is that the period of collection in the Drake Passage study was unbroken for 13 years. **Choice D** is incorrect because it is implied that there have been other studies of the region. If the data set is "the densest," then there is an implied comparison that there were other studies that had data that was not as dense.

10. **Level:** Hard | **Domain:** INFORMATION AND IDEAS
Skill/Knowledge: Central Ideas and Details

Key Explanation: Choice B is the best answer because Keel complains in the last sentence, "this decision will create two classes of Indian tribes: those who will benefit from Federal trust responsibility and those who will not." In other words, he feels that the decision has problems because some Native Americans qualify and some do not, so the "classes" or "groups" will be unequal in how they are treated.

Distractor Explanations: Choice A is incorrect because Keel does not explain how he felt about the original wording or how the policy varied from the original intent. **Choice C** is incorrect because the decision did not make any "new" methods or laws. It only restricted which groups of people the law applied to. **Choice D** is incorrect because "precedents" are legal cases that act as a guide for deciding future cases. The Carcieri decision, however, did not "facilitate" or "make easier" the process of "establishing" or "creating" tribal governments.

11. **Level:** Hard | **Domain:** INFORMATION AND IDEAS
Skill/Knowledge: Command of Evidence (Textual)

Key Explanation: Choice A is the best answer. The claim is that Dickenson "personifies books," which means that she gives books the characteristics of living people. **Choice A** refers to

"meeting" a book, like meeting a person, and that the book is "in the dress" or "wearing the clothes" of his time period, just like a person would.

Distractor Explanations: None of the other choices show books in a way that makes them seem like living creatures. **Choice B** only refers to what scholars are interested in, not the way books are. **Choice C** refers to time periods. **Choice D** is a weak choice because books are not mentioned; if "he" refers to a book, it could show that the book is familiar with facts from long ago. However, **Choice A** definitely refers to books having human qualities, so is a much better example of the claim.

12. **Level:** Medium | **Domain:** INFORMATION AND IDEAS
Skill/Knowledge: Command of Evidence (Textual)

Key Explanation: Choice C is the best answer because Sagan's quote is a warning that before assuming that there is life, "we will need to work hard to think of any non–biological process" that could explain "some features in the light spectrum that might be indicative of life." **Choice C** is a case that Sagan would warn against because it assumes that oxygen is caused by living creatures rather than considering and eliminating all other possible reasons that there may be oxygen present.

Distractor Explanations: Choice A is incorrect because it offers tangible proof of an organism rather than just guessing that there is life based on secondary signs. **Choice B** is incorrect because it shows that the scientist does not rashly assume that oxygen means there is life. Sagan would approve because the scientist indicates there are other options to explain the oxygen. **Choice D** is incorrect because it does not show that anyone is jumping to the conclusion that there is life before enough facts exist to prove that there is life.

13. **Level:** Medium | **Domain:** INFORMATION AND IDEAS

Skill/Knowledge: Command of Evidence (Quantitative)

Key Explanation: Choice D is the best answer. The example should be one that shows that there are options for nurses other than working in hospitals; particularly, the example should relate to the aging population. **Choice D** focuses on a group of registered nurses who have such an occupation: they work in nursing homes or residential care facilities where seniors often live when their health declines.

Distractor Explanations: Choice A is incorrect because it refers to employment other than working in a hospital, but it does not address the question of an aging population. Nurses in education most likely work with younger people starting out in their careers. **Choice B** is incorrect because it is too vague. It lists two different careers, but does not say what percentage of nurses work in them or how they relate to an aging population. **Choice D** is incorrect because it does not convey the information from the graph correctly. It refers to the percentage change in employment, but the graph refers to the percentage of the registered nurses employed at the time.

14. **Level:** Medium | **Domain:** INFORMATION AND IDEAS

Skill/Knowledge: Command of Evidence (Quantitative)

Key Explanation: Choice C is the best answer because it uses data from the graph to accurately complete the text. The graph shows Gender-interest stereotypes were stronger than gender-

ability stereotypes hence those who believed the stereotypes would be less interested in participating in any courses related to computer science or engineering.

Distractor Explanations: Choice A is incorrect because it doesn't accurately reflect the data from the graph. The graph indicates that girls who believed in the stereotypes would believe that they are less skilled but would also not be interested in participating in any courses related to computer science or engineering. The word "than" suggests that they more interested than skilled however the graph shows that gender-interest stereotypes were stronger than gender-ability stereotypes, meaning that they would be less interested than skilled and not less skilled than interested. **Choice B** is incorrect because it doesn't accurately reflect the data from the graph. The graph indicates that girls who believed in the stereotypes would believe that they are less skilled and not be interested in participating in any courses related to computer science or engineering. The word "equally" suggests that they interested and skilled at the same level however the graph shows that gender-interest stereotypes were stronger than gender-ability stereotypes, meaning that they would be less interested than skilled and not equally interested and skilled. **Choice D** is incorrect because it doesn't accurately reflect the data from the graph. The graph indicates that gender-interest stereotypes were stronger than gender-ability stereotypes. Hence, girls who believed in the stereotypes would be less interested in participating in any courses related to computer science or engineering.

15. **Level:** Medium | **Domain:** INFORMATION AND IDEAS

Skill/Knowledge: Inferences

Key Explanation: Choice A is correct. The text describes the functions that can be performed by a robot, such as collecting thousands of data samples with high precision and accuracy. However, the text also states that data and understanding is not the same. Therefore, this choice elaborates on this statement by explaining that there may be prerequisites, such as foundational knowledge, in order to truly understand the data.

Distractor Explanations: Choice B is incorrect because the text does not focus on the difference between accuracy and precision. Further, this choice is not an explanation that elaborates upon the statement in the previous sentence. Choice C is incorrect because the text suggests that robots are skilled in collecting data. This choice presents the opposite from the conclusion described in the text. Choice D is incorrect because this choice does not highlight the difference between data and understanding.

16. Level: Easy | Domain: STANDARD ENGLISH CONVENTIONS
Skill/Knowledge: Form, Structure, and Sense

Key Explanation: Choice B is the best answer because it is a plural possessive form. It shows that the "use" is something of the "cowry shells."

Distractor Explanations: Choice A is incorrect because it is a singular possessive word, but "cowry shells" is plural. "Currency" is singular, but it is not the correct referent in the context because "cowry shells" are the subject of the sentence; "they" also give a clue to the proper pronoun. Choice C is incorrect because it refers to a place rather than possession. Choice D is a contraction for "they are," which does not fit the grammatical structure preceding "use has declined."

17. Level: Easy | Domain: STANDARD ENGLISH CONVENTIONS
Skill/Knowledge: Form, Structure, and Sense

Key Explanation: Choice B is the best answer. The subject is the singular "Professor David Neumark," so a singular verb is needed for agreement.

Distractor Explanations: Choice A is incorrect because "in conjunction with Dr. William Wascher of the Federal Reserve Board" modifies "Professor David Neumark" rather than creating a verb with two people in it. Although it appears that a plural verb is needed, that is not the case. Choice C is incorrect because it is only a gerund rather than an active verb (such as "is dissenting,") so the result is a fragment. Choice D can be eliminated because it requires a plural subject.

18. Level: Easy | Domain: STANDARD ENGLISH CONVENTIONS
Skill/Knowledge: Boundaries

Key Explanation: Choice A is the best answer. "(or stratovolcano)" is another name for the composite formation of volcanoes, as shown by the "or." In other words, it is additional information describing the preceding item, "composite." Extra information in parentheses should be treated as part of the word it describes. In this case, there would be a comma after composite if there were no parentheses because it is part of a list joined by "and," so a comma should come after the parentheses.

Distractor Explanations: All of the other choices have incorrect punctuation for items in a list. For Choice B, items in parentheses are included as part of the word they describe, so they should not be divided into separate items using a comma after "composite." Choices C and D are incorrect because items in a list should be followed by a comma, but "and" is not. **Choice C** is also missing a comma after "stratovolcano)" and **Choice D** erroneously places the first comma after "composite" rather than after "stratovolcano)".

19. **Level:** Easy | **Domain:** STANDARD ENGLISH CONVENTIONS
    Skill/Knowledge: Boundaries

    Key Explanation: Choice C is the best answer. "People...granted" is the main idea, and "over...water" is another complete idea with a noun and verb. That idea is made secondary by the word "but." A clause that is secondary needs to be separated from the main idea using a comma.

    Distractor Explanations: It may appear that a semicolon is needed to separate ideas in a list, as there is a semicolon before "670 million." However, **Choice A** is incorrect because a semicolon must be preceded by complete ideas that can stand on their own. Also , "but" is left hanging at the end of the preceding idea. **Choice B** is incorrect because a semicolon must be followed by complete ideas that can stand on their own. Also , "but" creates a subordinate clause that can not stand alone. **Choice D** is incorrect because there should be a comma separating clauses from each other.

20. **Level:** Medium | **Domain:** STANDARD ENGLISH CONVENTIONS
    Skill/Knowledge: Boundaries

    Key Explanation: Choice A is the best answer. A pair of dashes can be used to add interesting but not essential information to a sentence. In this case, the names of the crops are not required, but could help the reader know what other cereal crops there are.

    Distractor Explanations: Choice B is incorrect because, while commas after "crops" and "sorghum" would also create an aside that describes "cereal crops," there should be no comma after "rye." That punctuation is because "rye and sorghum" forms a list of two items joined by "and," and such a list should not have a comma before the "and." **Choice C** is incorrect because "that" is the start of a relative clause that should not be divided from its noun with any punctuation. **Choice D** is incorrect because "that" is the start of a relative clause that should not be divided from its noun with any punctuation. However, a single dash could otherwise be used after a main clause to add more information such as the names of the grains.

21. **Level:** Easy | **Domain:** STANDARD ENGLISH CONVENTIONS
    Skill/Knowledge: Boundaries

    Key Explanation: Choice A is the best answer. A series of nouns joined by "and" should have a comma following each noun. Since "Greenland" is one place on the list where Inuit people live, it should be followed by a comma. No other punctuation is needed.

    Distractor Explanations: Choices B and **C** are incorrect because a colon should follow a complete clause, but the part preceding the colon cannot stand on its own as a sentence. "In" is left dangling. **Choice C** is also incorrect because there should be a comma after "Greenland." **Choice D** is incorrect because the part before and after a semicolon should both be complete clauses, but the following portion has no subject or verb.

22. **Level:** Easy | **Domain:** STANDARD ENGLISH CONVENTIONS
Skill/Knowledge: Boundaries

Key Explanation: The convention being tested is punctuation use between a sentence and an essential element. **Choice A** is the best answer because in this context, the essential element supplement "who feel valued and supported" provides necessary information about the noun "employees" and therefore should not be separated from the noun by punctuation.

Distractor Explanations: Choice B is incorrect because it uses a comma, which would suggest that the essential element supplement is optional and could be removed without changing the meaning of the sentence. **Choice C** uses a dash, which is not a standard way to introduce an essential element supplement. **Choice D** uses parentheses, which is not necessary or appropriate in this context.

23. **Level:** Easy | **Domain:** EXPRESSION OF IDEAS
Skill/Knowledge: Transitions

Key Explanation: Choice C is the best answer. The first sentence explains that some scientific fields overlap, and the following sentence gives a specific example of two fields that have points in common. **Choice C** is used to introduce an example or specific case of a general idea, so fits the context well.

Distractor Explanations: None of the other choices effectively shows that the following information is a particular case that is used to clarify the previous sentence. **Choice A** introduces an alternate possibility, not the same thing. **Choice B** shows that something happens despite something else, so provides an exception rather than a classic example. **Choice D** is used to introduce a summary or preference regarding the previous idea.

24. **Level:** Easy | **Domain:** EXPRESSION OF IDEAS
Skill/Knowledge: Transitions

Key Explanation: Choice A is the best answer. The previous sentence explains that echolocation is highly developed in some species. The following sentence says that other species have echolocation, but it is in a "limited form" or "not developed much at all." **Choice A** is used to qualify an earlier claim, so it fits the context of qualifying the idea that only a few animals have developed echolocation by saying that in reality, others also have it, albeit in a modified form.

Distractor Explanations: Choice B can be eliminated because it implies that the following statement is a consequence of the former statement(s). **Choice C** is used to show the logical result of an argument, so it does not effectively establish the relationship between ideas. A few species having limited echolocation is not necessarily a logical result of some species having echolocation. **Choice D** is used to introduce an idea that the reader might assume; in other words, the author feels it is obvious. However, it is probably not common knowledge that shrews and two bird species have modified echolocation.

25. **Level:** Easy | **Domain:** EXPRESSION OF IDEAS
Skill/Knowledge: Transitions

Key Explanation: Choice A is the best answer because it is used to establish a contrast between clauses in a sentence. In this case, it contrasts what "seems" or "appears" to be a large percentage with the much larger worldwide population. In other words, **Choice A** establishes that the percentage of bilingual speakers in the US is relatively small, as it is half that of the global average.

Distractor Explanations: None of the other choices effectively show the relationship between the first and second halves of the sentence. **Choice B** can be eliminated because it tries to establish a cause-and-effect relationship, when the following sentence is an effort to undermine the previous one. **Choice C** is grammatically incorrect. Its meaning of "even though" fits the context, but "despite" should be followed by a noun or noun phrase rather than a clause starting with "that." **Choice D** is incorrect because "since" introduces an argument that builds on the previous one(s), which is not the purpose of the following statement,

26. **Level:** Medium | **Domain:** EXPRESSION OF IDEAS
    Skill/Knowledge: Rhetorical Synthesis

    Key Explanation: Choice B is the best answer. The question asks for an "underlying theme" in some of Maya Angelou's books. In other words, it is asking for something that is similar to books that she wrote. The description of *I Know Why the Caged Bird Sings* says that it "reveals details about her private life up to the age of 17," or "tells about her youth," and the notes say that *Mom & Me & Mom* is about her relationship with her mother. In other words, both books tell about her personal life, which makes them "autobiographies."

    Distractor Explanations: Choice A is incorrect because, while it is true, it does not refer to a theme in books. Instead, it refers to a movie, *Down the Delta*. **Choice C** is incorrect because it also does not refer to a theme in books, only a theme in her life. There is no evidence that she actually wrote more than one unfinished book about world leaders. **Choice D** is incorrect because, while *I Know Why the Caged Bird Sings* was received well, there is no indication that her other books were received poorly or were not read by many people.

27. **Level:** Hard | **Domain:** EXPRESSION OF IDEAS
    Skill/Knowledge: Rhetorical Synthesis

    Key Explanation: Choice B is correct because it effectively highlights the unique features of both Bitcoin and Ethereum as drawn from the notes. Bitcoin's distinct aspect of longer transaction times and higher fees due to its decentralized nature is addressed. Simultaneously, it also underlines Ethereum's unique functionality of programmable smart contracts which makes it suited for advanced applications such as decentralized finance and non-fungible tokens. This answer not only distinguishes both cryptocurrencies but also gives prominence to their individual features, thus accomplishing the objective of emphasizing their uniqueness.

    Distractor Explanations: Choice A is incorrect because it fails to highlight the distinct features of both Bitcoin and Ethereum; while, instead, it emphasizes their common characteristics: their rising market values. **Choice C** is incorrect because it doesn't sufficiently highlight the unique characteristics of Bitcoin and Ethereum. Although it acknowledges that Bitcoin was the first decentralized cryptocurrency, it doesn't fully emphasize the individual unique features of each. It only partially covers Ethereum's smart contracts but lacks a detailed differentiation for Bitcoin. **Choice D** is incorrect as it only emphasizes one unique aspect of Bitcoin – its longer transaction times and higher fees due to its decentralized nature. While this information is accurate, it erroneously implies a comparison with Ethereum without specifying any unique features of the latter, thus failing to accomplish the objective of emphasizing the distinct features of both Bitcoin and Ethereum.

1. **Level:** Medium | **Domain:** CRAFT AND STRUCTURE
    Skill/Knowledge: Words in Context

    Key Explanation: Choice D is the best answer because the blank shows the cane toad's relationship to South America. **Choice D** means "native to" a specific place, so fits the context of saying that the toad came from South America but was "transported" or "moved" to Australia.

    Distractor Explanations: None of the other choices establishes the toad's relationship to South America. **Choice A** refers to an inborn or natural trait or characteristic, not a species. **Choice B** also refers to an inborn or natural trait or characteristic, not a species so it is incorrect. **Choice C** refers to an epidemic or wide–spread disease.

2. **Level:** Hard | **Domain:** CRAFT AND STRUCTURE
    Skill/Knowledge: Words in Context

    Key Explanation: Choice B is the correct option. "Demonstrated" usually refers to something that has been shown clearly. In this case, the fellowship is granted to those who have clearly shown their "exceptional capacity… in the arts."

    Distractor Explanations: Choice A is incorrect because "accomplish" refers to something that has been already achieved. However, capacity refers to the ability of a person (for example: "I do not have the capacity to work any harder"). Therefore, one cannot accomplish capacity in the sense that the text is implying. **Choices C** and **D** are incorrect because both options mean "giving up something." However, the fellowship would not be given to those who have given up exceptional capacity.

3. **Level:** Medium | **Domain:** CRAFT AND STRUCTURE
    Skill/Knowledge: Words in Context

    Key Explanation: Choice A is the correct option. Benefactor refers to someone who donates or supports one monetarily. Therefore, option A is the best choice because "patron" also refers to someone who offers monetary support.

    Distractor Explanations: All the other choices are incorrect because they do not refer to a person who supports others financially. The text mentions "first benefactor." **Choice B** refers to someone who establishes an institution, in this case, Harvard College. "First founder" is incorrect as there cannot be consecutive founders. **Choice C** is incorrect as an "antagonist" is an adversary and does not refer to someone who provides financial support. **Choice D** is incorrect because a "beneficiary" is someone who receives the benefit from a benefactor.

4. **Level:** Hard | **Domain:** CRAFT AND STRUCTURE
    Skill/Knowledge: Text Structure and Purpose

    Key Explanation: **Choice B** is the best answer as this sentence explains that it is Christmas the next day. The previous sentences show Della worried about money, but not why. This sentence illuminates the mystery and the reader begins to understand that she is trying to gather as much money as possible to purchase a Christmas present.

    Distractor Explanations: Choice A is incorrect because this sentence does not address that Della is frugal. The previous sentences might imply this, but this sentence shows a woman not concerned about money in order to be wise with it, but because she is going to spend it. **Choice C** is wrong there is no indication that Della despises Christmas. She is clearly frustrated that she does not have the money she would like to have for this gift-giving holiday, but not that she is frustrated with the holiday itself. **Choice D** is wrong because there is no indication of how she feels about this holiday positively either. Her feelings are negative and they are directed at her finances.

5. **Level:** Easy | **Domain:** CRAFT AND STRUCTURE
   Skill/Knowledge: Text Structure and Purpose

   Key Explanation: Choice C is the best answer because the result of the experiment is that "flames can ignite at extremely low temperatures." More specifically, the flames "can burn at 900 degrees in the International Space Station." That piece of information is not very helpful to the average reader, so the author gives a reference that the reader most likely knows, the temperature of something in a house on Earth. The reader can then see that the flame can burn at a third the temperature as one on Earth.

   Distractor Explanations: Choice A is incorrect because "motivation" is a "reason" or "goal." The goal is not a fact about gas stoves on Earth; the goal is described in the second sentence, "to gain valuable insight into the mechanisms of fire." **Choice B** is incorrect because "methodology" is the series of steps taken to perform an experiment. However, there is no indication of how the scientists lit flames in space. **Choice D** is incorrect because the underlined portion shows what happens on Earth, not in the experiments on the International Space Station.

6. **Level:** Hard | **Domain:** CRAFT AND STRUCTURE
   Skill/Knowledge: Text Structure and Purpose

   Key Explanation: Choice A is the best answer because the text "contrasts" or "shows the

difference" between two different things: the busy street below and the bright star above.

Distractor Explanations: Choice B is incorrect because the passage does not say that any actions are "futile" or "useless." The busy street image is hectic, but there is no claim that it has no point. **Choice C** is incorrect because there is no "problem" or "concern to be solved," and hence, there is also no solution or remedy in the text. **Choice D** is incorrect because while a star or street could be a metaphor, there is no hint about what they might represent in the text.

7. **Level:** Hard | **Domain:** INFORMATION AND IDEAS
   Skill/Knowledge: Central Ideas and Details

   Key Explanation: Choice D is the best answer because it accurately captures the main idea of the passage. The passage discusses the crucial role of the amygdala in processing emotions and emotional memories, its involvement in the limbic system, and its connection to the complex nature of human emotions and psychological disorders. The phrase "Studying the amygdala's function and connectivity with other brain regions provides valuable insights into the complex nature of human emotions and related psychological disorders" sums up the central idea of the passage.

   Distractor Explanations: Choice A is incorrect because it focuses solely on the regulation of emotions, behavior, and motivation, neglecting the other aspects mentioned in the passage such as processing emotional memories and the amygdala's connection to psychological disorders. **Choice B** is incorrect because it only highlights the consequences of amygdala dysfunction, without encompassing the broader discussion of the amygdala's role and significance. **Choice C**

is incorrect because it narrows down the main idea to the formation and storage of emotional memories, disregarding other key aspects discussed in the passage.

8. **Level:** Medium | **Domain:** INFORMATION AND IDEAS
   Skill/Knowledge: Central Ideas and Details

   Key Explanation: Choice D is the best answer because the passage says that Mann used personal interviews "to provide an insider's perspective." She was trying to get a clearer understanding of veganism from vegans themselves.

   Distractor Explanations: Choice A is incorrect because there is no evidence that Mann expected to find a "conflict" or "opposing views" between the interviews and scientific research. She was trying to blend the two to get a more rounded view of the topic as a whole. **Choice B** is incorrect because the health benefits were analyzed through scientific studies found in the literature review; Mann was not trying to "resolve a debate" so much as "combat stereotypes" by sharing different views. **Choice C** is incorrect because there is no evidence that "most" or "the largest percentage" of literature is "biased against" or "opposing" veganism.

9. **Level:** Medium | **Domain:** INFORMATION AND IDEAS
   Skill/Knowledge: Central Ideas and Details

   Key Explanation: Choice B is the best answer because the passage says he was "fortunate in that respect," meaning that he was lucky in becoming "a household name" or "really famous" because "fans celebrated his triumphs against the background of news from World War I and the

1918 influenza pandemic." In other words, fans liked his "triumphs" or "successes" as a contrast to the "grim" or "bad" times of a war and pandemic.

Distractor Explanations: Choice A is incorrect because the passage says that he started as a pitcher, but became famous when he was "an outfielder and powerful batter." Therefore, his fame was not because of his pitching. **Choices C and D** are incorrect because the passage only refers to the se events as the "background" of Ruth's "triumphs" or "successes." There is no discussion whether he participated in them or not.

10. **Level:** Hard | **Domain:** INFORMATION AND IDEAS
    Skill/Knowledge: Command of Evidence (Textual)

    Key Explanation: Choice A is correct. The study found that stress-induced cardiomyopathy impaired hearts that were then transplanted were able to quickly recover, suggesting that this dysfunction is only temporary. However, the finding that these hearts faced other cardiovascular issues 20 years later undermines the study's finding because this suggests the dysfunction is not temporary and can resurface.

    Distractor Explanations: Choice B is incorrect because this choice does not refute the fact that some impairment is temporary and the transplanted heart is able to function as normal. **Choice C** is incorrect because this choice does not refute the study's finding since it does not discuss underlying heart diseases like coronary artery disease. **Choice D** is incorrect because this choice does not refute the study's finding and it only suggests how recipients can promote good heart health.

11. **Level:** Hard | **Domain:** INFORMATION AND IDEAS

   Skill/Knowledge: Command of Evidence (Quantitative)

   Key Explanation: Choice C is the correct option. It accurately reflects the information in the text and graph by acknowledging that effective vaccines lead to a significant reduction in the likelihood of encountering a pandemic with a comparable fatality rate to COVID-19.

   Distractor Explanations: Choice A is incorrect because the graph clearly shows the significant difference in mortality rates if effective vaccines are administered early on in a pathogen outbreak similar to COVID-19. **Choice B** is incorrect because while it acknowledges some reduction, it might not accurately capture the substantial impact of vaccines described in the graph and text. **Choice D** is incorrect because it suggests that the mortality rate remains unchanged due to pathogen transformation. However, the text does not provide any information on the transformation of a new pathogen and how it might affect the mortality rate.

12. **Level:** Medium | **Domain:** INFORMATION AND IDEAS

   Skill/Knowledge: Command of Evidence (Quantitative)

   Key Explanation: Choice D is the correct option as it effectively complements the original text by using correct information about forest loss in temperate regions taken from the chart, thereby directly contrasting with the information about tropical regions provided in the sentence prior to the one to be completed.

   Distractor Explanations: Choice A is incorrect because it discusses the cause of tree loss in Europe due to logging for products like paper. However, it doesn't provide a direct comparison to the information presented about tropical regions and their primary causes of forest loss. **Choice B** is incorrect because it focuses on wildfires in Oceania and its smaller geographical area. The use of "In comparison" at the beginning of the sentence shows that the sentence must be a contrast to the previously provided information on clearing forests within the tropics. Choice B does not offer this comparison. **Choice C** is incorrect because it discusses the cause of forest loss in Africa due to shifting agriculture and does not offer a direct contrast with the tropical regions and their primary drivers of forest loss as stated in the previous sentence.

13. **Level:** Medium | **Domain:** INFORMATION AND IDEAS

   Skill/Knowledge: Inferences

   Key Explanation: Choice B is correct. Dr. Zeberg observed that Dupuytren's disease is rare in Africa and posited that the disease may be linked to Neanderthal DNA. The correct choice must present some sort of relationship between Neanderthal DNA, which is associated with the disease, to Africa. Since the disease is not commonly found in Africa, Africa must not have linkages to Neanderthal DNA. Therefore, B is the correct choice.

   Distractor Explanations: Choice A is incorrect because this choice does not present a relationship between Neanderthal DNA and Africa. **Choice C** is incorrect because this choice does not present a relationship between Neanderthal DNA and Africa. **Choice D** is incorrect because the text suggests that since Dupuytren's disease is not commonly found in Africa, Africa must not have linkages to Neanderthal DNA. This choice presents the opposite statement, so it is incorrect.

14. **Level:** Hard | **Domain:** INFORMATION AND IDEAS
Skill/Knowledge: Inferences

Key Explanation: Choice D is the best answer because the text is discussing the extreme temperatures on Mercury. The transition "in fact" is used to emphasize a point, and in this case, the blank portion needs to emphasize the previous idea of nights being cold. **Choice D** effectively does that by showing that despite the hot days, there may still be ice on the planet.

Distractor Explanations: All of the other choices can be eliminated because they offer a point that is off the topic of temperature and cold. **Choice A** refers to the orbit, **Choice B** to the speed, and **Choice C** to the size and appearance

15. **Level:** Medium | **Domain:** STANDARD ENGLISH CONVENTIONS
Skill/Knowledge: Form, Structure, and Sense

Key Explanation: Choice C is the correct answer. The convention being tested is plurals and possessives. In this context, "European Union's firefighting airplanes" is the correct possessive form to indicate that the firefighting aircraft belong to the European Union. The apostrophe is correctly placed before "s" to show possession by the European Union.

Distractor Explanations: Choice A is incorrect because it lacks the possessive apostrophe and uses "Unions" instead of "Union's." The apostrophe after "airplanes" is also incorrect and unnecessary. **Choice B** is incorrect because "European Union's

firefighting airplane's" has a redundant possessive apostrophe after "airplane." **Choice D** is incorrect because it lacks the possessive apostrophe and uses "Unions" instead of "Union's," and also has a redundant possessive apostrophe after "airplane."

16. **Level:** Medium | **Domain:** STANDARD ENGLISH CONVENTIONS
Skill/Knowledge: Form, Structure, and Sense

Key Explanation: Choice D is the best answer. "A classic image of colonial cooperation" is a modifier that needs to describe the noun that follows it. **Choice D** accurately shows that the image of cooperation refers to quilting bees.

Distractor Explanations: All of the other choices can be eliminated because the modifier "A classic image of colonial cooperation" refers to something illogical. In **Choice A**, it refers to a diary, but a diary is a personal account rather than a classic example of cooperating with other people. **Choices B** and **C** are incorrect because the subject is Martha Ballard, who is an individual person rather than an image of cooperation.

17. **Level:** Medium | **Domain:** STANDARD ENGLISH CONVENTIONS
Skill/Knowledge: Form, Structure, and Sense

Key Explanation: Choice D is the correct answer. The convention being tested is subject-verb agreement. Choice D is correct because the subject "a lifetime of exploration" is singular, and the singular verb "awaits" is the right choice. The sentence is discussing a general truth, and the present tense "awaits" fits well in this context.

Distractor Explanations: Choice A is incorrect because it uses the plural form "await," which is not suitable here. The subject "a lifetime of exploration" is singular, so the correct verb form should also be singular, which is "awaits." **Choice B** is incorrect because it uses the present perfect tense "has awaited," which doesn't fit well in this context. The present perfect tense is typically used to connect past actions to the present. The simple present tense is more appropriate for discussing a general truth as is the case in the sentence to be completed. **Choice C** is incorrect because it uses the present continuous tense which implies an ongoing action and not a general truth about what awaits those who seek the less-trodden path.

18. **Level:** Medium | **Domain:** STANDARD ENGLISH CONVENTIONS
Skill/Knowledge: Form, Structure, and Sense

Key Explanation: Choice C is the best answer. An s followed by an apostrophe is the correct way to indicate a plural possessive. It correctly shows that the efforts were made by more than one volunteer.

Distractor Explanations: Choice A is incorrect because "volunteers" is a plural noun that does not show any possession. **Choices A** and **D** are incorrect because "efforts" does not possess anything in the sentence, so should not have an apostrophe. **Choice B** is incorrect because an apostrophe followed by an s is the way to show possession of a singular thing, but the efforts span 125 years, so were done by more than one volunteer.

19. **Level:** Medium | **Domain:** STANDARD ENGLISH CONVENTIONS
Skill/Knowledge: Boundaries

Key Explanation: Choice A is the best answer. "Sacrificed XX for YY" is a standard idiom that refers to doing something at the expense of something else. No punctuation is needed.

Distractor Explanations: Choice B is incorrect because "accuracy" is the object of "sacrificed;" "for eloquence" is the reason that accuracy was given up. However, dashes are used to indicate additional information that is not part of the main clause, so they erroneously divide the object from its verb. **Choice C** is incorrect because a colon should not divide essential parts of the sentence from the main clause. In this case, the portion after the colon is necessary for correct understanding of what Longfellow did. **Choice D** is incorrect because "accuracy" is the object of "sacrificed;" "for eloquence" is the reason that accuracy was given up. However, parentheses are used to indicate additional information that is not part of the main clause, so they erroneously divide the object from its verb.

20. **Level:** Easy | **Domain:** STANDARD ENGLISH CONVENTIONS
Skill/Knowledge: Boundaries

Key Explanation: Choice D is the best answer. The ideas in the preceding and following portions are complete clauses that can stand on their own as sentences, so should be divided by a period and a capital letter "t".

Distractor Explanations: Choice A is incorrect because a semicolon should be preceded and followed by a complete clause that can stand on its own, but "and" subordinates the following portion. The second part cannot stand on its own. **Choice B** is incorrect because "because" subordinates the following portion, which cannot stand on its own as a sentence. **Choice C** is incorrect because it is a comma splice between two clauses that can each stand on their own.

21. **Level:** Medium | **Domain:** STANDARD
ENGLISH CONVENTIONS
Skill/Knowledge: Boundaries

Key Explanation: Choice B is the best answer.
The portions before and after the punctuation
are both independent clauses, meaning that they
could both stand on their own as sentences.
Therefore, they should be joined by a semicolon or
a period, which is not a given choice.

Distractor Explanations: Choice A is incorrect
because it creates a comma splice. **Choice C** is
incorrect because a colon is used to add more
information clarifying the clause before the
colon. In this case, the preceding portion is
about low levels of inflation, but the following
portion introduces a different topic, high levels
of inflation. **Choice D** is incorrect because it is a
run–on.

22. **Level:** Easy | **Domain:** EXPRESSION OF IDEAS
Skill/Knowledge: Transitions

Key Explanation: Choice B is the best answer.
The first sentence explains that Tingatinga's
career was very short. The second sentence offers
a contrast: he was one of the most important
painters in modern Africa. **Choice B** is used to
show that despite one thing happening, another
is true. It therefore fits the context of saying that
despite the short career, Tingatinga made a great
impact.

Distractor Explanations: None of the other
choices establishes a contrast between the
preceding and following ideas. **Choice A** is used
to introduce a logical result of the previous claim,
but it is more logical to expect little impact from
a short career. **Choices C** and **D** are both used to
add more detail to clarify the same topic rather
than change tone to something unexpected.

23. **Level:** Easy | **Domain:** EXPRESSION OF IDEAS
Skill/Knowledge: Transitions

Key Explanation: Choice D is the best answer.
The passage describes two types of search and
rescue dog, and the blank is the point at which
the topic changes from one type to the other, from
air scent to tracking. **Choice D** is used to show
that the following method is an "alternate" or
"different" case, so it fits the context of introducing
a second method.

Distractor Explanations: None of the other
choices shows that the following information
is the second of two possible methods. **Choice
A** is used to add another point to continue an
argument. **Choice B** is used to add specific detail
clarifying a general statement. **Choice C** is used
to add a qualification or restriction to a previous
claim.

24. **Level:** Easy | **Domain:** EXPRESSION OF IDEAS
Skill/Knowledge: Transitions

Key Explanation: Choice D is the best answer.
The previous sentence describes the price of
"monthly expenses" as being over $35. The
following sentence describes the "upkeep" or
"ongoing expenses," which are the same thing,
but uses a different way to express the money: it
discusses what alternate things a person could buy,
lattes. **Choice D** is used to rephrase or introduce
an idea in different words, so effectively shows that
the following is a different way of looking at the
figures in the previous sentence.

Distractor Explanations: Choice A is incorrect
because it is used to show a contrasting or
opposite idea, not rephrase the same point.
Choice B is used to show that something happens
in spite of something else, which does not fit the

discussion of equivalent concepts. **Choice C** is used to add more to the same argument, so in the context, would be used to add a new type of expense in caring for tropical fish.

25. **Level:** Hard | **Domain:** EXPRESSION OF IDEAS
Skill/Knowledge: Rhetorical Synthesis

Key Explanation: Choice B is correct because it effectively conveys the distinct operational strategies of both companies. By juxtaposing Company A's commitment to extensive research and development with Company B's rapid design and iteration model, this choice effectively illustrates their different approaches to attaining industry prominence.

Distractor Explanations: Choice A is incorrect because it primarily explores the customer bases of both companies without providing insight into their operational strategies or differences between them. While this could provide an interesting contrast regarding clientele, it does not help meet the student's goal of emphasizing strategic differences. **Choice C** is incorrect because it focuses solely on Company B's operational strategy, highlighting its rapid design and iteration model that led to its quick rise in the electronics industry. However, it doesn't address or compare this with Company A's operational strategy. Therefore, it does not successfully underscore the distinct strategies between the two companies. The focus is only on the achievement of one company without a comparison to the other, thereby falling short of the student's aim of emphasizing the strategic differences between the companies. **Choice D** is incorrect because it does not effectively highlight the contrasting operational strategies of the two companies. While it refers to Company A's extensive history and Company B's rapid rise, it fails to clearly compare their differing

methodologies. Specifically, it does not juxtapose Company A's commitment to comprehensive research and development with Company B's emphasis on rapid design and iteration, thereby not fully meeting the student's objective of underscoring the distinct operational strategies of these companies.

26. **Level:** Medium | **Domain:** EXPRESSION OF IDEAS
Skill/Knowledge: Rhetorical Synthesis

Key Explanation: Choice A is correct because it effectively balances the unique attributes of both digital and traditional businesses: digital businesses' broad customer access and efficiency with potential cyber risks; while traditional businesses' geographical restrictions but personal interactions.

Distractor Explanations: Choice B is incorrect because it doesn't address the full range of contrasts between digital and traditional businesses. It overlooks the advantages and challenges of both types of business beyond the investment issue. **Choice C** is incorrect because although it successfully draws some comparison between digital and traditional businesses, it doesn't adequately convey its purpose - to contrast the two in all possible aspects. By not including the geographical limitations of traditional businesses or the customer relationships they offer through direct transactions, it fails to fully capture the student's desire to emphasize the differences. **Choice D** is incorrect because it only addresses differences in geographical reach and cyber threats and does not take into account other factors such as efficiency and type of interactions that each business type provides.

27. **Level:** Hard | **Domain:** EXPRESSION OF IDEAS
Skill/Knowledge: Rhetorical Synthesis

Key Explanation: Choice A is correct because it effectively conveys the revolutionary nature of the Internet as a communication medium, drawing parallels between it and historical methods such as telegram and Pony Express to emphasize its global and instantaneous reach.

Distractor Explanations: Choice B is incorrect because it simply states that previous communication methods were not as fast as the Internet. However, it fails to highlight the revolutionary aspect of the Internet in transforming communication in a more comprehensive manner than just speed, which is the aim stated in the question stem. Instead, it focuses narrowly on the speed attribute, omitting the global reach and other transformative effects the Internet has had on communication. **Choice C** is incorrect because although this answer choice compares the Internet to Gutenberg's printing press, it does not state which of the two was more revolutionary; rather it highlights their shared significance as turning points. **Choice D** is incorrect because although it mentions the global reach and speed of the Internet, it fails to highlight its revolutionary nature. Instead, this choice focuses on its limitations relative to Pony Express and Telegram delivery systems instead of emphasizing how revolutionary the internet's attributes are.

1. **Level:** Medium | **Domain:** GEOMETRY AND TRIGONOMETRY
    Skill/Knowledge: Circles | **Testing point:** Working with transformations and the equation of a circle

    Key Explanation: Choice C is correct. The equation of a circle is given by $(x - h)^2 + (y - k)^2 = r^2$, where (h, k) is the center of the circle. In the initial equation, the center of the circle is $(3, -6)$ and in the transformed equation, the center of the circle is $(2, -4)$. To compare the equations, the equation of the second circle must be put into standard form by completing the square as shown below.
    $(x - 2)^2 + y^2 + 8y = 33$
    $(x - 2)^2 + y^2 + 8y + 16 = 33 + 16$
    $(x - 2)^2 + (y + 4)^2 = 33 + 16$
    $(x - 2)^2 + (y + 4)^2 = 49$.
    This yields $(2, -4)$ as the center of the transformed circle.
    Therefore, the transformation will be 1 to the left as the x coordinate moves from 3 to 2 and 2 up as the y coordinate moves from -6 to -4.

    Distractor Explanations: Choice A is incorrect because the x coordinate moves to the left rather than to the right. This answer may have been incorrectly selected if the student misinterpreted the standard form for the equation of a circle and thought that the x-coordinates of the centers of the circles are -3 and -2. **Choice B is incorrect.** This answer may have been incorrectly selected if the student assumed that the centers were (-3, 6) and (-2 and 4) through misinterpretation of the standard form of the equation of a circle and/or through completing the square incorrectly. **Choice D is incorrect** and may have been incorrectly selected by not completing the square correctly or incorrectly interpreting the center values in the standard equation for a circle

2. **Level:** Hard | **Domain:** ADVANCED MATH
    Skill/Knowledge: Nonlinear equations in one variable and systems of equations in two variables
    Testing point: How many solutions does an equation have

    Key Explanation: Choice B is correct. To solve this equation, first, use the foiling method to expand the left side of the equation and use the distributive property to expand the right side of the equation. Then combine like terms and solve the resulting linear equation as follows:
    $(x - 1)(x + 2) = x(x - 3)$
    $x^2 - x + 2x - 2 = x^2 - 3x$
    $x - 2 = -3x$
    $4x = 2$
    $x = \dfrac{1}{2}$ or 0.5
    This shows that the equation has only one solution.

    Distractor Explanations: Choice A is incorrect. This answer may be arrived at due to math miscalculations or conceptual errors. **Choice C** is incorrect. This answer may be arrived at due to math miscalculations or conceptual errors **Choice D is incorrect.** This answer may be arrived at if the student chooses to simply equate each parentheses to zero and finds 1, -2, 0, and 3 as the solutions.

3. **Level:** Easy | **Domain:** Algebra
    Skill/Knowledge: Linear equations in one variable
    Testing point: Solving equations of one variable

    Key Explanation: For a system of equations to have an infinite number of solutions, it means that the equations are identical and have the same slope and y-intercept.
    The first step is to use the distributive property to multiply out the terms on the left side of the equation, resulting in:

$3x - 18 - 2x - 4 = px - 5x - 22a$

Combining like terms yields

$x - 22 = px - 5x - 22$

Adding $5x$ to both sides yields:

$6x - 22 = px - 22$

Therefore p is equal to 6.

4. **Level:** Easy | **Domain:** ADVANCED MATH
   Skill/Knowledge: Nonlinear functions | **Testing point:** Determining the meaning in context with exponential equations

   Key Explanation: Choice C is correct. The format for an exponential growth equation is:

   Initial value $\times$ (1+growth rate as a decimal)^x
   The growth factor of the weeds on the farm is defined by 1 + the growth rate r.

   Therefore,

   $$1 + r = 1.995$$
   $$r = 0.995 \text{ or } 99.5\%,$$

   which would then make choice C correct.

   Distractor Explanations: Choice A is incorrect. The number of weeds on the farm, at the beginning, known as the initial value, was 1,300. **Choice B** is incorrect. This choice implies that the model is linear. However, the model is exponential. **Choice D** is incorrect because it implies that the model is linear and that 1,300 is the increase in weeds every x weeks, however, it is the initial number of weeds on the farm.

5. **Level:** Easy | **Domain:** ADVANCED MATH
   Skill/Knowledge: Equivalent expressions | **Testing point:** Binomial expressions

   Key Explanation: Choice A is correct. To solve this problem, first, use the exponent rules to combine both binomials in parentheses with one exponent. $((x - 2)(x + 2))^2$ using the identity

$(a + b)(a - b) = a^2 - b^2$, $(x - 2)(x + 2)$ can be simplified to $(x^2 - 4)$ and that would simplify to $(x^2 - 4)^2$.

Using the identity $(a - b)^2 = a^2 - 2ab + b^2$ the problem can be simplified to $(x^2 - 4)^2 = x^4 - 8x^2 + 16$, making **Choice A** the right option.

Distractor Explanations: Choice B is incorrect. This answer choice may be arrived at due to a common exponent conceptual error. **Choice C** is incorrect as this answer choice may be due to a miscalculation of $8x$ as positive. **Choice D** is incorrect due to both exponent conceptual and miscalculation errors.

6. **Level:** Easy | **Domain:** PROBLEM-SOLVING AND DATA ANALYSIS
   Skill/Knowledge: One-variable data: distributions and measures of center and spread | **Testing point:** Finding mean and median of grouped data

   Key Explanation: To calculate the median of the 27 foods, look for the middle number frequency wise of the data. If there are 27 items then the middle number is the 14th food which, based on the frequency table, has 180 calories. To find the mean number of calories, use the mean formula which can be found by taking the total number of calories divided by the number of food items. To find the total number of calories multiply each calorie content number in the table by its frequency, as follows:

   $(100 \times 6) + (180 \times 9) + (280 \times 11) + (350 \times 1) =$

   $\dfrac{5,650}{27} = 209.3$.

   Therefore the difference of the mean and median of the calorie content of the 27 foods would be $209.3 - 180 = 29.3$.

7. **Level:** Medium | **Domain:** ADVANCED MATH
Skill/Knowledge: Nonlinear functions | **Testing point:** Finding the *x–intercept*

Key Explanation: Choice C is correct. The *x–intercept* is found when *y* = 0, therefore:

$$x = 3^{0-1} + \frac{5}{3}$$

$$x = 3^{-1} + \frac{5}{3}$$

$$x = \frac{1}{3} + \frac{5}{3}, \text{ which makes } x = 2 \text{ making } \textbf{Choice C}$$

correct.

Distractor Explanations: Choice A is incorrect. The student might incorrectly think this equation is linear and therefore the $\frac{5}{3}$ represents the *y–intercept*. However, this is not the case. Also, the question has asked for the *x–intercept*. **Choice B** is incorrect and would be due to a conceptual or miscalculation error. **Choice D** is incorrect and would be due to a conceptual or miscalculation error.

8. **Level:** Hard | **Domain:** PROBLEM–SOLVING AND DATA ANALYSIS
Skill/Knowledge: Inferences from sample statistics and margin of error |
Testing point: Generalization of data from surveys

Key Explanation: Choice D is correct. 100% – 80% (who think statistics is the hardest subject) = 20%(who chose Physics as the hardest subject. Since only 11th graders in the math summer class were surveyed the data can only be generalized to the 11th graders in the math summer class. This then makes option D, the best option.

Distractor Explanations: Choice A is incorrect. It generalizes the survey to all students in the summer math class. **Choice B** is incorrect. It contradicts the given information.**Choice C** is incorrect. It contradicts the given information.

9. **Level:** Easy | **Domain:** ADVANCED MATH
Skill/Knowledge: Equivalent expressions |
Testing point: Manipulating quadratic equations

Key Explanation: First, expand out $(x + 3)^2$ to $(x + 3) \times (x + 3)$. Using the foiling method, multiply out the two binomial terms to get the following:
$-3 (x^2 + 6x + 9) + 9 + x = ax^2 + bx + c$
Use the distributive property to expand out the left side of the equation and then combine like terms to get the following: $-3x^2 - 17x - 18 = ax^2 + bx + c$
Therefore $a = -3$, $b = -17$ and $c = -18$; $a + b + c = (-3) + (-17) + (-18) = -38$

10. **Level:** Hard | **Domain:** ADVANCED MATH
Skill/Knowledge: Nonlinear functions | **Testing point:** Vertex form of a quadratic equation

Key Explanation: Choice C is correct. The maximum point of a quadratic equation is the vertex. Therefore, (3, 2) is the vertex of the parabola. The vertex form of a parabola is given by $a(x - h)^2 + k$, where (h, k) is the vertex of the parabola. This equation can be used to find the equation for a parabola. Therefore, $y = a(x - 3)^2 + 2$. The quadratic equation passes through the point (2, 0). Plugging this point into the vertex form equation for *x* and *y* yields
$$0 = a(2 - 3)^2 + 2$$
$$0 = a + 2$$
$$a = -2$$
$$y = -2(x - 3)^2 + 2$$
If *x* is a solution to the quadratic equation, *y* must

equal zero. Plugging in the answer choices into the vertex form equation is the fastest method. **Choice C** is the only answer that works. $0 = -2(4 - 3)2 + 2$ and thus $0 = 0$ results.

Distractor Explanations: Choice A is incorrect. This is the *y-intercept* of the equation. **Choice B** is incorrect. This is the value of a in the vertex form of a parabola equation. However, this option can also be a miscalculation. **Choice D** is incorrect. This can be the result of a conceptual or miscalculation error.

11. **Level:** Easy | **Domain:** ALGEBRA
    Skill/Knowledge: Linear functions | **Testing point:** Finding the slope of a line given two points

    Key Explanation: Choice C is correct. To find the slope of a line, the formula $\frac{y_2 - y_1}{x_2 - x_1}$ is used. Plugging in the x and y coordinates of the two given points $(0, 0)$ and $(3, 5)$ into the slope equation yields $\frac{5-0}{3-0} = \frac{5}{3}$

    Distractor Explanations: Choice A is incorrect and was determined by finding the change in x over the change in y instead of the change in y over the change in x. **Choice B** is incorrect and is the result of either miscalculation or conceptual errors. **Choice C** is incorrect and is the result of either miscalculation or conceptual errors.

12. **Level:** Hard | **Domain:** ADVANCED MATH
    Skill/Knowledge: Nonlinear equations in one variable and systems of equations in two variables
    Testing point: System of linear and quadratic inequalities

Key Explanation: Choice D is correct. To solve this problem, graph the system.

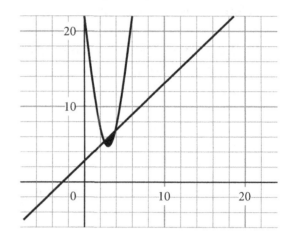

The solution for the system will be the region that is shaded. The minimum value of b can then be found by finding the vertex of the parabola $y = 2(x - 3)^2 + 5$. The vertex form of a parabola is given by $y = a(x - h)^2 + k$. Therefore, the vertex of the parabola is $(3, 5)$. The minimum y value of a concave up parabola can be found at the vertex. Therefore, the minimum value of b is 5.

Distractor Explanations: Choice A is incorrect. This answer would be the value of a and b if the vertex was incorrectly found to be $(-3, -5)$ **Choice B** is incorrect. This answer would be the value of a and b if the vertex was incorrectly found to be $(-3, -5)$. **Choice C** is incorrect. It is the minimum value of the system of inequalities.

13. **Level:** Easy | **Domain:** GEOMETRY AND TRIGONOMETRY
    Skill/Knowledge: Area and volume | **Testing point:** Volume of a sphere

    Key Explanation: The volume of a sphere is found using the formula $\frac{4}{3}\pi r^3 = \frac{4}{3}(3)^3\pi = 36\pi$

14. **Level:** Easy | **Domain:** ALGEBRA
Skill/Knowledge: Systems of two linear equations in two variables | **Testing point:** Systems of equations with no solution

Key Explanation: Choice A is correct. For a system of equations to have no solution, the system represents parallel lines with the same slope but different *y*–intercepts.

$3x - 4y = 8$

$px + 8y = -6$

To easily compare the slopes, the equations should be put into the slope–intercept form of a line $y = mx + b$ where m is the slope. By mathematical manipulation, doing this yields the equations:

$$y = \frac{3}{4}x - 2$$

$$y = \frac{-p}{8}x - \frac{3}{4}$$

Since parallel lines have the same slope, the equation $\frac{-p}{8} = \frac{3}{4}$ can be solved by *p*. Multiplying both sides of the equation by –8 yields $p = -6$, **Choice A**.

Distractor Explanations: Choice B is incorrect. It would make the system of equations incorrectly have 1 solution. These answer choices are determined by mathematical miscalculations or conceptual errors. **Choice C** is incorrect. It would make the system of equations incorrectly have 1 solution. The answer choices are determined by mathematical miscalculations or conceptual errors. **Choice D** is incorrect. It would make the system of equations incorrectly have 1 solution. This answer choices are determined by mathematical miscalculations or conceptual errors

15. **Level:** Easy | **Domain:** GEOMETRY AND TRIGONOMETRY
Skill/Knowledge: Circles | **Testing point:** Equation of a circle

Key Explanation: Choice D is correct. To find the center of the circle, we have to write the equation of the circle in its standard form $(x - h)^2 + (y - k)^2 = r^2$. This is done by completing the square for the *x*'s and the *y*'s in the equation.

$x^2 + 6x + 9 + y^2 - 6y + 9 = 63 + 9 + 9$

$(x + 3)^2 + (y - 3)^2 = 81$

This then gives the center of the circle as $(-3, 3)$.

Distractor Explanations: Choice A is incorrect. This is the negative of the center of the equation of the circle. **Choice B** is incorrect. It can be determined by incorrectly picking the coefficients of *x* and *y* without writing the equation in standard form. **Choice C** is incorrect. It can be determined by incorrectly picking the coefficients of *x* and *y* without writing the equation in standard form.

16. **Level:** Hard | **Domain:** ADVANCED MATH
Skill/Knowledge: Nonlinear equations in one variable and systems of equations in two variables
Testing point: Solving quadratic equations using the quadratic formula

Key Explanation: This quadratic equation can be solved using the quadratic formula

$$x = \frac{-b \pm \sqrt{b^2 - 4ac}}{2a}$$, where $a = 3$ and $b = -6$ and

$c = -11$.

Therefore:

$$x = \frac{-(-6) \pm \sqrt{(-6)^2 - 4(3)(-11)}}{2(3)}$$

$$x = \frac{6 \pm \sqrt{36 + 132}}{6}$$

$$x = \frac{6 \pm \sqrt{168}}{6}$$

$$x = \frac{6 \pm \sqrt{42\sqrt{4}}}{6}$$

$$x = \frac{6 \pm 2\sqrt{42}}{6}$$

$$x = \frac{3 \pm \sqrt{42}}{3}$$

Therefore $g = 42$.

17. **Level:** Easy | **Domain:** ALGEBRA
Skill/Knowledge: Linear inequalities in one or two variables | **Testing point:** Solving linear inequalities

Key Explanation: Choice D is correct. To solve the inequality, add x to both sides of the inequality.
$-2x + x \geq -4 - x + x$
$-x \geq -4$, Next, divide both sides of the equation by -1 which flips the inequality sign.
Only 5 is not less than 4.

Distractor Explanations: Choice A is incorrect as $2 \leq 4$ and is therefore also a solution to the above inequality. **Choice B** is incorrect as it is also a solution to the inequality $3 \leq$. **Choice C** is incorrect as it is a solution to the inequality $-4 = -4$.

18. **Level:** Easy | **Domain:** ADVANCED MATH
Skill/Knowledge: Nonlinear equations in one variable and systems of equations in two variables
Testing point: Solving square root equations

Key Explanation: Choice B is correct. The problem can be solved in 2 ways. The easiest and quickest way is to just substitute the answer choices and test to see which answer makes the equation true.

Substitute **Choice A**.

$\sqrt{2(2) + 5} = 2 - 5$

$\sqrt{9} = -3$,

This isn't true. Substitute **Choice B**.

$\sqrt{2(10) + 5} = 10 - 5$

$\sqrt{20 + 5} = 10 - 5$

$\sqrt{25} = 5$

This makes **Choice B** the only right option.

Distractor Explanations: Choice A is incorrect mathematically as shown above. **Choice C** is incorrect as it incorrectly states that 2 is one of the solutions. **Choice D** is incorrect. It can be due to a miscalculation error.

19. **Level:** Hard | **Domain:** ALGEBRA
Skill/Knowledge: Systems of two linear equations in two variables | **Testing point:** Solving simultaneous equations

Key Explanation: Cross multiplying $\frac{5}{x} = \frac{2}{y}$ yields

$5y = 2x$

The next step is to get the two terms on the left side of the second equation of the same common denominator of xy as follows:

$$\frac{4}{x} \times \left(\frac{y}{y}\right) - \frac{2}{y} \times \left(\frac{x}{x}\right) = \frac{4y - 2x}{xy} = -\frac{1}{5}$$

Cross multiplying the condensed second equation yields
$5(4y - 2x) = -xy = 20y - 10x = xy$
Using the first equation, $5y = 2x$, multiply each side by 4, resulting in $20y = 8x$
Substituting $8x$ for $20y$ in the second equation yields
$8x - 10x = xy$ or $-2x = xy$
Dividing both sides of the equation by x yields
$y = -2$

Substituting this value for y in the first equation yields

$5(-2) = 2x$

$-10 = 2x$

$x = -5$

Therefore, $xy = (-2)(-5) = 10$

20. **Level:** Easy | **Domain:** ADVANCED MATH
Skill/Knowledge: Equivalent expressions | **Testing point:** Remainder theorem

Key Explanation: Choice D is correct. A is the remainder when the function $3x^2 + 7x + 9$ is divided by $x - 2$. The remainder can be found when $f(2)$ is calculated. Because $-2 = 0$ yields $x = 2$ as a solution, it can be plugged into the given quadratic function as follows to find A:
$3(2)^2 + 7(2) + 9 = 12 + 14 + 9 = 35$.

Distractor Explanations: Choice A is incorrect, This is the answer incorrectly found through a conceptual or miscalculation error. **Choice B** is incorrect. This is the answer incorrectly found by plugging in -2 instead of 2 into the quadratic equation. **Choice C** is incorrect. This is the answer incorrectly found by adding coefficients together $(3 + 7 + 9)$ of the quadratic equation.

21. **Level:** Easy | **Domain:** PROBLEM-SOLVING AND DATA ANALYSIS
Skill/Knowledge: Inference from sample statistics and margin of error | **Testing point:** Margin of error

Key Explanation: Choice D is correct. Given that the sample mean mass is 67.9 *kgs*, the actual mean mass of the penguins in the zoo would lie between 67.9 *kgs* plus or minus 4.5 *kgs*, or 63.4 *kgs* and 72.*kgs*. This then makes **Choice D** correct.

Distractor Explanations: Choice A is incorrect as the mass of the penguins in the park cannot be found from the data available.
Choice B is incorrect as the mean mass does not state that the mass of all the penguins is 67.9 kgs.
Choice C is incorrect. Nothing can be concluded about the median mass of the penguins in the zoo.

22. **Level:** Hard | **Domain:** ALGEBRA
Skill/Knowledge: Linear equations in two variables | **Testing point:** Number of solutions in a linear system of two variables

Key Explanation: Choice D is correct. The first step is to use the distributive property to multiply out the terms on the left side of the equation as follows:
$3x - 9 + 2x + 2y = 5x + 2y - 9$
Combining like terms on the left side of the equation yields
$5x + 2y - 9 = 5x + 2y - 9$
Since the equations on the left and the right are the same, they represent the same line and thus have infinitely many solutions.

Distractor Explanations: Choice A is incorrect. To have zero solutions the equations would need to be parallel lines and thus have the same slope and different y-intercepts. That would mean that the coefficients of x and y will be equal however the constants will not. This is not the case in this problem. **Choice B** is incorrect. That would mean there would be one (x, y) solution to the system above. That is not the case as they represent the same line. **Choice C** is incorrect. Linear equations with two variables do not have 2 solutions.

1. **Level:** Medium | **Domain:** ADVANCED MATH
    Skill/Knowledge: Equivalent expressions | **Testing point:** Foiling out binomials and combining like terms

    Key Explanation: Choice D is correct. To solve the question, first, distribute out the two binomial expressions. The next step is to combine like terms and put the final expression in standard form.
    $3(x^2 + 10x + 25) - 2(x^2 - 10x + 25) + 2x$
    $3x^2 + 30x + 75 - 2x^2 + 20x - 50 + 2x$
    $x^2 + 52x + 25$

    Distractor Explanations: Choice A is incorrect. This answer can be arrived at if the foiling expansion is done incorrectly. **Choice B is incorrect.** This answer can be arrived at if a math miscalculation is done after the foiling out expansion is completed. **Choice C is incorrect.** This answers can be arrived at if the foiling expansion is done incorrectly.

2. **Level:** Medium | **Domain:** ADVANCED MATH
    Skill/Knowledge: Equivalent expressions | **Testing point:** Finding the least common denominator with binomial terms and combining

    Key Explanation: Choice A is correct. To solve this problem, the fractions need a common denominator to be added. The least common denominator is $(x - 2)(5 - x)$, which multiplies out to a denominator of $-x^2 + 7x - 10$. To get both terms of this expression over the same denominator, the numerator and denominator of the first term each must be multiplied by $(5 - x)$ and the numerator and denominator of the second term each must be multiplied by $(x - 2)$. Since the two terms are now over the same denominator, the numerators can be added as follows:
    $$\frac{5 - x + 2x(x - 2)}{(x - 2)(5 - x)},$$

    Using the foiling and distributive operations to multiply out and combine like terms, the final answer is: $\dfrac{2x^2 - 5x + 5}{-x^2 + 7x - 10}$.

    Distractor Explanations: Choice B is incorrect. This answer can be arrived at wrongly by adding the two fractions directly, which is a common conceptual error. **Choice C is incorrect.** This answer can be arrived at wrongly by adding the two fractions directly, which is a common conceptual error. **Choice D is incorrect.** This answer may be arrived at by finding the common multiple for the denominator and then just adding the original numerators directly without multiplying them by the binomials needed to get the common multiple for the denominator.

3. **Level:** Easy | **Domain:** ALGEBRA
    Skill/Knowledge: Systems of two linear equations in two variables | **Testing point:** Solving simultaneous equations

    Key Explanation: Solve for y by using the distributing property and the substitution method as follows:
    $3x - 6 + 5(-2(x - 5)) = 2$
    $3x - 6 - 10(x - 5) = 2$
    $3x - 6 - 10x + 50 = 2$
    $-7x + 44 = 2$
    $-7x = -42$
    $x = 6$
    Substitute $x = 6$ into the second equation to find y.
    $y = -2(6 - 5)$
    $y = -2$

4. **Level:** Easy | **Domain:** PROBLEM-SOLVING AND DATA ANALYSIS
    Skill/Knowledge: Two-variable data: models and scatterplots | **Testing point:** Line of best fit

Key Explanation: Choice A is correct. This question can be solved in several ways. The equation of the line of best fit can be determined by finding the slope and *y-intercept* from the graph directly and plugging those values into the *slope-intercept* equation of a line, $y = mx + b$. The elimination method can also be used. The slope and *y-intercept* of the line of best fit are both positive, which eliminates **Choices C** and **D**. The slope of the line of best fit is not steep so that eliminates **Choice B**.

Distractor Explanations: Choice B is incorrect because the slope of the line of best fit is $\dfrac{1}{4}$ and not 4. **Choice C** is incorrect because the *y-intercept* of the line of best fit is positive, not negative. **Choice D** is incorrect because the line of best fit has a positive slope and not a negative one.

5. **Level:** Medium | **Domain:** GEOMETRY AND TRIGONOMETRY
   Skill/Knowledge: Circles | **Testing point:** Arc length of a circle

   Key Explanation: Choice C is correct. The arc length of the circle can be found by using the equation arc length = $r\theta$, where r is the radius of the circle and theta is the degree in radians of the central angle that subtends the arc length desired.

   Therefore the arc length would be $6\left(\dfrac{7}{12}\pi\right) = \dfrac{7}{2}\pi$. The arc length can also be found by converting radians to degrees using the formula $\dfrac{\theta}{360}2\pi r$. This would still give the answer as $\dfrac{7}{2}\pi$ cm.

Distractor Explanations: Choice A is incorrect. This is the circumference of the whole circle. **Choice B** is incorrect. This is the area of the whole circle. **Choice D** is incorrect. This is the area of the sector that can be found using the formula $\dfrac{1}{2}r^2\theta$, where θ is the measure of the central degree in radians.

6. **Level:** Easy | **Domain:** ADVANCED MATH
   Skill/Knowledge: Nonlinear equations in one variable and systems of equations in two variables
   Testing point: Finding the sum of the roots in a quadratic equation

   Key Explanation: Choice A is correct. The first step is to simplify the equation by dividing out 2, the greatest common factor out of the equation, leaving $x^2 + 3x + 2 = 0$. The equation is in simplified form. The sum of the roots of a quadratic equation is equal to $\dfrac{-b}{a}$, where $a = 1$, $b = 3$.

   Therefore, the sum of the roots of the quadratic equation above would be $\dfrac{-3}{1} = -3$.

   Distractor Explanations: Choice B is incorrect and is the negative of the product of the roots and can be arrived at by using $\dfrac{-c}{a}$. **Choice C** is incorrect. This is the product of the roots given by $\dfrac{c}{a}$. **Choice D** is incorrect and is the negative value of the sum of roots i.e $\dfrac{b}{a}$.

7. **Level:** Medium | **Domain:** GEOMETRY AND TRIGONOMETRY
   Skill/Knowledge: Lines, angles, and triangles
   Testing point: Finding the sum of angles in a polygon and converting degrees to radians

Key Explanation: The sum of the interior angles in a polygon is $180 \times (n - 2)$, where n is the number of sides in the polygon. A heptagon has 7 sides, so the sum of its interior angles will be $180 \times (7 - 2) = 900°$.

A hexagon has 6 sides, so the sum of its interior angles will be $180 \times (6 - 2) = 720°$. The difference between the total number of degrees of the interior angles of the two shapes is $180°$. This number in radians would be π and $a = 1$.

8. **Level:** Medium | **Domain:** ALGEBRA
   Skill/Knowledge: Linear functions | **Testing point:** Finding equations of functions

   Key Explanation: Choice A is correct. The problem gives two points and asks what the function $f(x)$ is that best describes the points. Using points $(3, 2)$ and $(6, -3)$, the slope of the function, which is the change in the y coordinates over the change in the x coordinates, $\dfrac{(y_2 - y_1)}{(x_2 - x_1)}$, can be found as follows:

   $$\frac{2 - (-3)}{3 - 6} = \frac{5}{-3}$$

   The answer choices are in slope–intercept form, $y = mx + b$ where m represents the slope. The only answer choice that has a slope of $\dfrac{-5}{3}$ is **Choice A**.

   Distractor Explanations: Choice B is incorrect most likely due to a conceptual error. **Choice C** is incorrect and incorrectly states the slope formula as the change in x over the change in y. **Choice D** is incorrect as this is the equation of the line that is perpendicular to $f(x)$.

9. **Level:** Easy | **Domain:** ALGEBRA
   Skill/Knowledge: Linear equations in one variable
   Testing point: Solving for x

Key Explanation: Choice D is correct. To solve this problem, first divide both sides of the equation by 2 to get:

$$(x + 4) = \frac{18}{2}$$
$$(x + 4) = 9$$
$$x = 5$$

Therefore $(x + 6) = 5 + 6 = 11$

Distractor Explanations: Choice A is incorrect. It can be the result of a miscalculation. **Choice B** is incorrect. This is the value of x only. **Choice C** is incorrect. This is the value of $(x + 4)$.

10. **Level:** Medium | **Domain:** PROBLEM–SOLVING AND DATA ANALYSIS
    Skill/Knowledge: Ratios, rates, proportional relationships, and units | **Testing point:** Ratios

    Key Explanation: To solve this problem, let x equal the total number of people at the fair. Every group of 5 students and 3.5 parents has a total of 8.5 total people in it. Set up a proportion of ratio students to ratio total people and set it equal to the ratio of the total number of students to the total number of people as follows:

    $$\frac{5}{8.5} = \frac{2,000}{x}$$

    Cross multiplying gives the equation $5x = 2,000 \times 8.5$. Dividing both sides of the equation by 5 gives $x = 3,400$ students.

11. **Level:** Medium | **Domain:** PROBLEM–SOLVING AND DATA ANALYSIS
    Skill/Knowledge: Percentages | **Testing point:** Percent decrease

    Key Explanation: Choice A is correct. The percent decrease can be found by using the formula:

$$\frac{\text{difference between actual and predicted values}}{\text{original value}} \times 100.$$

Looking at the graph, the actual y values when $x = 4$ are 6 and 11. The predicted y value at $x = 4$ is 9. Since the question asked for the percent decrease from the actual value to the predicted value, the actual value needs to be higher and thus we would use the y value of 11 and not 6 at $x = 4$. Plugging in the y values of 11 and 9 into the equation yields $\frac{11-9}{11} \times 100 = 18.18\%$

Distractor Explanations: Choice B is incorrect as this answer is the percent increase from 9 to 11. **Choice C** is incorrect as this answer is the percent decrease from 9 to 6. **Choice D** is incorrect as this describes the percent increase from 6 to 9.

12. **Level:** Easy | **Domain:** ALGEBRA
    Skill/Knowledge: Linear inequalities in one or two variables | **Testing point:** Systems of linear inequalities

    Key Explanation: Choice B is correct. To solve the question, the fastest method would be to substitute the x and y coordinates of the answer choices into the system of inequalities and see which coordinate pair satisfies both inequalities. Plugging in the x and y values for **Choice B** makes both inequalities valid as follows:
    Inequality 1: $4 > -3(1) + 5$
                       $4 > -3 + 5$
                       $4 > 2$
    Inequality 2: $4 > 2(1)$
                       $4 > 2$

    Distractor Explanations: Choice A is incorrect. Plugging in this coordinate pair into the second inequality yields $4 > 4$, which is false. **Choice C** is incorrect. Plugging this coordinate pair into the second inequality yields $4 > 2(3) = 4 > 6$, which is false. **Choice D** is incorrect. Plugging this

coordinate pair into the second inequality yields $1 > 2(2) = 1 > 4$, which is false.

13. **Level:** Medium | **Domain:** ADVANCED MATH
    Skill/Knowledge: Nonlinear equations in one variable and systems of equations in two variables
    Testing point: Finding solutions for an absolute value equation

    Key Explanation: To solve this absolute value equation, first divide both sides of the equation by 3 to get: $|x - 4| = 2$. Then remove the absolute value and set up and solve the following 2 equations:
    $x - 4 = 2$ and $x - 4 = -2$
    $x = 6$ and $x = 2$

14. **Level:** Easy | **Domain:** GEOMETRY AND TRIGONOMETRY
    Skill/Knowledge: Area and volume | **Testing point:** Area of a trapezoid

    Key Explanation: Choice D is correct. Since segment AD is parallel to segment BC and AB = DC the shape is an isosceles trapezoid. To find the area of a trapezoid the formula $\frac{h}{2}(a+b)$, is used where h is the height of the trapezoid and a and b are the lengths of the two bases of the trapezoid.
    The height of the trapezoid can be found by using the Pythagorean theorem $a^2 + b^2 = c^2$, where a and b are the legs of the right triangle and c is its hypotenuse.

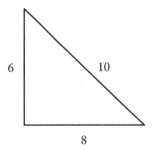

Using the pythagorean theorem $a^2 + 8^2 = 10^2$ or $a^2 = 36$, yielding $a = 6$. Thus the height of the trapezoid is 6. Plugging in the values for a, b, and h into the area of a trapezoid formula, yields

$$\frac{6}{2}(12 + 28) = 120$$

Therefore the area of the trapezoid would be 120.

Distractor Explanations: Choice A is incorrect. It is the value of the area of the two triangles alone **Choice B** is incorrect. This answer is the perimeter of the trapezoid. **Choice C** is incorrect. This answer can be determined if the shape is divided into a rectangle and two triangles. This answer is the area of the rectangle plus one triangle.

15. **Level: Easy | Domain:** ADVANCED MATH
Skill/Knowledge: Nonlinear equations in one variable and systems of equations in two variables
Testing point: Absolute values

Key Explanation: Choice C is correct. The first step is to combine the two absolute value terms into $|x + 3| = -2$. The next step is to divide both sides by -1 to get: $|x + 3| = 2$, The absolute value is equal to a positive number and therefore it has 2 solutions.

Distractor Explanations: Choice A is incorrect. To have 0 solutions in an absolute value equation, the absolute equation value has to be equal to a negative number. **Choice B** is incorrect. For an absolute value equation to have 1 solution it has to be equal to 0. **Choice D** is incorrect. There is sufficient information to answer the question.

16. **Level:** Medium | **Domain:** ALGEBRA
Skill/Knowledge: Linear equations in two variables | **Testing point:** Perpendicular lines

Key Explanation: The slope is found by putting the equation of the line into slope–intercept form of $y = mx + b$ as follows:
$5x - 6y + 30 = 0$
$-6y = -5x - 30$

$y = \frac{5}{6}x + 5$. The slope is then $\frac{5}{6}$, a line perpendicular to this will have the negative inverse of this slope which is $\frac{-6}{5}$.

17. **Level:** Easy | **Domain:** GEOMETRY AND TRIGONOMETRY
Skill/Knowledge: Right triangles and trigonometry
Testing point: Trigonometric identities

Key Explanation: Choice A is correct.
$\sin x = \cos(90° - x)$ and vice versa, therefore $\cos 72° = \sin(90° - 72°)$ This equates to $\sin 18°$.

Distractor Explanations: Choice B is incorrect as $\sin 72°$ is equal to $\cos 18°$. **Choice C** is incorrect. $\cos 18°$ is equal to $\sin 72°$. **Choice D** is incorrect. This choice may be selected due to a conceptual error.

18. **Level: Easy | Domain:** PROBLEM–SOLVING AND DATA ANALYSIS
Skill/Knowledge: Probability and conditional probability | **Testing point:** Probability Complement

Key Explanation: Choice C is correct. The sum of the probabilities of an event and its complement must add up to 1. Therefore, if the probability that it will rain is 0.26, the probability of no rain is $1 - 0.26 = 0.74$.

Distractor Explanations: Choice A is incorrect and can be due to a miscalculation or conceptual error. **Choice B** is incorrect and can be due to a miscalculation or conceptual error. **Choice D** is incorrect as a probability of 1 means that it is certain that it will not rain.

19. **Level:** Easy | **Domain:** ADVANCED MATH
Skill/Knowledge: Nonlinear functions | **Testing point:** Vertex form of a quadratic and minimum/maximum point

Key Explanation: The maximum t value of a concave down parabola for the quadratic equation $ax^2 + bx + c$ can be found using the formula $t = \dfrac{-b}{2a}$, which finds the x coordinate of the vertex of the parabola. In the equation above, a is 3 and $b = 9$ yielding,

$$t = \left(\frac{-9}{2(-3)} \right) = \frac{-9}{-6} = \frac{3}{2}$$

20. **Level:** Hard | **Domain:** GEOMETRY AND TRIGONOMETRY
Skill/Knowledge: Right triangles and trigonometry | **Testing point:** Special triangles

Key Explanation: Choice C is correct. The triangle PQR is a special triangle Triangle PQR is inscribed in a semicircle where the hypotenuse of triangle PQR is the diameter of the circle. This makes angle P a right angle. A triangle has 180 degrees and that would make angle R equal to 30 degrees. Therefore triangle PQR is a special triangle, more specifically a 30 – 60 – 90 special triangle. Since the radius of the circle is 7cm, this makes the diameter 14cm. The hypotenuse of triangle PQR is the diameter of the circle. In a 30 – 60 – 90 special triangle, the length of the side opposite the right angle, the hypotenuse, is two times the length of the side opposite the 30–degree angle. This makes side $PQ = 7cm$. The side opposite the 60–degree angle in this special triangle is the length of the side opposite the 30–degree angle times $\sqrt{3}$. Therefore the length of PR is equal to $7\sqrt{3}$.

Distractor Explanations:. Choice A is incorrect as it is the length of *PR*. **Choice B is incorrect.** This answer is due to a conceptual error confusing the ratios in sides of the 30 – 60 – 90 triangle with the 45 – 45 – 90 special triangle. **Choice D is incorrect.** This is the diameter of the circle and the value of the length of *RQ*.

21. **Level:** Medium | **Domain:** ALGEBRA
Skill/Knowledge: Linear inequalities in one or two variables | **Testing point:** Absolute value linear inequalities

Key Explanation: Choice A is correct. For the above inequality either $x + 3 > 4$ or $x + 3 < -4$ Solving $x + 3 > 4$ yields $x > 1$. Solving $x + 3 < -4$ yields $x < -7$. **Choice A** is the correct choice as it has the only value in the domain of the range of solutions to the inequality.

Distractor Explanations: Choice B is incorrect as they are not part of the range of solutions to the inequality. **Choice C is incorrect** as they are not part of the range of solutions to the inequality. **Choice D is incorrect** as they are not part of the range of solutions to the inequality.

22. **Level: Easy | Domain:** ALGEBRA
Skill/Knowledge: Systems of two linear equations in two variables | **Testing point:** Systems of equations

Key Explanation: Choice C is correct. To solve this problem, subtract the two equations. $3x + 4y = 31 - (2x + 3y = 22) = x + y = 9$, which is **Choice C.**

Distractor Explanations: Choice A is incorrect. This answer is the value of y. **Choice B is incorrect.** This answer is the value of x. **Choice D is incorrect.** It is due to conceptual or miscalculation errors.

This page is intentionally left blank

Chapter 5

Practice Test 4

You are about to begin a full-length Practice Test. The test has four modules. The time allotted for each module is marked at the beginning of the module. Work on one module at a time. Use a timer to keep track of the time limits for every module.

Try to take the Practice Test under real test conditions. Find a quiet place to work, and set aside enough time to complete the test without being disturbed. At the end of the test, check your answers by referring to the Answer Key and fill in your raw score in the scorecard below. Also, note down the time taken by you for completing each module.

Pay particular attention to the questions that were answered incorrectly. Read the answer explanations and understand how to solve them.

My Score Card (Raw Score)

	Reading and Writing		Math	
	Module 1	Module 2	Module 1	Module 2
Out of	27	27	22	22
My Score	_____	_____	_____	_____
Time Taken	_____	_____	_____	_____

TEST BEGINS ON THE NEXT PAGE

Reading and Writing Test

27 QUESTIONS | 32 MINUTES

DIRECTIONS

The questions in this section address a number of important reading and writing skills. Each question includes one or more passages, which may include a table or graph. Read each passage and question carefully, and then choose the best answer to the question based on the passage(s). All questions in this section are multiple–choice with four answer choices. Each question has a single best answer.

1

R.K. Narayan was a pioneer in Indian literature that was written in English. His stories often revolve around common people in the fictional town of Malgudi. His unassuming insights and gently humorous treatment of everyday life and interactions are _____ accessible to the average reader and give his writing a timeless appeal.

Which choice completes the text with the most logical and precise word or phrase?

A) readily

B) anxiously

C) contentedly

D) wryly

2

Many city councils in Germany impose strict regulations that aim to _____ noise pollution in residential areas. Violators face penalties, including fines and potential legal action. City Council officers explain that compliance with these rules is crucial to ensure a peaceful and harmonious environment for all residents.

Which choice completes the text with the most logical and precise word or phrase?

A) limit

B) exacerbate

C) overlook

D) intensify

3

The number of people in the US with myopia, or nearsightedness, has increased over 16 percent since 1971. However, the problem is much more _____ in Southeast Asia, where an estimated 80 to 90 percent of students with twelve years of schooling have the condition.

Which choice completes the text with the most logical and precise word or phrase?

A) pronounced

B) advocated

C) prescribed

D) articulated

4

The following text is adapted from F. Scott Fitzgerald's 1922 novel, *The Beautiful and the Damned.*

Anthony's recollections of the gallant Ulysses were vivid. After Henrietta Lebrune Patch had "joined another choir," as her widower huskily remarked from time to time, father and son lived up at grampa's in Tarrytown, and Ulysses came daily to Anthony's nursery and expelled pleasant, thick–smelling words for sometimes as much as an hour. He was continually promising Anthony hunting trips and fishing trips and excursions to Atlantic City, "oh, some time soon now;" but none of them ever materialized. One trip they did take; when Anthony was eleven they went abroad, to England and Switzerland, and there in the best hotel in Lucerne his father died with much sweating and grunting and crying aloud for air. In a panic of despair and terror, Anthony was brought back to America, wedded to a vague melancholy that was to stay beside him through the rest of his life.

Which choice best states the function of the underlined sentence in the text as a whole?

A) To foreshadow the trip in which Adam Ulysses passes away

B) To indicate the superficial nature of Anthony's father

C) To emphasize the deep interest that Adam Ulysses has for his son

D) To give an indication of Adam Ulysses' vast wealth

The Jiroft culture is a hypothetical society that lived in the third millennium BC in Iran. The first indication of the culture was found in 2001 when scientists evaluated confiscated artefacts, but many were skeptical of the find because it did not have an archaeological context and may contain forgeries. However, the site of Konar Sandal in Iran is now being excavated, and archaeologists have discovered two mounds, a citadel, and tablets with an unknown script that might prove a vital link to understanding whether the Jiroft culture actually existed.

What is the main purpose of the text?

A) It casts doubt on the existence of an ancient culture.

B) It reveals flaws in the theory that an ancient culture existed.

C) It outlines the current understanding of an ancient culture.

D) It presents incompatible findings regarding an ancient culture.

The following text is from Virginia Woolf's 1922 novel, Jacob's Room.

The house was flat, dark, and silent. Jacob was at home engaged upon a chess problem, the board being on a stool between his knees. One hand was fingering the hair at the back of his head. He slowly brought it forward and raised the white queen from her square; then put her down again on the same spot. He filled his pipe; ruminated; moved two pawns; advanced the white knight; then ruminated with one finger upon the bishop. Now Fanny Elmer passed beneath the window.

Which choice best states the main purpose of the text?

A) It hints that Jacob was more intent on the window than on chess.

B) It emphasizes Jacob's desire to improve his chess skills.

C) It shows the intensity with which Jacob concentrated on chess.

D) It establishes that Jacob and Fanny had a quarrel.

Text 1

Through recent advanced imaging techniques, neuroscientists have uncovered the complex networks of neurons responsible for cognitive processes such as memory and decision-making. These findings have deepened our understanding of the brain's plasticity and its ability to adapt and rewire itself in response to experiences and learning. However, much still remains to be learnt about the brain and how it functions.

Text 2

Our understanding of the brain encompasses diverse cellular and cognitive perspectives. David Marr's pioneering work provides a framework for comprehending brain networks. He emphasized the importance of defining the functional properties of brain processes, with a focus on behavioral observations as the initial step. While groundbreaking at the time, his work gave rise to subsequent questions about other cognitive processes.

Based on the texts, the author of Text 1 and the author of Text 2 would most likely agree with which statement?

A) Recent scientific research has uncovered the exact mechanisms through which the brain adapts and rewires itself in response to experiences and learning.

B) David Marr's work has revolutionized the understanding of cellular perspectives, consequently leading to a deeper understanding of the brain's plasticity.

C) Behavioral observations play only a minor role in illustrating the functional properties of brain processes compared to other approaches.

D) Recent scientific research has raised many more questions about the brain's functional processes.

8

Chili *(Capsicum spp.)* is a spice, a fruit widely grown around the world that is recognized for its nutraceutical (nutritional and medicinal) properties and economic value. In Benin, chili is the second cash gardening crop after the tomato. Its annual production is about 47.162 tons. Pepper plants produce the compound capsaicin, possibly to deter mammalian herbivores. In Benin, chili pepper is grown only for food partially in the cultivable lands of the coastal areas, where soil salinity and water irrigation can negatively affect the quantity and quality of the crop, and may also have a strong influence on the concentration of bioactive compounds of vegetables.

According to the text, what is the reason that the chili plant evolved to contain capsaicin in the fruit?

A) It adds flavor to human food dishes.

B) It is a part of herbal medicine remedies.

C) It increases the plant's absorption of nutrients.

D) It protects the plant from predation.

9

The following text is adapted from Herman Melville's 1851 novel, *Moby Dick; or The Whale.*

Now, when I say that I am in the habit of going to sea, I do not mean that I ever go to sea as a passenger. For to go as a passenger you must needs have a purse, and a purse is but a rag unless you have something in it. Besides, passengers get sea-sick—grow quarrelsome—don't sleep——no, I never go as a passenger; nor, though I am something of a salt, do I ever go to sea as a Commodore, or a Captain, or a Cook. I abandon the glory and distinction of such offices to those who like them. I always go to sea as a sailor, because they make a point of paying me for my trouble, whereas they never pay passengers a single penny that I ever heard of.

Based on the text, why does Ishmael avoid traveling aboard ship as a passenger?

A) He does not want excessive responsibilities.

B) He desires reimbursement for his efforts.

C) He sometimes enters periods of deep depression.

D) He hungers for recognition for his efforts.

10

Scientists studying at a site called Hegra in modern Jordan found the tomb of a woman called Hinat. Her name was identified in an inscription at the entrance which claims the tomb was bought by herself and belonging to her and her descendants. Archaeologists have found the remains of over 80 people buried inside, though none of them are identified. The tomb also contains many well-preserved artifacts that offer insight into the Nabataean culture that flourished in the region about 2,000 years ago.

Based on the passage, what is most likely true about Hinat?

A) She was a royal Nabataean personage.

B) She had her own tomb because she never married.

C) She is buried with many of her ancestors.

D) She was one of the 80 people buried in the tomb.

11

A medical research team conducted sex-specific analyses of measured blood pressure, a crucial indicator of cardiovascular risk. The dataset encompassed nearly 145,000 blood pressure measurements gathered over a span of 43 years from 32,833 study participants aged 5 to 98 years old. Instead of comparing men to women, the investigators focused on comparing women to women and men to men in order to identify distinctive patterns for each sex. This approach allowed researchers to observe high blood pressure and cardiovascular health progress over time and revealed that women experience elevated blood pressure at an earlier stage of life compared to men, indicating a higher risk of cardiovascular disease for young women with hypertension when compared to men of the same age.

Which finding, if true, would most directly undermine the study's finding?

A) While 6% of the general male population aged 50 years old are likely to suffer from a stroke, 4% of the general female population of the same age are likely to suffer from a stroke.

B) While 4% of the general male population aged 50 years old are likely to suffer from a stroke, 6% of the general female population of the same age are likely to suffer from a stroke.

C) Among people who have hypertension, women are 5% as likely as men to suffer from a stroke at the same age.

D) Among people who have hypertension, men are 5% as likely as women to suffer from a stroke at the same age.

CONTINUE

Nutrients Found Primarily in Animal Tissues

Nutrient	Function	Natural source	Alternate Source
B12	Used by nervous and circulatory systems	Fish, meat, dairy, eggs	Enriched grain products; some nutritional yeast
Creatine	Increases muscle performance	Animal tissue	Supplements; the body naturally makes small amounts
DHA	Mental health and brain development, especially in children	Fatty fish, fish oil	Microalgae
Taurine	Muscle function, bile production	Fish, meat, poultry, dairy products	Synthetic supplements

The vegan diet is one that is chosen by individuals for various reasons, including health and/or ethical reasons. In fact, it is evident that the vegan diet is much more than a diet itself, but has developed into a lifestyle, often associated with animal rights and environmental advocacy as well as a greater concern for physical activity and mindfulness. While many health benefits exist, it is essential for those who are vegan or are planning to become vegan to be educated about potential nutritional deficiencies to prevent adverse outcomes. For example, a vegan who is adverse to taking man–made supplements in any form _____

Which choice most effectively uses data from the table to complete the claim?

A) is likely to suffer from mental health disorders.

B) may suffer from insufficient levels of bile.

C) may be prone to various heart diseases.

D) could succumb to circulatory system disorders.

13

The Medicaid Disproportionate Share Hospital (DSH) payment program was created to pay higher insurance payouts to hospitals that served a significant number of patients on Medicaid, which is insurance eligible only for low-income individuals. The assumption was that these hospitals served both insured and uninsured low-income patients, so the hospitals should be subsidized for the costs of uninsured care that was provided. The reality was that hospitals began to compete for insured Medicaid patients to be able to enter the DSH program. Hospitals that actually served uninsured patients but did not meet the threshold to enter the DSH program were not compensated at all, having the unintended effect of _____

Which choice most logically completes the text?

A) encouraging patients to earn less to meet the low-income threshold.

B) compensating hospitals that served high-income individuals.

C) crowding out the target group it was meant to help.

D) compensating both the intended target group and the unintended target group.

14

Most students have heard of the charismatic 18t US president, Ulysses S. Grant. However, the name of his vice president, Schuyler Colfax, has mostly been relegated to history. In reality, he played an important role in passing the 13th Amendment, which abolished slavery. Not only did he actively promote his Abolitionist views, but he also voted in favor of the amendment when it came before the House of Representatives. His decision to vote was notable since the Speaker of the House typically remains silent except in the case of a tie. This implies that Colfax's vote for the 13th Amendment _____

Which choice most logically completes the text?

A) occurred because there was a tie in the House of Representatives.

B) was not considered valid because the Speaker of the House could not vote

C) greatly emphasized Colfax's commitment to the amendment

D) went against the opinions held by President U.S. Grant

15

Eagly's social role theory posits that prevalent gender stereotypes arise from the gender-based division of labor within a society. In Western cultures, men's increased involvement in powerful, higher-status roles and the disproportionate allocation of nurturing responsibilities to women _____ stereotypes linking agency to men and empathy to women.

Which choice completes the text so that it conforms to the conventions of Standard English?

A) have fostered

B) has fostered

C) fostered

D) fosters

16

When the Erie Canal was opened in 1825, it was 40 feet wide and 4 feet deep. Over half the original canal was taken out of use with the 1918 opening of a 120 feet wide and 12 feet deep section that _____ about ten years earlier to accommodate the larger barges of the modern era.

Which choice completes the text so that it conforms to the conventions of Standard English?

A) had been designed

B) had designed

C) designed

D) is designed

17

Unusual additions to a freshwater aquarium include pom-pom crabs, aptly named for the hair-like tufts on their pincers which make the crabs appear to be holding small pom-poms. Growing to about one inch long, _____ but they can be eaten by even small predatory fish.

Which choice completes the text so that it conforms to the conventions of Standard English?

A) a large tank is not required for these crabs,

B) it is not a large tank needed for the crabs,

C) these crabs do not require a large tank,

D) the requirements for these crabs do not include a large tank,

18

Pottery and ceramics are interchangeable words. They both refer to objects which are made from clay that is heated to make it harder. Earthenware is pottery that is baked at a low temperature. The result is porous and brittle. Earthenware is often glazed to enhance _____ durability and capacity to hold water.

Which choice completes the text so that it conforms to the conventions of Standard English?

A) its

B) it's

C) their

D) they're

19

The largest known fish species, the whale shark, is actually a slow-moving filter feeder that primarily subsists on plankton. Therefore, despite its _____ is not a threat to humans.

Which choice completes the text so that it conforms to the conventions of Standard English?

A) size. It

B) size it

C) size—it

D) size, it

20

Judy Blume is the author of many beloved children's _____ *Tales of a Fourth Grade Nothing.* Her frank discussions of childhood anxieties and family issues have made her a target of censors, so along with her writing, she has spent considerable time fighting to protect the freedom of speech.

Which choice completes the text so that it conforms to the conventions of Standard English?

A) stories such as:

B) stories, such as

C) stories, such as,

D) stories. Such as

21

When Austrian painter Gustav Klimt completed *The* _____ it was initially reviled as excessive due to its gold leaf, silver, and platinum. However, it is now considered one of the finest examples of the Art Nouveau style.

Which choice completes the text so that it conforms to the conventions of Standard English?

A) *Kiss (Der Kuss* in German)

B) *Kiss, (Der Kuss* in German)

C) *Kiss (Der Kuss* in German),

D) *Kiss, (Der Kuss* in German),

22

American author and inspirational _____ has shared his optimistic outlook with audiences around the world. His unusual approach to leadership is founded in cultural anthropology rather than business.

Which choice completes the text so that it conforms to the conventions of Standard English?

A) speaker Simon Sinek

B) speaker—Simon Sinek—

C) speaker, Simon Sinek

D) speaker Simon Sinek,

23

_____ slavery was abolished and Black American men were granted the right to vote in the 1860s, rights were slowly taken away so that conditions were inferior for people of color. It took almost 100 years for new federal laws to be passed that prevented discrimination based on race.

Which choice completes the text with the most logical transition?

A) Although

B) Since

C) Hence

D) Because

24

Water is by far the most common drink in the world. The next most popular is coffee, but that beverage is consumed in a variety of different ways. _____, it may be served hot, cold, or with additions such as milk or spices.

Which choice completes the text with the most logical transition?

A) Regardless,

B) Nevertheless,

C) Indeed,

D) Additionally,

25

Edgar Allen Poe's _Murders in the Rue Morgue_ is a detective story written in 1841. At the time it was written, it was praised as being exceptionally clever and considered quite a novelty. _____ it is considered the beginning of the detective fiction genre.

Which choice completes the text with the most logical transition?

A) Meanwhile,

B) Nevertheless,

C) Instead,

D) Today,

26

While researching a topic, a student has taken the following notes:

- The Treaty of Versailles signed between Germany and the Allied powers on June 28th, 1919, ended the war between them and placed heavy war reparations on Germany

- The Great Depression began as an economic slump that spread globally starting in 1929, leading to widespread unemployment and poverty in its wake.

- Adolf Hitler's rise to power in Germany was made easier by economic woes during the Great Depression and discontent with the Versailles Treaty terms.

- World War II began in 1939 due to Adolf Hitler's aggressive foreign policies and expansionist ideology.

- Following World War II, the Marshall Plan was instituted by the United States in 1948 to assist in rebuilding Western European economies and stop Soviet communism from spreading further.

The student wants to describe the chain of events from the Treaty of Versailles to the start of World War II. Which choice most effectively uses relevant information from the notes to accomplish this goal?

A) Following the signing of the Treaty of Versailles, the Great Depression caused global economic decline and ultimately contributed to Adolf Hitler's ascension and eventually World War II's beginning.

B) The Treaty of Versailles resulted in the Marshall Plan being implemented, effectively marking the end of World War II.

C) Adolf Hitler's aggressive ideologies sparked World War II in 1939, after which the U.S. implemented the Marshall Plan in 1948 to aid Western Europe's recovery and curb the spread of Soviet communism.

D) World War II was instigated by Hitler's rise to power, which had been facilitated by the global economic slump of the Great Depression.

27

While researching a topic, a student has taken the following notes:

- The first dynasty of Egypt was the first period after Lower and Upper Egypt were unified into one country by the first ruler.

- The seat of the first dynasty was Thinis.

- The exact dates are unknown, but were centered in the Bronze Age, most likely from 3100 B.C. to 2900 B.C.

- Tombs of the period were mostly made from wood, mud, and bricks; stones were typically used only for decoration, though some tombs were stone.

- The first ruler was Narmer and the last ruler `was Qa'a.

The student wants to introduce the first ruler of Egypt to someone unfamiliar with Egyptian dynasties. Which choice most effectively uses relevant information from the notes to accomplish this goal?

A) The rulers in the first dynasty of Egypt reigned from about 3100 B.C. to 2900 B.C., starting with Narmer and ending with Qa'a.

B) Narmer unified Lower and Upper Egypt into one country in around 3100 B.C. and became the first ruler of its first dynasty.

C) Narmer was the first ruler in Egypt during the Bronze Age and his tomb was made of wood, mud, and bricks.

D) The first dynasty of Egypt ruled from Thinis after Narmer joined Upper and Lower Egypt.

No Test Material On This Page

Reading and Writing Test

27 QUESTIONS | 32 MINUTES

DIRECTIONS

The questions in this section address a number of important reading and writing skills. Each question includes one or more passages, which may include a table or graph. Read each passage and question carefully, and then choose the best answer to the question based on the passage(s). All questions in this section are multiple-choice with four answer choices. Each question has a single best answer.

1

The following text is adapted from Fyodor Dostoevsky's 1848 novel, *White Nights and Other Stories.*

Suddenly, the inebriated gentleman set off and flew full speed in pursuit of my unknown lady. She was racing like the wind, but the staggering gentleman was overtaking—overtook her. In a flash I was on the other side of the street; in a flash the <u>obtrusive</u> gentleman had taken the position, had fallen back without a word.

As used in the text, what does the word "obtrusive" most nearly mean?

A) Obvious

B) Conspicuous

C) Deplorable

D) Inevitable

2

Ocean energy, as all other renewable sources of energy, can contribute to a more sustainable energy supply, but it is not environmentally friendly per se. The activities involved in manufacturing, operation, maintenance, and decommissioning of ocean energy devices will have various effects on the environment. Governments and society need a _____ understanding of the environmental implications of ocean energy systems before ocean energy systems are built, and also to reduce or adjust impacts to acceptable levels.

Which choice completes the text with the most logical and precise word or phrase?

A) vigorous

B) sturdy

C) robust

D) tough

3

The following text is from Charles Dickens's novel Oliver Twist, published serially between 1837 and 1839.

The donkey was in a state of profound <u>abstraction:</u> wondering, probably, whether he was destined to be regaled with a cabbage–stalk or two when he had disposed of the two sacks of soot with which the little cart was laden; so, without noticing the word of command, he jogged onward.

As used in the text, what does the word "abstraction" most nearly mean?

A) Generalization

B) Hypothesis

C) Intention

D) Preoccupation

4

The following text is adapted from Emily Dickinson's *Poems*, published after her death in 1886.

If I can stop one heart from breaking,

I shall not live in vain;

If I can ease one life the aching,

Or cool one pain,

Or help one fainting robin

Unto his nest again,

I shall not live in vain.

What is the main purpose of repeating the line "I shall not live in vain"?

A) It stresses how strongly the author feels about the subject.

B) It indicates that the author is close to her death.

C) It highlights the futile nature of certain tasks.

D) It shows that the author regrets not accomplishing certain goals.

5

The fearsome T-rex: one of the most well-known dinosaurs from the Jurassic era. With its short arms, large head, and razor-sharp teeth, its unique features stand out from its fellow dinosaurs in the minds of dinosaur enthusiasts. As it turns out, these characteristics do not just belong to the *Tyrannosaurus rex*. A recent study detailed that there were many other lesser-known dinosaurs with the same combination of traits that lived a substantial 20 million years before the infamous T-rex.

Which choice best states the function of the underlined sentence in the text as a whole?

A) It discusses a significant problem that the *Tyrannosaurus rex* faced during the Jurassic period

B) It argues that the *Tyrannosaurus rex* was the fiercest predator in the Jurassic era

C) It presents the *Tyrannosaurus rex* in order to compare it with another dinosaur species

D) It claims that the *Tyrannosaurus rex* had superior features to other species

6

Text 1

The Kuiper Belt is a region of space, shaped roughly like a donut, at the far reaches of our solar system. It is located outside the orbit of Neptune and contains over 2,000 identified objects, though scientists speculate that there may be millions more that have not been found yet due to its extreme distance from the sun. In 1930, the dwarf planet Pluto was the first object to be found in the Kuiper Belt, but it took many decades for the second, Pluto's moon, Charon, to be located in 1978.

Text 2

Objects in the Kuiper Belt are rocky bodies made from elements such as iron, and most of the ones found to date also are covered with ice that is composed of water or methane. In fact, some scientists speculate whether Earth's oceans were formed from water ice from comets in the Kuiper Belt. The quantity of ice greatly increases an object's reflectivity, making it easier to isolate objects made of such materials in telescopes that are trained on the distant reaches of our solar system.

Based on the texts, how would the author of Text 2 react to the claim in Text 1 that "there may be millions more that have not been found yet"?

A) By saying that many of the objects will be hard to find because they are not covered with reflective ice.

B) By claiming that it is easier to find large objects such as dwarf planets, so the remaining objects must all be small.

C) By pointing out that the objects that have been found are probably closer to the sun than the objects that have not yet been found.

D) By arguing that the number is greatly elevated over the actual number of objects which are in the Kuiper Belt.

Text 1

Prisons in the 1820s were unregulated and unhygienic, ... Dorothea Dix visited every public and private facility she could access, documenting the conditions she found. She then presented her findings to the legislature of Massachusetts, demanding that officials take action toward reform. Her reports—filled with dramatic accounts of prisoners flogged, starved, chained, and abused by their keepers, and left undressed and without heat or sanitation—shocked her audience and galvanized a movement that succeeded in improving conditions for the imprisoned and insane.

Text 2

Settlement house founder and peace activist Jane Addams (1860-1935) …, along with a college friend, Ellen Starr, moved in 1889 into an old mansion in an immigrant neighborhood of Chicago. Hull-House, which remained Addams's home for the rest of her life and became the center of an experiment in philanthropy, political action, and social science research, was a model for settlement work among the poor.

Based on the texts, how would Jane Addams in Text 2 most likely respond to Dix's actions to improve the conditions for the imprisoned and insane as illustrated in Text 1?

A) By disputing the idea that Dix could impose reform through documentation and reports instead of physically experiencing the conditions

B) By assenting the importance of political action in achieving reform but asserting the greater significance of a personal lifetime commitment to a social cause

C) By corroborating that thorough and honest research combined with political action are necessities when attempting social reform

D) By contesting the effectiveness of the non-scientific and dramatic nature of Dix's reports in achieving reform

8

The planet Venus is the second closest to the Sun in our solar system, but is generally hotter than the closest planet, Mercury—the average temperature is 462 degrees Celsius. That is because the atmosphere contains about 96 percent carbon dioxide, creating a greenhouse effect that is like having a giant blanket over the planet that retains the heat. The sulfuric acid in the atmosphere makes it very reflective, so Venus is the second brightest object in the night sky after the Moon.

According to the text, what is most likely true about the planet Mercury?

A) It does not have any sulfuric acid in its atmosphere.

B) Its temperature never exceeds 462 degrees Celsius.

C) It has less than 96 percent carbon dioxide in its atmosphere.

D) It is difficult to locate in the night sky because it is dark.

9

The following text is adapted from Mary Wollstonecraft Shelley's 1818 novel, Frankenstein; Or, the Modern Prometheus.

We sat late. We could not tear ourselves away from each other nor persuade ourselves to say the word "Farewell!" It was said, and we retired under the pretence of seeking repose, each fancying that the other was deceived; but when at morning's dawn I descended to the carriage which was to convey me away, they were all there—my father again to bless me, Clerval to press my hand once more, my Elizabeth to renew her entreaties that I would write often and to bestow the last feminine attentions on her playmate and friend.

Based on the text, what is most likely true about the narrator?

A) The narrator is a woman who grew up with Elizabeth.

B) The narrator is leaving home for the first time.

C) The narrator was trying to avoid the end of the journey.

D) The narrator will be absent for a long period.

CONTINUE

13

The following text is adapted from Jane Austin's 1811 novel, *Sense and Sensibility.*

Mrs. Dashwood waited only for the disposal of her effects at Norland before she set off to her new home; and this, as she was exceedingly rapid in the performance of everything that interested her, was soon done. The horses which were left her by her husband had been sold soon after his death, and an opportunity now offering of disposing of her carriage, she agreed to sell that likewise at the earnest advice of her eldest daughter. For the comfort of her children, had she consulted only her own wishes, she would have kept it; but the discretion of Elinor had prevailed. *Her* wisdom too limited the number of their servants to three; two maids and a man, with whom they were speedily provided from amongst those who had formed their establishment at Norland.

Based on the text, what can be inferred about the relationship between Mrs. Dashwood and her oldest daughter?

A) Mrs. Dashwood defers to her daughter's decisions.

B) Mrs. Dashwood usually tells her daughter what to do.

C) Both would prefer living apart from each other.

D) Both feel that the other is acting in error.

11

Examining children from two contrasting cultures, Elaine Liu and Sharon Xuejing Zuo observed their behavior at a shared school in Yunnan, China. Initially, Mosuo girls, adhering to their matrilineal society, displayed greater risk-taking tendencies than Mosuo boys, while Han girls, influenced by the patriarchal Han culture, exhibited less risk-taking compared to Han boys. However, this began to change as the children interacted with each other. Both groups experienced a shift: Mosuo girls became more risk-averse, while Han girls became more inclined to take risks. Liu believes the study's finding can have long-term economic consequences if it leads to women choosing riskier but more rewarding career paths.

Which finding, if true, would most directly undermine the implication of the study?

A) Upon graduation from the shared school, Mosuo girls became less risk-averse and Han girls became more risk-averse due to the lack of interaction between the two groups.

B) Mosuo boys became less risk-averse and Han boys became more risk-averse after interacting with one another.

C) Mosuo boys became more risk-averse and Han boys became less risk-averse after interacting with one another.

D) Upon graduation from the shared school, Mosuo girls remained more risk-averse and Han girls remained less risk-averse.

12

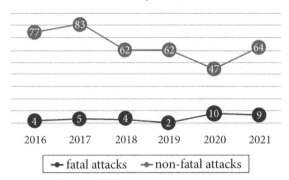

Shark attacks by Year (Global)

77 83 62 62 47 64

4 5 4 2 10 9

2016 2017 2018 2019 2020 2021

→ fatal attacks → non-fatal attacks

When people envision sharks, they often imagine deadly carnivores that attack people on sight. In reality, sharks tend to avoid encounters with humans unless provoked, and the actual number of deaths per year is typically below 10 for the entire world per year. Of course, it is incorrect to judge the number of dangerous encounters just by looking at deaths. For example, there were 9 deaths from shark attacks in 2021, _____

Which choice most effectively completes the example using data from the graph?

A) but fewer non–fatal attacks than earlier in the decade.

B) down by 1 from the previous year.

C) but there were 64 non–fatal attacks.

D) which was more than in 2018 and 2019 combined.

13

Togo 65,000
Madagascar 49,000
Eritrea 28,000
Burundi 56,000
Sierra Leone 30,000
Nigeria 634,000

0 100,000 200,000 300,000 400,000 500,000 600,000 700,000

■ Number of Tourists (2016)

Safari tourism in Africa highlights exotic creatures including elephants, lions, rhinos, hippos, and big game. However, the region is also replete with natural features or attractions that tourists gravitate toward, particularly those in search of outstanding scenic sites or who desire an environmental adventure. There are dozens of awe–inspiring national parks throughout Africa like Mt. Kilimanjaro in Tanzania and Zuma Rock in Nigeria. However, local conditions make it hard to travel in some places. For example, due to the infrastructure for accommodating visitors, travel in Togo in 2016 was: _____

Which choice most effectively uses data from the graph to illustrate the claim?

A) the highest of the selected countries represented in the figure.

B) greater than that of either Burundi or Nigeria.

C) lower than that of Nigeria but higher than that of Eritrea.

D) higher than it had been in the previous year.

14

A study in the US found that children who participate in individual sports are more likely to suffer from anxiety, depression, or other mental health struggles compared to both children who participate in team sports and children who do not participate in any sports at all. The study is one of the largest ever conducted in terms of the size of the database that was analyzed. However, while the study has proven a correlation between the type of sport and the mental health issues faced by children, the public should refrain from immediately steering kids away from individual sports because the study fails to prove causation. For instance, it is possible that _____

Which choice most logically completes the text?

A) children may feel isolated while playing individual sports, leading to feelings of anxiety and depression.

B) children that do not suffer from anxiety or depression are more likely to choose team sports over individual sports in the first place.

C) the study can prove causation by conducting a randomized controlled experiment.

D) the study can consider the mechanisms behind the correlation to propose a causal relationship.

15

Out of the Fortune 500 companies present in 1955, a staggering 88% no longer exist. Most of _____ unidentifiable and have either faded into obscurity or disappeared due to bankruptcies or mergers with other brands. With the shrinking lifespan of businesses, organizations must now exercise heightened vigilance to ensure innovation, thereby future-proofing their operations.

Which choice completes the text so that it conforms to the conventions of Standard English?

A) it is

B) this is

C) they are

D) them are

CONTINUE

16

Carbon emission credit programs are designed to reduce the overall amount of pollution released into the environment by limiting greenhouse gas emissions, encouraging technological innovation, and _____

Which choice completes the text so that it conforms to the conventions of Standard English?

A) it increases competition between enterprises for the credit rights.

B) increasing competition between enterprises for the right to use the credits.

C) the right to use the credits is something enterprises compete for.

D) increased competition between enterprises for the right to use the credits.

17

Plastic pollution arises when plastic items and particles (such as plastic bottles, and bags) accumulate within the Earth's environment, leading to negative impacts on both humans and wildlife, as well as their habitats. Though affordable and highly durable, _____ thoroughly damages the environment.

Which choice completes the text so that it conforms to the conventions of Standard English?

A) the purchase of plastic material

B) plastic material and its usage

C) purchasing of plastic material

D) plastic material or its purchase

18

Scientists have discovered a new species of lizard in the Andes mountains of _____ the color of its skin in response to temperature changes. According to the researchers, the lizard's ability to change color helps it regulate its body temperature and avoid predation.

Which choice completes the text so that it conforms to the conventions of Standard English?

A) Peru that is able to change

B) Peru: that is able to change

C) Peru - that is able to change

D) Peru, that is able to change

19

Success in the music industry is often attributed to natural talent and luck, but the reality is that many _____ have done so through perseverance, dedication, and hard work. Musicians who work hard not only improve their skills and craft, but also develop a strong work ethic, resilience, and a sense of purpose.

Which choice completes the text so that it conforms to the conventions of Standard English?

A) artists, who have achieved great things,

B) artists - who have achieved great things -

C) artists who have achieved great things

D) artists; who have achieved great things

20

Modern dance is a contemporary form of expression that evolved from the rigid structure of ballet to become naturalistic, with free and fluid movements that represent _____ feelings.

Which choice completes the text so that it conforms to the conventions of Standard English?

A) ideas emotions and

B) ideas, emotions, and

C) ideas, emotions and,

D) ideas; emotions; and

21

_____ massive stones erected around 2,500 B.C.— is one of the most famous Neolithic monuments in the world, though it was built on the site of a circle made of timber and pounded earth that had been built about 500 years earlier.

Which choice completes the text so that it conforms to the conventions of Standard English?

A) Stonehenge—a ring of

B) Stonehenge, a ring of—

C) Stonehenge, a ring of

D) Stonehenge: a ring of

22

Billy Joel is a singer and songwriter who is best known for the song "Piano Man." He started his music career in earnest when he found he did not have enough credits to graduate high school and claimed he did not care about finishing his education. _____ twenty–five years later he contacted his former school and wrote essays that allowed him to belatedly receive a degree.

Which choice completes the text with the most logical transition?

A) Inevitably,

B) Simultaneously,

C) Consequently,

D) Nonetheless,

23

The largest boat to date to sail the Great Lakes, the Edmund Fitzgerald, sank on November 10, 1975, northwest of Whitefish Point in Lake Superior. _____ its fame, the exact cause of the shipwreck has yet to be determined.

Which choice completes the text with the most logical transition?

A) Because of

B) Despite

C) Indeed,

D) Furthermore,

24

Several international space organizations monitor the position of space debris larger than 10 centimeters across to ensure safe space travel. _____ those efforts are not sufficient, as there are about twenty times as many smaller objects that are moving at speeds fast enough to damage even a heavily protected spacecraft.

Which choice completes the text with the most logical transition?

A) However,

B) Likewise,

C) Therefore,

D) Alternatively,

25

While researching a topic, a student has taken the following notes:

- In 1775, the American Revolution began, driven by colonists' dissatisfaction with British rule and its perceived unfair impositions on them.

- The "Shot Heard Around the World" at the battles of Lexington and Concord marked the initial military engagements in America's Revolution.

- In 1776, the Declaration of Independence marked a turning point in colonists' independence from British control.

- General George Washington led the Continental Army as it contributed to the ultimate triumph of the American Revolution.

- The American Revolution concluded in 1783 with the Treaty of Paris, recognizing US sovereignty over an area roughly defined by present-day Canada to the north, Florida to the south, and the Mississippi River on its western end.

The student wants to present an overview of the American Revolution's major events and their significance. Which choice most effectively uses relevant information from the notes to accomplish this goal?

A) The American Revolution, from its inception with the "Shot Heard Around the World" until it concluded with the Treaty of Paris, was an uprising against perceived British injustices that ultimately resulted in independence for America.

B) The American Revolution was marked by pivotal events such as the Lexington and Concord Battles, the Declaration of Independence, and the Treaty of Paris that helped define both identity and borders within America.

C) George Washington was an instrumental leader during the American Revolution, which was initiated by widespread dissatisfaction against British rule.

D) The American Revolution began with unrest against British rule, witnessed significant milestones such as the Declaration of Independence, and ultimately reached a successful conclusion with the Treaty of Paris.

26

While researching a topic, a student has taken the following notes:

- George Elton Mayo was an Australian psychologist, industrial researcher, and theorist who came up with a humanistic theory for management.

- Mayo's theory is based on the idea that repetition of tasks is boring and reduces innovation.

- Mayo's theory offers each worker a significant amount of freedom in completing tasks.

- The teamwork aspects of Mayo's theory can lead to high productivity and communication.

- Some workers feel greater stress and pressure because individual responsibilities are increased in environments where Mayo's theory is applied.

The student wants to introduce Mayo's theory to an audience who wants to increase innovation in the workplace. Which choice most effectively uses relevant information from the notes to accomplish this goal?

A) George Elton Mayo created a theory based on the idea that repetition of tasks is boring, so many companies see little innovation.

B) The theorist George Elton Mayo pointed out that workers given significant freedom complete their tasks and form good teams, but may feel great stress as a result.

C) A theory proposed by George Elton Mayo addresses the question of increasing innovation output by suggesting that workers get more freedom and consequently less repetition in completing tasks.

D) George Elton Mayo's humanistic theory can cause some workers stress, though it is outweighed by the many positive points related to innovation.

27

While researching a topic, a student has taken the following notes:

- The Berlin Wall, constructed in 1961 and dismantled after 28 years until 1989, served as a division between East and West Berlin until its fall.

- The Wall represented an iconic representation of the Iron Curtain - an ideological barrier dividing Western and communist Eastern Europe during the Cold War.

- Construction of the Wall began by East Germany or the German Democratic Republic to protect the socialist state from Western "fascists".

- The fall of the Berlin Wall can largely be attributed to political shifts and civil unrest in East Germany.

- Today, sections of the Wall serve as memorials and symbols of the end of the Cold War.

The student wants to emphasize the political motivations behind the construction and subsequent fall of the Berlin Wall. Which choice most effectively uses relevant information from the notes to accomplish this goal?

A) East Germany constructed the Berlin Wall to protect their socialist state against Western "fascists", while its fall was brought about by political changes and civil unrest within East Germany itself.

B) In 1989, the Berlin Wall which served as an Iron Curtain came tumbling down, marking an end to the Cold War era.

C) The Berlin Wall, a symbol of the Iron Curtain, was erected by East Germany to shield its socialist state from Western "fascists."

D) Now an iconic part of history, the Berlin Wall represented the stark political division between communist Eastern Europe and Western Europe during the Cold War era.

....

STOP

No Test Material On This Page

Math

22 QUESTIONS | 35 MINUTES

DIRECTIONS

The questions in this section address a number of important math skills. Use of a calculator is permitted for all questions.

NOTES

Unless otherwise indicated: • All variables and expressions represent real numbers. • Figures provided are drawn to scale. • All figures lie in a plane. • The domain of a given function is the set of all real numbers x for which $f(x)$ is a real number.

REFERENCE

$A = \pi r^2$
$C = 2\pi r$

$A = \ell w$

$A = \dfrac{1}{2} bh$

$c^2 = a^2 + b^2$

Special Right Triangles

$V = \ell w h$

$V = \pi r^2 h$

$V = \dfrac{4}{3}\pi r^3$

$V = \dfrac{1}{3}\pi r^2 h$

$V = \dfrac{1}{3}\ell w h$

The number of degrees of arc in a circle is 360.

The number of radians of arc in a circle is 2π.

The sum of the measures in degrees of the angles of a triangle is 180.

For **multiple–choice questions,** solve each problem, choose the correct answer from the choices provided, and then circle your answer in this book. Circle only one answer for each question. If you change your mind, completely erase the circle. You will not get credit for questions with more than one answer circled, or for questions with no answers circled.

For **student–produced response questions,** solve each problem and write your answer next to or under the question in the test book as described below.

- Once you've written your answer, circle it clearly. You will not receive credit for anything written outside the circle, or for any questions with more than one circled answer.

- If you find more than one correct answer, write and circle only one answer.

- Your answer can be up to 5 characters for a positive answer and up to 6 characters (including the negative sign) for a negative answer, but no more.

- If your answer is a fraction that is too long (over 5 characters for positive, 6 characters for negative), write the decimal equivalent.

- If your answer is a decimal that is too long (over 5 characters for positive, 6 characters for negative), truncate it or round at the fourth digit.

- If your answer is a mixed number (such as 3.!. 2), write it as an improper fraction (7/2) or its decimal equivalent (3.5).

- Don't include symbols such as a percent sign, comma, or dollar sign in your circled answer.

1

Which of the following represents the equation of the graph below?

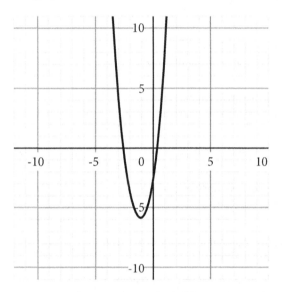

A) $y = 3x^2 - 6x - 3$

B) $y = -3x^2 + 6x - 3$

C) $y = 3x^2 + 6x - 3$

D) $y = -3x^2 - 6x - 3$

2

$$3x^2 - 12x - 15 = 0$$

What is the product of the solutions in the equation above?

3

A standard 52–card deck consists of 13 hearts, 13 spades, 13 cloves, and 13 diamonds. If the first card picked randomly is a heart and is not put back on the deck, what is the probability of picking a second heart card from the deck?

A) $\dfrac{13}{52}$

B) $\dfrac{12}{52}$

C) $\dfrac{12}{51}$

D) $\dfrac{39}{51}$

4

Which expression is equivalent to $6xy(y + 3x) - 2x(3xy + y^2)$?

A) $12xy^2 + 12x^2y$

B) $4xy^2 + 12x^2y$

C) $4xy^2 - 12\,x^2y$

D) $12x^2y - 4xy^2$

5

The price of a dress, which originally cost \$200, increased by 15% on 15th May 2021. Mary bought the same dress on the 23rd of May 2021 at a 30% discount. How much did she pay for the dress?

6

If $x^2 - y^2 = 12$ and $x - y = 2$, what is the value of $x + y$?

A) –2

B) 2

C) 4

D) 6

7

$$2x + y = 2$$

$$3y - x = 20$$

What is the value of xy for the system above?

A) –12

B) –3

C) –2

D) 6

8

$$2 |x + 4| = 12$$

What is the positive value of x for above equation?

9

A researcher collected a sample of 12 height samples from his local mall and wrote them down in meters.

The data he collected are 1.23, 1.45, 1.67, 1.53, 1.12, 1.23, 1.25, 1.39, 1.73, 1.84, 1.39, and 1.09.

Which of the following statements is correct when he collects a last–minute sample of 2.23m?

A) The mean and the range will increase and the median and standard deviation will decrease

B) The mean, range, and standard deviation will increase and the median remains the same

C) The mean, range, median, and standard deviation will increase

D) The mean, range, median and standard deviation will decrease

10

A circle is inscribed in a square. If the square has a side length of 14cm, what is the area of the circle?

A) 14π

B) 49π

C) 98π

D) 196π

11

$$f(x) = 3x + 5$$

What is the new *y-intercept* of the function $f(x)$ above if the line is moved 2 units to the left and 1 unit up?

12

$$-2y > -4$$

$$3x - y > 3$$

Which of the following coordinates is a solution to the above system of inequalities?

A) (1, 2)
B) (1, 3)
C) (2, 4)
D) (3, 1)

13

A circle has endpoints of a diameter with the coordinates of (−6, 10) and (2, 10). Which of the following is an equation for the circle?

A) $(x - 2)^2 + (y - 10)^2 = 16$

B) $(x + 2)^2 + (y - 10)^2 = 16$

C) $(x + 2)^2 + (y + 10)^2 = 16$

D) $(x - 2)^2 + (y + 10)^2 = 16$

14

If $f(x) = x + 2$ and $g(x) = 2x + 3$, find $f(g(2))$.

A) 4
B) 7
C) 9
D) 11

15

$$y = 300^x + 5$$

What is the *y-intercept* of the function above?

16

If the shaded region represents the solutions to an inequality, which of the following inequalities is represented by the graph below?

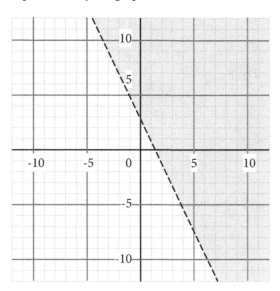

A) $y > 2x + 3$

B) $y > -2x + 3$

C) $y < -x + 3$

D) $y < -2x + 3$

17

Which of the following expressions is represented by the graph below?

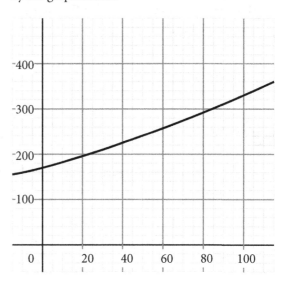

A) $400(1.03)^{0.2x}$

B) $180(0.97)^{0.2x}$

C) $180(1.03)^{0.2x}$

D) $400(0.97)^{0.2x}$

18

If $3x + 2(x + 4y) = ax + by$, what is the value of a?

A) 2

B) 3

C) 4

D) 5

19

$$-3y > -15$$

Using interval notation, what is the value of y in the inequality above ?

20

If $sin(3x) = cos(x + 10)$, what is the value of x in degrees?

A) 5°

B) 20°

C) 30°

D) 60°

21

Amanda is planning a trip and decides to save for it. She saves $10 dollars during the first week and doubles the amount she saves every week thereafter. Which type of function below best represents the amount that she will save in a given week?

A) Exponential growth

B) Linear growth

C) Exponential decay

D) Linear decay

22

If $4x + 8 = 24$, what is the value of x?

A) 3

B) 4

C) 6

D) 8

No Test Material On This Page

Math

22 QUESTIONS | 35 MINUTES

DIRECTIONS

The questions in this section address a number of important math skills. Use of a calculator is permitted for all questions.

NOTES

Unless otherwise indicated: • All variables and expressions represent real numbers. • Figures provided are drawn to scale. • All figures lie in a plane. • The domain of a given function is the set of all real numbers x for which $f(x)$ is a real number.

REFERENCE

$A = \pi r^2$ $A = \ell w$ $A = \frac{1}{2}bh$ $c^2 = a^2 + b^2$ Special Right Triangles
$C = 2\pi r$

$V = \ell wh$ $V = \pi r^2 h$ $V = \frac{4}{3}\pi r^3$ $V = \frac{1}{3}\pi r^2 h$ $V = \frac{1}{3}\ell wh$

The number of degrees of arc in a circle is 360.

The number of radians of arc in a circle is 2π.

The sum of the measures in degrees of the angles of a triangle is 180.

For **multiple-choice questions,** solve each problem, choose the correct answer from the choices provided, and then circle your answer in this book. Circle only one answer for each question. If you change your mind, completely erase the circle. You will not get credit for questions with more than one answer circled, or for questions with no answers circled.

For **student-produced response questions,** solve each problem and write your answer next to or under the question in the test book as described below.

- Once you've written your answer, circle it clearly. You will not receive credit for anything written outside the circle, or for any questions with more than one circled answer.

- If you find more than one correct answer, write and circle only one answer.

- Your answer can be up to 5 characters for a positive answer and up to 6 characters (including the negative sign) for a negative answer, but no more.

- If your answer is a fraction that is too long (over 5 characters for positive, 6 characters for negative), write the decimal equivalent.

- If your answer is a decimal that is too long (over 5 characters for positive, 6 characters for negative), truncate it or round at the fourth digit.

- If your answer is a mixed number (such as 3.!. 2), write it as an improper fraction (7/2) or its decimal equivalent (3.5).

- Don't include symbols such as a percent sign, comma, or dollar sign in your circled answer.

1

$7x + 28 = 112$, What is the value of $x + 4$?

A) −4

B) 8

C) 12

D) 16

2

The radius of a ball is three times the radius of its prototype. If the prototype has a volume of $10cm^3$, what is the volume of the ball?

3

$$y = 2x + k$$

$$y = x^2 - 10x + 30$$

If the system of equations above has one solution, what is the value of k?

A) −6

B) −3

C) 3

D) 6

4

If $\dfrac{27^{x-1}}{81^y} = 9$, what is the value of $6x - 8y$?

A) 2

B) 4

C) 5

D) 10

5

If the diagonal of a square is $16\sqrt{2}$, what is the perimeter of the square?

6

Which of the following graphs represents the
equation $12x + 4y = 8$?

A)

B)

C)

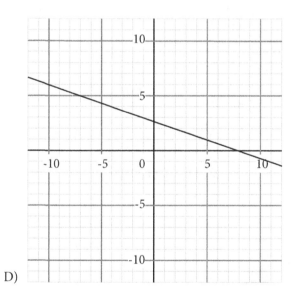

D)

7

$$\frac{3}{2}x + 5 = px + \frac{3}{2}$$

If the system of equations above

has no solution, what is the value of p

8

A researcher created a model $p(x)$, which is a function for the height of a girl in feet. Where t is in years and t is $2 \le t \le 5$. If $p(x) = 1.23(1.32)^t$, which of the following best represents the model in m months?

A) $p(x) = 1.23(1.32)^{12m}$

B) $p(x) = 1.23\left(\frac{1.32}{12}\right)^m$

C) $p(x) = 1.23(1.32)^{\frac{m}{12}}$

D) $p(x) = 1.23(1.32)^m$

9

If $\dfrac{-2x^2 + 5x + 10}{x - 3} = A + \dfrac{7}{x - 3}$, which of the following expressions best represents A?

A) $-2x - 1$

B) $2x + 3$

C) $-2x - 3$

D) $-2x^2 + 4x + 13$

10

If $3x = -5y$ and $2x + 3y = -1$, what is the value of x?

A) -8

B) -5

C) 2

D) 3

11

$$4x^2 - 12x + k = 0$$

What is the greatest possible integer value of k if the quadratic equation above has two distinct solutions?

12

$$3(x + 6) + x = 4x + 5$$

How many solutions does the equation above have?

A) 0

B) 1

C) 2

D) Infinite

13

$$\dfrac{1}{\dfrac{1}{x-2}+\dfrac{1}{x+2}}$$

Which of the following is equivalent to the expression above ?

A) $\dfrac{x^2-4}{2x}$

B) x

C) $\dfrac{2x}{x^2-4}$

D) $\dfrac{x^2+4}{2x}$

14

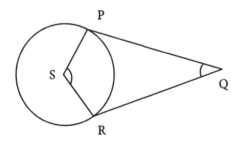

PQ and PR are tangents and points P and R lie on the circle. If $\angle PSR = 80°$ and $\angle PQR = a\pi$, what is the value of a?

A) $\dfrac{5}{18}$

B) $\dfrac{5}{9}$

C) $\dfrac{13}{18}$

D) 1

15

What is the area of a circle whose circumference is 12π?

16

$$3p^{\frac{1}{3}}\sqrt{p}$$

Which of the following expressions is equivalent to the expression above?

A) $3\sqrt[5]{p}$

B) $\sqrt[6]{3p^5}$

C) $3\sqrt[6]{p}$

D) $3\sqrt[6]{p^5}$

17

What is the volume of a cylinder with a radius of 9 *cm* and a height of 6 *cm*?

A) 81π

B) 108π

C) 270π

D) 486π

18

If lines $3x + 5y = 6$ and $-6x + py = 18$ are parallel, what is the value of p?

A) -10

B) 3

C) 5

D) 10

19

If $3xy(5x + 2) + 2y(3x - 1) = ax^2y + bxy + cy$, what is the value of b?

20

$$-2|x + 4| = -8$$

How many solutions does the absolute value equation above have?

A) None

B) One

C) Two

D) Infinite

21

If $xy = 5$ and $x^2 + y^2 = 45$, what is the value of $(x + y)^2$?

A) 9

B) 35

C) 55

D) 110

22

A study was conducted on 1,200 residents in a particular town. 950 of the residents surveyed owned a dog or a cat and the rest owned a different type of pet. If there are 62,500 residents in the town, approximately how many of them own a different type of pet?

A) 13,020

B) 49,480

C) 61,550

D) 62,500

STOP

This page is intentionally left blank

Answer Key

Reading and Writing

Module 1

Questions	Correct	Mark your correct answers
1.	A	
2.	A	
3.	A	
4.	B	
5.	C	
6.	A	
7.	D	
8.	D	
9.	B	
10.	C	
11.	D	
12.	D	
13.	B	
14.	C	
15.	A	
16.	A	
17.	C	
18.	A	
19.	D	
20.	B	
21.	C	
22.	A	
23.	A	
24.	C	
25.	D	
26.	A	
27.	B	

Module 2

Questions	Correct	Mark your correct answers
1.	C	
2.	C	
3.	D	
4.	A	
5.	C	
6.	A	
7.	C	
8.	C	
9.	D	
10.	A	
11.	C	
12.	C	
13.	A	
14.	B	
15.	D	
16.	B	
17.	B	
18.	B	
19.	C	
20.	B	
21.	A	
22.	D	
23.	B	
24.	A	
25.	B	
26.	C	
27.	A	

Math

Module 1

Questions	Correct	Mark your correct answers
1.	C	
2.	-5	
3.	C	
4.	B	
5.	161	
6.	D	
7.	A	
8.	2	
9.	B	
10.	B	
11.	12	
12.	D	
13.	B	
14.	C	
15.	6	
16.	B	
17.	C	
18.	D	
19.	$(-\infty, 5)$	
20.	B	
21.	A	
22.	B	

Module 2

Questions	Correct	Mark your correct answers
1.	D	
2.	270	
3.	A	
4.	D	
5.	64	
6.	C	
7.	$\frac{3}{2}$ or 1.5	
8.	C	
9.	A	
10.	B	
11.	8	
12.	A	
13.	A	
14.	C	
15.	36π	
16.	D	
17.	D	
18.	A	
19.	12	
20.	C	
21.	C	
22.	A	

1. **Level:** Medium | **Domain:** CRAFT AND STRUCTURE
    Skill/Knowledge: Words in Context

    Key Explanation: Choice A is the best answer. The blank describes the way in which the insights and treatment of everyday life are "accessible to the average reader." The passage says the insights are "unassuming" or "not flamboyant," and the treatment of everyday life and interactions is "gently humorous" or "pleasantly funny," which suggests the stories are probably very easy to read. **Choice A** means "effortlessly" or "easily," which fits the context that the average reader can enjoy the stories without working hard to understand them.

    Distractor Explanations: Choice B is incorrect because it refers to being full of worry, but there is no indication that the average reader would be worried about stories that are unassuming and pleasant. **Choice C** is incorrect because the reader may be content reading the stories, but the underlined word refers to the "accessibility" of the stories rather than to the reader. Accessibility is inanimate and therefore not content. **Choice D** is incorrect because it refers to dry, ironic humor, but the passage already states that his humor is "gentle."

2. **Level:** Medium | **Domain:** CRAFT AND STRUCTURE
    Skill/Knowledge: Words in Context

    Key Explanation: Choice A is the correct option as it aligns with the purpose of the regulations mentioned in the passage. The city councils aim to restrict or confine noise pollution, making this the correct answer.

    Distractor Explanations: Choice B is incorrect because to exacerbate means to make something worse or more severe, which is the opposite of what the city councils are trying to achieve by imposing regulations. **Choice C** is incorrect because to overlook means to fail to notice or consider something, which is not the intended action of the city councils. They are actively attempting to regulate noise pollution, not ignoring or neglecting it. **Choice D** is incorrect because to intensify means to make something stronger or more intense. This is the opposite of what the city councils are aiming for. They want to mitigate or lessen noise pollution, not make it stronger or more intense.

3. **Level:** Easy | **Domain:** CRAFT AND STRUCTURE
    Skill/Knowledge: Words in Context

    Key Explanation: Choice A is the best answer. The underlined word is an adjective which describes "the problem" as the problem exists in Southeast Asia. "Pronounced" refers to something which is conspicuous or noticeable. Therefore, it fits the context of saying that myopia is a more noticeable problem in Southeast Asia than in the US, as such a large percentage of students have it.

    Distractor Explanations: None of the other choices adequately describe "the problem" in Southeast Asia. **Choice B** refers to supporting a particular policy, but there is no indication that people want myopia, as it is a "problem." **Choice C** refers to something which is ordered to be done, such as taking a medical prescription. **Choice D** is incorrect because it refers to how clearly something is said.

4. **Level:** Medium | **Domain:** CRAFT AND STRUCTURE
    Skill/Knowledge: Text Structure and Purpose

Key Explanation: Choice B is the best answer because despite promising trips, "none of them ever materialized." This shows that Ulysses was more interested in talking than in following through with his word. That is the action of a "superficial" or "shallow" personality: saying one thing but not caring enough to do it.

Distractor Explanations: Choice A is incorrect because "foreshadowing" involves giving a clue of something that will happen in the future. However, the promised trips never happened, so they do not give any hint that Ulysses would take his son on a trip or that Ulysses would die. **Choice C** is incorrect because, if Ulysses really took an interest in his son, he would follow through on promises and spend time with the boy rather than getting the boy's hopes up and breaking them. **Choice D** is incorrect because the trips would cost a lot of money if the father and son really took them all, but the trips never happened. Therefore, it is possible that the father had very little money and was just talking about places he could only dream of visiting.

5.   **Domain:** CRAFT AND STRUCTURE
     Skill/Knowledge: Text Structure and Purpose

Key Explanation: Choice C is the best answer because the text describes when the Jiroft culture was first proposed and what evidence was available at the time. The text then describes a later finding—the excavations at Komar Sandal—which might strengthen the evidence for such a culture, but the link has not yet been decisively drawn, as the text says "might prove a vital link."

Distractor Explanations: Choice A is incorrect because the text starts by showing that there was doubt about the culture because the artefacts were not studied where they were found, but the

information from Komar Sandal implies that the culture may really have existed. **Choice B** is also incorrect because no "flaws" or "errors" are discussed about the theory; the text only says that the 2001 artefacts are not strong proof that it existed. **Choice D** is incorrect because there are no "incompatible" or "conflicting" findings, only recent evidence that supplements less strong earlier evidence.

6.   **Level:** Hard | **Domain:** CRAFT AND STRUCTURE
     Skill/Knowledge: Text Structure and Purpose

Key Explanation: Choice A is the best answer. Jacob was looking at the chess board, but uncertain about his moves, fingering his hair and lifting and replacing the same piece before making a few other moves which may or may not have been effective. The end sentence shows what he was actually waiting or hoping for: the sound of Fanny walking by.

Distractor Explanations: Choice B is incorrect because there is no indication of a desire to get better at chess, only to use time waiting. Though Jacob thinks about his moves, it is unclear whether they are effective or not. **Choice C** is incorrect because Jacob is not "intense" or "concentrating very hard." Instead, he is vacillating over moves and noticing things outside the room. **Choice D** is incorrect because it is clear that Jacob is waiting for Fanny, but not why. There is no clue that there was a "quarrel" or "argument."

7.   **Level:** Medium | **Domain:** CRAFT AND STRUCTURE
     Skill/Knowledge: Cross–Text Connections

Key Explanation: Choice D is the correct answer since it accurately reflects the information provided in both texts. Text 2 states that David Marr's pioneering work provided a framework for comprehending specific brain networks, but also acknowledges the subsequent questions that it led to. Text 1 also mentions that "much still remains to be learned about the brain and how it functions." Therefore, both authors are likely to agree that recent research has raised more questions about the brain's functional processes.

Distractor Explanations: Choice A is incorrect because both texts acknowledge that while significant progress has been made in understanding the brain's plasticity and its ability to adapt, there is still much more to learn about the exact mechanisms involved. **Choice B** is incorrect because while Text 2 acknowledges David Marr's contributions to understanding brain networks, it does not explicitly connect it to the brain's plasticity. **Choice C** is incorrect because both texts acknowledge the importance of behavioral observations in understanding the functional properties of brain processes. Therefore, the role of behavioral observations cannot be considered as minor.

8. **Level:** Easy | **Domain:** INFORMATION AND IDEAS
    Skill/Knowledge: Central Ideas and Details

    Key Explanation: Choice D is the best answer because "evolved" refers to the changes that the plant underwent over time. The text defines capsaicin and says that it is mostly contained in the fruit. The speculation is "possibly to deter mammalian herbivores." "Herbivores" are animals that eat plants, so the plants that contained capsaicin "stopped" or "deterred" predators from eating the chili. Over time, the plants with more capsaicin survived.

Distractor Explanations: Choice A is incorrect because it is a use that chilis have been adapted for by humans but is not why chili plants evolved with capsaicin in their fruit. **Choice B** is incorrect because it is a use that chilis have been adapted for by humans but is not why chili plants evolved with capsaicin in their fruit. **Choice C** is not mentioned anywhere in the text.

9. **Level:** Easy | **Domain:** INFORMATION AND IDEAS
    Skill/Knowledge: Central Ideas and Details

    Key Explanation: Choice B is the best answer because "reimbursement" refers to payment, and he explains how much he enjoys getting paid for traveling aboard a ship, "I always go to sea as a sailor, because they make a point of paying me for my trouble."

    Distractor Explanations: Choice A is incorrect because there is no reference to "excessive" or "too much" responsibility for passengers; the narrator does not mention the amount of work. **Choice C** is incorrect because it only describes what happens to passengers, not to Ishmael. **Choice D** is incorrect because the narrator does not want "recognition" or "fame." He indicates that he is happy to leave those "to those who like them."

10. **Level:** Hard | **Domain:** INFORMATION AND IDEAS
    Skill/Knowledge: Inferences

    Key Explanation: Choice C is correct. The text states that the target group of the program is to help hospitals that serve uninsured low-income patients and compensate them for the costs of this care. However, by qualifying these hospitals based on the amount of insured Medicaid patients they service, the program ended up compensating hospitals that competed to serve a significant amount of insured patients. Therefore, the unintended effect of the program is that the target group (hospitals serving uninsured patients) was crowded out and did not receive help from the program.

Distractor Explanations: Choice A is incorrect because this choice is about an unintended effect on the patients, while the text is about the incentives and effects on the hospitals. **Choice B** is incorrect because the text states that the program ended up serving hospitals with insured Medicaid patients. Patients are only eligible for Medicaid if they are deemed as low-income, so it is not accurate to say that the program compensated hospitals serving high-income individuals. **Choice D** is incorrect because the text states that the intended target group was not compensated from the program since the group was crowded out.

11. **Level:** Easy | **Domain:** INFORMATION AND IDEAS
    Skill/Knowledge: Central Ideas and Details

    Key Explanation: Choice D is the best answer. Since the tomb inscriptions say that the tomb belonged to Hinat, it is a logical assumption that she was buried there.

    Distractor Explanations: Choice A is incorrect. There is no evidence that Hinat was royal; if anything, the act of buying a tomb indicates that the populace did not make one for their ruler. **Choice B** is incorrect because, though she bought her own tomb, she had "descendants," which indicates that she had children. **Choice C** is incorrect because "ancestors" are the people who came before someone, so are the opposite of "descendants." There is no indication that anyone before Hinat was buried with her.

12. **Level:** Hard | **Domain:** INFORMATION AND IDEAS
    Skill/Knowledge: Command of Evidence (Textual)

    Key Explanation: Choice D is correct. The study found that there is a higher risk of cardiovascular disease for young women with hypertension, or high blood pressure, when compared to men of the same age. Therefore, among people who have hypertension, if men are more likely than women to suffer from a stroke at the same age, the study's finding is refuted.

    Distractor Explanations: Choice A is incorrect because this choice does not specifically address people with hypertension, which is the focus of the study. **Choice B** is incorrect because this choice does not make an observation about people with hypertension, which is discussed in the study's finding. **Choice C** is incorrect because this choice directly supports the study's finding.

13. **Level:** Medium | **Domain:** INFORMATION AND IDEAS
    Skill/Knowledge: Command of Evidence (Quantitative)

    Key Explanation: Choice B is the best answer because the "alternate source" column on the right–hand side lists only taurine as requiring a "synthetic" or "man–made" supplement. The other nutrients can be at least partly replaced by other sources. The second column of the chart lists "function." The functions of taurine are given as "muscle function, bile production." Someone who does not have enough taurine would therefore, have problems with muscles and bile. **Choice B** refers to "insufficient levels" or "not enough" bile, which relates to problems with producing bile.

    Distractor Explanations: None of the other choices are related to the function of taurine.

Choice **A** could be caused by a lack of DHA, which could be replaced using microalgae. **Choices C** and **D** could both be caused by a lack of B12, but that can be replaced using nutritional yeast.

14. **Level:** Easy | **Domain:** INFORMATION AND IDEAS
   Skill/Knowledge: Inferences

   Key Explanation: Choice C is the best answer. The passage says that the vote was "notable" or "important" because the Speaker "typically remains silent" or "usually does not vote." In other words, Colfax went against the normal protocol by voting. His decision shows that he was "committed" or "felt strongly" about the amendment to the point of breaking tradition to show his support of it.

   Distractor Explanations: Choice A is incorrect because the passage says that a vote is usually only cast "in the case of a tie." Since Colfax's vote was notable, it probably was not cast under those conditions or it would be considered average or not worth noticing. **Choice B** is incorrect because the passage says that the Speaker usually does not vote, but can if there is a tie. Therefore, it is possible to vote, though it may have been "not valid" or "not acceptable" for other reasons. **Choice D** is impossible to determine because there is not enough information in the passage to determine Grant's views on the subject.

15. **Level:** Medium | **Domain:** STANDARD ENGLISH CONVENTIONS
   Skill/Knowledge: Form, Structure, and Sense

   Key Explanation: Choice A is the correct answer. The convention being tested is subject-verb agreement. The present perfect tense "have

fostered" is correctly used in choice A with the plural subject "men's increased involvement… and the disproportionate allocation of nurturing responsibilities to women." Choice A indicates that the actions of men's increased involvement and disproportionate allocation of responsibilities have occurred in the past and continue to have an impact on the present.

Distractor Explanations: Choice B is incorrect because it uses the singular form "has fostered," which is incorrect because the subject "men's increased involvement" and "disproportionate allocation of nurturing responsibilities" are both plurals. The correct verb form should be plural to agree with the subject. **Choice C** is incorrect because it uses the simple past tense "fostered," which doesn't accurately convey the ongoing impact of the actions on gender stereotypes. **Choice D** is incorrect because it uses the simple present tense "fosters," which doesn't accurately convey that past actions (that have been completed) have resulted in prevalent gender stereotypes.

16. **Level:** Easy | **Domain:** STANDARD ENGLISH CONVENTIONS
   Skill/Knowledge: Form, Structure, and Sense

   Key Explanation: Choice A is the best answer. "Had" is used to show that something happened in the past before another action in the sentence; in this case, it shows that the design was made before the opening of the new section. "Been" makes the verb passive, showing that the design of the section was made by someone not mentioned in the passage; the section did not do the designing itself.

   Distractor Explanations: Choice B is incorrect because it doesn't establish that the plans had already been drawn out in the past. **Choice C** is incorrect because they are active verbs which erroneously show that the section did the act of designing. **Choice C** is also incorrect because it doesn't describe how the plans for the new section had been made before it had been constructed. **Choice D** is a present–tense verb, so it does not fit the context of an action which occurred in the past.

17. **Level:** Medium | **Domain:** STANDARD ENGLISH CONVENTIONS
Skill/Knowledge: Form, Structure, and Sense

Key Explanation: Choice C is the best answer. The beginning of the sentence, "growing to about one inch long," refers to the size of the crab. A modifier like this phrase needs to be followed directly by the noun it modifies. Since **Choice C** starts with "these crabs," it offers the correct order for the modifier and words that follow. In addition, "they" in the second half ("but they… predatory fish") properly refers to the subject of the sentence, "these crabs."

Distractor Explanations: All of the other choices can be eliminated because the preceding modifier, "growing to about one inch long," is not followed by a logical noun. Since "growing" indicates an animate object, it does not refer to the "large tank" in **Choice A**. **Choice B** starts with the placeholder "it," and **Choice D** illogically makes the modifier refer to "the requirements."

18. **Level:** Easy | **Domain:** STANDARD ENGLISH CONVENTIONS
Skill/Knowledge: Form, Structure, and Sense

Key Explanation: Choice A is the best answer. The subject is the singular "earthenware," as indicated by the singular verb "is." **Choice A** is

the singular possessive form showing that the durability and water–holding capacity belongs to the earthenware.

Distractor Explanations: Choice B is incorrect because it is a contraction for "it is" rather than a word showing possession. **Choice C** is incorrect because it is a plural possessive form, but "is" shows that "earthenware" is singular. **Choice D** is incorrect because it is a contraction for "they are."

19. **Level:** Easy | **Domain:** STANDARD ENGLISH CONVENTIONS
Skill/Knowledge: Boundaries

Key Explanation: Choice D is the best answer. The underlined portion connects the modifier "despite its size" with the main clause, "it is not a threat…" A comma needs to follow a modifier at the beginning of the sentence.

Distractor Explanations: Choice A is incorrect because "despite its size" is not a complete sentence; there is no active verb. **Choice B** is incorrect because there should be punctuation separating the main clause "it is not a threat…" from the phrases that modify it. Otherwise, the reader is unsure where one part of the sentence ends and the next begins. **Choice C** is incorrect because a single dash should follow a complete sentence, but the preceding portion cannot stand on its own.

20. **Level:** Medium | **Domain:** STANDARD ENGLISH CONVENTIONS
Skill/Knowledge: Boundaries

Key Explanation: Choice B is the best answer. "such …*Nothing*" adds more information to describe the previous noun, "many beloved children's stories." A comma correctly separates the noun from extra information that describes it but which is not essential for understanding the main part of the sentence.

Distractor Explanations: Choice A is incorrect because a colon should only follow a complete clause, but "such as" leaves the preceding idea unfinished. **Choice C** is incorrect because there should be no comma dividing "such as" from its object, the title of the book. **Choice D** is incorrect because the portion after the period is not a complete idea because there is no verb, so it cannot stand on its own as a sentence.

21. **Level:** Easy | **Domain:** STANDARD ENGLISH CONVENTIONS
    Skill/Knowledge: Boundaries

    Key Explanation: Choice C is the best answer. Parenthetical information should be treated as if it is part of the noun it describes, so in this case, *"Der Kuss* in German" should follow the same punctuation as *"The Kiss."* "When…*Kiss"* is a long modifier explaining the time of the main clause, "it was…platinum." A comma should come at the end of a modifier at the start of a sentence. Since the parenthetical information is included as part of the clause, the comma comes after it.

    Distractor Explanations: Choice A is incorrect because there is no comma separating the modifier of time from the main clause. **Choices B** and **D** are incorrect because the comma after "Kiss" divides the parenthetical information from the title it describes.

22. **Level:** Medium | **Domain:** STANDARD ENGLISH CONVENTIONS
    Skill/Knowledge: Boundaries

Key Explanation: Choice A is the best answer. "Simon Sinek" is necessary in the sentence to know which "American author and inspirational speaker" the sentence is writing about. Therefore, there should be no punctuation dividing the name from the rest of the main clause.

Distractor Explanations: Choice B is incorrect because "Simon Sinek" is not an aside but an essential part clarifying the subject of the sentence. Therefore, it should not be set aside from the main clause. **Choice C** is incorrect because "American author and inspirational speaker" is a subject, not a modifier. If it began with "an" or "the," then it is possible that the description could be used in that way at the start of the sentence. **Choice D** is incorrect because it divides the subject from its verb "has shared."

23. **Level:** Easy | **Domain:** EXPRESSION OF IDEAS
    Skill/Knowledge: Transitions

    Key Explanation: Choice A is the best answer. The sentence has two parts, one which says that Blacks were granted various rights, but the second part says that conditions grew worse for Blacks and other people of color. **Choice A** is used to show that the main clause occurs in spite of the clause modified by "although." Therefore, it fits the context of showing that conditions were bad in spite of slavery being abolished.

    Distractor Explanations: Choice B is incorrect because using "since" here doesn't concur with the following sentence, but proposes a contradiction instead. **Choice C** is grammatically incorrect because it is not used to subordinate a clause. **Choice D** can be eliminated because "because" is used to offer a logical reason for the main clause of the sentence. It does not establish the relationship between the parts of the sentence, because it is not logical that people who are given rights have those rights taken away again.

24. **Level:** Easy | **Domain:** EXPRESSION OF IDEAS
Skill/Knowledge: Transitions

Key Explanation: Choice C is the best answer. It is used to add information that emphasizes a previous claim, so fits the context of expanding on the claim that coffee is served many ways by giving examples of different ways it is served.

Distractor Explanations: Choice A can be eliminated because it is used to demonstrate that something occurs in spite of something that says it shouldn't. Similarly, **Choice B** is used to show that something happens despite something else, so it does not fit the context of adding examples to a claim. **Choice D** is used to add more information on a topic, but it does not fit this context because the information should be a new point that is related rather than more details like examples that expand on the original point.

25. **Level:** Medium | **Domain:** EXPRESSION OF IDEAS
Skill/Knowledge: Transitions

Key Explanation: Choice D is the best answer. The previous sentence describes how a story was viewed in 1841. The present tense in the following sentence shows that the sentence refers to the current time. **Choice D** correctly warns the reader that the time changes from the past to the present "now."

Distractor Explanations: Choice A is incorrect because it is used to show two things that happen at the same time, but the preceding and following sentences are in the past and present

tense, respectively. Therefore, they do not occur simultaneously. **Choice B** is used to show that something happens despite something else. It does not fit the context because it is logical rather than unexpected that a very unusual piece of writing was the beginning of a genre. **Choice C** is used to show an alternative, so is not used to introduce two things that are both true.

26. **Level:** Hard | **Domain:** EXPRESSION OF IDEAS
Skill/Knowledge: Rhetorical Synthesis

Key Explanation: Choice A is correct because it accurately recounts the chain of events described in the notes: the signing of the Treaty of Versailles, the onset of the Great Depression, Hitler's rise to power, and the beginning of World War II. This choice successfully synthesizes information from notes to meet the student's goal of outlining historical progression.

Distractor Explanations: Choice B is incorrect because it implies that the Treaty of Versailles directly led to the implementation of the Marshall Plan, bypassing key transitions such as the Great Depression and Hitler's rise to power. This may misrepresent history and leave out key transitions such as these. **Choice C** is incorrect it discusses implementation of the Marshall Plan, which was a post-war activity; whereas, the question is about the events until the start of the war. **Choice D** is incorrect because it inaccurately suggests that Hitler's rise to power directly instigated World War II, without acknowledging that the Treaty of Versailles and the Great Depression might also have had some role. The notes make it clear that these two events preceded and we cannot deny the possibility that they might have contributed to Hitler's rise to power.

27. **Level:** Medium | **Domain:** EXPRESSION OF IDEAS

Skill/Knowledge: Rhetorical Synthesis

Key Explanation: Choice B is the best answer because the question asks about the first ruler of Egypt. **Choice B** provides the most information about Narmer, including saying that he was the first ruler. **Choice B** includes relevant details about his unification of Upper and Lower Egypt and the approximate time the unification and his rule began.

Distractor Explanations: Choice A is incorrect because it describes the first dynasty more than the first ruler of the dynasty; it provides extra information at the expense of details that would add more about Narmer. **Choice C** is incorrect because the notes do not directly state that Narmer's tomb was made of these materials, only that the materials were common for the time. It is possible that Narmer's was one of the exceptions made from stone. **Choice D** is incorrect because it does not explain whether Narmer actually became the first ruler, so it is unclear who the first ruler was.

1. **Level:** Hard | **Domain:** CRAFT AND STRUCTURE
    Skill/Knowledge: Words in Context

    Key Explanation: Choice C is the best answer because it is a strong word that means "disreputable" or "offensive." "Obtrusive" refers to the "gentleman" that was following the girl, and **Choice C** clearly shows that the gentleman was not behaving properly as a gentleman should. **Choice C** conveys distinct contempt for the man's actions.

    Distractor Explanations: None of the other choices shows that the narrator took great offense at the gentleman's behavior. **Choice A** means "clear" or "apparent." **Choice B** refers to something that is easy to see or that calls attention to itself. **Choice D** refers to something that is certain to Happen.

2. **Level:** Medium | **Domain:** CRAFT AND STRUCTURE
    Skill/Knowledge: Words in Context

    Key Explanation: Choice C is the best answer because in the context, the blank describes the understanding that governments and society need before ocean energy deployment takes place. **Choice C** refers to something that is solid and able to withstand outside pressures. It shows that the understanding needs to be complete and not easy to crumble when the pressure of arguments is brought against it.

    Distractor Explanations: None of the other choices describe the understanding that governments and society need. **Choice A** refers to a living thing that is healthy and full of energy. **Choice B** refers to something that is physically able to withstand rough treatment. When used to describe something intangible, **Choice D** refers to something that is strict or uncompromising. It refers to things such as rules rather than the way something is understood.

3. **Level:** Hard | **Domain:** CRAFT AND STRUCTURE
    Skill/Knowledge: Words in Context

    Key Explanation: Choice D is the best answer. In this context, "abstraction" refers to the "state" or "mood" that the donkey was in. The passage shows that he did not notice "the word of command" but instead "jogged onward" or "continued" because he was wondering whether he would get a cabbage stalk or not. **Choice D** refers to having one's attention focused on something, so fits the context of saying the donkey was paying attention to whether he would get food or not rather than listening to commands.

    Distractor Explanations: Choice A is incorrect because it refers to making a judgment based on specific cases, but the donkey is not judging, nor is it making a final decision. **Choice B** refers to a working idea used as the basis for an experiment, but a "state" or "mood" is not a hypothesis. **Choice C** refers to a specific decision, but the donkey has not resolved to do anything, it is just wondering and jogging along.

4. **Level:** Hard | **Domain:** CRAFT AND STRUCTURE
    Skill/Knowledge: Text Structure and Purpose

    Key Explanation: Choice A is the best answer because "I shall not live in vain" can be paraphrased as "I would have fulfilled a useful purpose before dying." The repetition of this phrase shows that the author feels very strongly or seriously that she should do something useful before she dies, such as helping prevent a person from getting a broken heart or aiding a bird that has fallen from its nest.

Distractor Explanations: Choice B is incorrect because the author is not saying she is about to die, she is saying what she wants to accomplish before dying. **Choice C** is incorrect because the phrase highlights the importance of the tasks, but "futile" means "useless." **Choice D** is incorrect because there is no clue as to whether the author has "accomplished" or "completed" the things she mentions in the poem; she just stresses that they are important things to do.

5. **Level:** Easy | **Domain:** CRAFT AND STRUCTURE
   Skill/Knowledge: Text Structure and Purpose

   Key Explanation: Choice C is the best answer because later in the passage, the author suggests that there are other species with similar features to the *Tyrannosaurus rex*. The underlined sentence introduced the Tyrannosaurus rex so that it can be compared with other species in the following sentences.

   Distractor Explanations: Choice A is incorrect since any difficulties that the *Tyrannosaurus rex* faced are not described. Additionally, this answer choice ignores the comparison to other species that are brought up in the final sentences. **Choice B** is wrong because although the passage states that the T-rex was a "fearsome" predator, it does not state that it was the "fiercest" predator. The superlative adjective "fiercest" would mean that the T-rex is the most fierce predator of all the predators at the time. The passage does not state this. **Choice D** is wrong because the author does claim that the features of the *Tyrannosaurus rex* are superior, but are actually similar to another species.

6. **Level:** Medium | **Domain:** CRAFT AND STRUCTURE
   Skill/Knowledge: Cross–Text Connections

   Key Explanation: Choice A is the best answer. The author of Text 2 refers to the difficulty of identifying objects that are not covered with ice because such objects do not reflect light. Therefore, the objects that have not been found might not have ice, and therefore, they are harder to see.

   Distractor Explanations: Choice B is incorrect because the author of Text 2 does not refer to the size of the object in relation to how easy it is to isolate; it is possible that many large objects that are not covered with ice still have not been found. **Choice C** is incorrect because there is no discussion in Text 2 about the distance from the sun affecting whether it is easy to see objects or not. **Choice D** is incorrect because Text 2 implies that there are objects which have not been located, though there is no clue about how many objects there might be.

7. **Level:** Hard | **Domain:** INFORMATION AND IDEAS
   Skill/Knowledge: Cross–Text Connections

   Key Explanation: Choice C is the best answer because it describes the most likely way that Jane Addams (Text 2) would respond to Dix's actions to improve the conditions for the imprisoned and insane presented in Text 1. According to Text 1, Dix visited every public and private mental illness and prison facility she could to research and document in graphic detail the inhumane conditions, she then took political action and presented the information to legislature of Massachusetts which led to reform. Text 2 indicates that Addams was an advocate for social reform and dedicated her life to political action and social science research that would improve the lives of lower-class slums residents. This suggests that Addams would corroborate or support the methodology and actions used by Dix to achieve social reform.

Distractor Explanations: Choice A is incorrect because nothing in Text 2 suggests that Addams would dispute the effectiveness of research and documentation in achieving social reform. Text 2 confirms that Addams would support this type of action and she practiced it herself. **Choice B** is incorrect because Text 2 doesn't include any information suggesting that Addams placed greater significance on a personal lifetime commitment to social cause than using political action to achieve social reform. **Choice D** is incorrect because there's no information in Text 2 suggesting that Addams would contest or question the effectiveness of Dix's reports in achieving reform. Although Text 2 describes Addams's methodology more scientifically, it doesn't imply that Addams would be against shocking society into reformation using dramatic and emotional information.

8. **Level:** Hard | **Domain:** INFORMATION AND IDEAS
    Skill/Knowledge: Central Ideas and Details

    Key Explanation: Choice C is the best answer. The text points out that Venus is warm because it has a "giant blanket" of an atmosphere with so much carbon dioxide holding in the heat. If Mercury had such a blanket, then it would also hold in heat due to the greenhouse effect. Therefore, Mercury probably has less carbon dioxide, which is why it is less hot in general than Venus is, even though Mercury is closer to the Sun.

Distractor Explanations: Choice A is incorrect because Mercury could have some sulfuric acid in the atmosphere, though it presumably does not have as much as Venus, which is reflective and brighter because of the acid. **Choice B** is incorrect because "never" is too absolute. The passage only says that Venus is "generally hotter," which means that it can sometimes be less hot than Mercury. Plus, the "average" or "middle" temperature is 462 degrees Celsius, so it is possible that Mercury is sometimes hotter than that. **Choice D** is not discussed in the passage; it could be possible to locate Mercury easily. The passage only says that Venus is brighter.

9. **Level:** Medium | **Domain:** INFORMATION AND IDEAS
    Skill/Knowledge: Central Ideas and Details

    Key Explanation: Choice D is correct since the group did not want to say "farewell" and everyone went out to see the narrator off, it is logical to assume that the narrator is not leaving for a brief trip. Since Elizabeth asked for the narrator to write, there will be time to send letters.

    Distractor Explanations: Choice A is incorrect because the gender is not given; it is possible that the narrator is a man. **Choice B** is incorrect because the narrator could have traveled before. **Choice C** is incorrect because, while the narrator didn't want to leave the others, it is possible that the narrator was looking forward to the end of the journey and what would happen upon arrival.

10. **Level:** Hard | **Domain:** INFORMATION AND IDEAS
    Skill/Knowledge: Command of Evidence (Textual)

    Key Explanation: Choice A is correct. The implication of the study is that women may choose risky but rewarding careers, which can affect the economy in the long term. However, if the girls from the different cultures revert to their original level of risk aversion because they are no longer interacting with one another upon graduation, this implication is no longer valid.

Distractor Explanations: Choice B is incorrect because this choice mentions a finding about the Mosuo and Han boys, while the implication of the study is about the girls and their future career choices as women. **Choice C** is incorrect because this choice mentions a finding about the Mosuo and Han boys, while the implication of the study is about the girls and their future career choices as women. **Choice D** is incorrect because this choice directly supports the implication of the study.

11. **Level:** Medium | **Domain:** INFORMATION AND IDEAS
    Skill/Knowledge: Command of Evidence (Quantitative)

    Key Explanation: The unfinished sentence is giving an example to illustrate the claim in the previous sentence that "it is incorrect to judge the number of dangerous encounters just by looking at deaths." Therefore, the mission portion should emphasize a point that extends beyond deaths caused by sharks. **Choice C** effectively stresses the point because it shows that there were many more dangerous encounters in the same year, so to estimate the number of attacks, **Choice C** shows that it is better to look at all attacks rather than just fatal ones.

    Distractor Explanations: None of the other choices offer a good example to show that "it is incorrect to judge the number of dangerous encounters just by looking at deaths." **Choice A** is very vague and the reader does not know if

the number of non-fatal attacks is high or not. It could be almost identical to the number of deaths. **Choices B** and **D** only offer more detail about deaths, so they do not emphasize how looking at deaths gives an inaccurate idea of the number of dangerous encounters.

12. **Level:** Medium | **Domain:** INFORMATION AND IDEAS
    Skill/Knowledge: Command of Evidence (Quantitative)

    Key Explanation: Choice C is the best answer because the number of tourists in Togo in 2016 was 65,000. That number is lower than the one for Nigeria, 634,000, but higher than the number for Eritrea, 28,000.

    Distractor Explanations: Choice A is incorrect because, although Togo is the top row on the graph, it does not have the greatest number of tourists. That country is Nigeria in the bottom row, which had almost ten times as many visitors. **Choice B** is incorrect because the number for Togo is greater than that for Burundi, 56,000, but lower than that for Nigeria. **Choice D** is impossible to determine because the graph does not give the number of tourists for the previous year.

13. **Level:** Easy | **Domain:** INFORMATION AND IDEAS
    Skill/Knowledge: Central Ideas and Details

    Key Explanation: Choice A is the best answer because the comment that "an opportunity… kept it" explain that Elinor, the oldest daughter, convinces Mrs. Dashwood to sell the carriage despite the fact that Mrs. Dashwood herself wanted to keep it. In addition, Elinor suggests that Mrs. Dashwood limit their household to three servants. Mrs. Dashwood "defers" or "agrees" to the opinions of her daughter despite some apparent reluctance.

Distractor Explanations: Choice B is opposite of the relationship portrayed in the passage. **Choices C** and **D** are not supported by any evidence in the text.

14. **Level:** Hard | **Domain:** INFORMATION AND IDEAS
Skill/Knowledge: Inferences

Key Explanation: Choice B is correct. The previous sentence warns that correlation is not the same as causality and the public should not be quick to draw conclusions based on causality. This choice provides an example where the relationship is not a causal one. If children with better mental health are more likely to choose team sports in the first place, then it is not the participation in team sports that is causing lower levels of anxiety and depression. The children who play team sports are found to have better mental health because those are the types of children likely to play team sports at the outset.

Distractor Explanations: Choice A is incorrect because this choice provides an example of a mechanism behind a causal relationship. However, the previous sentence is commenting on how correlation is not proof of causality, so providing an example related to causality is not relevant here. **Choice C** is incorrect because this example is about how a study can prove causality. However, the previous sentence is commenting on how correlation is not proof of causality, so providing an example related to causality is not relevant here. **Choice D** is incorrect because this example is about how a study can prove causality. However, the previous sentence is commenting on how

correlation is not proof of causality, so providing an example related to causality is not relevant here.

15. **Level:** Medium | **Domain:** STANDARD ENGLISH CONVENTIONS
Skill/Knowledge: Form, Structure, and Sense

Key Explanation: Choice D is the correct answer. The convention being tested is the pronoun-antecedent agreement. In this case, the antecedent is "the Fortune 500 companies present in 1955." This antecedent is plural because it refers to multiple companies. Therefore, the correct pronoun to use is a plural pronoun, "them" being the correct option in this context. It is important to remember that "them" is an object pronoun, meaning that it can be used to replace the object in a sentence.

Distractor Explanations: Choice A is incorrect because the subject being referred to is plural ("Most of [the companies]"), hence, rendering the usage of the singular "it" incorrect. **Choice B** is incorrect because "this" does not have a clear antecedent, and the subject is plural. The usage of "is" further makes this option incorrect. **Choice C** is incorrect because "they" is used as a subject pronoun. This means that "they" can be used to replace a subject and not an object.

16. **Level:** Easy | **Domain:** STANDARD ENGLISH CONVENTIONS
Skill/Knowledge: Form, Structure, and Sense

Key Explanation: Choice B is the best answer. The underlined portion is part of a list joined by "and." Each part of such a list needs to have the same grammatical structure. In this case, the first two items are –ing verbs that show the method of the reduction following "by": "limiting...

emissions," and "encouraging...innovation." **Choice B** is another –ing verb, so fits the same structure.

Distractor Explanations: All of the other choices can be eliminated because they do not maintain the same structure as the other two items in the list joined by "and." **Choice A** is a complete clause, "it is...." **Choices C** and **D** are noun phrases, "the right..." and "increased competition...."

17. **Level:** Medium | **Domain:** STANDARD ENGLISH CONVENTIONS
Skill/Knowledge: Form, Structure, and Sense

Key Explanation: Choice B is the correct answer. The convention being tested is subject-modifier placement. **Choice B** is the only option where the modifier is placed next to the subject. Therefore, it correctly connects the idea of plastic material and how its usage damages the environment.

Distractor Explanations: Choice A is incorrect because the modifier and subject are not in alignment. It is not "the purchase of plastic material" that causes environmental damage but the plastic itself that causes pollution. This choice incorrectly changes the meaning of the sentence and also incorrectly implies that the purchase of plastic is durable. **Choice C** is incorrect because selecting this option would change the meaning of the sentence. It is not the "purchasing" action that is affordable and durable. It is plastic that has these characteristics. **Choice D** is incorrect because "plastic material or its purchase" changes the sentence's intended meaning. Using "plastic material or its usage" introduces a disjunctive construction, indicating a choice between two options. However, in the context of the sentence, the intention is to convey that plastic material, along with its usage, causes environmental

damage. Using a disjunctive construction here could imply that either the plastic material or its usage (but not both) causes the damage, which is not the intended meaning.

18. **Level:** Easy | **Domain:** STANDARD ENGLISH CONVENTIONS
Skill/Knowledge: Boundaries

Key Explanation: The convention being tested is punctuation use between a sentence and an essential element. **Choice A** is the best answer because the sentence is a complex sentence that has an essential element supplement introduced by the relative pronoun "that". This essential element provides necessary information about the new species of lizard that was discovered in the Andes mountains of Peru.

In such cases, it is standard English to not separate the essential element with any punctuation, including colons, dashes, or commas. Using any of these options would create an incorrect sentence structure, as they would create a pause or break that would separate the essential element from the rest of the sentence.

Distractor Explanations: Choice B is incorrect because it uses a colon to separate the clauses, which implies that the second clause explains or expands on the first clause. However, in this case, the second clause is providing additional information about the new species of lizard, not about Peru itself. **Choice C** is incorrect because it uses a dash to separate the clauses, which does not convey the appropriate relationship between the two clauses. Additionally, the use of a dash in this way creates an abrupt break in the sentence that is not necessary. **Choice D** is incorrect because using a comma, the identifying clause "that is able to change" is providing additional information about Peru, rather than simply describing the new species of lizard.

19. **Level:** Easy | **Domain:** STANDARD ENGLISH CONVENTIONS
Skill/Knowledge: Boundaries

Key Explanation: The convention being tested is punctuation use between a sentence and an essential element. **Choice C** is the best answer because in this context, the essential element supplement "who have achieved great things" provides necessary information about the noun "artists" and therefore should not be separated from the noun by punctuation.

Distractor Explanations: Choice A is incorrect because it uses a comma, which would suggest that the essential element supplement is optional and could be removed without changing the meaning of the sentence. **Choice B** uses a dash, which is not a standard way to introduce an essential element supplement. **Choice D** uses a semicolon, which is not necessary or appropriate in this context.

20. **Level:** Easy | **Domain:** STANDARD ENGLISH CONVENTIONS
Skill/Knowledge: Boundaries

Key Explanation: Choice B is the best answer. When three or more nouns are joined in a list using "and," there should be a comma after all the nouns that precede "and."

Distractor Explanations: All of the other choices can be eliminated because they are not standard punctuation for a list joined by "and." **Choice A** is incorrect because there is no punctuation at all to

show where one noun ends and the other begins. **Choice C is** incorrect because there should be a comma after the noun "emotions" but none after "and." **Choice D** is incorrect because semicolons are only used to join items in a list if there are commas within the ideas, but each noun is a single word.

21. **Level:** Medium | **Domain:** STANDARD ENGLISH CONVENTIONS
Skill/Knowledge: Boundaries

Key Explanation: Choice A is the best answer. "a ring of massive stones erected around 2,500 B.C." is added information that describes "Stonehenge." Added information needs to be separated from the main clause "Stonehenge is one of..." using the same punctuation at both ends. In this case, the end punctuation after "2,500 B.C." is a dash, so the added information should also be preceded with a dash.

Distractor Explanations: Choice B is incorrect because the dash divides "of" from its object. The resulting main clause is illogical: Stonehenge, a ring of is one of...." **Choice C** is incorrect because the punctuation needs to be the same at the start and end of information inserted into a sentence's main clause. It is possible to use commas, but there should also be one after "2,500 B.C." In addition, a single dash needs to follow a complete clause, but there is no active verb in the first section. **Choice D** is incorrect because a colon needs to follow an independent clause, but the preceding portion is only a noun.

22. **Level:** Easy | **Domain:** EXPRESSION OF IDEAS
Skill/Knowledge: Transitions

Key Explanation: Choice D is the best answer. The previous information says that Joel did not care about finishing a high school degree, but the following says that he later went to the effort of obtaining it. Choice D fits that context because it is used to show that the following information happened despite the previous claim. In other words, he finished a degree despite saying he did not care about getting one.

Distractor Explanations: Choices A and C are incorrect because they refer to the following happening as a certain or logical result of the previous claim. However, this text refers to something that happens unexpectedly; Joel got a degree although he said he did not want one. **Choice B** is incorrect because it signifies that the previous and following claims happen at the same time, but in this case, the events occur 25 years apart.

23. **Level:** Easy | **Domain:** EXPRESSION OF IDEAS
Skill/Knowledge: Transitions

Key Explanation: Choice B is the best answer because it is used to show that something happens even though something else happens. In this case, **Choice B** accurately shows that the main idea of the sentence, not finding the cause of the shipwreck, occurred even though the first idea in the sentence, the fame of the ship, existed. In other words, even though the shipwreck was famous, no one knows why it sank.

Distractor Explanations: Choice A is incorrect because it offers the first idea as a reason for the second, but it is not necessarily reasonable that something very famous is still a mystery. **Choices C and D** are incorrect because they do not grammatically fit in the context. They act as separate linking words, so the result is that "its fame" becomes an appositive, but "its fame" is not another way of saying "the exact cause."

24. **Level:** Easy | **Domain:** EXPRESSION OF IDEAS

Skill/Knowledge: Transitions

Key Explanation: Choice A is the best answer. The previous portion points out the actions that certain organizations are taking for safety, and the following portion says those actions are "not sufficient" or "not good enough." **Choice A** is used to show a contrast of ideas, so accurately cues the reader that the following idea casts doubt on the first claim.

Distractor Explanations: Choice B is incorrect because it is used to highlight a similarity, but the preceding and following ideas are opposite as far as ensuring safety for travel in space. **Choice C** is used to show a logical result of the preceding argument, but in this case, the idea that smaller items can cause damage is not a logical result of the previous discussion that steps are taken for safety reasons. **Choice D** is used to show another possibility or choice, so does not fit the context of describing the current situation and a problem with the current situation.

25. **Level:** Hard | **Domain:** EXPRESSION OF IDEAS
Skill/Knowledge: Rhetorical Synthesis

Key Explanation: Choice B is correct because it efficiently and concisely integrates key events such as the Lexington and Concord Battles, the Declaration of Independence, and the Treaty of Paris into an overall timeline tracing their significance to shaping America.

Distractor Explanations: Choice A is incorrect because it does not incorporate as many details from the student's notes as Choice B; specifically, it leaves out references to both the Declaration of Independence and General George Washington, two key components of the American Revolution. **Choice C** is incorrect because it primarily highlights the contributions of General Washington and events he could be associated with and neglects other significant events, including the Lexington and Concord battles, the Declaration of Independence, and the Treaty of Paris. While his role was crucial, this activity does not cover everything happening during that era, and major milestones were missed out of consideration. **Choice D** is incorrect and serves as an excellent diversion because it highlights several key events; however, it fails to mention the Battles of Lexington and Concord which triggered World War One as well as General Washington's key role.

26. **Level:** Medium | **Domain:** EXPRESSION OF IDEAS
    Skill/Knowledge: Rhetorical Synthesis

    Key Explanation: Choice C is the best answer. The audience is concerned about improving innovation, and **Choice C** directly "addresses" or "responds to" that question by offering a solution based on Mayo's theory: giving workers more freedom.

    Distractor Explanations: Choice A is incorrect because it only discusses why innovation does not occur; it does not offer any solutions for increasing innovation or solving the problem of boredom. **Choice B** is incorrect because it does not show how Mayo's theory affects innovation; it points out a way to get tasks done, but not necessarily in a creative way. Furthermore, it points out a problem that could negate any benefits of the theory. **Choice D** is extremely vague; it says that there are positive points regarding innovation, but the audience does not know what these positive points are. The negative aspect of stress may not outweigh the benefits as far as the audience is concerned; the audience does not have enough information to make a clear judgment.

27. **Level:** Medium | **Domain:** EXPRESSION OF

IDEAS
Skill/Knowledge: Rhetorical Synthesis

Key Explanation: Choice A is correct because it effectively depicts both the construction and fall of the Berlin Wall, linking these events directly to political motivations and changes within East Germany.

Distractor Explanations: Choice B is incorrect because it incorrectly emphasizes the fall of the wall as an event marking the end of the Cold War and does not address its political motivations, which was part of the student's goal setting. **Choice C** is incorrect because it doesn't fully address the student's goal to emphasize both the construction and the fall of the Berlin Wall. While it correctly mentions the political motivation behind the wall's construction, it fails to mention the political changes and civil unrest in East Germany that led to its fall. Therefore, it only partially meets the criteria set by the student. **Choice D** is incorrect because though it touches upon the political symbolism of the Wall, it fails to emphasize its construction and eventual fall - two points that the student intended to emphasize.

1. **Level:** Medium | **Domain:** ADVANCED MATH
Skill/Knowledge: Nonlinear functions | **Testing point:** Determining the equation of a parabola from its graph

Key Explanation: Choice C is correct. The general equation of a parabola is given by $y = a(x - h)^2 + k$ where (h, k) is the vertex. Based on the graph, the vertex of the parabola is at $(-1, -6)$. Substituting the coordinate of the vertex to the general equation yields $y = a(x + 1)^2 - 6$. Since the graph opens upward, the leading coefficient is greater than zero. This means that a is positive and based on the choices, a is equal to 3. Substituting 3 to the equation of the parabola yields $y = 3(x + 1)^2 - 6$. Expanding the right side of the equation yields $y = 3x^2 + 6x - 3$.

Distractor Explanations: Choice A is incorrect and may result from an error in expanding the equation of the parabola. **Choice B** is incorrect because a is negative, which means that the graph opens downward. **Choice D** is incorrect because a is negative, which means that the graph opens downward.

2. **Level:** Easy | **Domain:** ADVANCED MATH
Skill/Knowledge: Nonlinear functions | **Testing point:** Determining the products of the solutions to a quadratic equation

Key Explanation: To find the product of the solutions, use the formula $\left(\dfrac{c}{a} \right)$, where a is the coefficient of x^2 and c is the constant. From the given equation $a = 3$ and $c = -15$. Therefore, the product of the solutions is $\left(\dfrac{-15}{3} \right)$, which is equal to -5.

3. **Level:** Medium | **Domain:** PROBLEM-SOLVING AND DATA ANALYSIS
Skill/Knowledge: Probability and conditional probability | **Testing point:** Calculating probability of simple events

Key Explanation: Choice C is correct. The probability of a simple event occurring can be calculated using the formula $p = \dfrac{no.\ of\ favorable\ outcomes}{total\ no.\ of\ possible\ outcomes}$. Since a heart is picked at first and is not put back in the deck, there are only 12 hearts left in a deck of now 51 cards. The probability of picking a heart card for the second time would then, therefore, be $\dfrac{12}{51}$, which is 12 heart cards out of the 51 cards on the deck.

Distractor Explanations: Choice A is incorrect. This would be the probability of picking the first heart from the deck of 52 cards. **Choice B** is incorrect and may result from not subtracting the first card picked from the initial total number of cards. **Choice D** is incorrect because it represents the probability of not picking a second heart.

4. **Level:** Easy | **Domain:** ADVANCED MATH
Skill/Knowledge: Equivalent expressions | **Testing point:** Matching coefficients

Key Explanation: Choice B is correct. To solve this, use the distributive property which yields $6xy^2 + 18x^2y - 6x^2y - 2xy^2$.
Combining like terms yields $4xy^2 + 12x^2y$.

Distractor Explanations: Choice A is incorrect and may result from a conceptual or calculation error. **Choice C** is incorrect and may result from a conceptual or calculation error. **Choice D** is incorrect and may result from a conceptual or calculation error.

5. **Level:** Easy | **Domain:** PROBLEM-SOLVING AND DATA ANALYSIS
Skill/Knowledge: Percentages | **Testing point:** Using discounts and percentage increase

Key Explanation: Since the price of the dress first increases by 15%, then it becomes $115\% \times 200 = 230$. Therefore, the price after 15th May is \$230. However, she bought it at a discounted price. Applying the discount, the amount that she paid for the dress is $70\% \times 230 = \$161$.

6. **Level:** Easy | **Domain:** ADVANCED MATH
Skill/Knowledge: Nonlinear equations in one variable and systems of equations in two variables
Testing point: Using the difference of two squares to solve a system of equations

Key Explanation: Choice D is correct. The first equation contains the difference of two squares which is in the form of $a^2 - b^2$. This can be factored into $(a + b)(a - b)$.
Therefore,
$(x - y)(x + y) = x^2 - y^2$.
The first equation then becomes
$(x - y)(x + y) = 12$. Substituting the value of $(x - y)$ from the second equation into the first equation yields $2(x + y) = 12$.
Dividing both sides of the equation by 2 yields $(x + y) = 6$.

Distractor Explanations: Choice A is incorrect and may result from solving the value of $y - x$.
Choice B is incorrect and may result from solving the value of y. **Choice C** is incorrect and may result from solving the value of x.

7. **Level:** Medium | **Domain:** ALGEBRA
Skill/Knowledge: Systems of two linear equations in two variables | **Testing point:** Solving system of linear equations for x and y

Key Explanation: Choice A is correct. Solve for the value of x and y by using the elimination method.
Multiplying to the first equation yields
$3(2x + y = 2)$ or $6x + 3y = 6$.
Subtracting the second equation from the first equation yields $6x + 3y - 3y + x = 6 - 20$.
Combining like terms yields $7x = -14$. Dividing both sides of the equation by 7 yields $x = -2$. To find y, replace x with the value -2 in the first equation.
This yields $6(-2) + 3y = 6$ or $-12 + 3y = 6$.
Adding 12 to both sides of the equation yields $3y = 18$.
Dividing both sides of the equation by 3 yields $y = 6$.
The value of $xy = (-2)(6) = -12$.

Distractor Explanations: Choice B is incorrect because it would be the value of $\frac{y}{x}$. **Choice C** is incorrect because this is the value of x. **Choice D** is incorrect because this is the value y.

8. **Level:** Medium | **Domain:** ADVANCED MATH
Skill/Knowledge: Nonlinear equations in one variable and systems of equations in two variables
Testing point: Solving absolute value equations

Key Explanation: Isolate the absolute value by dividing both sides of the equation by 2.
This yields $\frac{2|x+4|}{2} = \frac{12}{2}$ or $|x + 4| = 6$.
Solve the values of x by equating the content of the absolute value to the positive and negative values of the constant.
Determine the first value of x using $x + 4 = 6$.
Subtracting 4 from both sides of the equation

yields $x = 2$.

Determine the second value of x using $x + 4 = -6$. Subtracting 4 from both sides of the equation yields $x = -10$.

Since the problem only requires the positive value of x, the answer is 2.

9. **Level:** Easy | **Domain:** PROBLEM–SOLVING AND DATA ANALYSIS
Skill/Knowledge: One–variable data: distributions and measures of center and spread
Testing point: Evaluating and comparing measures of center and spread

Key Explanation: Choice B is correct. The data being added would be an outlier on the higher end of the data set. The add–on changes the maximum of the data set and this would mean that the range would increase. The outlier would also increase the mean. The median will remain the same and will still be 1.39 because it is the 7th number in the new set of data. The standard deviation will increase as the data point is an outlier.

Distractor Explanations: Choice A is incorrect. This is a false statement.**Choice C** is incorrect. This is a false statement.**Choice D** is incorrect. This is a false statement.

10. **Level:** Medium | **Domain:** GEOMETRY AND TRIGONOMETRY
Skill/Knowledge: Area and volume | **Testing point:** Area of a circle in an inscribed polygon

Key Explanation: Choice B is correct. Since the circle is inscribed in a square, the side length of the square is equivalent to the diameter of the circle. Therefore, if the diameter is $14cm$, the radius would be half, which is $7cm$. The area would therefore be $7^2\pi$ or 49π.

Distractor Explanations: Choice A is incorrect because this is the circumference of the circle. **Choice C** is incorrect because this is twice the value of the circle's area. **Choice D** is incorrect. It is the area of a circle if the radius is $14cm$.

11. **Level:** Hard | **Domain:** ALGEBRA
Skill/Knowledge: Linear functions | **Testing point:** Using linear transformations

Key Explanation: The function $f(x)$ translated 2 units to the left will become $f(x + 2)$.
This yields $y = 3(x + 2) + 5$ or $y = 3x + 11$.
The function $f(x)$ translated 1 unit up will become $f(x) + 1$.
This yields $y = 3x + 11 + 1$ or $y = 3x + 12$.
Therefore, the new y-intercept is 12.

12. **Level:** Medium | **Domain:** ALGEBRA
Skill/Knowledge: Linear inequalities in one or two variables | **Testing point:** Finding the solutions to an inequality

Key Explanation: Choice D is correct. To find the solution, substitute the choices for each inequality and verify if the statements are true or false.
Plugging in **Choice D** (3, 1) to the first inequality yields $(-2)(1) > -4$ or $2 > -4$ which is true.
Plugging (3, 1) into the second inequality yields $3(3) - 1 > 3$ or $5 > 3$ which is also true.
Since both statements are true when the point (3, 1) is plugged into both inequalities, then the correct answer is **Choice D**.

Distractor Explanations: Choice A is incorrect. Plugging in (1, 2) to both inequalities yields $-4 > -4$ and $1 > 3$ which are both false statements. **Choice B** is incorrect. Plugging in (1, 3) to both inequalities yields $-6 > -4$ and $0 > 3$ which are both false statements. **Choice C** is incorrect. Plugging in (2, 4) to both inequalities yields –8 > –4 and 2 > 3 which are both false statements.

13. **Level:** Medium | **Domain:** GEOMETRY AND TRIGONOMETRY
    Skill/Knowledge: Circles | **Testing point:** Using the midpoint formula and the equation of a circle

    Key Explanation: Choice B is correct. The standard equation of a circle is given by $(x – h)^2 + (y – k)^2 = r^2$ where (h, k) is the center and r is the radius. The endpoints of the circle are (–6, 10) and (2, 10). The midpoint of these two points would be $\left(\dfrac{-6+2}{2}, \dfrac{10+10}{2}\right) = (-2,10)$ which is also the coordinates of the center of the circle. The radius of the circle can be solved by calculating the distance between the center and one of the endpoints of the diameter. Substituting (2, 10) and (–2, 10) to the formula $\sqrt{\left(y_2 - y_1\right)^2 + (x_1 - x_2)^2}$ yields

    $\sqrt{\left(10-10\right)^2 + (-2-2)^2} = 4$

    4 would therefore be the radius.
    Plugging in the coordinates of the center and the radius to the standard equation yields $(x + 2)^2 + (y – 10)^2 = 16$.

    Distractor Explanations: Choice A is incorrect and may result due to conceptual errors such as identifying the center from the equation of the circle. **Choice C** is incorrect and may result due to conceptual errors such as identifying the center from the equation of the circle. **Choice D** is incorrect and may result due to conceptual errors such as identifying the center from the equation of the circle.

14. **Level:** Medium | **Domain:** ALGEBRA
    Skill/Knowledge: Linear functions | **Testing point:** Finding the value of a composite function

    Key Explanation: Choice C is correct. To solve this, calculate for $g(2)$ first.
    Substituting 2 to $g(x)$ yields $g(2) = 2(2) + 3$ or $g(2) = 4 + 3$.
    Combining like terms yields $g(2) = 7$.
    Since $g(2) = 7$, then $f(g(2)) = f(7)$.
    Substituting 7 yields $f(7) = 7 + 2$ or $f(7) = 9$.

    Distractor Explanations: Choice A is incorrect because this is the value of $f(2)$. **Choice B** is incorrect because this is the value of $g(2)$. **Choice D** is incorrect because this would be the value of $g(f(2))$.

15. **Level:** Medium | **Domain:** ADVANCED MATH
    Skill/Knowledge: Nonlinear functions | **Testing point:** Solving for the y–intercept in a nonlinear function

    Key Explanation: The y–intercept is when $x = 0$. Substituting 0 for x in the given equation yields $y = 300^0 + 5$.
    Any number raised to the power of 0 is equal to 1. The equation becomes, $y = 1 + 5$ or $y = 6$.
    Therefore, the y–intercept is 6.

16. **Level:** Easy | **Domain:** ALGEBRA
    Skill/Knowledge: Linear inequalities in one or two variables | **Testing point:** Finding the equation of an inequality from its graph

    Key Explanation: Choice B is correct. The solutions to the inequality are above the line which would mean that the y values are greater. This means that the equation will be in the form of $y > mx + b$. Hence, the possible answer is either **choice A** or **B**. Since the dash line falls down from left to right, the value of the *slope*(m) is negative. Between **Choices A** and **B**, only **Choice A** has a negative slope. Therefore, the graph represents the inequality $y > -2x + 3$.

Distractor Explanations: Choice A is incorrect because it has a positive slope. **Choice C** is incorrect because it uses less than symbols for the inequalities. **Choice D** is incorrect because it uses less than symbols for the inequalities.

17. **Level:** Easy | **Domain:** ADVANCED MATH
Skill/Knowledge: Nonlinear functions | **Testing point:** Finding exponential functions from graphs

Key Explanation: Choice C is correct. Since the graph rises from left to right, it is an exponential growth function in the form of $f(x) = a(1 + r)^x$ where a is the initial amount, r is the growth rate, and x is the number of time intervals. Since the graph represents an exponential growth function, $(1 + r) > 1$. Hence, the possible answers are **Choices A** or **C** because $1.03 > 1$. To determine the correct answer between **Choice A** and **C**, find the value of a. Looking at the graph, it intersects at $(0, 180)$ which means that the y–intercept is 180. Thus, the initial amount is 180 or $a = 180$. Therefore, the correct answer is **Choice C.**

Distractor Explanations: Choice A is incorrect. It has y–intercepts greater than 180. **Choice B** is incorrect. It represents a decaying exponential function. **Choice D** is incorrect. It has y–intercepts greater than 180.

18. **Level:** Easy | **Domain:** ALGEBRA
Skill/Knowledge: Linear equations in two variables | **Testing point:** Matching coefficients

Key Explanation: Choice D is correct. To solve this, use the distributive property to simplify the left side of the equation.

This yields $3x + 2x + 8y = ax + by$.
Combining like terms yields $5x + 8y = ax + by$.
Matching the coefficients yields $a = 5$.

Distractor Explanations: Choice A is incorrect and may result from a conceptual or calculation error. **Choice B** is incorrect and may result from a conceptual or calculation error. **Choice C** is incorrect and may result from a conceptual or calculation error.

19. **Level:** Easy | **Domain:** ALGEBRA
Skill/Knowledge: Linear inequalities in one or two variables | **Testing point:** Writing the solution of an inequality in interval notation

Key Explanation: To solve for this inequality, divide both sides by -3 which yields $\frac{-3y}{-3} > \frac{-15}{-3}$ or $y < 5$. Since y can be any number less than 5, its value approaches negative infinity. Therefore, the interval notation is $(-\infty, 5)$.

20. **Level:** Easy | **Domain:** GEOMETRY AND TRIGONOMETRY
Skill/Knowledge: Right triangles and trigonometry | **Testing point:** Using trigonometric identities

Key Explanation: Choice B is correct. Since $sin(3x) = cos(x + 10)$, the two angles $(3x)$ and $(x + 10)$ are complementary and add up to 90°. Therefore, $(3x) + (x + 10) = 90$.
Combining like terms yields $4x + 10 = 90$.
Subtracting 10 from both sides of the equation yields $4x = 80$.
Dividing both sides of the equation by 4 yields $x = 20°$.

Distractor Explanations: Choice A is incorrect and may result from a conceptual or calculation error. **Choice C** is incorrect and may result from solving the value of $(x + 10)$. **Choice D** is incorrect and may result from solving the value of $3x$.

21. **Level:** Easy | **Domain:** ADVANCED MATH
Skill/Knowledge: Nonlinear functions | **Testing point:** Determining the type of equation from data given

Key Explanation: Choice A is correct. Since Amanda doubles the amount of money she will save every week, the amount that she puts in every week grows exponentially. This exponential growth can be represented by the *model s* = $10(2)$ ^{t}, where t is time in weeks and s is the amount that she will save in the given week.

Distractor Explanations: Choices B is incorrect. The function is exponential and not linear. **Choice C** is incorrect. The amount she saves per week increases exponentially and does not decrease. **Choices D** is incorrect. The function is exponential and not linear.

22. **Level:** Easy | **Domain:** ALGEBRA
Skill/Knowledge: Linear equations in one variable
Testing point: Solving for x in a linear equation

Key Explanation: Choice B is correct. The value of x can be solved by subtracting 8 from both sides which yields $4x + 8 - 8 = 24 - 8$ or $4x = 16$. Dividing both sides of the equation by 4 yields $x = 4$.

Distractor Explanations: Choice A is incorrect and may result from a conceptual or calculation error. **Choice C** is incorrect and may result from

a conceptual or calculation error. **Choice D** is incorrect and may result from a conceptual or calculation error.

1. **Level:** Easy | **Domain:** ALGEBRA
   Skill/Knowledge: Linear equations in one variable
   Testing point: Solving for x in a linear equation

   Key Explanation: Choice D is correct. To solve for this, start by factoring out the 7 which yields $7(x + 4) = 112$. Then divide both sides of the equation by 7 which yields $(x + 4) = \dfrac{112}{7}$ or $x + 4 = 16$.

   Distractor Explanations: Choice A is incorrect and may result from solving the value of x when $x + 4 = 0$. **Choice B** is incorrect and may result from a miscalculation or conceptual error. **Choice C** is incorrect and may result from only solving for the value of x.

2. **Level:** Medium | **Domain:** GEOMETRY AND TRIGONOMETRY
   Skill/Knowledge: Area and volume | **Testing point:** Using ratios similar figures

   Key Explanation: The ratio of the radius of the ball to that of the prototype is $3 : 1$. Since the volume of a sphere is directly proportional to the cube of its radius $(V \propto r^3)$, the ratio of their volumes should be $3^3 : 1^3$ or $27 : 1$. And given that the volume of the prototype is $10 cm^3$, the volume of the ball will be $27 \times 10 = 270 cm^3$.

3. **Level:** Easy | **Domain:** ADVANCED MATH
   Skill/Knowledge: Nonlinear equations in one variable and systems of equations in two variables
   Testing point: Using the discriminant to find the number of solutions of a quadratic equation

   Key Explanation: Choice A is correct. A quadratic with one solution has a discriminant equal to 0 which means $b^2 - 4ac = 0$.

To get the values of a, b, and c, equate the two equations which yield $2x + k = x^2 - 10x + 30$. Subtracting $2x$ and k from both sides of the equation yields $0 = x^2 - 12x + 30 - k$. This means that $a = 1$, $b = -12$, and $c = 30 - k$. Substituting the values of a, b, and c to the discriminant yields $(-12)^2 - 4 (1)(30 - k) = 0$. Using the distributive property yields $144 - 120 + 4k = 0$. Combining like terms yields $24 + 4k = 0$. Subtracting 24 from both sides of the equation yields $4k = -24$. Dividing both sides of the equation by 4 yields $k = -6$.

Distractor Explanations: Choice B is incorrect and could be a result of miscalculation or conceptual error. **Choice C** is incorrect and could be a result of miscalculation or conceptual error. **Choice D** is incorrect because this is the negative value of k.

4. **Level:** Hard | **Domain:** ADVANCED MATH
   Skill/Knowledge: Nonlinear equations in one variable and systems of equations in two variables
   Testing point: Using exponent rules

   Key Explanation: Choice D is correct.
   To solve for this, equate the exponents by making the bases the same. Since 9, 27 and 81 are multiples of 3, then every base will be converted to 3. This yields $9 = 3^2$, $27 = 3^3$, and $81 = 3^4$. Hence the equation will now become $\dfrac{3^{3(x-1)}}{3^{4y}} = 3^2$ or

   $$\dfrac{3^{3x-3}}{3^{4y}} = 3^2.$$

   Since the terms on the left side of the equation are being divided, the exponents will be subtracted. This yields $3^{3x-3-4y} = 3^2$. Equating the exponents yields $3x - 3 - 4y = 2$. Adding 3 to both sides of

the equation yields $3x - 4y = 5$. To find the value of $6x - 8y$, multiply both sides of the equation by 2 which yields $2(3x - 4y) = 2(5)$.
Using the distributive property yields $6x - 8y = 10$.

Distractor Explanations: Choice A is incorrect and may result from solving the value of $\dfrac{6x - 8y}{5}$.

Choice B is incorrect and may result from solving the value of $\dfrac{2(6x - 8y)}{5}$. **Choice C** is incorrect and may result from solving the value of $3x - 4y$.

5. **Level:** Medium | **Domain:** GEOMETRY AND TRIGONOMETRY
    Skill/Knowledge: Right triangles and trigonometry | **Testing point:** Using the pythagorean theorem

    Key Explanation: The sides of a square are equal. Therefore, if the sides are s, then the diagonal will be $s\sqrt{2}$, which can be proven using the Pythagorean theorem $a^2 + b^2 = c^2$. Since $s\sqrt{2} = 16\sqrt{2}$, then $s = 16$. The perimeter of a square can be found by $4s$ which is $4(16) = 64$.

6. **Level:** Easy | **Domain:** ALGEBRA
    Skill/Knowledge: Linear functions | **Testing point:** Matching a linear equation to its graph

    Key Explanation: Choice C is correct. Rewrite the given equation into slope–intercept form of $y = mx + b$ where m is the slope of the line and b is the y–intercept.
    Subtracting $12x$ from both sides of the equation yields $4y = -12x + 8$.
    Dividing both sides of the equation by 4 yields $y = -3x + 2$. Thus, the slope of the line is -3 and a y–intercept of 2. Since the slope is negative, the graph goes down from left to right. Hence, the

answer can only be **choice C** or **D**. To determine the correct answer between the two choices, solve for the x–intercept by substituting 0 to y in the equation. This yields $0 = -3x + 2$. Adding $3x$ to both sides of the equation yields $3x = 2$. Dividing 3 from both sides of the equation yields $x = \dfrac{2}{3}$.
Since **choice C** is the only graph that has a y–intercept of 2, an x–intercept of $\dfrac{2}{3}$, and a negative slope, it is the correct answer.

Distractor Explanations: Choice A is incorrect because it represents a linear equation with a positive slope. **Choice B** is incorrect because it represents a linear equation with a positive slope. **Choice D** is incorrect because it has an x–intercept of 6.

7. **Level:** Easy | **Domain:** ALGEBRA
    Skill/Knowledge: Systems of two linear equations in two variables | **Testing point:** Working with parallel lines and linear systems with no solution

    Key Explanation: To have no solutions means that the lines are parallel and have the same slope. The slope of the first linear equation is $\dfrac{3}{2}$. Since p represents the slope of the second equation, then $p = \dfrac{3}{2}$ which makes both lines parallel.

8. **Level:** Hard | **Domain:** ADVANCED MATH
    Skill/Knowledge: Nonlinear functions | **Testing point:** Using exponential growth equation

    Key Explanation: Choice C is correct. The original equation requires t in years. Since a year has 12 months, then $\dfrac{m}{12} = t$. This can be best represented by the model in C.

Distractor Explanations: Choices A, is incorrect and may result from a conceptual error. **Choice B** is incorrect and may result from a conceptual error. **Choice D** is incorrect and may result from a conceptual error.

9. **Level:** Medium | **Domain:** ADVANCED MATH
    Skill/Knowledge: Equivalent expressions
    Testing point: Rewriting the equation and solving for the variable

    Key Explanation: Choice A is correct. Solve for A by isolating it and then simplifying the equation. Subtracting $\dfrac{7}{x-3}$ from both sides of the equation yields $\dfrac{-2x^2+5x+10}{x-3} - \dfrac{7}{x-3} = A$

    or $\dfrac{-2x^2+5x+3}{x-3} = A$. Factoring the numerator on the left side of the equation yields $\dfrac{(-2x-1)(x-3)}{x-3} = A$. Canceling out $(x-3)$ yields $-2x - 1 = A$ or $A = -2x - 1$.

    Distractor Explanations: Choice B is incorrect and may result due to calculation errors. **Choice C** is incorrect and may result from solving the value of $-A$. **Choice D** is incorrect. This would be the difference between $-2x^2 + 5x + 10$ and $x - 3$.

10. **Level:** Easy | **Domain:** ALGEBRA
    Skill/Knowledge: Systems of two linear equations in two variables | **Testing point:** Solving the system of linear equations

    Key Explanation: Choice B is correct. Solve the system of equations by solving for y in the first equation and substituting it to the second equation.
    Dividing both sides of the first equation by -5

yields $-\dfrac{3}{5}x = y$.

Substituting y to the second equation yields

$2x + 3(-\dfrac{3}{5}x) = -1$ or $2x - \dfrac{9}{5}x = -1$.

Combining like terms yields $\dfrac{1}{5}x = -1$.
Multiplying 5 to both sides of the equation yields $x = -5$.

Distractor Explanations: Choice A is incorrect and may result due to a calculation or conceptual error. **Choice C** is incorrect and may result due to a calculation or conceptual error. **Choice D** is incorrect. This is the value of y.

11. **Level:** Hard | **Domain:** ADVANCED MATH
    Skill/Knowledge: Nonlinear equations in one variable and systems of equations in two variables
    Testing point: Using the discriminant to find the number of solutions to a quadratic equation.

    Key Explanation: For a quadratic equation to have two distinct solutions, the discriminant $b^2 - 4ac$ must be positive. In the given equation, $a = 4$, $b = -12$, and $c = k$.
    Substituting the values of a, b and c to get the discriminant yields $(-12)^2 - 4(4)(k)$ or $144 - 16k$. Since the discriminant must be positive, it must be greater than zero which is represented by $144 - 16k > 0$.
    Adding $16k$ to both sides of the inequality yields $144 > 16k$.
    Dividing 16 from both sides of the inequality yields $9 > k$ or $k < 9$.
    The next integer number lower than 9 is 8.
    Therefore, the correct answer is 8.

12. **Level:** Easy | **Domain:** ALGEBRA
    Skill/Knowledge: Linear equations in one variable
    Testing point: Finding the solutions to a linear equation

    Key Explanation: Choice A is correct. Using the distributive property to simplify the equation yields $3x + 18 + x = 4x + 5$ or $4x + 18 = 4x + 5$. Subtracting $4x$ from both sides of the equation yields $18 = 5$ or $13 = 0$ which is a false statement. This implies that there is no solution.

    Distractor Explanations: Choice B is incorrect. For a linear equation to have one solution, the value of the variable can be solved. **Choice C is incorrect.** Linear systems do not have 2 solutions. **Choice D is incorrect.** For a linear system to have infinite solutions, the simplified equation must be a true statement.

13. **Level:** Hard | **Domain:** ADVANCED MATH
    Skill/Knowledge: Equivalent expressions
    Testing point: Adding rational expressions with fractions

    Key Explanation: Choice A is correct.
    Simplify the denominator first.

    This yields $\dfrac{1}{x-2} + \dfrac{1}{x+2} = \dfrac{x+2+x-2}{x^2-4} = \dfrac{2x}{x^2-4}$

    Simplifying the whole fraction yields

    $\dfrac{1}{\frac{2x}{x^2-4}} = \dfrac{x^2-4}{2x}$

    Distractor Explanations: Choice B is incorrect and may result from an error in adding the contents in the denominator x. **Choice C** is incorrect because it is only the simplified denominator, not the whole fraction. **Choice D** is incorrect and may result from miscalculation or conceptual errors.

14. **Level:** Hard | **Domain:** GEOMETRY AND TRIGONOMETRY
    Skill/Knowledge: Circles
    Testing point: Using circle theorems and converting degrees to radians

    Key Explanation: Choice C is correct. The measure of a circumscribed angle and its corresponding central angle are supplementary. Hence, $\angle\,\mathrm{PSR} + \angle\,\mathrm{PQR} = 180°$. Substituting the value of the central angle $\angle\,\mathrm{PSR}$ yields $80° + \angle\,\mathrm{PQR} = 180°$. Subtracting $80°$ from both sides of the equation yields $\angle\,\mathrm{PQR} = 100°$. Converting the value of $\angle\,\mathrm{PQR}$ to radians yields $100° \times \dfrac{\pi}{180°} = \dfrac{5}{9}\pi$. Since $\angle\,\mathrm{PQR} = a\pi$, then $a = \dfrac{5}{9}$.

    Distractor Explanations: Choice A is incorrect and may result from a conceptual or calculation error. **Choice B** is incorrect and may result from a conceptual or calculation error. **Choice D** is incorrect and may result from a conceptual or calculation error.

15. **Level:** Easy | **Domain:** GEOMETRY AND TRIGONOMETRY
    Skill/Knowledge: Circles | **Testing point:** Finding the area of a circle given its circumference

    Key Explanation: The circumference of a circle is found by the formula πD where D is the diameter of the circle. Since the circumference is 12π then $D = 12$. The radius is therefore 6, and the area of the circle is $\pi r^2 = \pi(6)^2 = 36\pi$.

16. **Level:** Easy | **Domain:** ADVANCED MATH
    Skill/Knowledge: Equivalent expressions
    Testing point: Converting from exponents to radicals

Key Explanation: Choice D is correct. Expressing the radical as exponent yields $3p^{\frac{1}{3}}p^{\frac{1}{2}}$. Since the same variables are being multiplied, their exponents will be added.

Hence, $\frac{1}{3} + \frac{1}{2} = \frac{5}{6}$.

The expression now becomes $3p^{\frac{5}{6}}$. Converting the exponent back to radical yields $3\sqrt[6]{p^5}$.

Distractor Explanations: Choice A is incorrect and may result from a conceptual or calculation error. **Choice B is** incorrect and may result from a conceptual or calculation error. **Choice C is** incorrect and may result from a conceptual or calculation error.

17. **Level:** Easy | **Domain:** GEOMETRY AND TRIGONOMETRY
    Skill/Knowledge: Area and volume | **Testing point:** Finding the volume of a cylinder

Key Explanation: Choice D is correct. The volume of a cylinder is found using the formula $V = \pi r^2 h$ where r is the radius and h is the height. Substituting the given radius and height to the formula yields $V = \pi 9^2 6 = 486\pi$.

Distractor Explanations: Choice A is incorrect and may result from solving the area of one base of the cylinder. **Choice B is** incorrect and may result from solving the lateral area of the cylinder. **Choice C is** incorrect and may result from solving the surface area of the cylinder.

18. **Level:** Hard | **Domain:** ALGEBRA
    Skill/Knowledge: Linear equations in two variables | **Testing point:** Working with parallel lines and their equations

Key Explanation: Choice A is correct. For lines to be parallel, they must have proportional coefficients of x and y. To make the coefficients of x to be the same, multiply the first equation by –2. This yields $-2(3x + 5y = 6)$ or $-6x - 10y = -12$. Matching the coefficients of y in $-6x - 10y = -12$ and $-6x + py = 18$ yields $p = -10$.

Distractor Explanations: Choice B is incorrect and may result from a conceptual or calculation error. **Choice C is** incorrect and may result from a conceptual or calculation error. **Choice D is** incorrect. It is the negative of option A.

19. **Level:** Easy | **Domain:** ADVANCED MATH
    Skill/Knowledge: Equivalent expressions
    Testing point: Matching coefficients

Key Explanation: Using the distributive property, the left side of the equation becomes $15x^2y + 6xy + 6xy - 2y$. Combining like terms yields $15x^2y + 12xy - 2y = ax^2y + bxy + cy$. Matching the coefficients yields $a = 15$, $b = 12$, and $c = -2$. Therefore, b is equal to 12.

20. **Level :** Easy | **Domain:** ADVANCED MATH
    Skill/Knowledge: Nonlinear equations in one variable and systems of equations in two variables
    Testing point: Finding the number of solutions of an absolute value equation

Key Explanation: Choice C is correct. Isolating the absolute value and simplifying the equation yields $|x + 4| = \frac{-8}{-2}$ or $|x + 4| = 4$. Since the absolute value is being compared with a positive number, it has two solutions.

Distractor Explanations: Choice A is incorrect. For an absolute value to have 0 or no solution, the absolute value should be less than or equal to a negative number. **Choice B** is incorrect. For an absolute value to have 1 solution, it should be equal to zero. **Choice D** is incorrect. For an absolute value to have infinite solutions, it should be greater than a negative number.

21. **Level:** Easy | **Domain:** ADVANCED MATH
    Skill/Knowledge: Nonlinear equations in one variable and systems of equations in two variables
    Testing point: Using exponent rules and FOILing method to find value of quadratic expression

    Key Explanation: Choice C is correct. Expanding the expression $(x + y)^2$ yields $x^2 + 2xy + y^2$.
    Since $x^2 + y^2 = 45$, the expression becomes $45 + 2xy$.
    Since $xy = 5$, the expression becomes $45 + 2(5)$ or 55.
    Therefore, $(x + y)^2 = 55$.

    Distractor Explanations: Choice A is incorrect and may result from solving the value of $\dfrac{x^2 + y^2}{xy}$.
    Choice B is incorrect and may result from solving the value of $(x - y)^2$. **Choice D** is incorrect and may result from solving the value of $2(x + y)^2$.

22. **Level:** Easy | **Domain:** PROBLEM–SOLVING AND DATA ANALYTICS
    Skills/Knowledge: Inference from sample statistics and margin of error | **Testing Point:** Inferring from a sample to a population

    Key Explanation: Choice A is correct. From the data surveyed, $1,200 - 950 = 250$ residents own a different type of pet. We can infer that

$\dfrac{250}{1,200} \times 62,500 = 13,020$ residents in the town own a different type of pet.

Distractor Explanations: Choice B is incorrect. This is the approximate number of residents in the town that own either a dog or a cat. **Choice C** is incorrect. This is the difference between the number of residents in the survey that owned a cat or a dog and the total number of residents in the town ($62,500 - 950$). **Choice D** is incorrect. This option is the total number of residents in the town.

Chapter 6

Practice Test 5

You are about to begin a full-length Practice Test. The test has four modules. The time allotted for each module is marked at the beginning of the module. Work on one module at a time. Use a timer to keep track of the time limits for every module.

Try to take the Practice Test under real test conditions. Find a quiet place to work, and set aside enough time to complete the test without being disturbed. At the end of the test, check your answers by referring to the Answer Key and fill in your raw score in the scorecard below. Also, note down the time taken by you for completing each module.

Pay particular attention to the questions that were answered incorrectly. Read the answer explanations and understand how to solve them.

My Score Card (Raw Score)

	Reading and Writing		Math	
	Module 1	Module 2	Module 1	Module 2
Out of	27	27	22	22
My Score	_____	_____	_____	_____
Time Taken	_____	_____	_____	_____

TEST BEGINS ON THE NEXT PAGE

Reading and Writing Test

27 QUESTIONS | 32 MINUTES

DIRECTIONS

The questions in this section address a number of important reading and writing skills. Each question includes one or more passages, which may include a table or graph. Read each passage and question carefully, and then choose the best answer to the question based on the passage(s). All questions in this section are multiple–choice with four answer choices. Each question has a single best answer.

1

The idea of a credit card was first proposed in 1887 by Edward Bellamy in a novel titled Looking Backward. Different institutions offered cards for limited purposes after that, but the first modern credit card with revolving payments was _____ in 1958 by Bank of America in Fresno, California.

Which choice completes the text with the most logical and precise word or phrase?

A) dispatched

B) issued

C) consigned

D) allocated

2

The following text is adapted from Jane Austen's 1811 novel, Sense and Sensibility.

Mr. John Dashwood told his mother again and again how exceedingly sorry he was that she had taken a house at such a distance from Norland as to prevent his being of any service to her in removing her furniture. He really felt conscientiously vexed on the occasion; for the very exertion to which he had limited the performance of his promise to his father was by this arrangement rendered impractical. Instead, the furniture was all sent around by water.

As used in the text, what does the word "removing" most nearly mean?

A) Transferring

B) Detaching

C) Dismissing

D) Separating

3

Caravaggio was an Italian painter active around 1600. His style was very distinct and enchanting, combining realism and high lighting contrasts in a way that added drama and intensity to the scenes portrayed. His peculiar use of shadow was a prime influence on the work of later generations of Baroque artists who also explored artistic extremes.

As used in the text, what does the word "peculiar" most nearly mean?

A) Singular

B) Abnormal

C) Indisposed

D) Discernible

4

The parents of the first female self–made millionaire, Madam J. Walker, were slaves, but she made a fortune selling cosmetics and hair care products. Throughout her life, she supported Black organizations and artists. Her philanthropy continued after her death, as two–thirds of her legacy was set aside to _____ charities.

Which choice completes the text with the most logical and precise word or phrase?

A) enforce

B) concede

C) endow

D) accord

5

The following text is adapted from Alexandre Dumas's 1849 novel, *The Three Musketeers*.

It was, then, into the midst of this tumult and disorder that our young man advanced with a beating heart, ranging his long rapier up his lanky leg, and keeping one hand on the edge of his cap, with that half–smile of the embarrassed provincial who wishes to put on a good face. When he had passed one group he began to breathe more freely; but he could not help observing that they turned round to look at him, and for the first time in his life, D'Artagnan, who had till that day entertained a very good opinion of himself, felt ridiculous.

What is the main purpose of the underlined portion in the overall structure of the text?

A) It warns the reader of a coming conflict.

B) It indicates a temporal change in the passage.

C) It describes the appearance of a scene.

D) It stresses the emotional state of a character.

6

The following text is from Leo Tolstoy's 1873 novel, "Anna Karenina."

Levin had meant to tell his brother of his determination to get married, and to ask his advice; he had indeed firmly resolved to do so. But after seeing his brother, listening to his conversation with the professor, hearing afterwards the unconsciously patronizing tone in which his brother questioned him about agricultural matters, Levin felt that he could not for some reason begin to talk to him of his intention of marrying. He felt that his brother would not look at it as he would have wished him to.

Which choice best states the function of the underlined sentence in the text as a whole?

A) It explains the purpose of the conversation with the professor.

B) It adds to the sense of inferiority which causes Levin to change his mind.

C) It elaborates on an obstacle preventing Levin from getting married.

D) It introduces a problem that Levin and his brother frequently disagreed about.

7

A very rare meteorological event is called thundersnow. This uncommon event occurs when there are strong updrafts in cold weather. The mechanics are basically the same as those which cause thunderstorms, but the results are lightning and thunder with falling snow or hail instead of rain. Thundersnow clouds tend to be lower than thunderstorm clouds, and the effect is most common over large bodies of water like the Great Lakes in the Northwestern United States and Utah's Great Salt Lake, though they can occur elsewhere. Often the sounds of the thunder are muted due to the presence of snow.

What is the main purpose of the text?

A) It explains an unusual phenomenon.

B) It identifies locations to see a phenomenon.

C) It describes why a phenomenon occurs.

It outlines a scientific dilemma.

8

Text 1

On August 5, 2013, a live television broadcast from London showed two food critics tasting a hamburger patty cooked by chef Richard Geown. The importance of this event was that the hamburger was the first public tasting of cultured meat, meaning meat that was raised from cells in a laboratory. This sample took two years and cost $300,000 to produce, but its creator, Mark Post, is sure there is potential for such foods in the market.

Text 2

Cultured meat is regarded with skepticism in many circles. Will people readily consume animal meat raised in a laboratory? No animals are slaughtered, but the concept is still repulsive to many. Even so, many companies are jumping on the bandwagon to produce different meats, and the first sales occurred in December 2020, when a Singapore restaurant included cultured meat in its offerings.

Which choice best describes the relationship between the texts?

A) Text 1 describes the introduction of a product, and Text 2 explains later developments.

B) Text 1 describes the positive reception of a product, and Text 2 brings up reservations.

C) Both texts refer to the difficulty in creating a new product.

D) Both texts discuss the public's reaction to a new product.

9

Text 1

Prior to 1972, polar bear populations were severely reduced by hunters and trappers, causing concern about the survival of the majestic apex species. However, an international agreement regulating commercial hunting enacted in 1973 changed odds for the hearty animals. Now, the total number of polar bears has rebounded to healthy levels that demonstrate that the species is no longer in imminent danger of extinction.

Text 2

Sea ice is essential for all parts of the polar bear lifecycle—and it is melting at a faster rate than ever before due to climate change. It is important to note that as of 2019, although two of the nineteen known populations increased in numbers, four had declined and there was not enough data on eight.

Based on the texts, after his experiments, how would the author of Text 2 most likely describe the view of the author of Text 1?

A) Limited, because it only addresses one aspect of the threats against polar bears.

B) Inspiring, because it provides evidence that polar bear populations are increasing.

C) Erroneous, because it inaccurately reported the total number of polar bears.

D) Worrisome, because it hints that efforts to protect polar bears are only partially successful.

10

This passage is adapted from Mark Twain's 1903 story, "The $30,000 Bequest."

Saladin's wife, Electra, was a capable helpmeet, although—like himself—a dreamer of dreams and a private dabbler in romance. The first thing she did after her marriage was buy an acre of ground on the edge of the town, and pay cash for it—twenty–five dollars, all her fortune. Saladin had less, by fifteen. She instituted a vegetable garden there, and got it farmed on shares by the nearest neighbor. Out of Saladin's first year's wage she put thirty dollars in the savings–bank, sixty out of his second, a hundred out of his third. By the time two children had arrived, she banked two hundred a year from the salary. When she had been married seven years, she built a pretty and comfortable house in the midst of her garden–acre and moved her family in.

What is the main idea of the text?

A) Electra was more capable at finances than her husband was.

B) Electra and Saladin were too romantic to be practical.

C) Saladin was taking advantage of Electra's money.

D) Electra has excellent thrift and planning ability.

11

John Milton is one of the most famous poets from the 1600s. Though his writing is sometimes archaic to modern readers, the sentiments still ring close to the heart. For instance, he claims at the preface of his 1637 poem "Lycidas" that "the Author bewails a learned Friend": _____

Which quotation from "Lycidas" most effectively illustrates the claim?

A) "YET once more, O ye Laurels, and once more / Ye Myrtles brown, with Ivy never–sear, / I com to pluck your Berries harsh and crude,"

B) "For we were nurst upon the self–same hill, / Fed the same flock by fountain, shade, and rill."

C) "But O the heavy change, now thou art gon, / Now thou art gon, and never must return!"

D) "Fame is the spur that the clear spirit doth raise / (That last infirmity of Noble mind) /To scorn delights, and live laborious days"

12

A study examined the mental health of children with chronic health issues over a span of several years. A sample of approximately 7000 children was analyzed to explore the prevalence of mental health disorders such as anxiety and depression alongside chronic illnesses. The assessment of chronic illness relied on mothers' evaluations of their child's health at ages 10 and 13, encompassing minor health problems as well. Findings revealed that children with chronic health conditions were twice as likely as the control group to exhibit mental health disorders at ages 10 and 13, and 60% more likely at age 15.

Which finding, if true, would most directly undermine the conclusion of the study?

A) Children with mental health disorders are likely to develop chronic health conditions due to an overall weakened immune system.

B) Children with chronic health conditions are likely to develop mental health disorders due to long stays in hospitals or other forms of isolation from their peers.

C) Children with chronic health conditions are likely to develop mental health disorders due to low self-esteem and a weakened immune system.

D) Mental health disorders are also associated with chronic health conditions among teenage children and working-age adults.

13

Percentage of Australian population born overseas at the time of census, 1911 to 2016

A Western Sydney University survey revealed 80% positivity toward cultural diversity. Despite Australia's multicultural perception, its actual diversity rank is low, partly due to the 1901 "White Australia" policy. Colonial concerns about increasing migrants from China and the Pacific in the late 19th century led to strict immigration laws, including the Immigration Restriction Act. Aimed at limiting non-white immigration, this law was rooted in colonial legislation. Overseas-born residents may have increased post-World War II, but_____

Which choice most effectively completes the text using information from the graph?

A) before the dismantling of the White Australia policy, Australia was a predominantly White country, with only 9% overseas-born residents in 1947.

B) prior to the war, this policy resulted in a rapid decrease in overseas-born residents, from almost 17% before 1920 to a low of almost 9% in 1947.

C) not significantly enough to make a difference to the overall population of Australia.

D) even after the dismantling of the White Australia policy, Australia's diversity rank is low.

14

A group of researchers from Peking University have been documenting tall trees in the Tibet Autonomous region as part of a project to understand and protect the region's environmental diversity through conservation efforts. The tallest trees ever documented in Asia include a 272-foot-tall (83 m) fir tree in southwest China and a 252-foot (77 m) tree in Medog County. Outside of Asia, the tallest tree in the world is a 381-foot (116 m) coastal redwood in the Redwood National Park in California. Recently, a 335 feet (102 meters) tall cypress tree in Bome County, China was discovered, _____.

Which choice most logically completes the text?

A) now believed to be the second-tallest tree in Asia and the tallest tree in the world.

B) now believed to be the tallest tree in Asia and the second-tallest tree in the world.

C) almost reaching the height of the Statue of Liberty, which stands at 305 feet (93 m).

D) now believed to be the tallest tree in Asia.

15

Contrary to popular belief, fish do drink water while living in water. Fish can drink some water through their mouths, but most of the water is absorbed through the fish's skin and gills using a process called osmosis. The cells in the fish's body must balance out the levels of water with their external environment, so water moves between the body of water the fish is residing in and the cell membranes in the fish's body from areas with low levels of salt to areas with high levels of salt until a balance is achieved. Therefore, the amount of water absorbed by a fish is based on the _____

Which choice most logically completes the text?

A) speed of osmosis.

B) levels of water consumed by the fish.

C) number of cells in its body.

D) saltiness of its habitat.

16

Kinkaku–ji, also known as the Golden Pavilion, is one of the most popular tourist sites in Kyoto despite _____ in a fire set by an arsonist in 1950; a replica was later rebuilt on the same pattern as the original.

Which choice completes the text so that it conforms to the conventions of Standard English?

A) completely destroying

B) it was destroyed completely

C) to have been completely destroyed

D) having been completely destroyed

17

With its intricate mechanical design and precision engineering, a car is a complex yet remarkable mode of transportation. From its engine's combustion to the transmission's power distribution, various components play a crucial role in ensuring the vehicle's motion. For a car to move forward, _____ must have enough force to push its own weight on the road out of the way. This propels the vehicle forward, enabling it to overcome resistance and reach its desired destination efficiently and smoothly.

Which choice completes the text so that it conforms to the conventions of Standard English?

A) you

B) it

C) we

D) they

18

First performed in England in 1984, _____ It is most notable because all the cast sing and act their parts on roller skates.

Which choice completes the text so that it conforms to the conventions of Standard English?

A) Richard Stilgoe and Andrew Lloyd Webber wrote the lyrics and music, respectively, for the musical *Starlight Express*.

B) Richard Stilgoe wrote the lyrics for *Starlight Express* and Andrew Lloyd Webber wrote the music.

C) Andrew Lloyd Webber wrote the music and Richard Stilgoe wrote the lyrics for the musical *Starlight Express*.

D) *Starlight Express* is a musical with lyrics by Richard Stilgoe and music by Andrew Lloyd Webber.

19

A survey is a process of collecting a small but representative sampling of responses on a given topic and extrapolating that information to what a larger group might think about it, since many _____ fall into basic patterns when looked at as a whole.

Which choice completes the text so that it conforms to the conventions of Standard English?

A) peoples' opinions

B) people's opinions

C) people's opinions'

D) peoples' opinions'

20

The sousaphone—invented in 1893 by J.W. Pepper at the request of band leader John Philip _____ a brass instrument related to the tuba and often used in marching bands because it is easier to carry and directs sound over the head of other band members.

Which choice completes the text so that it conforms to the conventions of Standard English?

A) Sousa is

B) Sousa is—

C) Sousa, is

D) Sousa—is

21

There has been scholarly debate about the exact definition of Aztec, but it loosely refers to a culture that flourished in Mexico between approximately 1300 and 1521. The Aztec Empire was formed in 1427 of three separate _____ Tlacopan.

Which choice completes the text so that it conforms to the conventions of Standard English?

A) city–states: Tenochtitlan, Texcoco, and,

B) city–states: Tenochtitlan; Texcoco; and

C) city–states Tenochtitlan, Texcoco, and

D) city–states: Tenochtitlan, Texcoco, and

22

In 1961, Jenny Johnson wrote the beloved poem "Warning," which is now best known by its first _____ I am an old woman, I shall wear purple."

Which choice completes the text so that it conforms to the conventions of Standard English?

A) line "when

B) line, "when

C) line, those are "when

D) line, it is "when

23

Many researchers have identified a correlation between the consumption of nuts and longevity. _____ it has yet to be established whether the nuts actually impact lifespan or whether people who already have healthier lifestyles tend to include nuts in their diets.

Which choice completes the text with the most logical transition?

A) Therefore,

B) However,

C) Indeed,

D) Similarly,

24

The Egyptian leader known as King Tut died around 1323 B.C. when he was only 18 or 19 years old. Archaeologists debate over the cause of his death, saying it could have been caused by malaria, a hippopotamus attack, a chariot race injury, or murder. _____ the death was unexpected: he was buried in a tomb that was designed for another person.

Which choice completes the text with the most logical transition?

A) Therefore,

B) As a result,

C) Alternatively,

D) In any event,

25

After Christopher Columbus's ships were stranded in Jamaica, the indigenous people grew tired of providing food and Columbus was worried about the safety of his crew. _____ he used information from an almanac about an upcoming lunar eclipse to intimidate the natives.

Which choice completes the text with the most logical transition?

A) Nevertheless,

B) In other words,

C) Likewise,

D) Therefore,

26

While researching a topic, a student has taken the following notes:

- B.F. Keith lived from 1846 to 1914 and owned and operated hundreds of vaudeville theaters around the United States.

- Keith did not approve of the common theatrical trend of vulgarity and insisted that his performers offered decent acts with no swear words.

- The theaters were lavish and entertained spectators with their palace–like, elegant ornamentation, as opposed to simple structures of older theaters.

- Ushers had authority to remove audience members who heckled the performers.

- Edwin Albee was Keith's invaluable partner and assumed control of the theaters after Keith's death.

The student wants to emphasize what differentiated Keith's theaters from others at the time. Which choice most effectively uses relevant information from the notes to accomplish this goal?

A) B.F. Keith (1846–1914) owned more theaters than others in the era and built ones that were extremely ornamented.

B) Compared to other theaters in that period, B.F. Keith's theaters offered more polite performances and the theaters themselves were very elaborate.

C) B.F. Keith ran vaudeville shows rather than other performances until his death in 1914, when Edwin Albee took over his hundreds of elegant theaters.

D) B.F. Keith disapproved of acts with swear words or audiences that heckled performers, so prohibited those in his gorgeously ornamented theaters.

27

While researching a topic, a student has taken the following notes:

- Social constructivism asserts that reality is formed through human action.

- People actively create or build their own representations of objective reality.

- Behaviorism asserts that human behavior is determined by conditioning rather than through the active construction of reality.

- Behaviorists maintain that all forms of human behavior can be explained through environmental forces rather than internal forces.

- Constructivists and behaviorists both recognize the pivotal role that environmental influences play in shaping individuals' behaviors and understanding.

The student wants to emphasize the similarity in ideas between social constructivism and behaviorism. Which choice most effectively uses relevant information from the notes to accomplish this goal?

A) Both social constructivism and behaviorism view individuals as active participants in their environment, with social constructivism emphasizing reality construction while behaviorism emphasizes conditioning as conditioning agents.

B) While social constructivism emphasizes the active construction of reality and behaviorism focuses on conditioning, both theories agree on one core tenet: environmental influences play a critical role in shaping individuals' behaviors and understandings.

C) Behaviorism, like social constructivism, believes that an individual's environment plays a powerful role in shaping his or her understanding of the world.

D) Social constructivism, similar to behaviorism, recognizes the significance of the environment on human behavior through various mechanisms.

No Test Material On This Page

Reading and Writing Test

27 QUESTIONS | 32 MINUTES

DIRECTIONS

The questions in this section address a number of important reading and writing skills. Each question includes one or more passages, which may include a table or graph. Read each passage and question carefully, and then choose the best answer to the question based on the passage(s). All questions in this section are multiple-choice with four answer choices. Each question has a single best answer.

1

Though her invention was originally mocked as foolish, Marion Donovan _____ childcare by inventing the disposable diaper, freeing housewives from hours of labor. In the past, women had to not only clean the diaper but also furniture and clothes when the cloth padding leaked. The disposable diaper's absorbent padding and close-fitting cover completely changed how babies could be raised.

Which choice completes the text with the most logical and precise word or phrase?

A) rebuilt

B) reorganized

C) reclassified

D) revolutionized

2

In the experiment, the date of appearance of the first flowers was noted for each treatment of salt that stressed the plant; thus, the number of days it took for each plant to make its first flower from the start of the stress <u>application</u> was covered. Fruit ripening, number, size, and fresh mass were also evaluated.

As used in the text, what does the word "application" most nearly mean?

A) Significance

B) Diligence

C) Request

D) Execution

3

James Abbot McNeill Whistler's famous 1871 painting known as *Whistler's Mother* has been considered one of the classics of American art. Originally titled *Arrangement in Grey and Black #1,* the strong composition of Anna Whistler exemplifies the artist's _____ at manipulating subtle colors.

Which choice completes the text with the most logical and precise word or phrase?

A) susceptibility

B) adroitness

C) engagement

D) diversion

4

The popular 1943 film *Lassie Come Home* was based on a book written in 1940 by Eric Knight about a female dog named Lassie who had a deep emotional connection with the boy who owned her. <u>The fictional dog was supposedly first introduced in an earlier short story that Knight wrote.</u> However, in 1859, Elizabeth Gaskell published "The Half Brothers," a similar short story featuring a dog named Lassie that saved two boys lost in a snowstorm.

What is the main purpose of the underlined portion in the overall structure of the text?

A) It casts doubt on the veracity of a claim.

B) It questions the similarity between two stories.

C) It emphasizes that a character was fictional.

D) It highlights the popularity of an earlier work.

Spike Lee is a movie director known for his nuanced depictions of Black characters, but in the past, movies were far less sensitive about the multiple facets of people of color. The first Black man who starred in a major motion picture was Sam Lucas, who played a role in the 1914 production of *Uncle Tom's Cabin*. Prior to that time, Black characters were played by White actors in face paint. Throughout the following years, Black actors received roles, but primarily as maids, servants, or jungle savages, until the late 19th century, when daring directors pushed the stereotyped boundaries.

What is the primary function of the underlined portion in the overall structure of the text?

A) It hints that a common stereotype is flawed.

B) It offers an example to use as a comparison.

C) It introduces the person who pioneered a change.

D) It brings up a problem that took time to resolve.

Mas Subramanian, a solid–state materials scientist, was trying to create a magnetic substance that could be used in computer hard drives. One of his creations was not at all magnetic, but instead was a bright shade of blue. Subramanian realized that every cloud has a silver lining and started to find ways to market the new pigment. As opposed to most other sources of blue, his material was stable and non–toxic.

What is the main purpose of the phrase "every cloud has a silver lining"?

A) To provide a metaphor showing that the material was gaseous like a cloud

B) To indicate that Subramanian realized that the seeming failure had benefits

C) To establish that the pigment could be used to make silver as well as blue

D) To show that the material could be rendered magnetic by adding other substances

7

Text 1 is adapted from Charles Stearns's 1849 treatise, "The Way to Abolish Slavery."
Text 2 is adapted from Catharine Beecher's 1837 letter, "Slavery and Abolitionism, with
Reference to the Duty of American Females."

Text 1:

The Government of the United States creates no slaves; it only recognises as lawful the
slavery existing in the several States, or to use the words of the Constitution, "held to
service or labor, under the laws thereof." The *laws* of the several slave–holding States are
made the standard for the general government's action upon this subject. No quibble can
possibly evade this, for it is not necessary to prove that a runaway slave justly owes service
to his master, but only if he does, under *the laws of his master*. What then is necessary to
be done to remove this prop from under the colossal statue of slavery? Plainly, to repeal
all laws recognising its existence.

Text 2:

Now what is it that makes a man cease to be a slave and become free? It is not kind
treatment from a master; it is not paying wages to the slave. It always signifies *that legal*
act, which, by the laws of the land, changes a slave to a freeman. No exception can be
made for those who live in the States where the act of emancipation, by a master, makes a
slave the property of the State, to be sold for the benefit of the State.

Which choice best describes how Stearns (Text 1) would most likely react to Beecher's
(Text 2) assertion that some slaves are not freed because they live in states that consider
emancipated slaves the property of the state?

A) Stearns would argue that such a case is only possible with adequate paperwork.

B) Stearns would argue that is one more reason that all slavery laws should be
    eliminated.

C) Stearns would argue that slavery is an integral part of the U.S. Constitution.

D) Stearns would argue that if such slaves left the state, they would then be free.

8

Coywolves first appeared in the early part of the 20th century near Canada's Algonquin Provincial Park. They are hybrids between wolves and western coyotes; some studies have also identified genetic material from domestic dogs in coywolves. They are extremely adaptable to a wide variety of habitats and are now flourishing in different areas. Biologists estimate that there may be over one million coywolves dispersed across Eastern North America from Canada to Virginia. In general, the coywolf has a larger body, longer legs, shorter ears, and a larger, stronger jaw than a regular coyote.

Based on the text, what is true about coywolves?

A) They are more common in Canada than other places.

B) They are more closely related to coyotes than wolves.

C) They were hybridized by Canadian people in the early 20th century.

D) They may be found in different environmental conditions.

9

Jessica Nabongo is the first black woman known to have visited all 195 countries in the world; she has been to 10 different territories as well. The last country on her list was the Seychelles, which she visited in 2019. During her travels, she was appalled by the poverty and at the way poor countries supported the burden of the world's waste. Now Nabongo, who is Ugandan–American, is an advocate for ethical and sustainable travel, and has written a book about her adventures called *The Catch Me If You Can*.

According to the text, what is true about Jessica Nabongo?

A) She was born in Uganda and moved to America.

B) She is the author of a book about traveling around the world.

C) She visited 195 countries before visiting 10 territories.

D) She felt that the Seychelles had too much poverty.

10

The automobile company Volkswagen proposed an advertising campaign called The Fun Theory under the assumption that the best way to change people's behaviors was by adding an element of fun. To test the theory, researchers measured the number of passengers in a Swedish subway station who were willing to walk on stairs that made piano sounds for every step as opposed to a regular escalator next to it. Measuring use before and after converting the staircase, results indicated a 66% increase.

Which choice best states the main idea of the text?

A) Volkswagen has created an effective new advertising strategy.

B) People are willing to change behaviors when fun is used as an incentive.

C) More people prefer taking stairs to using an escalator.

D) Staircases should be converted so that they sound like a piano.

11

Argentina's Iguazu National Park contains one of the most spectacular waterfalls in the world. Water drops in multiple cascades up to 80 meters high, forming a crescent about 2,700 meters in diameter. Named a national park in 1934 and a UNESCO World Heritage Site in 1984, the park is considered a world treasure for more than its beauty: _____

Which quotation most effectively illustrates the claim?

A) its conservation has a generous budget and is conducted by rangers and other professionals.

B) it is located on a basaltic line that forms the border between Argentina and Brazil.

C) the spray from the falls creates a unique microclimate with over 2,000 species of plants.

D) most of the region has been severely altered due to logging and agriculture.

12

Total Increase in Iron Content in Cells

Total Increase in Iron content in cells

Figures adapted from "Biallelic HEPHL1 variants impair ferroxidase activity and cause an abnormal hair phenotype" by Prashant Sharma et al., PLOS Genetics, 2019.

HEPHL1 belongs to a family of proteins known as Multi–Copper Oxidases (MCOs) that catalyze the oxidation of iron so that it can bind to a circulating protein called transferrin which distributes the iron throughout the body. One unique property of MCOs is the presence of three copper–binding sites that can house six copper atoms. To help us explore the physiological consequences of the loss of HEPHL1 activity more thoroughly, we used a gene–targeting approach to make mice with a disrupted *Hephl1* gene. Interestingly, all mice that had a complete deletion of both copies of their *Hephl1* gene had short, curled whiskers throughout their life. We found that the iron uptake increase difference between the cells of the mouse with no HEPHL1 and the cells of the control mouse was significant: _____ .

Which choice most effectively uses data from the table to complete the statement?

A) about 1.1 nmoles/mg of protein

B) at almost 2.1 nmoles/mg of protein

C) nearly 2.7 nmoles/mg of protein

D) around 3.8 nmoles/mg of protein

13

5 countries and their share of population that cannot afford a healthy diet, 2021

Malawi — 95.9%
Niger — 92%
Rwanda — 82%
India — 74.1%
Indonesia — 70.8%

Source: World Bank, adapted from Herforth et al. (2022)
OurWorldInData.org/food-prices • CC BY

▶2017 ————————————o 2021

The majority of countries establish 'food-based dietary guidelines' outlining ideal dietary patterns. These guidelines encompass optimal food group proportions, including fruits, vegetables, meat, and dairy, for sustained well-being. Researchers discovered that adopting healthy diets costs over four times as much as a basic, calorie-sufficient one. Furthermore, the researchers examined the most budget-friendly approaches to align with these country-specific dietary guidelines. Globally, maintaining a nutritious diet averaged at $3.54 per day. However, when considering affordability as allocating 52% of income towards food, a staggering three billion individuals are unable to afford such a diet. Particularly _____

Which choice most effectively completes the text using information from the graph?

A) in nations liked Malawi, Niger, and Rwanda, more than 80% of the population cannot afford a healthy diet

B) in nations liked India, cultural dietary preferences, especially the preference towards vegetarian diets, do not always align with healthy eating patterns.

C) in economically advanced nations like India, a healthy diet is attainable for the majority of the population.

D) across various income levels, the accessibility of nutritious diets varies greatly in Indonesia, leading to disparities in health outcomes

BMI, or body mass index, is a rough estimation of the amount of body fat based on inputs like height and weight. Many doctors use BMI as an indicator for the likelihood to develop serious diseases, such as heart disease. However, critics have called out that doctors should refrain from using BMI for potential diagnosis. BMI can only identify the potential amount of body fat, not where the fat is stored in the body, which is the relevant indicator for specific diseases. For instance, _____

Which choice most logically completes the text?

A) those with fat stored in the upper body are more at risk for type 2 diabetes and coronary artery disease than those with fat stored in the lower body.

B) those with high levels of body fat are more at risk for type 2 diabetes and coronary artery disease than those with lower levels of body fat.

C) taller and thinner patients are more at risk for type 2 diabetes and coronary artery disease.

D) shorter and thinner patients are more at risk for type 2 diabetes and coronary artery disease.

Soccer balls are a surprisingly complex yet remarkable sports equipment. Starting with their aerodynamic surface to the internal bladder's air pressure, various components play a crucial role in ensuring the balls' flight. For soccer balls to move forward during a powerful kick, _____ must have enough force applied to them. This propels the balls forward, enabling them to travel swiftly and accurately towards their intended targets.

Which choice completes the text so that it conforms to the conventions of Standard English?

A) you

B) it

C) we

D) they

Built between 1960 and 1970 in Egypt, the Aswan Dam, now known as the Aswan High Dam, was erected across the Nile River to control flooding, increase water storage, and _____

Which choice completes the text so that it conforms to the conventions of Standard English?

A) generate hydroelectricity.

B) it generates hydroelectricity.

C) hydroelectricity is also generated.

D) to generate hydroelectricity.

17

The Audubon Society was named for one of the most eminent early American ornithologists, John James Audubon. Though Audubon himself made drawings of dead birds, members of the society _____ to the conservation of birds and their habitats.

Which choice completes the text so that it conforms to the conventions of Standard English?

A) is dedicated

B) are dedicated

C) dedicating

D) has been dedicated

18

Geologists have meticulously documented how geological forces interact with the cyclic nature of rain in regions but _____ also have started to explore the intriguing connections between geological processes and climate change patterns. The landscape in Chile's Atacama desert is a direct result of the cyclic nature of rain in this region, which has sculpted the terrain over millions of years. Most can't help but marvel at the intricate features that showcase the enduring power of nature's sculpting hand over millions of years.

Which choice completes the text so that it conforms to the conventions of Standard English?

A) they

B) he

C) it

D) she

19

Popular since the 1700s, _____ is the name of a spice compound made, as the name suggests, from seven spices, though the exact composition varies.

Which choice completes the text so that it conforms to the conventions of Standard English?

A) *shichimi* (Japanese for "seven spices")

B) *shichimi* , (Japanese for "seven spices")

C) *shichimi* (Japanese for "seven spices"),

D) *shichimi* , (Japanese for "seven spices"),

20

Dinosaurs lived on Earth for about 165 years until the Cretaceous Period, so many of the familiar _____ were actually separated by long periods of time.

Which choice completes the text so that it conforms to the conventions of Standard English?

A) species like stegosaurs and tyrannosaurs

B) species, like stegosaurs and tyrannosaurs

C) species, like stegosaurs, and tyrannosaurs,

D) species like: stegosaurs and tyrannosaurs

CONTINUE ➡

21

Saturn's moon Europa has an extremely smooth surface which indicates that there may be a water ocean beneath _____ such an ocean could theoretically exist despite the extremely cold temperatures due to the gravitational pull of Saturn.

Which choice completes the text so that it conforms to the conventions of Standard English?

A) it

B) it,

C) it;

D) it. And

22

The Frank Lloyd Wright building of the Guggenheim Museum is an architectural masterpiece best known for its Grand Ramp, a gentle spiral walkway that leads the visitor to every floor in a stately manner. What is little known is that as the plans evolved over the sixteen years of _____ was eliminated from the design.

Which choice completes the text so that it conforms to the conventions of Standard English?

A) construction, a smaller, much steeper ramp

B) construction a smaller, much steeper ramp,

C) construction a smaller, much steeper, ramp

D) construction a smaller much steeper ramp

23

Seeing eye dogs require the most rigorous training of all forms of working dogs. _____ they must learn to alert their handlers to potential dangers that could hurt the owner but not necessarily the dog, such as walking under a low branch.

Which choice completes the text with the most logical transition?

A) Nevertheless,

B) Therefore,

C) Specifically,

D) Similarly,

24

"Civil disobedience" is a term popularized in the United States by Henry David Thoreau's essay *Civil Disobedience*. That publication inspired Mahatma Gandhi in the 1920s to actively refuse to obey the laws of India in a non–violent way. _____ Martin Luther King, Jr., used similar techniques to promote the Civil Rights Movement in the United States in the 1960s.

Which choice completes the text with the most logical transition?

A) In conclusion,

B) Subsequently,

C) For instance,

D) Nonetheless,

25

Cashews are popular nuts eaten as snacks around the world, but are not sold in the shells, because the shells contain caustic oil compounds that trigger contact dermatitis. _____ the shell creates a rash on the skin.

Which choice completes the text with the most logical transition?

A) In other words,

B) Likewise,

C) Conversely,

D) On the other hand,

While researching a topic, a student has taken the following notes:

- Heat islands are urban areas that are 1–7 degrees Fahrenheit hotter than the surrounding areas during the day.

- Nighttime temperatures may be 2–5 degrees hotter

- Heat islands are caused by synthetic materials in buildings and roads that absorb and emit more heat than natural areas like plants or water

- The effect can be mitigated by planting trees

- Lightening the color of surfaces such as roofs can reduce the temperature differences.

- Heat islands do not directly increase global warming but can indirectly do so through factors such as using more air conditioners.

The student wants to offer an audience that does not know what a heat island is some practical solutions for reducing the effect. Which choice most effectively uses relevant information from the notes to accomplish this goal?

A) Heat islands do not increase global warming and their effect can be reduced by using air conditioners.

B) Heat islands, which are urban areas hotter than their surroundings by up to 7 degrees, are caused by using many synthetic materials in buildings and roads.

C) Heat islands are 1–7 degrees Fahrenheit hotter during the day and 2–5 degrees hotter at night, but that effect can be reduced by planting trees.

D) Heat islands, urban areas that are hotter than the surroundings, can be lessened in intensity by steps such as planting trees or painting roofs and other surfaces a lighter color.

27

While researching a topic, a student has taken the following notes:

- Wildlife corridors are areas that are designed to link habitats together.

- The goal is to promote biodiversity and safe movement of species so populations can intermingle and have a larger gene pool rather than become isolated.

- Animals can use wildlife corridors to find food, water, and other resources.

- The concept is consistent with farming, forestry, and conservation efforts because corridors can take different forms.

- Various options include "stepping stones" of native vegetation, bridges for animals to cross roads, and removal of fences around private property.

The student wants to convince people in a farming community to create a wildlife corridor to protect a native species of deer. Which choice most effectively uses relevant information from the notes to accomplish this goal?

A) We can protect the native deer using a wildlife corridor because it can link habitats for the deer to find food and mates while still allowing farmers to do their jobs.

B) We can create a wildlife corridor for the native deer so they can thrive and contribute to conservation efforts in the region.

C) Wildlife corridors are a good solution because they allow the native deer to move around safely, intermingle, and find food, through a system of bridges, native vegetation, and so on.

D) A wildlife corridor can take different forms and achieve the goal of preserving the gene pool of the native deer species.

STOP

No Test Material On This Page

No Test Material On This Page

Math

22 QUESTIONS | 35 MINUTES

DIRECTIONS

The questions in this section address a number of important math skills. Use of a calculator is permitted for all questions.

NOTES

Unless otherwise indicated: • All variables and expressions represent real numbers. • Figures provided are drawn to scale. • All figures lie in a plane. • The domain of a given function is the set of all real numbers x for which $f(x)$ is a real number.

REFERENCE

$A = \pi r^2$
$C = 2\pi r$

$A = \ell w$

$A = \frac{1}{2}bh$

$c^2 = a^2 + b^2$

Special Right Triangles

$V = \ell wh$

$V = \pi r^2 h$

$V = \frac{4}{3}\pi r^3$

$V = \frac{1}{3}\pi r^2 h$

$V = \frac{1}{3}\ell wh$

The number of degrees of arc in a circle is 360.

The number of radians of arc in a circle is 2π.

The sum of the measures in degrees of the angles of a triangle is 180.

For **multiple-choice questions,** solve each problem, choose the correct answer from the choices provided, and then circle your answer in this book. Circle only one answer for each question. If you change your mind, completely erase the circle. You will not get credit for questions with more than one answer circled, or for questions with no answers circled.

For **student-produced response questions,** solve each problem and write your answer next to or under the question in the test book as described below.

- Once you've written your answer, circle it clearly. You will not receive credit for anything written outside the circle, or for any questions with more than one circled answer.

- If you find more than one correct answer, write and circle only one answer.

- Your answer can be up to 5 characters for a positive answer and up to 6 characters (including the negative sign) for a negative answer, but no more.

- If your answer is a fraction that is too long (over 5 characters for positive, 6 characters for negative), write the decimal equivalent.

- If your answer is a decimal that is too long (over 5 characters for positive, 6 characters for negative), truncate it or round at the fourth digit.

- If your answer is a mixed number (such as 3.!. 2), write it as an improper fraction (7/2) or its decimal equivalent (3.5).

- Don't include symbols such as a percent sign, comma, or dollar sign in your circled answer.

CONTINUE

1

Alley bought a piece of land for $47,890. It increased in value every year by 2%. Which of the following best describes the model of the price of the land every year after she bought it if t is the number of years after she bought the land?

A) $47,890(1.02)^t$

B) $47,890 + 0.02^t$

C) $47,890(0.98)^t$

D) $47,890(1.02)^t$

2

If $ax + bx - b + a = 5x - 2$, what is the value of $a^2 - b^2$?

A) −10

B) −2

C) 3

D) 5

3

$$y = 3x^2 - 6x - 21$$

If one of the solution to the quadratic equation above is $1 + 2\sqrt{k}$, what is the value of k?

4

If the length of a rectangle is $6cm$ less than its width x, what is the length of the rectangle given that its area is $27cm^2$?

A) 3

B) 6

C) 9

D) 21

5

$$7x + 14 = 7$$

Which of the following equations is equivalent to the above?

A) $3x + 6 = 3$

B) $x - 2 = 1$

C) $x = 3$

D) $7x = 7$

6

$$|x + 3| < 7$$

How many possible integer values of x does the inequality above have?

7

The function $p(x)$ is defined by $p(x) = \left\{\dfrac{1}{8}\right\}^{-x}$,

what is the value of $P\left(\dfrac{1}{3}\right)$?

A) $\dfrac{1}{512}$

B) $\dfrac{1}{2}$

C) 2

D) 512

8

Which of the following is a factor of
$f(x) = 6x^2 - 17x + 10$?

A) $6x + 5$

B) $x + 5$

C) $x - 2$

D) $x - 5$

9

Which of the following is true about the two data sets above?

A) The mean of data set A is less than the mean of data set B

B) Data set A has more values than data set B

C) The median of data set A is greater than the median of data set B

D) The median of data set B is greater than the median of data set A

10

In the xy plane, the graph of the quadratic function f is a parabola with the vertex $(-2, 5)$. The function $g(x)$ is defined when the function $f(x)$ is translated 3 units to the left and 1 unit up. If (h, k) is the vertex of $g(x)$, what is the value of h?

11

For how many points does the line of best fit predict a lower value than the actual point?

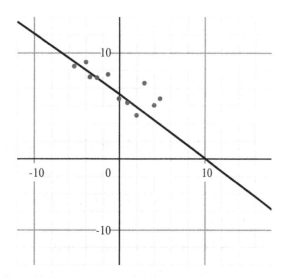

A) 3

B) 5

C) 6

D) 11

12

For all values of $x > 0$, which of the following is equivalent to $\left(x+\sqrt{2}\right)^2\left(x-\sqrt{2}\right)^2$?

A) $x^2 + 4x + 4$

B) $x^4 + 4x^2 - 4$

C) $2x^2 + 4$

D) $x^4 - 4x^2 + 4$

13

A baker has the graph below which models its daily expenditure for the month of August. Which of the following expressions best describes the equation of the function?

A) $y = 231 - 4.85x$

B) $y = 231 + 0.85x$

C) $y = 4.85x - 231$

D) $y = 4.85x + 231$

14

A school has 24 girls and 20 boys. If $\dfrac{3}{5}$ of the boys are on the track team and $\dfrac{3}{4}$ of the girls are not on the track team, what percentage of the students are on the track team? (round off to the nearest whole number)

15

$$y > 2(x - 2)^2 - 2$$

$$y \geq -1$$

If (a, b) are solutions to the system of inequalities above, what is the minimum value of b?

A) -2

B) -1

C) 0

D) 2

16

Which of the following equations is equivalent to $2x^2 + 28x = -98$?

I. $2(x + 7)^2 = 0$

II. $2(x - 7)^2 = 0$

A) I

B) All of them

C) II

D) Neither of them

17

$$3y - 2x = 6$$
$$5y - 4x = 8$$

If the system of equations above has a solution (x, y), what is the value of $2x + y$?

18

A survey was conducted in a school on the change of uniforms. The conclusion of the survey was that 53 students of the 97 students surveyed are in favor of the proposed change. If there are 2,300 students in the school, approximately how many students are not in favor of the change in school uniform?

A) 1,043

B) 1,093

C) 1,256

D) 2,300

19

$$y = 3x + 5 - \frac{8}{3}(x + 3) \text{ and } y = px + 4$$

If the system above has no solution, what is the value of p?

A) $\dfrac{1}{3}$

B) $\dfrac{2}{3}$

C) 1

D) $\dfrac{5}{3}$

CONTINUE

20

$$y = 5(x - 2) + x + 3 \text{ and } y = k(x - 2) + 2x + 1$$

If the system above has infinite solutions, what is the value of k?

21

A square is inscribed in a circle. If the circle has a radius of $12cm$. what is the length of one side of the square?

A) $4\sqrt{3}$

B) $12\sqrt{3}$

C) 12

D) 24

22

x	0	1	2	3
y	4	4	4	4

The table above represents the equation $y = 2k$. What is the value of k?

A) 1

B) 2

C) 4

D) 8

No Test Material On This Page

Math

22 QUESTIONS | 35 MINUTES

$A = \pi r^2$ $A = \ell w$ $A = \frac{1}{2} bh$ $c^2 = a^2 + b^2$ Special Right Triangles

$C = 2\pi r$

$V = \ell wh$ $V = \pi r^2 h$ $V = \frac{4}{3}\pi r^3$ $V = \frac{1}{3}\pi r^2 h$ $V = \frac{1}{3}\ell wh$

The number of degrees of arc in a circle is 360.

The number of radians of arc in a circle is 2π.

The sum of the measures in degrees of the angles of a triangle is 180.

For **multiple–choice questions,** solve each problem, choose the correct answer from the choices provided, and then circle your answer in this book. Circle only one answer for each question. If you change your mind, completely erase the circle. You will not get credit for questions with more than one answer circled, or for questions with no answers circled.

For **student–produced response questions,** solve each problem and write your answer next to or under the question in the test book as described below.

- Once you've written your answer, circle it clearly. You will not receive credit for anything written outside the circle, or for any questions with more than one circled answer.

- If you find more than one correct answer, write and circle only one answer.

- Your answer can be up to 5 characters for a positive answer and up to 6 characters (including the negative sign) for a negative answer, but no more.

- If your answer is a fraction that is too long (over 5 characters for positive, 6 characters for negative), write the decimal equivalent.

- If your answer is a decimal that is too long (over 5 characters for positive, 6 characters for negative), truncate it or round at the fourth digit.

- If your answer is a mixed number (such as 3.!. 2), write it as an improper fraction (7/2) or its decimal equivalent (3.5).

- Don't include symbols such as a percent sign, comma, or dollar sign in your circled answer.

CONTINUE

1

$$3x^2 - 19x + 6 = 0$$

Which of the following is a solution for the equation above ?

A) -6

B) $-\dfrac{1}{3}$

C) $\dfrac{1}{3}$

D) 2

2

$$x^2 - 8x + y^2 + 10y = 8$$

In the equation of a circle given above, what would be the value of its diameter?

A) 7

B) 14

C) 16

D) 49

3

If $f(x) = -2x - 6$, what is the value of $|f(2)|$?

4

Which of the following is equivalent to $tan(90 - x)°$?

A) $\dfrac{sin\,x}{cos\,x}$

B) $\dfrac{cos\,x}{sin\,x}$

C) $\dfrac{cos\,(90-x)°}{sin\,(90-x)°}$

D) $-tan\,x$

5

Alina started a savings account with \$113. She would earn a simple interest of 6.8% on her deposit monthly. The equation below represents the total amount of money $A(t)$ in her savings account in t months. What does 7.684 represent in this context?

$$A(t) = 113 + 7.684t$$

A) The amount of interest earned after t months

B) The total amount in the account after t months

C) The amount of interest earned every month

D) The interest earned every year.

6

$$6x - 3y = 2$$

The above equation is part of a system of equations. If the system has no solution, which of the following could be the equation of the second line in the system?

A) $2x - 3y = 4$

B) $-2x + y = 4$

C) $-2x + y = \dfrac{-2}{3}$

D) $3x - \dfrac{3}{2}y = 1$

7

If $p(x) = 2x^2 - 6x + 5$, what is the value of $p(2)$?

8

Which of the following is the equation of a line that passes through the origin and point (6, 5)?

A) $5y = 6x$

B) $6y = 5x$

C) $y = 5x + 6$

D) $y = 6x + 5$

9

Which of the following is the equation of the graph below?

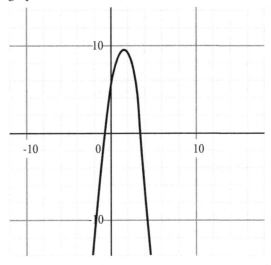

A) $y = 2x^2 - 6x + 5$

B) $y = 2x^2 + 6x + 5$

C) $y = -2x^2 - 6x + 5$

D) $y = -2x^2 + 6x + 5$

10

If a quadrilateral has the following interior angles $x°$, $(x + 40)°$, $(x + 50)°$, $(x - 10)°$, what is the value of x?

11

If triangle ABD is a right triangle, what is the value of sin CAD?

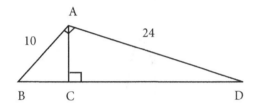

A) $\dfrac{12}{13}$

B) $\dfrac{12}{5}$

C) $\dfrac{5}{13}$

D) $\dfrac{5}{12}$

12

Which of the following expressions is equivalent to $7wp(2w + 5)$?

A) $14w^2p + 35$

B) $14w^2p + 35wp$

C) $14w^2 + 35p$

D) $9w^2p + 35pw$

13

The volume of sphere A is 27 times that of sphere B. If sphere B has a radius of $4cm$, what is the radius of sphere A?

14

A weather forecast report predicted that there is a 43% chance of rain on Monday. The report also indicated that it is twice as likely to rain on Thursday than on Monday. What is the probability that it won't rain on Thursday?

A) 0.14

B) 0.43

C) 0.57

D) 0.86

15

$$\frac{16^x}{4^x} > 2^6$$

What is the least possible integer value of x for the inequality above?

A) 0

B) 2

C) 3

D) 4

16

Given that $3(ax - b) + 4(bx - a) = x - 6$, what is the value of a?

17

What is the volume of a cone with a radius of $12cm$ and a height 6 more than its radius?

A) 864π

B) 960π

C) $1,080\pi$

D) $2,160\pi$

18

$$4x - 3y = 6$$

What is the slope of the equation of the line above?

A) $\dfrac{4}{3}$

B) 4

C) $\dfrac{3}{4}$

D) $\dfrac{-4}{3}$

19

If the circumference of a circle is 20π, what is the value of the angle that is subtended by an arc length of 3π?

20

Thirty students are required to pay a total of p dollars for a field trip. If 28 students paid before the day of the trip, how much was already paid in total?

A) $28p$

B) $\dfrac{14}{15}p$

C) $30p$

D) $\dfrac{p}{30}$

21

If the equation of a circle with a center $(-3, 5)$ and a radius of $6cm$ is written in the form $ax^2 + bx + cy^2 + dy + e = 0$, what is the value of e?

A) -2

B) 9

C) 25

D) 36

22

$$-3(x + 2) < 2(x - 8)$$

Which of the choices above is a possible value of x for the given linear inequality?

A) 0

B) 1

C) 2

D) 3

STOP

This page is intentionally left blank

Answer Key

Reading and Writing

Module 1

Questions	Correct	Mark your correct answers
1.	B	
2.	A	
3.	A	
4.	C	
5.	D	
6.	B	
7.	A	
8.	A	
9.	A	
10.	D	
11.	C	
12.	A	
13.	B	
14.	D	
15.	D	
16.	D	
17.	B	
18.	D	
19.	B	
20.	D	
21.	D	
22.	B	
23.	B	
24.	D	
25.	D	
26.	B	
27.	B	

Module 2

Questions	Correct	Mark your correct answers
1.	D	
2.	D	
3.	B	
4.	A	
5.	B	
6.	B	
7.	B	
8.	D	
9.	B	
10.	B	
11.	C	
12.	A	
13.	A	
14.	A	
15.	D	
16.	A	
17.	B	
18.	A	
19.	A	
20.	A	
21.	C	
22.	A	
23.	C	
24.	B	
25.	A	
26.	D	
27.	A	

Math

Module 1

Questions	Correct	Mark your correct answers
1.	A	
2.	A	
3.	2	
4.	A	
5.	A	
6.	13	
7.	C	
8.	C	
9.	D	
10.	-5	
11.	C	
12.	D	
13.	A	
14.	41	
15.	B	
16.	A	
17.	10	
18.	A	
19.	A	
20.	4	
21.	B	
22.	B	

Module 2

Questions	Correct	Mark your correct answers
1.	C	
2.	B	
3.	10	
4.	B	
5.	C	
6.	B	
7.	1	
8.	B	
9.	D	
10.	70	
11.	A	
12.	B	
13.	12	
14.	A	
15.	D	
16.	3	
17.	A	
18.	A	
19.	54	
20.	B	
21.	A	
22.	D	

1. **Level:** Medium | **Domain:** CRAFT AND STRUCTURE
   Skill/Knowledge: Words in Context

   Key Explanation: Choice B is the best answer. The blank is a verb that shows what the Bank of America did to the first modern credit card. Choice B refers to distributing something for use or sale, so aptly shows that the credit cards were first given out to customers in 1958.

   Distractor Explanations: Choice A is incorrect because it refers to sending something away with a purpose, such as sending an order to an army. It does not refer to selling something or making something available to many people. **Choice C** is incorrect because it refers to putting something into someone's care. **Choice D** refers to distributing the parts of a whole, such as allocating funds.

2. **Level:** Easy | **Domain:** CRAFT AND STRUCTURE
   Skill/Knowledge: Words in Context

   Key Explanation: Choice A is the best answer because "removing" is a verb that shows what Mr. Dashwood cannot do to the furniture. **Choice A** refers to carrying objects from one place to another, which fits the context of saying that Mr. Dashwood cannot "be of service" or "help" his mother move the furniture to a new house that is too far away.

   Distractor Explanations: None of the other choices fits the context of explaining that Mr. Dashwood cannot help take the furniture to a faraway place. **Choice B** refers to to disconnecting something, such as removing a part that is fastened in some way so it is incorrect. **Choice C** refers to ordering or sending something away. None of these choices contain the idea of taking

the possessions to a new location. **Choice D** is incorrect because it also refers to an inborn or natural trait or characteristic, not a species.

3. **Level:** Hard | **Domain:** CRAFT AND STRUCTURE
   Skill/Knowledge: Words in Context

   Key Explanation: Choice A is the best answer. "Peculiar" is used to describe Caravaggio's style, which is elsewhere described as "distinct" or "characteristic" of his work. Choice A refers to something unique or one-of-a-kind, which fits the context of art that was very notable and later adopted by a different school of artists

   Distractor Explanations: Choice B is incorrect because it has a negative connotation that implies that the writer does not like it, whereas the writer refers to the work as "enchanting" or "fascinating," indicating that there is a positive quality to it. **Choice C** is incorrect because it relates to feeling unwell or slightly sick, a very different meaning of "peculiar." **Choice D** is incorrect because it refers to something which is possible to see. Although Caravaggio's use of shadows was possible to see, the author is referring to a different, special quality that Baroque artists later used.

4. **Level:** Hard | **Domain:** CRAFT AND STRUCTURE
   Skill/Knowledge: Words in Context

   Key Explanation: Choice C is the best answer. "Endow" refers to formally giving money to someone or something, so fits the context of explaining that much of her "legacy" or "money given to people in a will" went to charities.

   Distractor Explanations: None of the other choices adequately explain what happened between the legacy and charities. **Choice A** refers to forcing someone to comply with laws or rules. **Choice B** refers to surrendering or yielding something, but the charities were not surrendered to anything. **Choice D** is incorrect because it refers to giving power or recognition, not money.

5. **Level:** Hard | **Domain:** CRAFT AND STRUCTURE
   Skill/Knowledge: Text Structure and Purpose

   Key Explanation: Choice D is the best answer. The fact that D'Artagnan notices that people turn around to look stresses that he is very nervous about appearing like an "embarrassed provincial." He realized that they saw through his front and "felt ridiculous." By mentioning the fact that he saw them, it is clear to the reader why his "very good opinion of himself" changed.

   Distractor Explanations: Choice A is incorrect because there is no conflict in the text. **Choice B** is incorrect because a "temporal change" is a shift in time, but the time sequence remains consistent. **Choice C** is incorrect because the reader has no idea what the scene really is; one knows D'Artagnan is walking by a group of people, but there is no clue how many or where they are.

6. **Level:** Medium | **Domain:** CRAFT AND STRUCTURE
   Skill/Knowledge: Text Structure and Purpose

   Key Explanation: Choice B is the best answer. The passage starts by saying that Levin planned to tell his brother about the marriage, and ends by saying he did not because he was afraid his brother would not view it favorably. The underlined portion gives part of the reason Levin changed his mind: his brother used an "unconsciously patronizing tone" or "spoke as if

he looked down on Levin without intending to do so." Therefore, Levin felt "inferior" or "too low" to discuss an important topic.

Distractor Explanations: Choice A is incorrect because the topic of the conversation with the professor is not given; the conversation about agriculture came "afterwards" or "later," and was presumably between Levin and his brother rather than the professor. **Choice C** is incorrect because there is no indication that the conversation about agriculture was an "obstacle" or "barrier" that prevented Levin from getting married; the details could have related to anything agricultural. Instead, the conversation was conducted in a tone which made him feel like he should bring up the topic at a different time. **Choice D** is incorrect because there is no indication that Levin and his brother "frequently" or "often" disagreed about agriculture. In fact, they might not have disagreed in this case, either. The brother just talked in a "patronizing" or "belittling" way.

7. **Level:** Easy | **Domain:** INFORMATION AND IDEAS
   Skill/Knowledge: Text Structure and Purpose

   Key Explanation: Choice A is the best answer. The passage says that thundersnow, a "meteorological event" or "weather phenomenon" is rare, then explains what it is and how it is different from a thunderstorm. Therefore, the main purpose is to introduce a reader to the unusual weather event.

   Distractor Explanations: Choice B is incorrect because only one sentence in the passage says that thundersnow is most common over "large bodies of water" and gives examples, but also says that the event occurs elsewhere. There is not enough information to know what kinds of other places are suitable, so **Choice B** is not the main purpose of the passage. **Choice C** is incorrect because "why" or "the reasons for" the effect are not discussed. The passage only says that the formation occurs in the same way that thunderstorms do. **Choice D** is incorrect because a "dilemma" is a problem, but there is no discussion of a problem that needs solved.

8. **Level:** Easy | **Domain:** CRAFT AND STRUCTURE
   Skill/Knowledge: Cross–Text Connections

   Key Explanation: Choice A is the best answer because Text 1 describes the "first public tasting of cultured meat" in 2013, and Text 2 explains the "later development" or "thing which occurred afterwards" by saying that the "first sales occurred in December 2020."

   Distractor Explanations: Choice B is incorrect because Text 1 does not actually say how anyone viewed the product, only that it was first tasted on television. **Choice C** is incorrect because only Text 1 says that it was expensive to develop. Text 2 refers to "skepticism" or "concern" about the product, but does not discuss how it was "created" or "made." **Choice D** is incorrect because Text 2 refers to the public's reaction of "skepticism," but Text 1 never says what people other than the creator thought of the product.

9. **Level:** Medium | **Domain:** CRAFT AND STRUCTURE
   Skill/Knowledge: Cross–Text Connections

   Key Explanation: Choice A is the best answer. Text 1 claims that polar bear populations are not threatened any longer because there was a ban on hunting. However, Text 2 points out that climate change is a severe problem. The author of the

Text 2 further distinguishes between changes in different populations, which indicates that while the numbers may be increasing overall, there may be serious losses in genetic diversity if some of the populations die out. Therefore, the author of Text 2 would probably say that Text 1 shows a "limited" or "insufficient" analysis of the complete situation.

Distractor Explanations: Choice B is incorrect because, while Text 1 does say that total numbers have "rebounded" or "returned to previous levels," the author of Text 2 points out that some populations have not. In addition, the author of Text 1 does not mention the problem of global warming, which Text 2 points out is eliminating sea ice essential to the survival of the polar bears. Therefore, the author of Text 2 would probably not find the text "inspiring" or "uplifting," but rather "incomplete" or "in error." **Choice C** is incorrect because, while the author of Text 2 might say that Text 1 is "erroneous" or "wrong" in claiming that polar bears are not "in imminent danger of extinction" or "threatened," the reason is not correct. The author of Text 2 might say that the total number is correct, but it is more important to look at numbers in different populations. **Choice D** is incorrect because Text 1 does not imply that efforts to conserve polar bears are "only partially successful." Rather, Text 1 indicates that efforts were successful and now there is little concern at all. The author of Text 2 would be worried about climate change, not about the positive information regarding hunting given in Text 1.

10. **Level:** Medium | **Domain:** INFORMATION AND IDEAS
    Skill/Knowledge: Central Ideas and Details

    Key Explanation: Choice D is the best answer because the passage focuses on how Electra increases her savings from $25 to buy a plot of land to having enough money after seven years to build a house for her family. "Thrift" refers to the ability to manage money well, so accurately describes Electra.

Distractor Explanations: Choice A is incorrect because the text points out that Electra had more money than her husband to begin with, but since she is saving increasing amounts after they got married, he is at least capable of earning money. It is possible he is also saving more on his own, too. **Choice B** is the opposite of the correct answer. The text says that they were romantic, but "practical" refers to making good decisions about everyday life, and the couple save enough for a nice house. **Choice C** is incorrect because there is no indication that Saladin is "taking advantage" or "using" Electra's money; she is saving the money he earned, so he is contributing to the family finances.

11. **Level:** Hard | **Domain:** INFORMATION AND IDEAS
    Skill/Knowledge: Command of Evidence (Textual)

    Key Explanation: Choice C is the best answer. The claim is that the author "bewails" or "expresses great regret" about a friend in the poem. **Choice C** says "thou art gone," meaning "you are no longer here." The following line, "and never must return" gives more of a clue to what happened: if the friend cannot return, he is probably dead. In other words, **Choice C** shows that there was a "heavy" or "horrible" change in that the friend died and the author is very sad.

    Distractor Explanations: Choice A is incorrect because it only refers to picking plants, not to any reason for doing so. **Choice B** is incorrect because it only reinforces that they are friends who "nurst upon the self–same hill" or "grew up together," and

"fed the same flock," meaning that they worked together. The friendship is established but there is no indication of mourning or sorrow. **Choice D** refers to fame, not to friendship or sorrow, so is incorrect.

12. **Level:** Hard | **Domain:** INFORMATION AND IDEAS
    Skill/Knowledge: Command of Evidence (Textual)

    Key Explanation: Choice A is correct. The study states that children with chronic health conditions are more likely to develop mental health disorders a few years later. However, if children who already have mental health disorders are actually predisposed to developing chronic health conditions, the conclusion of the study is inaccurate.

    Distractor Explanations: Choice B is incorrect because this choice supports the conclusion of the study and attempts to explain the mechanisms behind the finding. **Choice C** is incorrect because this choice supports the conclusion of the study and attempts to explain the mechanisms behind the finding. **Choice D** is incorrect because this choice discusses the relationship between chronic health conditions and mental health disorders among teenagers and adults, which neither supports nor undermines the conclusion of the study, which is about young children.

13. **Level:** Hard | **Domain:** INFORMATION AND IDEAS
    Skill/Knowledge: Command of Evidence (Quantitative)

    Key Explanation: Choice B is the correct option as it effectively completes the text by highlighting the impact of the White Australia policy on overseas-born residents and how their percentage decreased significantly from the pre-war period to 1947. It uses information from the graph to provide a contrast that is required since "but" is used before the blank.

Distractor Explanations: Choice A is incorrect because it provides information about the percentage of overseas-born residents in 1947 but doesn't directly address the trend after World War II in relation to the context provided earlier in the sentence. **Choice C** is incorrect because it doesn't provide specific information about the changes in overseas-born residents post-World War II and doesn't directly address the contrast that is required in the text. **Choice D** is incorrect because while it uses information from to text, it focuses on Australia's diversity rank, instead of addressing the context of the sentence to be completed.

14. **Level:** Hard | **Domain:** INFORMATION AND IDEAS
    Skill/Knowledge: Inferences

Key Explanation: Choice D is correct. Previously, the tallest tree in Asia stood at 272 feet tall. The recently discovered cypress tree stands at 335 feet tall, making it the tallest tree in Asia.

Distractor Explanations: Choice A is incorrect because the text suggests that the cypress tree is now the tallest tree in Asia, not the second-tallest tree. Further, the tallest tree in the world is the coastal redwood, not the cypress tree. **Choice B** is incorrect because there is not sufficient evidence in the text to say that the cypress tree is the second-tallest tree in the world. **Choice C** is incorrect. If the Statue of Liberty is 305 feet, the 335 feet tall cypress tree would already be taller than the Statue of Liberty.

15. **Level:** Hard | **Domain:** INFORMATION AND IDEAS
    Skill/Knowledge: Inferences

Key Explanation: Choice D is correct. The process of osmosis described involves water moving from low-salt areas to high-salt areas. Fishes are able to absorb water through their skin and gills. Therefore, when a fish is in a habitat where the salt levels in the water are higher than the salt levels in its body, the fish will absorb less water. On the other hand, fish will absorb more water when the salt levels in the water are lower than the salt levels in the fish's body. Therefore, the amount of water absorbed by the fish is based on the level of salt in its habitat.

Distractor Explanations: Choice A is incorrect because the text does not discuss the speed of osmosis as a factor in the amount of water a fish absorbs. **Choice B** is incorrect because the question itself is about the amount of water consumed by the fish, so this choice would lead to a sentence with circular reasoning. **Choice C** is incorrect because the text does not discuss the number of cells in the fish's body as a factor in the amount of water a fish absorbs.

16. **Level:** Medium | **Domain:** STANDARD ENGLISH CONVENTIONS
    Skill/Knowledge: Form, Structure, and Sense

Key Explanation: Choice D is the best answer because it is a passive past perfect form. That form shows that something else did the act of destroying to the subject; in this case, the arsonist destroyed the pavilion.

Distractor Explanations: Choice A is incorrect because it is an active form, but the pavilion did not do the act of destroying, the arsonist did.

Choice B is incorrect because "despite" should not be followed by a clause with a noun and verb. Choice C is incorrect because "despite" should not be followed by an infinitive verb.

17. **Level:** Medium | **Domain:** STANDARD ENGLISH CONVENTIONS
Skill/Knowledge: Form, Structure, and Sense

Key Explanation: Choice B, "it," is the best answer. In the passage, the phrase "For a car to move forward" indicates that the text is referring to the car itself. Therefore, the pronoun "it" correctly refers back to the car, representing the subject in the sentence. The sentence thus reads "For a car to move forward, it must have enough force to push its own weight on the road out of the way." This use of "it" conforms to the conventions of Standard English and maintains the logical continuity of the passage.

Distractor Explanations: Choice A is incorrect because it creates a pronoun-antecedent disagreement. The antecedent in the sentence is "a car," which is singular, but the pronoun "you" is plural, referring to multiple people or readers. To maintain proper pronoun-antecedent agreement, the correct pronoun should be singular to match the singular antecedent "a car." **Choice C** is incorrect because it results in a pronoun-antecedent disagreement. The antecedent, " a car," is singular, while the pronoun "we" is plural, indicating multiple people. For consistency and proper pronoun-antecedent agreement, the pronoun should be singular to refer to the singular antecedent "a car". **Choice D** is incorrect because it creates a pronoun-antecedent disagreement. The antecedent "a car" is singular, while the pronoun "they" is plural, referring to multiple individuals or entities. To maintain pronoun-antecedent agreement, the correct pronoun should be

singular, matching the singular antecdentt, " car".

18. **Level:** Medium | **Domain:** STANDARD ENGLISH CONVENTIONS
Skill/Knowledge: Form, Structure, and Sense

Key Explanation: Choice D is the best answer. "First performed in England in 1984" is a modifier that describes *Starlight Express*, so it needs to be followed by the noun it modifies. **Choice D** correctly puts the parts of the sentence in order with *Starlight Express* at the start of the main clause.

Distractor Explanations: All of the other choices can be eliminated because "First performed in England in 1984" illogically refers to a person rather than the musical 8 In **Choice A**, the modifier refers to both Stilgoe and Webber. In **Choice B**, it refers to Stilgoe, and in **Choice C** it refers to Webber.

19. **Level:** Medium | **Domain:** STANDARD ENGLISH CONVENTIONS
Skill/Knowledge: Form, Structure, and Sense

Key Explanation: Choice B is the best answer. "People" is plural, and since it ends with an "e," there needs to be an apostrophe and "s" to show that the opinions belong to the people.

Distractor Explanations: Choice A is incorrect because "peoples'" is not the correct plural apostrophe, as "people" already refers to more than one person. **Choice C** is incorrect because "opinions" shouldn't reflect any possession in this context, so the apostrophe after s is unsuitable. **Choice D** is also incorrect because neither is "peoples" the correct plural of people, nor should "opinions" denote possession of anything

20. **Level:** Medium | **Domain:** STANDARD ENGLISH CONVENTIONS
Skill/Knowledge: Boundaries

Key Explanation: Choice D is the best answer. "Invented in…Sousa" is an added piece of information to the main idea that "the sousaphone is a brass instrument…." Such information could be included with commas at each end, in parentheses, or with dashes at each end, but must use the same punctuation at both ends. Since "invented" is preceded by a dash, "Sousa" needs to be followed by one.

Distractor Explanations: Choice A is incorrect because a single dash in a sentence needs to follow a complete clause, but "The sousaphone" is just a noun. **Choice B** is incorrect because "is" is placed in the aside and away from the main clause, leaving the main clause without a verb. That problem can be more easily seen by writing the sentence without the words between the dashes: "the sousaphone is a brass instrument…." **Choice C** is incorrect because it uses a comma rather than a dash, so the punctuation at the start and end of the aside are not consistent.

21. **Level:** Easy | **Domain:** STANDARD ENGLISH CONVENTIONS
Skill/Knowledge: Boundaries

Key Explanation: Choice D is the best answer. "Tenochtitlan, Texcoco, and Tlacopan" are added information to describe the previous noun, "three separate city-states." They are not essential to understand the meaning of the noun, so need to be divided from the noun they refer to with a comma. There should also be a comma after "Tenochtitlan" and "Texcoco" because they are three items in a list joined by "and." Such lists need to have a comma after each item.

Distractor Explanations: In **Choices A** and **B**, a colon is not incorrect after "city–states" because the previous sentence can stand on its own and the following information adds detail to that sentence. However, **Choice A** is incorrect because "and" in a list is not followed by a comma. **Choice B** is incorrect because single words need to be separated by commas in a list, not by semicolons (semicolons are only used when the items in the list are multiple words with commas). **Choice C** is incorrect because a comma is necessary to divide "city–states" from the names of the city–states; a noun cannot be followed directly by another noun without punctuation showing how they relate to each other.

22. **Level:** Easy | **Domain:** STANDARD ENGLISH CONVENTIONS
Skill/Knowledge: Boundaries

Key Explanation: Choice B is the best answer because a comma needs to divide non–essential information from a noun that it describes. In this case, there is only one first line of the poem, so the actual words in the line are helpful but not necessary to understand the noun.

Distractor Explanations: Choice A is incorrect because there should be a comma after "line" because the words from the poem are not necessary to understand the sentence. **Choices C** and **D** are incorrect because they create a comma splice between two clauses. Both the parts before and after the comma can stand on their own as sentences.

23. **Level:** Easy | **Domain:** EXPRESSION OF IDEAS
Skill/Knowledge: Transitions

Key Explanation: Choice B is the best answer because it is used to show an exception or change the tone of a passage. The preceding sentence says nuts are related to a longer life, but the following says that it is unclear whether the nuts actually cause the longer life. **Choice B** therefore effectively shows that there is doubt related to the first claim.

Distractor Explanations: None of the other choices accurately show that the tone changes between sentences. **Choice A** is used to show the result of the first claim, not to show an exception. **Choice C** is used to emphasize the first point with supporting information. **Choice D** is used to highlight a common idea between two concepts that are related.

24. **Level:** Medium | **Domain:** EXPRESSION OF IDEAS
    Skill/Knowledge: Transitions

    Key Explanation: Choice D is the best answer because it is used to show that something happened despite possible ambiguity over previous claims. The previous sentence refers to a range of hypotheses about why King Tut died, which demonstrates ambiguity about the death. The second sentence shows a situation that is common to each of the possible scenarios; the death was fast.

    Distractor Explanations: Choice A is incorrect because the passage doesn't talk of anything which states that his death was expected. Similarly, **Choice B** is incorrect because it is used to introduce the logical conclusion of a previous claim. However, the fact that the death was unexpected is not necessarily logical given the options listed ; for example, he could have lived a long time after an injury or illness. **Choice C** is incorrect because it is used to give another option or possibility. However, the following sentence discusses something that is true in all of the cases,

not something which is separate from one of the theories. For example, being murdered is a form of unexpected death.

25. **Level:** Easy | **Domain:** EXPRESSION OF IDEAS
    Skill/Knowledge: Transitions

    Key Explanation: Choice D is the best answer because it is used to introduce the result of a series of events. In this context, **Choice D** aptly introduces the result of intimidating the natives because Columbus was worried that the natives might harm his crew or stop providing food. If they were intimidated, they would continue giving necessary supplies without rebelling.

    Distractor Explanations: Choice A is incorrect because it is used to show that something happens despite something else, but in this case, the second is a direct result of the first. **Choice B** is used to paraphrase the preceding idea, so does not fit the context of continuing a story. **Choice C** is used to identify similarities in a comparison rather than show how one event was stopped by another.

26. **Level:** Medium | **Domain:** EXPRESSION OF IDEAS
    Skill/Knowledge: Rhetorical Synthesis

    Key Explanation: Choice B is the best answer because it clearly meets the student's goal of "differentiating" or "showing the contrasts" between Keith's theaters and others. **Choice B** highlights two main differences from the notes. One is that the performances were "polite" because they did not have vulgarity, swear words, or audiences that heckled. The other is that the theaters were elaborate by comparison to "other theaters in that period."

Distractor Explanations: Choice A is incorrect because it only says Keith owned more theaters; there is nothing which shows how those theaters are different from other people's. Keith's theaters were elaborate, but **Choice A** does not show that other theaters were simple. **Choice C** is incorrect because there is no mention of the type of performances that other people's theaters ran; in addition, the fact that Albee took over does not offer a contrast for what happened in other situations. **Choice D** is incorrect because it only says what Keith preferred and did; there is no contrast to show how his decisions led to differences from other theaters.

27. **Level:** Medium | **Domain:** EXPRESSION OF IDEAS

    Skill/Knowledge: Rhetorical Synthesis

    Key Explanation: Choice B is correct because it elucidates the central similarity between social constructivism and behaviorism: the shared belief in the significant influence of the environment on individual behaviors and understandings. It successfully synthesized all information provided in notes to highlight similarities in ideas between both theories.

    Distractor Explanations: Choice A is incorrect because though it may be factually accurate, it highlights more the differences than the similarities among theories, thus conflicting with a student's stated goal to emphasize shared ideas. **Choice C** is not the best available choice because while it correctly identifies that both theories recognize the role of the environment in shaping understanding, it does not accurately reflect the distinct ways in which behaviorism and social constructivism perceive this influence. Behaviorism attributes this influence

to conditioning, while social constructivism emphasizes the active construction of reality. Thus, this choice falls short of capturing the nuanced similarity between the two theories as presented in the notes. **Choice D** is incorrect because it is less precise. It does not identify how each theory interprets environmental influences on each theory's perceptions and thus falls short in emphasizing common concepts between theories.

1. **Level:** Medium| **Domain:** CRAFT AND STRUCTURE
Skill/Knowledge: Words in Context

Key Explanation: Choice D is the best answer because the blank portion shows what "Donovan" did to "childcare." **Choice D** refers to a great change or improvement, so fits the context of saying that disposable diapers completely changed the way children could be raised.

Distractor Explanations: None of the other choices accurately show what "Donovan" did to "childcare." **Choice A** refers to putting something back together, but childcare has not been damaged or fallen apart from a better state. **Choice B** refers to changing the structure of an institution or rearranging objects in a place, and **Choice C** refers to changing the name or identification of something.

2. **Level:** Medium | **Domain:** CRAFT AND STRUCTURE
Skill/Knowledge: Words in Context

Key Explanation: Choice D is the best answer because "application" refers to the starting point of the salt stress. **Choice D** refers to the carrying out of a course of action, so aptly shows that the number of days from the action of creating stress until the appearance of the first flowers was recorded.

Distractor Explanations: None of the other choices fits the context of indicating when the salt process began. **Choice A** refers to "meaning" or "importance. **Choice B** refers to putting in hard effort over a long period. **Choice C** refers to asking for something.

3. **Level:** Hard | **Domain:** CRAFT AND STRUCTURE
Skill/Knowledge: Words in Context

Key Explanation: Choice B is the best answer. "Adroitness" means "skill" or "talent," so shows that the composition "exemplifies" or "stands as a model of" the artist's ability to manipulate or control color.

Distractor Explanations: None of the other choices adequately explain what the manipulation of subtle colors refers to. **Choice A** refers to the state of being easily harmed by something, but Whistler was not harmed by the colors. **Choice C** refers to an agreement to do something, such as meet a person. **Choice D** refers to something that distracts from a serious activity.

4. **Level:** Medium | **Domain:** CRAFT AND STRUCTURE
Skill/Knowledge: Text Structure and Purpose

Key Explanation: Choice A is the best answer because "casting doubt" refers to showing that something may not be true; "veracity" is "truth." The underlined word also has the same meaning: it shows that something is said but that there is doubt about whether the claim is true or not. The claim is that Knight created the Lassie character, but the following sentence shows there is doubt: Gaskell wrote about such a character almost a century earlier. In other words, the underlined portion indicates that the author feels that maybe Gaskell was the creator and not Knight, as others said.

Distractor Explanations: Choice B is incorrect because the underlined portion does not "question" or "cast doubt" on the idea that the stories have a lot in common; instead, the underlined portion emphasizes that they are similar by hinting that maybe Knight copied the character. **Choice C** is incorrect because the underlined portion does not modify or cast doubt upon "fictional," it modifies "first introduced." **Choice D** is incorrect because there is no indication that Gaskell's story was popular or widely read at all.

5. **Level:** Medium | **Domain:** CRAFT AND STRUCTURE
   Skill/Knowledge: Text Structure and Purpose

   Key Explanation: Choice B is the best answer because the example is that Lee is a sensitive director who shows "nuances" or "subtleties" about Black characters. The following portion is a "contrast" or "difference" because it shows how other people stereotyped black actors to specific roles or even painted White people to look like Black ones.

   Distractor Explanations: Choice A is incorrect because there is no mention of a stereotype in the underlined portion; the rest of the text points out that Blacks were reduced to stereotypical roles. **Choice C** is incorrect because there is no evidence that Lee "pioneered" or "started" a change; the text only says that his work is different from that of directors in the past. **Choice D** is incorrect because the problem of Black stereotypes is not mentioned in the underlined portion, so the underlined portion does not show that it took time to "resolve" or "fix" it.

6. **Level:** Easy | **Domain:** CRAFT AND STRUCTURE
   Skill/Knowledge: Text Structure and Purpose

   Key Explanation: Choice B is the best answer. "Every cloud has a silver lining" is an idiom which means that everything which at first looks bad actually has something good about it. In this case, the material that Subramanian made was not magnetic and could not be used for the purpose he wanted, but he saw the possibility that he could "market" or "sell" it and earn money because of its other properties.

   Distractor Explanations: Choice A is incorrect because the idiom is not used literally, but figuratively. A "pigment" is a coloring agent like a powder, not a cloud. **Choice C** is incorrect because there is no indication that the pigment could make other colors, only that it was useful for making blue because it had properties most other blues did not. **Choice D** is incorrect because "market the new pigment" shows that Subramanian is taking advantage of or selling the color, not the quality of magnetism. There is no sign that adding something else will make it magnetic after all.

7. **Level:** Medium | **Domain:** CRAFT AND STRUCTURE
   Skill/Knowledge: Cross–Text Connections

   Key Explanation: Choice B is the best answer because Stearns says that slavery is only possible because laws governing slavery exist. The fact that the slave is owned by the state is one piece of legislation, so it supports the claim that slavery continues due to legislation rather than just the wishes of the slave and owner.

   Distractor Explanations: Choice A is incorrect because Stearns says that the law is the only thing to be considered. Therefore, if the law says that emancipated slaves are state property, it doesn't matter if the former slave has any paperwork showing otherwise. **Choice C** is incorrect because Stearns says that the U.S. Constitution supports laws of the states, but does not support slavery *per se*. **Choice D** is incorrect because Stearns says that the slaves are subjected to the laws of their masters. In the scenario given, the master would be the state, so running away would not protect the slave from the laws of that state.

8. **Level:** Easy | **Domain:** INFORMATION AND IDEAS
Skill/Knowledge: Central Ideas and Details

Key Explanation: Choice D is the best answer because the passage states that "They are extremely adaptable to a wide variety of habitats" and "are now flourishing in different areas." In other words, coywolves are able to "adapt" or "change" enough to live in many different "habitats" or "natural surroundings." Hence, they are in a range of "environmental conditions."

Distractor Explanations: Choice A is incorrect because the text offers no comparison of which place has the most coywolves; it only says that they live in many habitats in Canada and other places. **Choice B** is incorrect because there is no indication of how closely related coywolves are to any species; it could be that they have one wolf parent and one coyote parent. **Choice C** is incorrect because the passage only says that coywolves "first appeared" in Canada in the 20th century. It is unclear whether anyone bred them or whether they hybridized naturally in the wild.

9. **Level:** Easy | **Domain:** INFORMATION AND IDEAS
Skill/Knowledge: Central Ideas and Details

Key Explanation: Choice B is the best answer because the final sentence says that Nabongo "has written a book about her adventures." Since "her adventures" refers to traveling to all the countries in the world, she is an "author" or "writer" of such a book.

Distractor Explanations: Choice A is incorrect because the text does not say which country Nabongo was born in; the fact that she is Ugandan–American could mean she was born in the U.S. to Ugandan parents. **Choice C** is incorrect because there is no indication of which order Nabongo visited the locations. **Choice D** is incorrect because the text does not give Nabongo's opinion just of the Seychelles, only of her travels in general.

10. **Level:** Easy | **Domain:** INFORMATION AND IDEAS
Skill/Knowledge: Central Ideas and Details

Key Explanation: Choice B is the best answer. The first sentence explains the idea of The Fun Theory and the second sentence explains how the company proposed to test the theory. The final sentence gives the results: a large percentage of people changed their behaviors due to the fun factor which was introduced.

Distractor Explanations: Choice A is incorrect because the passage says that the experiment was designed to test a theory used in an advertising campaign, but does not explain the results of the campaign. It is possible that no additional cars were sold as a result of it. **Choice C** is incorrect because the passage does not say that more people took the stairs than the escalator, only that the use of stairs increased. It is possible that the use of the escalator was still higher than the stairs. **Choice D** is incorrect because there is no discussion that other places should adopt the same type of piano stairs; the passage only says that the stairs were effective in changing behavior in this experiment.

11. **Level:** Hard | **Domain:** INFORMATION AND IDEAS
Skill/Knowledge: Command of Evidence (Textual)

Key Explanation: Choice C is the best answer. The claim is that the park is "considered a world treasure for more than its beauty" or "valuable for things other than the way it looks." **Choice C** gives an important reason that people might want to conserve it: the climate is "unique" or "one of a kind" that is high in biodiversity, as illustrated by the huge number of plants in the area.

Distractor Explanations: Choice A is incorrect because it only says that the site is preserved; it does not give a reason why. **Choice B** is incorrect because there is no reason that a country boundary is a world heritage site of great value; this choice could be acceptable if there were reasons showing why the basaltic line is special, but not as it stands. **Choice D** is incorrect because it gives a reason that the park might have lost value. If the park has also been damaged, then the conservation value is decreased.

12. **Level:** Medium | **Domain:** INFORMATION AND IDEAS
Skill/Knowledge: Command of Evidence (Quantitative)

Key Explanation: Choice A is the best answer because the statement describes the "difference in the iron uptake increase." Therefore, the correct answer is derived by subtracting the smaller column from the larger. The smaller column is the control mouse, which has a value of about 2.7. The larger represents the mouse with no HEPHL1 genes, which has a value of about 3.8.

The difference is 3.8−2.7=1.1. Even if the values are changed by a few decimal points, **Choice A** is the closest approximate.

Distractor Explanations: None of the other choices shows the "difference in the iron uptake increase." **Choice B** would represent a difference larger than 2 of the lines on the y–axis, but there is only one line (the one for 3 nmoles) between the two bars. **Choice C** refers to the total increase for the control mouse, not the difference between the control mouse and the mouse with no HEPHL1. **Choice D** refers to the total increase of the mouse with no HEPHL1.

13. **Level:** Hard | **Domain:** INFORMATION AND IDEAS
Skill/Knowledge: Command of Evidence (Quantitative)

Key Explanation: Choice A is the correct option as it effectively uses information given in the graph to complete the sentence. It specifies the countries (Malawi, Niger, and Rwanda) where a significant portion of the population is unable to afford a healthy diet, which aligns with the information in the graph.

Distractor Explanations: Choice B is incorrect because it discusses cultural dietary preferences in India but does not directly use information from the graph about the percentage of the population unable to afford a healthy diet to complete the text. **Choice C** is incorrect because it presents a contradictory statement, as it claims a healthy diet is attainable for the majority of the population in India, which goes against the information provided in the graph. **Choice D** is incorrect because it discusses the accessibility of nutritious diets in Indonesia as a result of a disparity in come across the country. However, it does not directly include information from the graph to complete the text.

14. **Level:** Hard | **Domain:** INFORMATION AND IDEAS
Skill/Knowledge: Inferences

Key Explanation: Choice A is correct. The text states that doctors should not use BMI to diagnose diseases because BMI cannot detect where body fat is stored. Therefore, the example here should illustrate diseases where the location of body fat is important. This choice is the most logical one since it mentions how type 2 diabetes and coronary artery disease risk is higher when body fat is stored in the upper body.

Distractor Explanations: Choice B is incorrect because this choice does not highlight how the location of body fat is important in identifying specific disease risk. **Choice C** is incorrect because this choice does not comment on the location or even amount of body fat. This choice only relates to the factors that can be used to calculate body fat: height and weight. **Choice C** is incorrect because this choice does not comment on the location or even amount of body fat. This choice only relates to height and weight, which are used to calculate the amount of body fat.

15. **Level:** Medium | **Domain:** STANDARD ENGLISH CONVENTIONS
Skill/Knowledge: Form, Structure, and Sense

Key Explanation: Choice D is the best answer. In the passage, the phrase "For soccer balls to move forward during a powerful kick" indicates that the text is referring to the soccer balls themselves. Therefore, the pronoun "they" correctly refers back to the soccer balls, representing the plural subject in the sentence. The sentence reads: "For soccer

balls to move forward during a powerful kick, they must have enough force applied to them." This use of "they" conforms to the conventions of Standard English and maintains the logical continuity of the passage.

Distractor Explanations: Choice A is incorrect because it changes the subject of the sentence, addressing the reader directly. The sentence is discussing soccer balls' ability to move forward during a powerful kick, not the reader's ability, so using "you" would be grammatically incorrect and inconsistent with the context of the passage. **Choice B** is incorrect because it refers to a singular object, while the passage discusses multiple soccer balls. Using "it" would be grammatically incorrect because it would not agree with the plural antecedent "soccer balls." **Choice C** is incorrect because it involves the reader or the author in the sentence. However, the passage is not talking about "our" or "we" as the ones kicking the balls, but rather focusing on the soccer balls themselves as the subject of the sentence.

16. **Level:** Easy | **Domain:** STANDARD ENGLISH CONVENTIONS
Skill/Knowledge: Form, Structure, and Sense

Key Explanation: Choice A is the best answer. The underlined portion is one item in a list joined by "and," and such lists need to have the same grammatical structure in each item. The first two items are infinitive verbs that follow "to" and show the purpose of the dam: "control" and "increase." **Choice A** maintains the same structure with the infinitive "generate."

Distractor Explanations: All of the other choices are incorrect because they are not parallel with the other items in the list joined by "and." **Choice B** includes the noun "it." **Choice C** changes the order of the words into a clause, and **Choice D** repeats "to," which is not repeated with "increase water storage."

17. **Level:** Easy | **Domain:** STANDARD ENGLISH CONVENTIONS
Skill/Knowledge: Form, Structure, and Sense

Key Explanation: Choice B is the best answer. The underlined portion is a verb that needs to agree with the subject, which is the plural word "members."

Distractor Explanations: Choice A is incorrect because it is a singular verb. Similarly, **Choice D** is also incorrect because it is a singular verb. Though the preceding word, "the society" is singular, the subject is actually plural, "members of the society." **Choice C** is incorrect because the underlined portion is part of the main clause; "though" subordinates the first half of the sentence. Therefore, an active verb is necessary to make a complete clause, but "dedicating" is a gerund.

18. **Level:** Easy | **Domain:** STANDARD ENGLISH CONVENTIONS
Skill/Knowledge: Form, Structure, and Sense

Key Explanation: Choice A is the best answer. The word "Geologists" is a plural noun, and the pronoun "they" agrees with it, providing the correct pronoun-antecedent agreement. Additionally, "they" correctly indicates that multiple geologists are involved in exploring the intriguing connections between geological processes and climate change patterns.

Distractor Explanations: Choice B is incorrect because "he" is a singular pronoun and does not match the plural noun "Geologists" in the sentence. **Choice C** is incorrect because "it" would

refer to a singular object or concept, which is not appropriate in the context of geologists exploring connections between geological processes and climate change patterns. **Choice D** is incorrect because "she" is also a singular pronoun and does not agree with the plural noun "Geologists." There is no indication in the sentence that a specific female geologist is being referred to.

19. **Level:** Easy | **Domain:** STANDARD ENGLISH CONVENTIONS
Skill/Knowledge: Boundaries

Key Explanation: Choice A is the best answer because parenthetical information should be considered part of the word it refers to in the sentence and the punctuation should follow the regular punctuation of that part of speech. In this case, the facts in the parentheses describe the subject "shichimi", so should be considered part of the subject. No commas are needed between the subject and the following verb "is."

Distractor Explanations: All of the other choices are incorrect because they include unnecessary commas. In **Choice B** and **Choice D**, the commas separate the noun from the parenthetical information that describe it. In **Choice C** and **Choice D**, the commas divide the subject and its verb.

20. **Level:** Easy | **Domain:** STANDARD ENGLISH CONVENTIONS
Skill/Knowledge: Boundaries

Key Explanation: Choice A is the best answer. "Like stegosaurs and tyrannosaurs" is used to explain what is meant by "familiar species," so does not have to be separated from the sentence with any punctuation.

Distractor Explanations: Choice B is incorrect because "were" is the verb that goes with "familiar species." If there is only one comma, then "like... of time" becomes a modifier of "species" and there is no verb in the main clause. **Choice C** is incorrect because "like stegosaurs and tyrannosaurs" could be separated from "species" and the main sentence with commas at both ends, but in that case, there should be no comma after "stegosaurs." Two nouns joined by "and" should not be separated with punctuation. **Choice D** is incorrect because a colon needs to follow a complete sentence, but the preceding portion has no verb to go with "species."

21. **Level:** Easy | **Domain:** STANDARD ENGLISH CONVENTIONS
    Skill/Knowledge: Boundaries

    Key Explanation: Choice C is the best answer. The portions before and after the underlined section are both able to stand on their own as sentences, so can be joined with a period or semicolon.

    Distractor Explanations: Choice A is incorrect because it creates a run-on. **Choice B** is incorrect because it creates a comma splice. **Choice D** is incorrect because "and" turns the following portion into a dependent clause that cannot stand on its own as a sentence.

22. **Level:** Medium | **Domain:** STANDARD ENGLISH CONVENTIONS
    Skill/Knowledge: Boundaries

    Key Explanation: Choice A is the best answer. "What is little known is that as the plans evolved over the sixteen years of construction" is a modifier separate from the main idea, "a ramp

was eliminated." Additional information needs to be divided from the main clause with a comma, as indicated by the comma after "construction." A comma should also follow "smaller" because it is part of a series of adjectives modifying the verb "ramp."

Distractor Explanations: None of the other choices correctly divides the sentence. **Choices B, C,** and **D** do not have the comma after "construction" that is necessary to identify where the modifier ends and the main clause starts. **Choice B** includes an unnecessary comma after "ramp," separating that noun from its verb, "was eliminated." The comma after "steeper" in **Choice C** is possible if "much steeper" is used to add description to the word "smaller," but there is still a comma lacking after "construction." **Choice D** is missing all punctuation.

23. **Level:** Medium | **Domain:** EXPRESSION OF IDEAS
    Skill/Knowledge: Transitions

    Key Explanation: Choice C is the best answer because it is used to give a detail related to a previous claim. In the context, the general idea of rigorous training is expanded upon with an example of one form of such rigorous training: the dog needs to learn to alert the owner in a special circumstance.

    Distractor Explanations: None of the other choices establish the relationship that the second sentence gives an example that illustrates the first sentence. **Choice A** is used to show that something happened despite the previous claim. **Choice B** is used to show the result of the previous claim. **Choice D** is used to point out a similarity between two different examples.

24. **Level:** Easy | **Domain:** EXPRESSION OF IDEAS
Skill/Knowledge: Transitions

Key Explanation: Choice B is the best answer because it is used to show that the following thing comes chronologically after the previous discussion. It fits the context of showing that Gandhi used civil disobedience in the 1920s and King used it in the 1960s.

Distractor Explanations: Choice A is incorrect because it is used to introduce the results of an argument, but the fact that King used civil disobedience does not necessarily follow from the points that Thoreau wrote about it and Gandhi practiced it. **Choice C** is incorrect because it is used to give an example. While the following portion is an example of civil disobedience, it is not an example of the previous sentence, Gandhi's use of the technique. Therefore, the transition is misplaced at this point. **Choice D** shows that something happens despite something else. However, King's use of civil disobedience did not necessarily happen because Gandhi used it; King might have drawn some inspiration from the previous event.

25. **Level:** Medium | **Domain:** EXPRESSION OF IDEAS
Skill/Knowledge: Transitions

Key Explanation: Choice A is the best answer because it is used to offer a paraphrase or different wording of a previous idea. In this case, it offers a simple explanation "the shell creates a rash" to clarify the earlier claim that the shells "trigger contact dermatitis" because of oils that are "caustic" or "cause a burning sensation."

Distractor Explanations: Choice B is incorrect because it is used to show something similar between a comparison of two items that have common elements but that are not the same. It is not used to explain the same idea in different words. **Choice C** is incorrect because the following statement is simplifying what the previous statement said, not contradicting it. Similarly, **Choice D** is incorrect because it is used to introduce the opposite possibility, but the context only gives different words for the same thing.

26. **Level:** Easy | **Domain:** EXPRESSION OF IDEAS
Skill/Knowledge: Rhetorical Synthesis

Key Explanation: Choice D is the best answer because it gives a concise definition of "heat islands" for an audience that does not know what they are. **Choice D** then achieves the student's goal of offering solutions by summarizing the fourth and fifth bullet points.

Distractor Explanations: Choice A is incorrect because it mistakenly offers air conditioners as a solution for heat islands, but the notes only say that air conditioners contribute to the problem of global warming. **Choice B** is incorrect because it only explains what heat islands are; it does not offer any solutions as per the student's goal. **Choice C** is incorrect because an audience that does not know what a heat island is will not know the meaning after reading the statement. It does not include the crucial definition that they are hotter urban areas. Though **Choice C** does offer one way to solve the problem, the reader does not know why it helps.

27. **Level:** Hard | **Domain:** EXPRESSION OF IDEAS
Skill/Knowledge: Rhetorical Synthesis

Key Explanation: Choice A is the best answer because it is the most convincing argument for a farming community: it shows how the deer can be protected, yet it also shows the people that the student is trying to convince that they will not be harmed in the process. The farmers can "do their jobs" rather than lose land or work because of the new plan.

Distractor Explanations: All of the other choices are incorrect because they show how the plan benefits deer, but they do not address the potential concerns of a farming community about such problems as losing part of their property to the corridor or how to continue farming if there are more deer habitats in the area. Therefore, they are not as convincing an argument for the student to use in trying to get the people to agree to a wildlife corridor.

1. **Level:** Easy | **Domain:** ADVANCED MATH
   Skill/Knowledge: Nonlinear functions | **Testing point:** Writing exponential function equation from data

   Key Explanation: Choice A is correct. The initial value of the land is $47,890, which increases by 2% every year. This suggests that the function is exponential growth. The exponential growth formula is $f(x) = a(1 + r)^x$ where a is the initial value, r is the growth rate and x is the time. In this situation, $a = 47{,}890$, $r = 0.02$, and $x = t$. Substituting these values to the formula yields $f(x) = 47{,}890(1.02)^t$. Making A the correct option.

   Distractor Explanations: Choice B is incorrect. The option is linear functions, however, the model equation in the question is exponential. **Choice C** is incorrect. This is a decreasing exponential function since the factor 0.98 is less than 1. **Choice D** is incorrect. The option is linear functions, however, the model equation in the question is exponential

2. **Level:** Medium | **Domain:** ALGEBRA
   Skill/Knowledge: Linear equations in one variable
   Testing point: Matching coefficients

   Key Explanation: Choice A is correct. Grouping the left side of the equation yields $(ax + bx) + (a - b) = 5x - 2$. Factoring out x from the first group yields $x(a + b) + (a - b) = 5x - 2$. Matching coefficients and constants on both sides of the equation yields $(a + b) = 5$ and $(a - b) = -2$. Factoring the given expression $(a^2 - b^2)$ yields $a^2 - b^2 = (a + b)(a - b)$. Substituting the values of $(a + b)$ and $(a - b)$ yields $a^2 - b^2 = (5)(-2) = -10$.

   Distractor Explanations: Choice B is incorrect. This is the value of $a - b$.

   Choice C is incorrect. This is the value of $(a + b) + (a - b)$. **Choice D** is incorrect. This is the value of $a + b$.

3. **Level:** Medium | **Domain:** ADVANCED MATH
   Skill/Knowledge: Nonlinear functions
   Testing point: Solving for a quadratic equation using the quadratic formula

   Key Explanation: To solve for this quadratic equation, use the quadratic formula
   $$x = \frac{-b \pm \sqrt{b^2 - 4ac}}{2a},$$
   where $a = 3$, $b = -6$ and $c = -21$.
   Substituting the given values yields
   $$x = \frac{-(-6) \pm \sqrt{(-6)^2 - 4(3)(-21)}}{2(3)} \text{ or } x = \frac{6 \pm \sqrt{288}}{6}.$$
   Simplifying the equation yields $x = 1 \pm \dfrac{12\sqrt{2}}{6}$ or
   $x = 1 \pm 2\sqrt{2}$.
   Matching the two expressions yields
   $1 \pm 2\sqrt{2} = 1 + 2\sqrt{k}$. Therefore, $k = 2$.

4. **Level:** Easy | **Domain:** GEOMETRY AND TRIGONOMETRY
   Skill/Knowledge: Area and volume | **Testing point:** Finding the area of a rectangle

   Key Explanation: Choice A is correct. The length of the rectangle is $(x - 6)$ and the width is x. The area of a rectangle is given by length $\times$ width which is $x(x - 6) = 27$.
   Using distributive property yields $x^2 - 6x = 27$. Subtracting 27 from both sides of the equation yields $x^2 - 6x - 27 = 0$. Solve the quadratic equation either by using the quadratic formula or by using the factor method.
   Factoring $x^2 - 6x - 27 = 0$ yields $(x + 3)(x - 9) = 0$. Equating $(x + 3)$ to zero yields $x + 3 = 0$ or $x = -3$.

Equating $(x - 9)$ to zero yields $x - 9 = 0$ or $x = 9$. Since the width cannot be negative, the width would therefore be 9. Solving for the length of the rectangle yields $9 - 6 = 3$.

Distractor Explanations: Choice B is incorrect. This is the difference between the length and the width of the rectangle. **Choice C** is incorrect. This is the value of x or the width of the rectangle. **Choice D** is incorrect and may result from a conceptual or calculation error.

5. **Level:** Easy | **Domain:** ALGEBRA
   Skill/Knowledge: Linear equations in one variable
   Testing point: Solving for x in a linear equation

   Key Explanation: Choice A is correct. Solve for x first in the given equation $7x + 14 = 7$. Subtracting 14 from both sides of the equation yields $7x = 7 - 14$ or $7x = -7$. Dividing both sides of the equation by 7 yields $x = -1$. The equivalent equation will also have the same value of x. Solve the value of x in choice A by subtracting 6 from both sides of the equation which yields $3x = 3 - 6$ or $3x = -3$. Dividing both sides of the equation by 3 yields $x = -1$. Therefore, $3x + 6 = 3$ is equal to $7x + 14 = 7$.

   Distractor Explanations: Choice B is incorrect. Solving the value of x from both equations yields $x = 3$. **Choice C** is incorrect. Solving the value of x from both equations yields $x = 3$. **Choice D** is incorrect. Solving the value of x from $7x = 7$ yields $x = 1$.

6. **Level :** Hard | **Domain:** ALGEBRA
   Skill/Knowledge : Linear inequalities in one or two variables | **Testing point :** Solving absolute value inequalities

Key Explanation: To solve for the values of x, make two inequalities of absolute value for the positive and negative values.

$^+\lvert x + 3 \rvert < {}^+7$	$-\lvert x + 3 \rvert < {}^+7$
$x + 3 < 7$	$-x - 3 < 7$
$x + 3 - 3 < 7 - 3$	$-x - 3 + 3 < 7 + 3$
$x < 4$	$-x < 10$, divide both sides by -1
	$x > -10$

Hence, $-10 < x < 4$. The integers between -10 and 4 are $-9, -8, -7, -6, -5, -4, -3, -2, -1, 0, 1, 2$ and 3. Therefore, there are 13 integer solutions in the given inequality.

7. **Level:** Easy | **Domain:** ADVANCED MATH
   Skill/Knowledge: Nonlinear functions | **Testing point:** Finding a value of an exponential function

   Key Explanation: Choice C is correct.
   Substituting $\dfrac{1}{3}$ to the given equation yields

   $$p\left(\frac{1}{3}\right) = \left\{\frac{1}{8}\right\}^{\frac{-1}{3}} = 8^{\frac{1}{3}} = \sqrt[3]{8} = 2$$

   Therefore, $p\left(\dfrac{1}{3}\right) = 2$.

   Distractor Explanations: Choice A is incorrect. This option may be a result of finding $p(3)$. **Choice B** is incorrect and may result from solving the value of $p\left(-\dfrac{1}{3}\right)$. **Choice D** is incorrect. This option may be a result of finding $p(-3)$.

8. **Level:** Medium | **Domain:** ADVANCED MATH
   Skill/Knowledge: Nonlinear functions | **Testing point:** Using the factor theorem

   Key Explanation: Choice C is correct. Factor theorem states that if $f(a) = 0$, then $x - a$ is a factor of $f(x)$. In **Choice C**, $a = 2$. Substituting 2 to the given equation yields $f(2) = 6(2)^2 - 17(2) + 10$. Using distributive property yields $f(2) = 24 - 34 +$

10 or $f(2) = 0$. This means that $x - 2$ is a factor of $f(x)$.

Distractor Explanations: Choice A is incorrect. Substituting $-\frac{5}{6}$ to the given equation yields

$$f\left(-\frac{5}{6}\right) = 6\left(-\frac{5}{6}\right)^2 - 17\left(-\frac{5}{6}\right) + 10 = \frac{25}{6} + \frac{85}{3}$$

Choice B is incorrect. Substituting -5 to the given equation yields 245. **Choice D** is incorrect. Substituting 5 to the given equation yields 75.

9. **Level:** Easy | **Domain:** PROBLEM–SOLVING AND DATA ANALYTICS
   Skill/Knowledge: One–variable data: distributions and measures of center and spread | **Testing point:** Interpreting box and whisker plots

   Key Explanation: Choice D is correct. The median in a box and whisker plot is represented by the line in the box (interquartile range). From the above, data set A has a median of data set B has a greater median compared to data set A.

   Distractor Explanations: Choice A is incorrect. The mean and number of data or frequency cannot be found from a box and whisker plot representation. **Choice B** is incorrect. The mean and number of data or frequency cannot be found from a box and whisker plot representation. **Choice C** is incorrect. This statement is false.

10. **Level :** Easy | **Domain:** ADVANCED MATH
    Skill/Knowledge: Nonlinear equations in one variable and systems of equations in two variables
    Testing point: Finding the vertex of a parabola through a transformation

    Key Explanation: The vertex of $f(x)$ is $(-2, 5)$. Translating the parabola 3 units to the left and 1 unit up would result in $(-5, 6)$, which is the vertex of $g(x)$.
    Therefore, the value of h is -5.

11. **Level:** Easy | **Domain:** PROBLEM–SOLVING AND DATA ANALYSIS
    Skill/Knowledge: Two–variable data: models and scatterplots | **Testing point:** Using the line of best fit

    Key Explanation: Choice C is correct. The points above the line of best fit have a higher value than the values predicted by the line of best fit. There are 6 points above the line.

    Distractor Explanations: Choice A is incorrect. This option may result from conceptual errors. **Choice B** is incorrect and may result from counting the points below the line. **Choice D** is incorrect and may result from counting the total points in the scatter plot.

12. **Level:** Easy | **Domain:** ADVANCED MATH
    Skill/Knowledge: Equivalent expressions | **Testing point:** Using the difference of two squared with binomial expressions

    Key Explanation: Choice D is correct. Rewriting the expression $(x + \sqrt{2})^2 (x - \sqrt{2})^2$ yields $\left[(x + \sqrt{2})(x - \sqrt{2})\right]^2$.

    Using $(a + b)(a - b) = a^2 - b^2$ yields $\left[(x + \sqrt{2})(x - \sqrt{2})\right]^2 = (x^2 - (\sqrt{2})^2)^2$. Simplifying the radicals yields $(x^2 - 2)^2$. Expanding the expression yields $x^4 - 4x^2 + 4$.

    Distractor Explanations: Choice A is incorrect and may result from a conceptual or calculation error. **Choice B** is incorrect and may result from a conceptual or calculation error. **Choice C** is incorrect and may result from a conceptual or calculation error.

13. **Level:** Easy | **Domain:** ALGEBRA
Skill/Knowledge: Linear functions | **Testing point:** Finding the equation of a line from a graph

Key Explanation: Choice A is correct. The graph decreases from left to right. This means that the line has a negative slope. Looking at the choices, only **Choice A** has a negative slope of –4.85. Therefore, $y = 231 – 4.85x$ is the equation of the graph.

Distractor Explanations: Choice B is incorrect. The equation have positive values of slopes. **Choice C** is incorrect. The equation have positive values of slopes **Choice D** is incorrect. The equation have positive values of slopes

14. **Level :** Medium | **Domain:** PROBLEM SOLVING AND DATA ANALYSIS
Skill/Knowledge: Percentages | **Testing point:** Using proportions and percentages

Key Explanation:

	Girls	Boys
On the track team	6	$\frac{3}{5} \times 20 = 12$
Not on the track team	$\frac{3}{4} \times 24 = 18$	8
	24	20

From the table, the number of students on the track team would be 6 + 12 = 18 out of the 44 students. In percentage form this would be $\frac{18}{44} \times 100 = 40.909\%$ or 41% rounded off to the nearest whole number.

15. **Level:** Easy | **Domain:** ADVANCED MATH
Skill/Knowledge: Nonlinear equations in one variable and systems of equations in two variables

Testing point: Solving for quadratic and linear inequalities

Key Explanation: Choice B is correct. The inequality $y > 2(x – 2)^2 – 2$ has a graph of parabola. This means that it is in the form $y > a(x – h)^2 + k$ where (h, k) is the vertex. Hence, the vertex is at $(2, –2)$. Since the value a is positive, the parabola opens upwards. This means that the lowest point of the graph is the vertex. Hence, the value of y must be greater than –2.

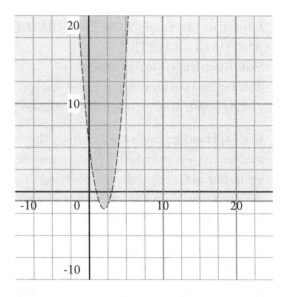

However, the second inequality states that $y \geq –1$, making –1 the least value of y.

Distractor Explanations: Choice A is incorrect. The option is not part of the solutions of the system. **Choices C** is incorrect. These are solutions to the system. However, they are not the least value of y. **Choices D** is incorrect. These are solutions to the system. However, they are not the least value of y.

16. **Level:** Hard | **Domain:** ADVANCED MATH
Skill/Knowledge: Equivalent expressions | **Testing point:** Factoring a quadratic

Key Explanation: Choice A is correct. Adding 98 to both sides of the equation yields $2x^2 + 28x + 98 = 0$. Factoring out 2 yields $2(x^2 + 14x + 49) = 0$. Using the model $(a + b)^2 = a^2 + 2ab + b^2$, the expression $(x^2 + 14x + 49)$ can be written as $(x + 7)^2$. Hence, the equation becomes $2(x + 7)^2 = 0$. Therefore, only equation 1 is equal to the given equation.

Distractor Explanations: Choice B is incorrect. This is because equation is not equivalent to the given equation. **Choice C** is incorrect. This is because equation is not equivalent to the given equation. **Choice D** is incorrect. This is because only equation 2 is not equivalent and not both of them.

17. **Level :** Easy | **Domain:** ALGEBRA
    Skill/Knowledge: Systems of two linear equations in two variables | **Testing point:** Solving simultaneous equations

    Key Explanation: The system of equations above can be solved either by substitution or elimination. Using elimination method, the 1st equation is multiplied by 2 which yields $2(3y – 2x = 6)$ or $6y – 4x = 12$.
    Subtract the two equations yields $y = 4$.
    Substituting the value of y to the first equation yields $3(4) – 2x = 6$ or $12 – 2x = 6$.
    Adding $2x$ and subtracting 6 from both sides of the equation yields $12 – 6 = 2x$ or $6 = 2x$.
    Dividing both sides of the equation by 2 yields $3 = x$ or $x = 3$.
    Therefore, $2x + y$ is $2(3) + 4 = 6 + 4 = 10$.

18. **Level :** Medium | **Domain:** PROBLEM SOLVING AND DATA ANALYSIS
    Skill/Knowledge: Inference from sample statistics and margin of error | **Testing point:** Making inferences from sample to population

Key Explanation: Choice A is correct. From the survey, $\frac{53}{97}$ of the students surveyed are in favor of changing the school uniform. This means that 97 – 53 = 44 or 44 of 97 students are not in favor of changing the school uniform. To approximate the number of students in school that are not in favor of the change would be $\frac{44}{97} \times 2,300 = 1,043$.

Distractor Explanations: Choice C is incorrect. This would be the approximate number of students in school that are in favor of the change in uniform. **Choice B** is incorrect. This option may result from miscalculation or conceptual error. **Choice D** is incorrect. This is the total number of students in the school.

19. **Level :** Easy | **Domain:** ALGEBRA
    Skill/Knowledge: Systems of two linear equations in two variables | **Testing point:** Working with systems of linear equations with no solution

    Key Explanation: Choice A is correct. A system of equations with no solutions means that the lines are parallel. They have the same slope but different y intercepts. Using distributive property yields

    $$3x + 5 - \frac{8}{3}x - 8 = px + 4$$

    Simplifying the left side of the equation yields $\frac{1}{3}x - 3 = px + 4$. Matching the coefficients of x yields $p = \frac{1}{3}$.

    Distractor Explanations: Choice B is incorrect. This option would result in having a system of equations with one solution. **Choice C is** incorrect. This option would result in having a system of equations with one solution. **Choice D is** incorrect. This option would result in having a system of equations with one solution.

20. **Level :** Medium | **Domain:** ALGEBRA
Skill/Knowledge: Linear equations in two variables | **Testing point:** Solving a system of equations with Infinite solutions

Key Explanation: A system of equations with infinite solutions are equations of the same line and have both the same slope and y–intercept. Using distributive property yields $5x - 10 + x + 3 = kx - 2k + 2x + 1$.
Combining and grouping like terms yields $6x - 7 = (kx + 2x) + (-2k + 1)$.
Matching the constants yields $-7 = -2k + 1$.
Adding 7 and $2k$ to both sides of the equation yields $2k = 8$.
Dividing both sides of the equation by 2 yields $k = 4$.

21. **Level :** Easy | **Domain:** GEOMETRY AND TRIGONOMETRY
Skill/Knowledge: Lines, angles, and triangles | **Testing point:** Working with inscribed shapes and special triangles

Key Explanation: Choice B is correct. The diameter of the circle is equal to the diagonal length of the square. The diameter is $12 \times 2 = 24 \ cm$, which means that the diagonal of the square is also 24. And since the diagonal length is equal to $s\sqrt{2}$ where s is the side length of the square, then $s\sqrt{2} = 24$. Solving for s by dividing both sides of the equation by $\sqrt{2}$ yields $s = \dfrac{24}{\sqrt{2}}$ Rationalizing the denominator yields

$s = \dfrac{24}{\sqrt{2}} \times \dfrac{\sqrt{2}}{\sqrt{2}} = \dfrac{24\sqrt{2}}{2} = 12\sqrt{2}$. Therefore, $s = 12\sqrt{2}$

Distractor Explanations: Choice A is incorrect. This is the value of the radius of the circle. **Choice C** is incorrect. This option would be a result of

misconception and conceptual error. **Choice D** is incorrect. This is the value of the diameter of the circle.

22. **Level :** Hard | **Domain:** ALGEBRA
Skill/Knowledge: Linear equations in two variables | **Testing point:** Determining the equation of a line from data

Key Explanation: Choice B is correct. The value is constant for all values of x given; thus the equation of the line would be $y = 4$. Substituting the value of y to the given equation yields $4 = 2k$. Dividing both sides of the equation by 2 yields $2 = k$ or $k = 2$.

Distractor Explanations: Choice A is incorrect. This option may be due to conceptual and miscalculation errors. **Choice C** is incorrect. This is the value of the constant $2k$. **Choice D** is incorrect. This option may be due to conceptual and miscalculation errors.

1. **Level:** Medium | **Domain:** ADVANCED MATH
Skill/Knowledge: Nonlinear equations in one variable and systems of equations in two variables
Testing point: Solving quadratic equations

Key Explanation: Choice C is correct. Quadratic equations can be solved either by using the quadratic formula or by solving using the factor method.
Using the factor method, first find the product of the highest degree term and the constant which will be $3x^2 \times 6 = 18x^2$.
The factors of $18x^2$ that will add up to be equal to the middle term $-19x$ are $-x$ and $-18x$.
Splitting the middle term yields $3x^2 - x - 18x + 6 = 0$.
Grouping the equation yields $(3x^2 - x) - (18x - 6) = 0$.
Factoring the equation yields $x(3x - 1) - 6(3x - 1) = 0$.
Factoring out $(3x - 1)$ yields $(3x - 1)(x - 6) = 0$.
Equating $(x - 6)$ to zero yields $x - 6 = 0$ or $x = 6$.

Equating $(3x - 1)$ to zero yields $3x - 1 = 0$ or $x = \frac{1}{3}$ Since $\frac{1}{3}$ is in the options, then **Choice C** is the correct answer.

Distractor Explanations: Choice A is incorrect. This is the negative value of the solution $x=6$. **Choice B is incorrect.** This is the negative value of the solution $x = \frac{1}{3}$. **Choice D is incorrect.** This is the value of the products of the solutions/roots which is $\frac{c}{a}$.

2. **Level :** Medium | **Domain:** GEOMETRY AND TRIGONOMETRY
Skill/Knowledge : Circles | **Testing point :** Completing the square and using the equation of a circle

Key Explanation: Choice B is correct. Diameter is twice the radius. To find the radius of the circle, rewrite the given equation in standard form $(x - h)^2 + (y - k)^2 = r^2$ where (h, k) is the center of the circle and r is its radius. Completing the squares yields $(x - 4)^2 - \left(\frac{-8}{2}\right)^2 + (y + 5)^2 - \left(\frac{10}{2}\right)^2 = 8$ or
$(x - 4)^2 - 16 + (y + 5)^2 - 25 = 8$. Adding 25 and 16 to both sides of the equation yields $(x - 4)^2 + (y + 5)^2 = 8 + 25 + 16$ or $(x - 4)^2 + (y + 5)^2 = 49$.
Since $r^2 = 49$, then $r = 7$.
The diameter would then be $2(7) = 14$.

Distractor Explanations: Choice A is incorrect. This is the value of the radius of the circle given above. **Choice C is incorrect.** This assumes that 8 is the radius of the circle and that the diameter would be $2(8) = 16$. **Choice D is incorrect.** This can be a result of not getting the square root of the constant in the equation.

3. **Level :** Easy | **Domain:** ALGEBRA
Skill/Knowledge: Linear functions | **Testing point :** Solving for the absolute value of a linear function $f(x)$, given x

Key Explanation: To find $f(2)$, substitute 2 in place of x in the equation which yields $f(2) = -2(2) - 6$.
Simplifying the equation yields $f(2) = -4 - 6$ or $f(2) = -10$.
$|f(2)|$ is the absolute value of $f(2)$.
Therefore, $|-10| = 10$.

4. **Level:** Hard | **Domain:** GEOMETRY AND TRIGONOMETRY
Skill/Knowledge: Right triangles and trigonometry | **Testing point:** Using trigonometric identities

Key Explanation: Choice B is correct. Converting the tangent function to sine and cosine functions yields $\tan(90-x)° = \dfrac{\sin(90-x)°}{\cos(90-x)°}$. Since the sine of an angle is equal to the cosine of its complementary angle and vice versa, $\sin x = \cos(90-x)$ and $\cos x = \sin(90-x)$. Substituting the equivalent identities yields $\tan(90-x) = \dfrac{\cos x}{\sin x}$. Therefore, the correct answer is **Choice B**.

Distractor Explanations: Choice A is incorrect and may result from solving the equivalent identity of $\tan x$ and $\dfrac{1}{\tan x}$ respectively. **Choice C** is incorrect and may result from solving the equivalent identity of $\tan x$ and $\dfrac{1}{\tan x}$ respectively. **Choice D** is incorrect and may result from solving the equivalent identity of $\tan(-x)$.

5. **Level:** Easy | **Domain:** ALGEBRA
    Skill/Knowledge: Linear functions | **Testing point:** Meaning in context in linear equation

    Key Explanation: Choice C is correct. Alina earns an interest monthly based on her deposit. This makes the model equation for her savings account linear. 7.684 in this context, is the amount of interest she earns monthly which can be obtained by multiplying the interest rate with the principal amount. This yields $(6.8\% \times 113) = 7.684$. Thus making option C correct.

    Distractor Explanations: Choice A is incorrect. The amount of interest earned after t months would be represented by $7.684t$. **Choice B** is incorrect. The total amount in the account after t months would be represented by the function $A(t)$. **Choice D** is incorrect. The interest earned per year is $92.208.

6. **Level:** Medium | **Domain:** ALGEBRA
    Skill/Knowledge: Systems of two linear equations in two variables | **Testing point:** Finding equation that makes system have no solutions

    Key Explanation: Choice B is correct. A system of equations with no solution are systems that have parallel lines and therefore have the same slope and different *y-intercepts*. To find the slope and *y-intercept* of the given equation, the equation has to be in the slope–intercept form $y = mx + c$. Subtracting $-6x$ from the equation yields $-3y = -6x + 2$. Dividing -3 from both sides of the equation yields $y = 2x - \dfrac{2}{3}$. The slope is 2 and the *y-intercept* is $-\dfrac{2}{3}$. Rewriting **Choice C** in slope intercept form yields $y = 2x + 4$. Since it has the same slope and different *y-intercept* with the given line, both lines are parallel and will have no solutions.

    Distractor Explanations: Choice A is incorrect. The line has a different slope of $\dfrac{2}{3}$, which makes the system have one solution. **Choice C** is incorrect. The line has a slope of 2 and y–intercept is $-\dfrac{2}{3}$ which is the same as the given line. Hence, the line is collinear which makes the system have infinite solutions. **Choice D** is incorrect. The line has a slope of 2 and y–intercept is $-\dfrac{2}{3}$ which is the same as the given line. Hence, the line is collinear which makes the system have infinite solutions.

7. **Level : Easy | Domain: ADVANCED MATH**
    Skill/Knowledge: Nonlinear functions | **Testing point:** Solving for $p(x)$ given x in a quadratic function

Key Explanation: To find $p(2)$, substitute 2 in place of x. This yields $p(2) = 2(2)^2 - 6(2) + 5$. Simplifying the equation yields $p(2) = 8 - 12 + 5$ or $p(2) = 1$.

8. **Level:** Easy | **Domain:** ALGEBRA
   Skill/Knowledge: Linear equations in two variables | **Testing point:** Finding the equation of the line given two points

   Key Explanation: Choice B is correct. To find the equation of the line, first find the slope of the line. Substituting $(6, 5)$ and $(0, 0)$ to the slope formula

   $m = \dfrac{y_2 - y_1}{x_2 - x_1}$ yields $m = \dfrac{0 - 5}{0 - 6} = \dfrac{5}{6}$. Substituting the

   slope to the slope–intercept form $y = mx + b$ yields

   $y = \dfrac{5}{6}x + b$. Since the line passes through the

   origin, the y–intercept is zero which means $b = 0$.

   Hence, the equation of the line is $y = \dfrac{5}{6}x$ or

   $6y = 5x$, which makes B the correct option.

   Distractor Explanations: Choice A is incorrect and may result from finding the equation of the line that passes through the origin and point $(5, 6)$. **Choice C** is incorrect. This line do not pass through the origin and point $(6, 5)$. **Choice D** is incorrect. This line do not pass through the origin and point $(6, 5)$.

9. **Level:** Easy | **Domain:** ADVANCED MATH
   Skill/Knowledge: Nonlinear functions | **Testing point:** Determining a quadratic equation from its graph

   Key Explanation: Choice D is correct. The graph opens downwards and this makes a (the coefficient of x^2) negative. Hence, the possible answer is either **Choice C** or **D**. To determine which is

correct between **Choice C** and **Choice D**, check the value of h for each equation using the formula

$\dfrac{-b}{2a}$ where b is the coefficient of x. Since the vertex

of the graph is in the first quadrant, then h must

be positive. Solving h in **Choice C** yields $\dfrac{-(-6)}{2(-2)}$

or $-\dfrac{3}{2}$. Hence, **Choice C** is incorrect. Solving h in

choice D yields $\dfrac{-(6)}{2(-2)}$ or $\dfrac{3}{2}$. Therefore, **Choice D**

is the correct answer.

Distractor Explanations: Choice A is incorrect. The graph of this equation opens upwards since the coefficient of x^2 is positive. **Choice B is** incorrect. The graph of this equation opens upwards since the coefficient of x^2 is positive. **Choice C** is incorrect because the value of h is negative.

10. **Level:** Easy | **Domain:** GEOMETRY AND TRIGONOMETRY
    Skill/Knowledge: Lines, angles and triangles | **Testing point:** Using the sum of the interior angles of a polygon formula

    Key Explanation: A quadrilateral is a four sided figure. The sum of the interior angles can be found by $180(n-2)$ where n is the number of sides. Substituting 4 yields $180(4 - 2) = 360°$. Adding the given angles yields $x + x + 40 + x + 50 + x - 10 = 360$. Combining like terms yields $4x + 80 = 360$. Subtracting 80 from both sides of the equation yields $4x + 80 - 80 = 360 - 80$ or $4x = 280$. Dividing both sides of the equation by 4 yields $x = 70°$.

11. **Level:** Medium | **Domain:** GEOMETRY AND TRIGONOMETRY
    Skill/Knowledge: Right triangles and trigonometry | **Testing point:** Using SOHCAHTOA in similar right triangles

    Key Explanation: Choice A is correct. Triangle *ABD* and Triangle *ACD* are similar right triangles. This makes angle *CAD* and angle *DBA* equal. Therefore, sin *CAD* = sin *DBA*.

    Since sin $DBA = \dfrac{O}{H} = \dfrac{AD}{BD}$, then sin $CAD = \dfrac{AD}{BD}$

    BD is the hypotenuse for triangle *ABD* which can be calculated using Pythagorean Theorem $a^2 + b^2 = c^2$, where *a* and *b* are the legs and *c* is the hypotenuse of the right triangle. Applying this to triangle *ABD* yields $AB^2 + AD^2 = BD^2$. Substituting the values of *AB* and *AD* yields $10^2 + 24^2 = BD^2$. Simplifying the left side of the equation yields $676 = BD^2$. Getting the square root of both sides of the equation yields $\sqrt{676} = BD$ or $26 = BD$. Substituting the value of *AD* and *BD* to sin $CAD = \dfrac{AD}{BD}$ yields sin $CAD = \dfrac{24}{26}$ or sin $CAD = \dfrac{12}{13}$.

    Distractor Explanations: Choice B is incorrect. This option is the value of tan *CAD*. **Choice C** is incorrect. This option is the value of cos *CAD*. **Choice D** is incorrect. This option is the value of tan *CDA*.

12. **Level:** Easy | **Domain:** ADVANCED MATH
    Skill/Knowledge: Equivalent expressions |
    Testing point: Using the distributive property

    Key Explanation: Choice B is correct. Using distributive property yields $7wp(2w) + 7wp(5)$. Simplifying the expression yields $14w^2p + 35wp$.

Distractor Explanations: Choice A is incorrect and may result from a conceptual or calculation error. **Choice C** is incorrect and may result from a conceptual or calculation error. **Choice D** is incorrect and may result from a conceptual or calculation error.

13. **Level :** Easy | **Domain:** GEOMETRY AND TRIGONOMETRY
    Skill/Knowledge: Area and volume | **Testing point:** Using volumes of similar shapes

    Key Explanation: The ratio of volume of sphere *A* and sphere *B* is 27 : 1. The ratio of the radius would be $\sqrt[3]{27} : \sqrt[3]{1} = 3 : 1$.
    Sphere *B* has a radius of 4 *cm*.
    Applying the ratio of 3 : 1, this would make the radius of sphere *A* $3 \times 4 = 12$.

14. **Level:** Hard | **Domain:** PROBLEM−SOLVING AND DATA ANALYSIS
    Skill/Knowledge: Probability and conditional probability | **Testing point:** Calculating probabilities

    Key Explanation: Choice A is correct.

	Rain	No rain
Monday	43%	57%
Thursday	86%	14%

    Probability is equal to one or 100% (if in percentage form), therefore the chance that it won't rain on Monday will be 100% − 43% = 57%. Since it is twice as likely to rain on Thursday than on Monday, the chance that it will rain on Thursday will be 2(43%) = 86%. Hence, the chance that it would not rain on Thursday is 100% − 86% = 14% or 0.14.

    Distractor Explanations: Choice B is incorrect. This is the value of the probability that it would rain on Monday. **Choice C** is incorrect as this is the chance that it would not rain on Monday. **Choice D** is incorrect as this is the chance that it would rain on Thursday.

15. **Level:** Hard | **Domain:** ADVANCED MATH
Skill/Knowledge: Nonlinear equations in one variable and systems of equations in two variables
Testing point: Solving nonlinear inequalities

Key Explanation: Choice D is correct. To solve the following system, the bases have to be the same. Since 16 and 4 are multiples of 2, 16^x becomes 2^{4x} and 4^x becomes 2^{2x}. This yields $\dfrac{2^{4x}}{2^{2x}} > 2$. Since the terms on the left side of the inequality are divided, their exponents will be subtracted which will yield $2^{4x-2x} > 2^6$ or $2^{2x} > 2^6$. Since the bases are the same, then $2x > 6$. Dividing both sides of the inequality by 2 yields $x > 3$. 4 is the next integer greater than 3.

Distractor Explanations: Choice A is incorrect as they are all less than 3 or equal to 3. **Choice B** is incorrect as they are all less than 3 or equal to 3. **Choice C** is incorrect as they are all less than 3 or equal to 3.

16. **Level :** Hard | **Domain:** ADVANCED MATH
Skill/Knowledge: Equivalent expressions | **Testing point:** Matching coefficients and solving systems of equations

Key Explanation: Using distributive property yields $3ax - 3b + 4bx - 4a = x - 6$. Grouping like terms yields $(3a + 4b)x + (-3b - 4a) = x - 6$. Matching the coefficients of x and the constants to make two equations yields $3a + 4b = 1$ and $-4a - 3b = -6$. Using the elimination method to find the value of a and b, multiply the 1st equation by 4 and the 2nd equation by 3. This yields $4(3a + 4b = 1)$ or $12a + 16b = 4$ and $3(-4a - 3b = -6)$ or $-12a - 9b = -18$. Adding the two

equations yields $7b = -14$. Dividing both sides of the equation by 7 yields $b = -2$. Substituting the value of b to the 1st equation yields $3a + 4(-2) = 1$ or $3a - 8 = 1$. Adding 8 to both sides of the equation yields $3a = 9$. Dividing both sides of the equation by 3 yields $a = 3$.

17. **Level:** Easy | **Domain:** GEOMETRY AND TRIGONOMETRY
Skill/Knowledge: Area and volume | **Testing point:** Finding the volume of a cone.

Key Explanation: Choice A is correct. The volume of a cone is given by the formula $\left(\dfrac{1}{3}\pi r^2 h\right)$ where r is the radius and h is the height. Since the height is 6 more than the radius, $h = 12 + 6 = 8$. Substituting the values to the formula yields $\dfrac{1}{3}\pi(12)^2(18) = 864\pi$.

Distractor Explanations: Choice B is incorrect because this gives the volume of a cylinder with the given parameters. **Choice C** is incorrect. This option may result from miscalculation or by using the wrong formula. **Choice D** is incorrect. This option may result from miscalculation or by using the wrong formula.

18. **Level:** Easy | **Domain:** ALGEBRA
Skill/Knowledge: Linear equations in two variables | **Testing point:** Finding the slope of a line from an equation

Key Explanation: Choice A is correct. To find the slope of the line, rewrite the equation in slope intercept form $y = mx + c$, where m is the slope and c is the y-intercept. Adding 3y and subtracting 6 from both sides of the equation yields $4x - 6 = 3y$. Dividing both sides of the equation by 3 yields

$\frac{4}{3}x - 2 = y$ or $y = \frac{4}{3}x - 2$. Therefore, the slope of the line is $\frac{4}{3}$.

Distractor Explanations: Choice B is incorrect because this is the coefficient of x when the equation of the line is in general form. **Choice C** is incorrect and may result from a conceptual or calculation error. **Choice D** is incorrect and may result from a conceptual or calculation error.

19. **Level : Medium | Domain:** GEOMETRY AND TRIGONOMETRY
    Skill/Knowledge: Circles | **Testing point:** Calculating angle measure given arc length

    Key Explanation: The arc length is a fraction of the circumference. The arc would therefore be $\frac{3\pi}{20\pi} = \frac{3}{20}$. Multiplying it to the full angle of a circle yields $\frac{3}{20} \times 360° = 54°$.

20. **Level:** Easy | **Domain:** PROBLEM SOLVING AND DATA ANALYSIS
    Skill/Knowledge: Ratios, rates, proportional relationships, and units | **Testing point:** Using inverse proportions

    Key Explanation: Choice B is correct. The price per student would be $\frac{p}{30}$. If 28 students paid before the day of the trip, then this can be represented by $\frac{p}{30} \times 28 = \frac{28p}{30}$ or $\frac{14}{15p}$.

    Distractor Explanations: Choice A is incorrect and may result from assuming that p is the price per student. **Choice C** is incorrect and may result from assuming that p is the price per student. **Choice D** is incorrect and may result from solving the price per student.

21. **Level:** Hard | **Domain:** GEOMETRY AND TRIGONOMETRY
    Skill/Knowledge: Circles | **Testing point:** Finding the equation of a circle

    Key Explanation: Choice A is correct. The standard form of the equation of a circle is $(x - h)^2 + (y - k)^2 = r^2$, where (h, k) is the center of the circle and r is the radius. Substituting the given data yields $(x + 3)^2 + (y - 5)^2 = 6^2$. Expanding the equation yields $x^2 + 6x + 9 + y^2 - 10y + 25 = 36$. Subtracting 36 from both sides of the equation yields $x^2 + 6x + y^2 - 10y + 34 - 36 = 0$. Matching the constant in $x^2 + 6x + y^2 - 10y - 2 = ax^2 + bx + cy^2 + dy + e$ yields $e = -2$.

    Distractor Explanations: Choice B is incorrect. This option may result from conceptual errors. **Choice C** is incorrect. This option may result from conceptual errors. **Choice D** is incorrect. This is the value of $r^2 = 6^2 = 36$, however it is not the value of e.

22. **Level:** Medium | **Domain:** ALGEBRA
    Skill/Knowledge: Linear inequalities in one or two variables | **Testing point:** Solving for a linear inequality

    Key Explanation: Choice D is correct. Using distributive property yields $-3x - 6 < 2x - 16$. Adding 6 and subtracting $2x$ from both sides of the inequality yields $-3x - 6 - 2x + 6 < 2x - 16 + 6 - 2x - 5x < -10$. Dividing both sides of the inequality by -5 yields $x > 2$. Since 3 is greater than 2, it is the correct answer.

    Distractor Explanations: Choice A is incorrect. This value is less than or equal to 2. **Choice B** is incorrect. This value is less than or equal to 2. **Choice C** is incorrect. This value is less than or equal to 2.

Made in United States
North Haven, CT
02 March 2024

49447414R00226